Challenge to Imperialism

About the Book and Author

Challenge to Imperialism is the first comprehensive analysis of the Zimbabwean struggle for independence in its international context. Based on extensive research in the southern African region and on interviews with the ZANU and ZAPU leaders in exile during the war, this study is an analysis of the crucial support given to the Zimbabwean nationalists by the five Frontline States—Angola, Botswana, Mozambique, Tanzania, and Zambia.

The book begins with a summary of the variable relations among the Frontline States and between those states and the Zimbabwean nationalists. More than once, Frontline governments put Zimbabwean nationalists in their own jails as tensions arose over leadership, conduct of the war, and terms for peace. Yet the Frontline States maintained their support in spite of the extremely high cost to their own economic development.

How could these weak and economically dependent states confront the dominant interests in the region? Was Lancaster House simply a capitulation to imperialist interests, a constitution forced on the nationalists by the beleaguered Frontline States?

This theoretical analysis addresses the complexity of these questions and suggests lessons for the current struggles in Namibia and in South Africa. Further, Dr. Thompson discusses the formation of the Southern African Development Coordination Conference (SADCC) as an attempt to transform the Zimbabwean political victory into regional economic cooperation.

This study of the political and economic background of Zimbabwean independence is important not only to those concerned about Zimbabwe and southern Africa, but also to those interested in the nature of liberation struggles and in the role of the state in developing countries.

Carol B. Thompson is an associate professor of political science at the University of Southern California, Los Angeles. She taught at the University of Dar es Salaam, Tanzania, during 1977–1979 and has been a research associate at the University of Zimbabwe during 1984–1986.

Challenge to Imperialism

The Frontline States in the Liberation of Zimbabwe

Carol B. Thompson

WITHDRAWN

Westview Press / Boulder and London

This Westview softcover edition was manufactured on our own premises using equipment and methods that allow us to keep even specialized books in stock. It is printed on acid-free paper and bound in softcovers that carry the highest rating of the National Association of State Textbook Administrators, in consultation with the Association of American Publishers and the Book Manufacturers' Institute.

Published in 1986 in the United States of America by Westview Press, Inc.; Frederick A. Praeger, Publisher; 5500 Central Avenue, Boulder, Colorado 80301

Published in 1985 in Zimbabwe by Zimbabwe Publishing House Ltd.

Library of Congress Cataloging-in-Publication Data
Thompson, Carol B.
  Challenge to imperialism.
  1. Africa, Southern—Foreign relations—Zimbabwe.
2. Zimbabwe—Foreign relations—Africa, Southern.
3. Zimbabwe—Politics and government. 4. Southern
Africa Development Co-ordination Conference.
I. Title
DT747.Z55T48 1986   327.6068   85-32317
ISBN 0-8133-7168-6

Printed and bound in the United States of America

The paper used in this publication meets the minimum requirements of the American National Standard for Permanence of Paper for Printed Library Materials Z39.48-1984.

6   5   4   3   2   1

To my parents, who taught me to care

Contents

Acknowledgments

Radical change of any status quo is a difficult and long process, frequently with more steps back toward the familiar than forward toward the vision. As the status quo is transformed, so is the vision, changing to adapt to realities and to new ideas. However, many cry out that the transformation of the vision is betrayal of 'real' goal; others welcome the newest idea as at last the 'final victory'. I have learned much from friends in Zimbabwe, Mozambique, Tanzania and from other Southern Africans about their continuing struggles for equality and justice; I am most indebted to them. Organized and disciplined efforts — political, economic, diplomatic and yes, military if necessary — do make a difference in the quality of life of a people. My hope is that we in the United States can learn from the real successes and bitter failures of Southern Africans to find ways to transform our status quo.

The analysis has benefited greatly from criticisms of many from the very first stages of the research. Intense debates among colleagues about simply 'what happened' and about theories to help explain the process have greatly clarified issues. Of course, errors remain which are my own; the continuing dialogue will correct them and elaborate the theories.

Because the book is about the interaction of several governments, I found it necessary to check details with those more expert than I for specific countries. I am indebted to the knowledge and advice of many, including Tony Avirgan, Gerald Bender, Amon Chaligha, Harry Goulbourne, Martha Honey, William Minter, James Mittelman, Jack Parson and Ben Turok.

Several colleagues gave criticism of the entire manuscript at various stages. I would like to thank most of all Allen Isaacman, who sacrificed much time from his own important work to read many drafts. Larry Bowman and Joel Samoff also spent numerous hours guiding the analysis.

Two colleagues who were especially important in offering invaluable critique, but also daily encouragement as best friends, are Nora Hamilton and Mark Kann.

The book would not have been possible without the daily contact with reality and constant understanding offered by my niece, Shari Gentry. One who has shared every stage of the debates and writing, and more important, the struggle for liberation in Southern Africa is Bud Day. He understands most of all.

Carol B. Thompson

Abbreviations

ANC–South Africa	African National Congress of South Africa
ANC	African National Council in Zimbabwe; in 1976 it became the UANC
CAF	Central African Federation
DARE	Dare re Chimurenga ('Council of Revolution' in Shona) — ZANU war council
FNLA	National Front for the Liberation of Angola
Frelimo	Front for the Liberation of Mozambique
Frolizi	Front for the Liberation of Zimbabwe
MOLINACO	National Liberation Movement of the Comores
MPLA	Popular Movement for the Liberation of Angola
PAIGC	African Independence Party of Guinea and Cape Verde Islands
PF	Patriotic Front (ZANU and ZAPU)
UANC	United African National Council
UDI	Unilateral Declaration of Independence
UNITA	National Union for the Total Liberation of Angola
UNLF	Uganda National Liberation Front
ZANLA	Zimbabwe African National Liberation Army of ZANU
ZANU	Zimbabwe African National Union
ZAPU	Zimbabwe African People's Union
ZIPA	Zimbabwe People's Army
ZIPRA	Zimbabwe People's Revolutionary Army of ZAPU

All dollar figures are in US$ unless otherwise stated.
Although the British colony of Southern Rhodesia did not legally change its name after the unilateral declaration of independence in 1965, it was popularly known as 'Rhodesia'. This text uses the shorter form of Rhodesia.

The Frontline States

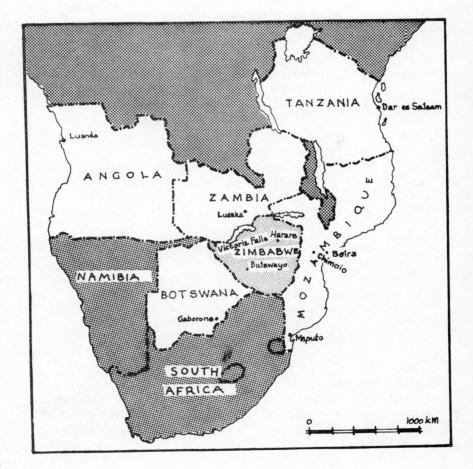

CHAPTER 1

Introduction

I don't believe in black majority rule
ever — not in a thousand years. I think it
would be a disaster for Rhodesia.

> Ian Smith
> Prime Minister, Rhodesia
> March 1975

It seemed like a dream when we won the
elections! We had thought that through
armed struggle we would achieve victory
perhaps in 1981 or 1982, but the reality
of independence came earlier than that.

> Robert Mugabe
> Prime Minister, Zimbabwe
> November 1981

As Rhodesia became Zimbabwe on 18 April 1980 the new government lowered the British, not the Rhodesian, flag. The raising of the new Zimbabwean flag hailed the successful struggle of the Zimbabwean majority against white minority rule. The lowered British flag symbolised the role of the Frontline States – Angola, Botswana, Mozambique, Tanzania, Zambia – in support of that struggle.

When the white settlers unilaterally declared independence for Rhodesia from British colonial rule on 11 November 1965, the British government refused to intervene against the illegal regime and only partially invoked economic sanctions. After their formation in 1974, the Frontline States, through support of guerrilla warfare and through diplomatic pressure, insisted that Britain resume responsibility for independence of its colony. As a small power alliance, the five states provided a united 'frontline' behind the Zimbabwean nationalists' demand for majority control of the state and of the economy.

This Zimbabwean demand required the use of military force, begun only after a long history of unsuccessful negotiations and peaceful petitions. Ian Smith, leader of the Rhodesian Front party, went to Lancaster House in 1979 and agreed to internationally supervised elections, only when the guerrillas were able to control much of the rural areas and the economy could no longer support a war effort costing more than $1 million per day. The victory of Zimbabwe belongs to its people, whose long and difficult struggle against a highly industrialised state with sophisticated military weaponry finally forced the Smith government to negotiate.

The guerrilla army, however, did not win a final military victory; instead, peace was negotiated on the 'second front', a term the late guerrilla military commander Josiah Tongogara gave to the Lancaster House discussions. The nationalists had followed the dual policy supported by the Frontline States: armed struggle and negotiations.

The Role Of The Frontline States

The Zimbabweans won their own independence, but they were not alone. The focus of this study is on the Frontline States, the five neighbours that aided the Zimbabwean liberation movement, much to their own economic and political peril. The Frontline States played three important roles in promoting majority rule for Zimbabwe. First, the military forces depended on guerrilla bases and training camps initially in one (Tanzania) and ultimately four (Angola, Mozambique, Tanzania, Zambia) of the Frontline States. (As will be discussed in Chapter 3, only Botswana was constrained from offering vital military support.) The alliance provided rear base logistical support and training for guerrillas, sanctuaries for refugees, weapons, food, clothing and medicine. International aid from outside the region was also important, but the Frontline States clearly carried the major burden – in terms of both capital and casualties – of the international support for the nationalists.

Equally important, the Frontline States provided a diplomatic base for the Zimbabwean nationalists. Pledging a united stand in support of Zimbabwean independence, they initiated the negotiating conferences that eventually led to Lancaster House. Mobilising, first,

African support through the Organisation of African Unity (OAU), and then wide international support for the nationalists, the Frontline was decisive in exposing the diplomatic manoeuvres of the Rhodesian regime and its allies to establish a neo-colonial government of black leaders dependent on the white minority, rather than the African majority, for their power.

A third key role of the Frontline States was to keep the nationalists united in their demands. A well-known tactic in war is to divide the enemy, and the Smith regime often tried to take advantage of important historical differences among the nationalists. These divisions – ideological, tactical, ethnic – were not unique to the Zimbabwean nationalists, but typical of any guerrilla struggle for liberation. The Frontline States helped the nationalists work through some of the differences and find ways to present a united front to Smith across the negotiating table. The role of the Frontline States was crucial to the united front which finally won the negotiated settlement, primarily because the two nationalist groups were never fully integrated: the nationalists always retained two armies and such divisions remained a legacy for the new government to resolve. However, Smith's inability to divide the political leaders of the guerrilla forces, Robert Mugabe (Zimbabwe African National Union – ZANU) and Joshua Nkomo (Zimbabwe African People's Union – ZAPU) was an important factor in his defeat.

The Western powers of Britain, the United States, and South Africa gave substantial and vital economic support to the white minority regime until the day of its demise.[1] An abundance of strategic minerals, combined with cheap labour and minimal taxes, made the nation attractive to investors. Foreign corporations systematically violated the economic sanctions voted by the United Nations to protest the unilateral declaration of independence, Furthermore, South Africa's white minority regime saw Rhodesia as an important economic and political ally, one that could strengthen South Africa's trade and investment in the region.

The Frontline States were not directly challenging international capitalism, as Western critics contended; the nature of the Zimbabwean economy was to be determined by the Zimbabwean people, during and after the armed struggle. Rather, the Frontline States supported national liberation: majority rule, sufficient state power to control national resources, and support for parties not beholden to South Africa for achieving power. That they could sustain this challenge is surprising, given the fact that all five states are economically dependent on British and American capital, and three of the five (Botswana, Mozambique, Zambia) have economies closely integrated with South Africa's. Despite the tremendous economic leverage the Western powers exerted in Southern Africa, they were unable to withstand the challenge of a few relatively poor and dependent African states. The small alliance won a major victory. In analysing the three roles of the Frontline States, the first problem is, therefore, to explain how these poor and weak states were able to challenge dominant interests in the region.

The 1979 negotiated settlement raises a second major problem. Critics of the negotiations say the war ended because the dominant powers achieved everything they wanted: the Frontline States were not 'successful'; the Western powers maintained or even strengthened their control in the Southern African region. An African government in Zimbabwe provides greater political stability for foreign investment, which the new state must accept for economic viability. This study addresses that problem as a hypothesis, not a premise: did the negotiations and elections compromise the goals of the nationalists? With a negotiated settlement that leaves state structures still very much intact, it would be more difficult for the Zimbabweans to realise their victory. Prime Minister Mugabe readily admits that many problems of the government would not exist if there had been a clear military victory: 'Previously we had hoped that the war would go on to final victory. If that happened, then obviously we wouldn't have Ian Smith here and would never have had General Walls [Commander of the Rhodesian Army]. Quite a number of people would have been brought to trial. But this is not the way that things went.'[2] To understand the reasons for the negotiations and to evaluate their possible impact on the new nation of Zimbabwe, it is necessary to understand the political-economic role of the Frontline States in that struggle.

The third major problem for investigation arises from the success of the independence struggle; it raises the question of the future of the Frontline States in the Southern African region. The national struggle for an independent Zimbabwe was political. The independence victory did not defeat imperialism in the Southern African region. As stated earlier, nationalist goals, which the Frontline supported, were modest: majority rule based on one person-one vote with the government in power not beholden to South Africa and with legal capability to take control of production. Yet these political goals became the basis for economic co-operation to transform the Southern African region. As a central state geographically, and one whose industrial production is second only to South Africa in the region, the political independence of Zimbabwe was viewed as a crucial step toward the economic independence of each of the Frontline States. The five states, joined now by Zimbabwe, Lesotho, Swaziland and Malawi, proposed regional economic co-ordination to end their dependence on South Africa, in particular, and on foreign capital in general. The co-operation is too nascent to evaluate its outcome, but this study will assess the obstacles which must be overcome to achieve its goals.

In summary, this study addresses these problems in the Frontline States' role in support of Zimbabwean political independence by investigating the following questions: 1) How were the Frontline States able to sustain their support for the Zimbabwean nationalists in spite of economic reprisals and direct armed attacks by Rhodesia and South Africa? 2)What factors obliged the white majority regime to negotiate and did negotiations compromise the goals of the nationalists? 3)Based on political co-operation of the Frontline States, the new regional economic co-ordination is proposed as a means for economic liberation; what is the likelihood that regional economic co-operation will promote local control over the productive sectors?

Theoretical Approaches To The Study

In analysing the role of the Frontline States in the liberation of Zimbabwe, two major theoretical issues emerge: the importance of the internationalisation of capital and the centrality of the role of the state. These issues are not new, but the experience of the Frontline States suggests further elaboration of the theories.

Since World War II, internationalisation of capital, through transnational corporations and international bank consortia, has increased to unprecedented levels. This dramatic growth from the centres of advanced capitalism spawned political-economic theories which emphasised the difficulty of newly independent states to weaken economic links which systematically removed capital from their national control. Political independence became regarded as simply an inexpensive variation on the theme of colonialism; neo-colonialism or dependency described the subórdinate economic position of states too weak to challenge their exploitation by the dominant powers. In this period of monopoly capitalism, growth in the concentration and power of the monopoly sectors seemed to breach the wave of political independence of African and Asian colonies. Political independence was described as an indicator of the strength of monopoly capital: it no longer needed to command political control to maintain economic control over raw materials, cheap labour, and new markets.

Emphasising the international economic context of monopoly capital, dependency theories were important in challenging analyses which treated the peripheral states as isolated entities – divorced from their histories of underdevelopment and from the contemporary world economy. They clarified the structural constraints on the peripheral economies and specified economic exchange variables which could perpetuate subordination of those economies. However, what the theories ignore is as important as what they include. Dependency theories designate economic restraints, but cannot analyse the causes or the political effects. Indicators of dependence are used in this study as a description of the international economic linkages of the Frontline States; in short, the theories help to designate international economic pressures which circumscribe the Frontline economies, but they cannot explain the ability of the Frontline to challenge the regional political-economic status quo.

Internationalisation of capital integrates not only economic exchange but also the international division of labour. The spectacular increase in the internationalisation of capital, therefore, was perhaps a sign of its strength but also set off contradictions which challenged its hegemony. One source of antagonism is the rivalry among capitalists themselves. They formed new institutions such as the Trilateral Commission and the international bank consortia to ameliorate this rivalry.[3] More serious contradictions, however, which are the subject of this study, are the challenges arising from the subordinate classes in the periphery. To understand these contradictions, analysis of the peripheral capitalist state becomes crucial. To assert its importance is not to reify the state, but to recognise it as an arena for class struggle.

The state has always been central to the social formation. In emphasising the importance of the dominance of monopoly capital, dependency theories simply lost sight of the importance of the political in the class struggle. In the early stages of mercantile capital, for example, the state aided primitive accumulation which allowed the emerging bourgeoisie to challenge the hegemony of the feudal lords.[4] As Marx analysed, the state also was important in passing laws to ameliorate the class contradictions arising from the sordid labour conditions in industrialised England. These laws were instrumental in changing capitalist attention from absolute surplus value to improving production techniques and efficiency in order to increase relative surplus value. Under *laissez faire* capital, the state was necessary to appear as the disinterested arbiter to regulate contracts and work conditions between labour and capital. Under monopoly capital, the state has entered the sphere of production while retaining its juridico-political functions, in an attempt to delimit the crises of capitalist production: declining profits, stagflation, soaring unemployment.

This study accepts the importance of the international economic context, but it reaffirms the importance of the state in a social formation. The state can be the site of the class struggle, for juridical control and political hegemony are powerful instruments in the class struggle. The state is definitely worth fighting for. But control of the state is only a necessary, not a sufficient, condition for promoting political and economic transformations of peripheral capitalism.

Part of the reluctance of the Frontline States to sustain the armed struggle without negotiations is that they knew from their own histories that not even war will destroy the structures that are a legacy of the colonial political economy. They must be transformed after the guns are laid down. Very few revolutionary governments have successfully broken away from capitalist domination entrenched by years of colonialism. Although the revolutionary parties of Angola and Mozambique won fully their demands from the Portuguese colonialists, the history of 400 years of economic structures subordinated to the development of other economies weighs heavily on their ability to change. The army and the judiciary are the first to be transformed; as repressive state apparatuses, they must serve the new authority.

The more difficult question is: how must the centralised bureaucracy, the commercial sector, and the productive sector be changed, and at what rate? The Mozambique government nationalised petty trading and then turned it back to private entrepreneurs saying the state cannot be concerned with selling toothpaste. Angola has taken majority ownership of corporations running the commanding heights of its economy but, for obvious reasons of capital investment and lack of skilled personnel, has refrained from outright nationalisation. The international division of labour retards national control of production. National revolution may put a new government in power. Social revolution may even put a new class in power. But neither national nor social revolution automatically changes the international economic structures which encase the new state.

It is necessary, therefore, to analyse the role of the state in the periphery to investigate the successes and limitations of the Frontline States. Several differences among the states produced tensions along the Frontline: support for one nationalist group over another, degree of support of the armed struggle, willingness to compromise with minority rights, ability to withstand attacks from Rhodesia and South Africa. Because of the importance of the Frontline in material and logistical support, these differences were as significant to the outcome as the differences among the Zimbabwean nationalists. To understand the vagaries of Frontline support and the tensions which almost split them apart, the central task is to analyse national class alliances and their relationship to each state.

Theories of relative state autonomy raise the question of the relationship of the state to the dominant class. They facilitate comparison and contrast of national social formations which, in turn, help to explain the different roles each state played in the Frontline. It is hypothesised that the successful support of the ZANU-ZAPU nationalists (instead of a Bishop Muzorewa) was possible because four of the five states were able to assert relative autonomy from the dominant classes – although in different ways and certainly to different degrees. Even though the state in Botswana could not claim relative autonomy, the importance of its ideological support will be demonstrated. The analysis uses the theories in a consciously critical way, in order to assess their limitations. As will be discussed in Chapter 6, the theories are highly controversial, because like many of their predecessors, they are partial; they cannot fully explain Frontline hesitancies and successes. However, by focusing on the role of the state in the class struggle within the context of international capital, the theories do indicate directions for further inquiry – and even offer partial answers as a basis for continuing the debate. This study helps to elaborate the theories of relative state autonomy. The theories do facilitate understanding of the Frontline States, but the analysis also develops the theory.

Focus Of The Study

This study enters the Zimbabwean independence struggle at the very end, the last six years of what could be defined as a 15-year struggle (from Unilateral Declaration of Independence – UDI – in 1965) or even a 90-year struggle (from the arrival of white settlers under the leadership of Cecil John Rhodes in 1890). Why? Why bother with analysis of the independence movement when the focus is so narrow?

First, this study is not a history of nationalist organising, peacefully and then militarily, against minority rule. There are several writers much closer to the conflict for at least the last 15 years who are documenting the inside story.[5] Hopefully, others will join them.

Nor is the study an account of guerrilla warfare. The armed struggle began with sabotage in the 1960's to scare the whites into compromise. Organised guerrilla warfare began in earnest in 1966-1967. Full evaluation of the strategy and tactics are needed to determine military successes and failures: this analysis would assist the next struggle in which oppressed peoples are forced into taking up arms to survive. Certainly, Zimbabwean commanders will pass on their legacy.

The study is, rather, an account of the support of Zimbabwean nationalist demands by their neighbours. This support expanded and intensified after the liberation of the Portuguese colonies of Mozambique and Angola, the final stage of which was precipitated by the Portuguese *coup d'etat* on 25 April 1974. Their independence surrounded Rhodesia – except for a small stretch less than 250 kilometres contingent to South Africa – with independent black states hostile to white minority rule on the African continent.

In 1974 the armed struggle was several years old, but important military and political leaders had been languishing in Smith's jails for ten years. The first successful act of the Frontline States was to obtain their release. And this is where the study begins.

Negotiations led by Britain had failed; Smith was intransigent. However, the independence of the Portuguese colonies altered the political and economic status quo of the Southern African region. The leaders of the independent African states moved to increase their material and diplomatic support of their Zimbabwean neighbours.

Chapters 2 and 3 set the historical context for the subsequent analysis. Not simply an enumeration of the events in the liberation struggle, they introduce the major themes of the negotiating conferences. First, in Chapter 2, the debate between the white minority government and the African nationalists is outlined. The controversy was not limited to the question of colour, of black versus white; the issue was more fundamentally about minority control of production: land, minerals, manufacturing. The minority government became willing to share political power but wanted to maintain full control of economic production, a proposal which was unacceptable to the Zimbabwean nationalists. Second, the chapter analyses tensions between the nationalists and the Frontline States as they try to offer a united front to the white regime. The strategies for achieving shared goals were often at variance, with the Frontline States at times putting nationalist leaders in their own jails. In Chapter 3, the tensions along the Frontline itself are explored. As stated above, the states are quite diverse and the minority government took every opportunity to profit from their divisions. In addition, a discussion of the cost of the war to each of the Frontline States reveals the high price – in terms of both development retarded and development diverted – of their support for the liberation struggle. These findings accentuate further the question of how the Frontline States were able to sustain their support.

Chapters 4 and 5 present the international economic context of the struggle. The analysis begins with an empirical investigation of the relationship between the Frontline States and their adversaries. Indicators of productive structure, trade, and capital transfer for each Frontline State are presented to show the dominant pattern in the region. To document the strategic interest of Western capital in Rhodesia, Chapter 5 investigates the extent and variety of foreign capital involvement in the Rhodesian economy. The white settlers declared unilateral independence, but they were not economically independent from foreign capital. Rhodesia, after UDI and the imposition of international sanctions, could not have survived without support from Britain, South Africa and the United States. The historical dominance of these economies over Rhodesia is analysed empirically. While foreign capital was dominant, it was increasingly constrained as the Frontline States promoted international isolation of the Rhodesian economy. The general decline of the hegemony of the advanced capitalist powers, symbolised by the defeat of the United States in Vietnam and of South Africa in Angola during the first year of Frontline negotiations, was a weakness that the Frontline States were able to exploit.

Given the economic vulnerability of the Frontline States and the contradictions in their struggle, Chapters 6 and 7 employ the theories of relative state autonomy to help explain the Frontline States' success. They delineate the reasons for the ability of the states to challenge the dominant economic powers in the region.

The Frontline States are in the process of trying to transform their political success into economic independence. Chapter 8 investigates the Southern African Development Co-ordination Conference (SADCC) which was formed after the independence of Zimbabwe. At this point the SADCC countries (nine in the region) are unified mainly by similar problems: mutual underdevelopment and the desire to overcome their close integration into the South African economy. But the potential is great; rich in minerals, the region could be an important industrial area. Zimbabwe is not yet free from colonial linkages which impede its development, and the problems are similar for the other states. SADCC is a co-ordinated effort to turn the political success of Zimbabwean independence into eventual economic independence for the Southern African region.

Notes

1. These three were by no means the only supporters of Rhodesia; certainly, the Federal Republic of Germany, France, Japan, Portugal, Switzerland and others continued economic relations with the minority regime. But, as discussed in Chapter 5, South Africa, Britain, and the US were by far the largest financial supporters, and the most important politically.
2. Interview by Anthony Lewis, November 1981, Broadcast on Public Broadcasting Service (PBS), 5 January 1982.
3. Holly Sklar, ed., *Trilateralism: The Trilateral Commission and Elite Planning for World Management* (Boston: South End Press, 1980).
   Carol B. Thompson, 'The Politicization of Monopoly Capital: The Trilateral Commission and International Bank Consortia,' *Transition*, 2, no. 1 (May 1979).
4. For a more detailed discussion of this point, see Harry Goulbourne, 'The Problem of the State in Backward Capitalist Societies', *Africa Development* (Dakar), 6, no. 1 (1981), pp. 51-53.
5. The most recent accounts of mobilisation for the guerrilla struggle are the following:
   David Martin and Phyllis Johnson, *The Struggle for Zimbabwe* (London: Faber and Faber and Harare: Zimbabwe Publishing House, 1981).
   Maurice Nyagumbo, *With the People* (London: Allison and Busby, 1980).
   Michael Raeburn, *Black Fire! Accounts of the Guerrilla War in Rhodesia* (London: Julian Friedman, 1978).

CHAPTER 2

The Alliance In Action

To understand the role of the Frontline States in the liberation of Zimbabwe, it is necessary to highlight and analyse the events in which they figure prominently in both the war and the negotiations for a Zimbabwean settlement. This chapter begins the discussion of the historical developments in the conflict from the inception of the Frontline, but it is not simply a historical description. Three major themes are analysed: 1) nature of the changing conflict between the Rhodesian government and the Zimbabwean nationalists; 2) quest for unity among the Zimbabwean nationalists; 3) serious disagreements between the Frontline and the nationalists. A careful look at the negotiating conferences is essential, for they are like signposts, indicating points of contention and of compromise. With these understandings, we can begin to assess the accomplishments of the Frontline States and the limitations to those successes.

Origins Of The Frontline States

In April 1974 the military *coup d'etat* in Portugal toppled not only the Caetano dictatorship in Lisbon but also the political status quo in Southern Africa. The armed struggles in the Portuguese African colonies precipitated the coup, for the Portuguese army refused to continue to fight wars they could not win. The guerrilla wars in all three of the colonies – Angola, Guinea-Bissau, Mozambique – were highly successful against the low morale of the overly extended Portuguese army. By the time of the coup, Frelimo (Front for the Liberation of Mozambique) had liberated one-third of Mozambique and had opened a passage into Rhodesia through Tete province as early as 1970. ZANLA (Zimbabwe African National Liberation Army), the military arm of ZANU, began operating from these liberated areas, with Frelimo's assistance, in 1971. Rhodesia had also been helping its ally, sending troops into Mozambique to fight with the Portuguese against Frelimo before 1970. Both sides viewed the struggle of the white minorities in Mozambique and in Rhodesia as one. Samora Machel, leader of Frelimo, said in 1970, 'Some of us, when we look at the situation in Mozambique, realise that if we liberate Mozambique tomorrow, that will not be the end. The liberation of Mozambique without the liberation of Zimbabwe is meaningless.'[1] With the independence of the Portuguese colonies, the minority regimes of Rhodesia and South Africa could no longer rely on those territories as buffer zones to independent black Africa; they had to face states whose leadership pledged their support for majority rule in the whole region.

As important was the economic threat of an independent Mozambique and Angola. Frelimo's forces had been threatening the transport line from Umtali, Rhodesia, to Beira before the April *coup d'etat*; with the new government in Mozambique the line to Maputo, over which the oil was shipped to keep the Rhodesian war economy running, would also be cut off. The situation would make Rhodesia totally dependent on South Africa for an outlet to the sea. South Africa also had close economic links with Mozambique. Seventy per cent of the ore from its rich Witwatersrand was shipped through Maputo; the new Cabora Basa dam was to supply electricity to the mines; and the Portuguese had provided as many as 350,000 Mozambican men to work in the South African mines. In addition, South African corporations had major investments in the iron ore and diamond mines of Angola.

Prime Minister Vorster responded to this drastically altered political and economic situation in a practical way. In a speech on 24 October 1974 he stated that Southern Africa had reached the crossroads where it had to choose between peace and escalation of strife; the consequences of the latter choice were easily foreseeable and the 'toll of major confrontation would be too high for Southern Africa to pay.'[2] He backed up his words with practical action: he opened discussions with Frelimo instead of supporting a coup attempt by Portuguese settlers against the transitional Frelimo government. President Kaunda immediately responded to the speech, during celebrations of the tenth anniversary of Zambian independence on 25 October, calling it the 'voice of reason.' The two speeches were the first public indication of talks that had been going on between Zambian and South African officials since April. (It is notable that Lonrho, a British corporation which had considerable investments in Rhodesia, South Africa and Zambia, was instrumental as a mediator in these talks.) Meeting in secret, representatives from both Zambia and South Africa hoped to find avenues to a negotiated settlement in Rhodesia. On 8 October they had drawn up a document, 'Towards the Summit: An Approach to Peaceful Change in Southern Africa.' As the title implies, the emphasis was on peaceful, for it discussed a six-month scenario to establish the basic requirements for a negotiated settlement in Rhodesia, such as 'ensuring that ZANU and ZAPU desist from armed struggle . . .' Further, it made promises for Frelimo and SWAPO (fighting for the independence of Namibia) about their relations with South Africa without having consulted either of them.[3]

President Kaunda was anxious for a peaceful solution to Rhodesia for moral and practical reasons. Disappointed over the armed strife among the liberation groups in Angola, he did not like the idea of a protracted war in Rhodesia that might also end up with Africans killing each other. The practical reason was the fundamental need for Zambia to be able to transport its copper to the sea and to import basic commodities. The Benguela Railroad was periodically closed because of the fighting in Angola; Kaunda was concerned that enforcement of economic sanctions against Rhodesia by an independent Mozambique would also cut Zambia's link to the sea through Beira. Hopeful that the altered status quo in Southern Africa was sufficient impetus for the white minority regime to negotiate, he decided to take the risk of compromising in order to promote a peaceful solution to the Rhodesian conflict.

The leaders of Botswana, Tanzania, and Frelimo agreed to share Kaunda's risk-taking (but did not accept the 8 October document). They joined together to formulate a united policy for negotiations with the Rhodesian government. Their first demand was the immediate release of the Zimbabwean nationalist leaders who had been in Smith's prisons for ten years. By 8 November 1974 Smith, under pressure from South Africa, paroled selected nationalist leaders to attend talks in Lusaka.[4] This parole and subsequent release (December) of the Zimbabwean nationalists was the first success of the group that would later be called the Frontline States.*

Smith acquitted the nationalists to obtain agreement for his demands for a ceasefire and for no preconditions to a constitutional

---

*Angola would join the Frontline States only after the 'Second War of National Liberation' in April 1976.

conference. Immediately, the points of contention emerged. The Frontline States hoped Smith was agreeing to negotiate majority rule; no preconditions to him meant that the question of majority rule was not necessarily a topic on the agenda. He would talk of more political power for the African majority but not majority rule. Further, the Frontline States' bargain for the release of the leaders was immediately criticised by the Organisation of African Unity (OAU) because some members feared the border states were negotiating peace at any price. The Smith-Vorster forces were hopeful they were.

The OAU criticism was based on previous experiences of negotiations with South Africa which had ended in total intransigence on the part of the apartheid regime. In April 1968 Vorster and Kaunda had exchanged emissaries and messages in an attempt to find common grounds for talks on Rhodesia. By October, 'dialogue' had come into the South African vocabulary. The Presidents of the Ivory Coast, Senegal, Liberia and Malawi (Houphouet-Boigny, Senghor, Tolbert, and Banda) all promoted dialogue with South Africa as the alternative to violent confrontation. They asserted that trade and co-operation with independent African states would help to liberalise South Africa's domestic policy. Other OAU members pointed out that if South Africa wanted dialogue it could start at home with the African leaders who were in its prisons. The issue became divisive within the OAU.

Kaunda was one of those who criticised the leaders who were willing to trade and receive capital from South Africa. In 1971 Vorster tried to destroy Kaunda's credibility by publicly stating that he too was part of the 'dialogue.' Kaunda responded by publishing the 1968-69 letters to show that although he had agreed to talk with Vorster, he had demanded changes in apartheid as conditions for regular exchange between the two countries.[5] The published letters exposed Vorster as misrepresenting the exchange and further discredited his attempt to normalise relations with independent Africa. 'Dialogue' of 1968-71 became a euphemism for the international legitimisation of apartheid. Although eager for trade relations and air transport rights with independent Africa, South Africa was not willing to transform apartheid. The government gained economic advantages without making concessions about its race policies. In 1974, therefore, it is understandable that some of the African states started to accuse the four states' response as another capitulation to South Africa. The criticism at first seemed well placed, for the initial activities of the new entente were purely negotiations with the Smith and Vorster regimes. The Zimbabwean nationalists were divided, and the armed struggle was weak.

The four, however, did not intend to compromise their opposition against minority rule. The basis of the 'dialogue' had been the Lusaka Declaration, which urged peaceful methods of struggle, with armed struggle only if absolutely necessary:

> We have always preferred, and we still prefer, to achieve liberation without physical violence. We would prefer to negotiate rather than destroy, to talk rather than to kill. We do not advocate violence, we advocate an end to the violence against human dignity which is now being perpetrated by the oppressor of Africa. If peaceful programmes to emancipation were possible, or if changed circumstances were to make it possible in the future, we would urge our brothers in the resistance movements to use peaceful methods of struggle even at the cost of some compromise on the timing of change.[6]

Tanzania and Zambia had signed the Lusaka Declaration but argued that peaceful negotiations did not require trade and capital exchange with the apartheid regime. They later fully supported the 1971 Mogadishu Declaration which rejected 'dialogue' and reaffirmed the armed struggle:

> ...there is no way left to the liberation of Southern Africa except armed struggle to which we already give and will increasingly continue to give our fullest support, that the policy of dialogue advocated by a small group of African leaders which has already been rejected by the OAU is again rejected because it is a ploy to hoodwink the African people . . . We condemn the African countries which, in establishing diplomatic and other relations with South Africa and Portugal, have betrayed the African freedom struggle.[7]

The argument in the OAU about whether the four states were legitimising apartheid by negotiating with South Africa intensified in the first months of 1975. The Zambian Foreign Minister stated the debate was finally silenced by exposing the critics: they came from countries which had regular trade relations with South Africa.[8] At the Ninth Extraordinary Session of the OAU Council of Ministers (Dar es Salaam, April 1975), the issue was debated and resolved. The Frontline States won formal recognition as an ad-hoc committee of the Assembly of the Heads of States of the OAU. More important than the formal recognition, the Council issued the Dar es Salaam Declaration which supported the negotiations the border states had been pursuing:

> As long as the objective of majority rule before independence is not compromised, the OAU would support all efforts made by the Zimbabwe nationalists to win independence by peaceful means. This may mean a holding of a Constitutional Conference where the nationalist forces will negotiate with the Smith regime. If that takes place, the OAU has the duty to do everything possible to assist the success of such negotiations, until and unless the Zimbabwe nationalists themselves are convinced that talks with Smith have failed. In this event, the freedom fighters will have to intensify the armed struggle with the material, financial and diplomatic assistance of independent Africa.[9]

Legacy Of Previous Negotiations For Majority Rule

The four states turned to South Africa because they assessed that South African influence would be crucial to bringing Smith to agree to majority rule. About 2,000 South African police had been helping Smith since 1967 and further military support would be necessary if the war escalated. Prime Minister Vorster and Head of Bureau of State Security, General Hendrik van den Bergh, were open to negotiations, rather than to escalation. The South Africans put pressure on Smith several times during this period, the first time being their insistence that he release the nationalists from prison. They viewed the Rhodesian situation as different from their own. With the white population in Rhodesia only 3 percent of the total, a greater role for Africans would have to be found as the growing economy required more skilled personnel. The South Africans were not talking about majority rule; they wanted Smith to look for a formula by which to share political rule in order to maintain economic control and stability. The South African leaders considered Smith's political intransigence a serious threat to economic stability; they wanted him to talk with the nationalists.

These overtures to South Africa by the Frontline States were only after Britain, the colonial power, had repeatedly failed to convince Smith to accept substantive constitutional changes. The British Labour and Conservative Parties had worked out six principles which were then accepted by the Commonwealth as the basis for constitutional negotiations:

1. guarantee of the principle and intention of unimpeded progress to majority rule;

2. guarantee against retrogressive amendments to the Constitution;

3. immediate improvements in the political status of the African population;

4. progress towards ending racial discrimination;

5. British government to be satisfied that the basis for independence is acceptable to the people of Rhodesia as a whole;

6. regardless of race, no oppression of majority by minority or minority by majority.

Prime Minister Harold Wilson had met with Ian Smith on the HMS *Tiger* (December 1966) and the HMS *Fearless* (October 1968) to discuss them. Smith accepted the proposals in principle but would not abandon the 1965 UDI constitution during the transition. In short, he accepted the principles but not the mechanism necessary to implement them. The British Foreign Secretary, Sir Alec Douglas-Home, met with Smith in Salisbury in November 1971 and an agreement was reached, which the British government interpreted as fulfilling the six principles. The Pearce Commission was then sent to Rhodesia to survey African opinion; their leaders had been excluded from the talks about the proposed constitution which postponed majority rule to the distant future.[10] Bishop Abel Muzorewa, with a mandate from the imprisoned ZANU and ZAPU leaders, led a successful campaign to oppose the proposal of independence before majority rule. As the Commission travelled around the country, they heard a resounding shout of 'No independence before majority rule,' later to be known as the NIBMAR position.

Smith was encouraged, not discouraged, by the talks, for he asserted that the Rhodesian position had became stronger. As he stated in the House of Assembly on 5 April 1973:

> I believe it would be appropriate to point out . . . that on every occasion on which we have held talks we have strengthened our position. We came back from HMS *Fearless* with terms which, for us, were an improvement on what we had been offered on HMS *Tiger*. Then, in turn, the Constitution negotiated in 1971 . . . is an improvement on what we were offered on *Fearless*. I must warn people who are clamouring for fresh negotiations,

that if these were to take place, there would be new demands which I would make on the British government . . . and we would emerge stronger than before.[11]

After the African rejection of the 1972 constitutional proposals, the British government, in practical terms, relinquished all responsibility as the colonial power to the hands of Smith. As will be discussed in Chapter 5, sanctions were not effective; political pressure ceased; the British government appeared to have accepted the unilateral declaration of independence of its rebel colony.

The willingness of each of the Frontline States to try to resolve the hostility was consistent with the development of their policies, emanating from their own anti-colonial struggles. Presidents Julius Nyerere, Kenneth Kaunda and Sir Seretse Khama led independence struggles that identified closely with social democracy. Their independence movements were based on high moral principles for racial and social justice; colonial political structures had to be changed because they violated basic human values of racial equality. Further, the strategies that the movements pursued were based on Gandhian principles of moral persuasion with non-violent resistance if necessary. The leaders all led strikes and boycotts to convince the British government that self-rule was necessary. Their non-violent confrontations exposed the contradictions between the social democracy professed by the British Labour Party and the treatment of Africans as subject and inferior peoples. The moral convictions directed the strategy of their own political struggles.

After winning the struggle to end minority colonial rule, the Tanganyikan government, at independence in 1961, refused to join the British Commonwealth unless South Africa withdrew; South Africa was subsequently asked to leave. In 1965 Tanzania (Tanganyika changed to the United Republic of Tanzania, one year after its uniting with Zanzibar) broke diplomatic relations with Britain because it did nothing to nullify the UDI proclaimed by white Rhodesians. As a result Tanzania lost £7.5 million (approximately $21 million) aid from Britain which was considered essential for the 1964-1969 development plan. Frelimo affirms that its war against Portuguese colonialism could not have been won without Tanzanian support. Tanzania sacrificed much for the liberation of Mozambique by offering guerrilla training bases and material support. The Tanzanian leaders viewed the Zimbabwean struggle as yet another step necessary to eradicate racism and minority control in Southern Africa. Tanzanian support for racial justice has been consistent for the last two decades.

Zambia was born in the struggle to resist subordination to white Rhodesia in the Central African Federation (CAF). The CAF, established in 1953, consisted of Northern Rhodesia (Zambia), Nyasaland (Malawi) and Southern Rhodesia. But the African majority in the British Protectorates — Northern Rhodesia and Nyasaland — rebelled against political and economic subordination to the white minority of Southern Rhodesia and the Federation broke up in 1963. Using populist appeals such as the platform of Humanism, Zambian leaders pledged support for the African majority in Rhodesia. Racial justice was not to stop at the border.

As an independent state whose economy was captured by the South African Customs Union, Botswana was situated between the two minority regimes. With the escalation of the Zimbabwean hostilities, Botswana's position would quickly become untenable, for it was quite vulnerable to any economic or military reprisals that could be taken by either Rhodesia or South Africa. At the same time, however, because its economy was captured by the South African Customs Union, the Botswanan leaders knew well how hollow political independence was without economic control over production. An independent Zimbabwe would facilitate Botswana's own economic release from South African hegemony. Caught in the middle, both geographically and economically, Botswana was limited in its ability to help the Zimbabwean liberation struggle. The strong will of the Batswana to preserve their independence, first articulated by their most prominent leaders in the late nineteenth century, surprised many observers who doubted the country's ability to adopt a principled stand because of its economic vulnerability. President Khama told the Development Committee of the European parliament:

> My country depends on those minority-ruled regimes whose policies we deplore . . . The beef that we sell to the Community is transported to the sea through South Africa. Our whole economic life and transportation system are bound up with those of Rhodesia and South Africa. This is the extent to which we find ourselves at the mercy of the regimes against which we support the liberation struggle.[12]

In spite of this vulnerability, the Botswanan leaders chose to become a Frontline State.

As stated earlier, the revolutionary struggle in Angola and Mozambique precipitated the discussion for change in Zimbabwe. They fought Portuguese colonialism for about a decade during which time the leaders had many contacts with both ZANU and ZAPU. In fact, leaders of ZAPU had been organising for independence before Frelimo and the MPLA were formed. But the armed struggle was slower to develop in Zimbabwe. First, Zambia was not independent until 1964 so no contiguous territory was available from which to launch incursions into Rhodesia. Second, it was difficult to infiltrate arms and men into Rhodesia across the Zambezi River even after Zambia became independent. The river border between Zambia and Rhodesia was a natural setting for ambush by the Rhodesians as the guerrillas tried to cross. Frelimo offered a passageway through Tete to ZANU and ZAPU by 1970. ZAPU was going through a leadership crisis at the time and could not send forces; ZANU was ready to go in and therefore started its operations from a liberated sector of Tete. With long personal, political and military contacts between the MPLA and Frelimo leadership and the Zimbabwean nationalists, joining the Frontline States as the newly independent states of Angola and Mozambique was a logical continuation of the exchanges.

In spite of this history of shared struggle against racism and colonialism, the terms accepted by the Frontline States for the release of the nationalists created two immediate crises between the Frontline and the nationalists. One condition for the release of the nationalists was an immediate ceasefire. The Frontline States decided it was a necessary gesture for negotiating in good faith. But ZANU had been escalating the guerrilla war in the north-east and knew that Smith was willing to negotiate only because of their recent successes against his forces. To halt the armed struggle would remove the incentive for him to talk. They were angry with the Frontline Presidents for this concession, made without consulting them, and immediately argued against it.

The second crisis was the demand for the nationalists to dissolve their individual parties and to unite under one. The Frontline assessed that if negotiations were to be successful with Smith, the nationalists had to unite and present him with unified demands across the negotiating table. At this point, the MPLA was not yet part of the Frontline because of its own difficulties with two other guerrilla forces in the transitional government to an independent Angola; the Frontline leaders, especially Kaunda and Nyerere, did not want to see

Zimbabwe torn apart by similar factions among the guerrillas. Ignoring Zimbabwean history, they demanded not simply a united front, but a single party. The Zimbabwean nationalists were divided into four groups at the time of their release: ZANU, ZAPU, FROLIZI (Front for the Liberation of Zimbabwe), ANC (African National Council).[13] When the Frontline States insisted on a unified party against Rhodesia, the nationalists resisted. ZANU refused the Frontline demand that the groups dissolve their own parties into one and that they pick one leader. The one leader was likely to be Joshua Nkomo, whose command they had chosen to leave (see pp. 44–46). Finally, after much heated debate with the Frontline Presidents, they agreed to a united front. Their parties were not dissolved but put under an umbrella ANC, with Bishop Abel Muzorewa as the compromise head. On 7 December 1974 they issued a unity statement in which they agreed to 'merge their respective organs and structures into the ANC' within four months. They also, however, recognised 'the inevitability of continued armed struggle and all other forms of struggle until the total liberation of Zimbabwe.'[14]

The Frontline States' initiative opened a path for a negotiated settlement, but also immediately put obstacles in that path which set up tensions between themselves and the nationalists. However, although the Frontline was economically vulnerable to their more powerful neighbours, they did not 'sell out' as their critics had predicted. They were interested in trying to save lives by negotiating majority rule. If Ian Smith had been willing in 1974 to negotiate transition to majority rule as he did in 1979, tens of thousands of Zimbabwean, Zambian, Mozambican, Tanzanian, Angolan, and Botswanan lives would have been saved. But the white regime, still supported by its Western allies, could be persuaded only by five more years of warfare.

Tactical Changes By The Rhodesian Government

The unilateral declaration of independence (UDI) proclaimed white settler refusal to accept one person, one vote. The subsequent diplomatic discussion over majority rule had two stages, for Smith changed his tactics as the war mounted and the international community increased pressure. At first, Smith refused to accept 'majority rule in my lifetime.' In June 1974, before the formation of the Frontline States, Smith talked with Bishop Muzorewa of the ANC. He proposed to discuss majority rule in 40-50 years, not sooner;

Muzorewa refused to discuss it. Right after the umbrella ANC was formed, Smith had a series of talks with Joshua Nkomo. On 19 March 1975, they broke down because Smith was talking about majority rule in ten to fifteen years. He considered this time span as a reasonable basis for discussion with the newly released nationalists. When the talks failed, Smith angrily reiterated that there would be no majority rule 'in a thousand years.' Not until April 1976 when US Secretary of State Henry Kissinger began his shuttle diplomacy in Southern Africa did Smith agree to majority rule within two years. It was a major breakthrough and the only real success of Kissinger's shuttles. By August, however, Smith tried to renounce that agreement. The drastic reduction in transition time for majority rule from fifty (1974) to two (1976) years resulted from the successful guerrilla warfare and the international diplomatic isolation of the minority regime. Both the war and the international outcry were escalating.

The tactical change that Smith made as the pressure mounted was to change the definition of majority rule. Smith manoeuvred to make it look as though he was accepting majority rule within 'two years,' but in fact, he was accepting only the semantics of majority rule, not the substance. The Frontline States were clear about what they meant by majority rule, as President Nyerere summarised: 'The purpose of Africa's independence struggles is the freedom of Africa and Africans. Our independent governments . . . must be the instruments through which the peoples of Africa develop themselves and their countries and enlarge their freedom until it means a life of dignity for every individual African.'[15]

Rhodesian tactics to extend the time to majority rule and then to change the definition of majority rule, involved five attempts for internal settlement:

1. 1969 — While in Smith's jail, Ndabaningi Sithole agreed to renounce the armed struggle not only personally, but for the party he then led, ZANU, in return for the release of ZANU members. The other party members in jail condemned the deal. No release took place.

2. 1975 — After the Victoria Falls conference in August, Smith opened bilateral talks with Joshua Nkomo. A series of talks between the two, supported by Zambia, continued until 19 March 1976 when both parties announced they had reached an impasse; Smith, clearly, was not willing to discuss a short transition period to majority rule.

3. 1976 — After the abortive Geneva Conference in October,

Smith brought Chiefs Chirau and Ndiweni into his government. Owing their status totally to Smith, the manoeuvre did not succeed in establishing legitimacy for the regime.

4. 1978 — During the discussions about the Anglo-American proposals at the Malta conferences, Smith staged his own 'settlement.' In March, Muzorewa, Sithole and Chirau agreed to a new constitution for Zimbabwe-Rhodesia.

5. 1978 — Smith started secret talks in August with Nkomo to bring him into the March settlement, with Muzorewa, Sithole, and Chirau, in an obvious effort to make it look more respectable. The negotiations broke off when Mugabe denounced the secret talks and Nkomo refused to compromise.

At first the settlements were simply an attempt to bring a few black faces into the government. For the third settlement Smith even tried to legitimise chiefs who owed their status to his sponsorship as the 'fair' representatives of the African majority. In later attempts, he began to talk of shared political power with leaders elected by a limited, but larger, franchised African voting population. Throughout these discussions, majority rule meant only shared political power with the whites retaining veto power in parliament, control of the army, police, judiciary and civil service and total control over the economy 'Majority rule with minority rights' became the semantic camouflage for white blocking power in parliament and white monopoly of the productive forces. By the time of the 1978 internal settlement with Muzorewa, the rhetoric and the programme had been refined; Smith even agreed to universal suffrage for the Africans with their right to choose an African prime minister. Although Nkomo entered into talks on two occasions, ZAPU remained allied with ZANU in the position that they were not fighting for a few seats in parliament, but for land: 'We have a strange situation in our country where three percent of the population, on account of their race, have seized 50 percent of the land through many and diverse techniques. Do you protect property in the possession of thieves?'[16] To the nationalist forces, majority rule meant no less than majority control of the productive forces of the economy, a mandate by the people for the party they chose to run the state *and* the economy.

Disagreeing with Smith's initial refusal to discuss majority rule with the Zimbabweans, South African Prime Minister Vorster did put pressure on Smith to release them from prison and to engage in talks. But the South African government's policy changed as Smith gradually moved toward some form of shared political power. In May 1976, after Smith had refused any compromise at the 1975 Victoria Falls conference and the guerrilla war was escalating, South African Secretary of Information, Eschel Rhoodie, an influential member of the government and a close friend of Vorster, stated, 'We will not under any circumstances undertake an upholding operation. Military intervention by South Africa to uphold the Rhodesian government is absolutely out of the question.'[17] By the second all-parties conference in Geneva in October 1976, Vorster was prompting Smith to accept shared power. He felt that Smith was lying to him and simply using his auspices to maintain a hard line. They were supplying Rhodesia with trade links by breaking international sanctions and had their troops in Rhodesia,but they told Smith that his position was untenable. When Smith did change his strategy from refusal of majority rule to changing the definition of majority rule, Vorster rallied support behind him stating in parliament in January 1977 that 'it would be wrong in principle to exert pressure on Smith . . . I am not prepared to do anything dishonourable.' He noted that Smith had to convince his cabinet to accept the Kissinger plan which led to Geneva while 'Nkomo and Mugabe are not responsible to anybody and they can change their stance all the time.'[18] The South African leader's attitude softened even more by the time Smith succeeded in bringing Muzorewa, Sithole and Chirau into the government. As will be discussed in Chapter 5, South Africa gave considerable support to the Rhodesian army: aircraft with pilots, soldiers, heavy equipment, and low interest loans. South Africa's key role strategically gave the government leverage to convince Smith to enter the talks and then to encourage him to find a formula to bring Africans into the legislature and executive without relinquishing white control of the state apparatus or of the economy. Although South Africa was an ally of Rhodesia and the key to Smith surviving as long as he did, the South African government was quicker in realising that the end of the war was possible only if the Zimbabweans assessed they had some political role. Both the South African and Rhodesian governments, however, were incorrect in assuming that token government positions for Africans and no change in the economy would suffice.

Negotiating Conferences: Camouflage Or Compromise?

Victoria Falls

In 1975 South Africa only pressured Smith to attend the first all-parties conference at Victoria Falls. After months of personal meetings between Smith and the released nationalist leaders ('talks about talks'), the conference, held on 25 August in a train on the Victoria Falls bridge between Rhodesia and Zambia, was to start the process for the constitutional conference as the first step toward majority rule. President Kaunda led the Frontline negotiations and was hoping South Africa would pressure Smith to agree to steps for a constitutional conference. But the meeting seems to have been as much for promoting South African international prestige as for negotiating any change in the Rhodesian government. Prime Minister Vorster was delighted that the South African regime received international attention as an 'arbiter' in the negotiation. (When Vorster arrived, a sign held by a member of the Zambian United National Independence Party (UNIP) read, 'Vorster becomes great in Africa today.') The delegation from Mozambique was not even informed that Vorster would be at the meeting, and they were furious when they saw him, South African Foreign Minister, Hilgard Muller and General van den Bergh at the Musi-O-Tunya Hotel on the Zambian side of the falls. Smith had been using the ceasefire, enforced on the guerrillas by the Frontline, to move equipment and troops to his advantage. With no armed struggle to pressure Smith, he was not even willing to grant amnesty to six key members of the executive of the umbrella ANC, including Sithole and James Chikerema (leader of Frolizi), so they could return to Rhodesia to negotiate a constitutional conference; he remained intransigent about the long transition time to majority rule and about continuing dominance and control by the Rhodesian Front party during the transition. The talks lasted only a few hours.[19]

The role of 'arbiter' that South Africa was trying to play at Victoria Falls is rather ironic since at the time of the conference it had begun its invasion of Angola. In alliance with two guerrilla forces, FNLA (National Front for the Liberation of Angola) and UNITA (National Union for the Total Independence of Angola), the South Africans were trying to prevent the MPLA from forming the government of Angola at independence which was scheduled for 11 November 1975. The invasion was turned back later only a few hundred miles outside of Luanda when Cuban forces were invited by the MPLA to help them withstand the attack. The South African strategy was to promote a moderate black government that would not be hostile to apartheid, and they decided that a full scale invasion was necessary to help those factions (FNLA and UNITA) to win. South Africa had the same goal for Zimbabwe, but was interested in trying to negotiate such a government.

The Angolan 'second war of liberation' also divided the Frontline States. The Presidents had strongly supported the Alvor (15 January 1975) and Nakuru Agreements (16-21 June 1975) in which the three parties pledged themselves to a unity government. But as unity clearly became impossible, Machel maintained his historical close links with the MPLA. Nyerere hesitated — hoping for unity — but also backed the MPLA as the party most capable of ruling. Although Kaunda had supported both the MPLA and UNITA throughout the liberation struggle, he was angry over massive Soviet arms to the MPLA and continued to call for no foreign intervention in Angola. This division within the Frontline was serious. Kaunda only belatedly recognised the new government on 15 April 1976. (Angola was admitted to the OAU on 11 February 1976.) It was in April when Angola joined the Frontline States to support Zimbabwean liberation. The important message of the Angolan crisis to the Frontline was not to let the divisions among the Zimbabwean nationalists deteriorate to open war against each other.

Discussions about Zimbabwean independence made little progress during the full-scale war in Angola. In February 1976, British Foreign Secretary James Callaghan sent officials to Salisbury who found Smith unwilling to negotiate. On 22 March Callaghan offered proposals as preconditions for a constitutional conference: principle of majority rule, elections in 18 months to two years, negotiations not to be protracted, independence only after majority rule, and no attempt to impede progress to majority rule and elections. Smith found the conditions extreme.

Only one month after South Africa withdrew from Angola, US Secretary of State Henry Kissinger arrived in Southern Africa in April 1976. Mozambique had closed its border (March) to Rhodesian traffic to enforce international sanctions. The second 'internal' settlement talks of Smith had collapsed (14 March) because Joshua Nkomo would not agree to the time for transition. Further, by January 1976, the Zimbabwe People's Army (ZIPA) had been formed from ZANLA and ZIPRA forces and was escalating the war. During his two-week tour of Africa, Kissinger made a major policy speech in Lusaka on 27 April 1976. He declared US support for majority rule in Rhodesia, for independence in Namibia, and for termination of

CHART

NEGOTIATIONS FOR ZIMBABWE SETTLEMENT

Conference	Date	Participants	Origins	Negotiation Results
Victoria Falls	August 1975	Vorster-Smith Kaunda Umbrella ANC (ZANU, ZAPU, Frolizi, ANC)	1. Independence of Portuguese colonies 2. Smith release of Zimbabwe nationalist leaders 3. Promised South African withdrawal of troops 4. Ceasefire by guerrillas	FAILURE — over issues of 1. Transition time to majority rule 2. Authority of interim government
Geneva	October-December 1976	Britain Smith ANC (Muzorewa) Patriotic Front (ZANU-ZAPU) Sithole (contending to represent ZANU)	1. Successful defeat of South Africa in Angola resulting in 2. Intensification of war by ZIPA (ZANU-ZAPU) 3. Kissinger initiatives	FAILURE — over issues of composition and authority of interim government: 1. Role of British Resident Commissioner for transition 2. Selection of Council of Ministers 3. Composition of security forces for transition

Malta I	February 1978			FAILURE — over issues of Anglo-American failure to bring Smith to negotiating table even after PF concessions including: a. British Resident Commissioner with Governing Council b. UN to supervise elections c. British officials in senior civil servant posts for transition d. Limited amnesty for Rhodesian leaders
Malta II (Venue: Dar es Salaam)	April 1978	Britain-US Frontline States Patriotic Front	Intensification of guerrilla war after Zambia released ZANU leaders (1976) and after crisis with ZANU/ZAPU (ZIPA) resolved	
Lancaster House (London)	September-December 1979	Britain Muzorewa-Smith (Sithole) Patriotic Front	1. Formation of 'Zimbabwe-Rhodesia' 2. Further guerrilla successes 3. Election of Conservatives in Britain with threat to recognise 'Zimbabwe-Rhodesia' 4. Commonwealth Conference pressure on Britain to call conference	SUCCESS — compromises on 1. Length of transition, size of observer force, election date 2. Number of guerrilla assembly points 3. Armed forces given equal status for transition 4. White minority over-represented in parliament 5. Compensation for land and pensions guaranteed

apartheid in Southern Africa. He offered his offices to facilitate negotiations.

On 24 June while South Africa was still experiencing internal turmoil after the 16 June Soweto uprisings, Kissinger met Vorster in Bavaria. They were the first high level meetings between South Africa and the United States since World War II. The meetings were to discuss negotiations for Rhodesia but South Africa also wanted an end to the US arms embargo and to curbs on government credit to South Africa.

Smith asked for talks with the United States to explain the Rhodesian position but also told the *Washington Post* in an interview on 25 August 1976 that a timetable for majority rule was 'illogical'; progress could only be made by achievement 'not by a clock or calendar.'

After a second conference with Prime Minister Vorster in Zurich, Kissinger made a second trip to Southern Africa in September. As he travelled to Tanzania and Zambia (President Machel did not see him), the Presidents told him to commit Smith to majority rule but not to set up steps for negotiation because such details could only be worked out between the nationalists and Smith. They warned him of viewing the conflict only as a Cold War confrontation with Moscow, stating he must consider the African historical context. Finally, they pledged themselves to military support of the nationalists unless the transition to majority rule could be worked out.

When Kissinger met with Smith in Pretoria on 19 September, Smith did agree to majority rule in two years, the only real breakthrough of the shuttles. But, in spite of warnings by the Frontline Presidents to leave the details to another all-parties conference, Kissinger supported a five-point proposal (repeating the two year limit to majority rule proposed by British Foreign Minister James Callaghan):

1. the attainment of majority rule within two years;

2. the immediate formation of an interim government, comprising two bodies — a Council of State made up of equal numbers of blacks and whites and a Council of Ministers appointed by the Council of State;

Responsibility of the Council of State: white chairman (with no special vote) to direct the Council in drafting a constitution and supervising elections for majority rule.

Responsibility of the Council of Ministers: black majority (with a black first minister) to take charge of government departments;

The Ministers of Defence and of Law and Order would be white.

3. British legislation to permit the elections for majority rule and the transition to independence;

4. the end of world economic sanctions against Rhodesia and the cessation of guerrilla activities upon formation of the interim government;

5. a programme of foreign economic support to ensure combined Rhodesian economic growth.[20]

On 24 September 1976 Smith announced on Rhodesian television that he accepted these principles.

Meeting in Lusaka on 26 September, the Frontline States rejected the proposals, calling them 'legalising colonialist and racist structures of power.'[21] President Nyerere, in particular, was angry because he had refused to discuss details and now details were being presented as an agreed plan. President Machel summarised the Frontline view of the Kissinger shuttles, 'You see in Zimbabwe today we have an armed struggle, that is the secondary school. When it becomes a revolutionary struggle, that is the university, and Dr Kissinger is coming to close the university before they can get there.'[22]

The Frontline condemned the proposals and asked Britain to call an all-parties conference to discuss how to achieve majority rule in two years. Later the Frontline Presidents found that Kissinger had sent them different messages about his talks with Smith. The arrogance of such a manoeuvre incensed the leaders. The State Department acknowledged on 27 September that 'major details' of the proposal had not been previously accepted by the African leaders. The leaders had accepted the majority-rule plan as a basis for further negotiations, while Smith had presented the programme to the Rhodesian public as a concrete settlement.

Geneva

The African call for an all-parties conference was to Britain. Realising that South Africa was now putting little pressure on Smith and that the Americans were preoccupied with Cold War considerations, the nationalists and the Frontline States once again called for Britain to take the lead as the colonial power; refusing to recognise UDI, the African leaders considered Britain to be the legitimate colonial power in Rhodesia. At the formation of the Frontline States in December 1974, they did not want Britain to step back into the negotiations because they had been disappointed in Britain's previous record of acquiescent support for Smith's UDI. In April 1975, Nyerere had told the British Foreign Office that it was not necessary yet for them to step in and that the Frontline States would request their arbitration when it was desired. Calling on Britain to chair an all-parties conference in the fall of 1976, the African leaders were requesting Britain to resume its role as the colonial power.

The Geneva Conference opened on 28 October 1976 chaired by the British ambassador to the UN, Ivor Richard. Smith arrived declaring the six proposals as non-negotiable. He left the conference for a full month and returned only to reiterate that the proposals were not negotiable. He and his deputy rejected the nationalists' counter proposals for a Council of Ministers to rule Rhodesia during transition with a clear majority of ZANU-ZAPU representatives and a British Resident Commissioner to oversee the implementation of the transition agreements. Smith insisted that the executive, the military and the police stay in white hands during the transition. The nationalists stalemated the talks for a while by demanding independence by 1 September 1977 but then compromised to 1 March 1978. Richard adjourned the conference on 12 December as a total stalemate. Smith regarded the request for a British Resident Commissioner during the transition as 'ghastly'. Few of the positions changed during the Geneva Conference, and both sides considered the talks a failure. The most significant change was the merger of ZANU-ZAPU, to be discussed later, into the Patriotic Front just before their attendance at the conference.

It was only after this conference that Smith began to modify his definition of 'majority rule.' He proposed to change 'hurtful discriminatory measures.' This change in rhetoric was important, for Smith was showing that he finally was listening to his allies, agreeing that some reforms had to be made to encourage a few Africans into co-operating with the government. The most significant signal was a constitutional change of the 1969 Land Tenure Act. All rural land, except the Tribal Trust Lands reserved for Africans, became open to purchase by all races on a commercial basis. Africans could buy farms in the European areas and Europeans could buy land in the African Purchase Areas. In reality, the inequity changed little, for only a few Africans could afford to purchase 'European land.' However, these amendments created a crisis in the Rhodesian Front party, for the right wing wanted to preserve the status quo. Twelve Rhodesian

Front MP's (who subsequently resigned), refused to vote for the amendment and it passed with the necessary two-thirds vote only when six African MP's voted in favour, although the other African MP's rejected it as constituting little change. Smith replaced his appeals for 'high standards' with references to a 'broad-based government.' Sports in schools were desegregated, as were some restaurants. During 1977, therefore, Smith was busy clearing out some of the obstacles to an internal settlement, to make it feasible for African leaders to join his government in the movement for reform (but not for fundamental change).

Anglo-American Proposals

Early in 1977 David Owen became British Foreign Secretary, and Andrew Young, US Ambassador to the UN, began to represent the new Carter administration in African affairs. Young flew to Nigeria in February 1977, just one month after Jimmy Carter became President, and discussed Nigerian views about the Rhodesian negotiations. By August, Young and Owen were on their own shuttle tour of Southern Africa. New Anglo-American proposals were formally presented in September, after being secretly discussed since March. The new initiative by the envoys of Britain and the United States did not alter at all American and British capital interests in Rhodesia. As is analysed in detail in Chapter 5, both private corporate and official government economic transactions were supportive of the white minority regime until the very end of the war. What needs to be explained here is why the Anglo-Americans increased their involvement in the negotiations, which eventually led to Lancaster House.

The clear impetus for the Anglo-American proposals was the escalation of the guerrilla war by 1977. After the release of the ZANU detainees (especially Commander Josiah Tongogara) in Zambia in October 1976 and the resolution of the conflict within ZIPA, ZANU was able to escalate the war drastically. As Machel stated, 'Only three months after the war was escalated, the Anglo-American proposals were presented.'

In addition, it appeared to the American government that the Soviets were successfully increasing their influence in the African continent.[24] In March 1977 Soviet President Podgorny and Fidel Castro both toured Southern Africa. Castro received a hero's welcome wherever he went. Although this was the first state visit of a

top-ranking Soviet official to Southern Africa, the reception for
Podgorny was mixed: in Tanzania, President Nyerere kept the visit at
a low profile. He castigated the Soviets for refusing to recognise and
aid ZANU on an equal basis with ZAPU; the Soviets continued to send
arms only to ZAPU. In contrast, the Mozambican government signed
a 30-year Treaty of Cooperation and Friendship with the USSR that
included a mutual defence pact.[25] Further, by mid 1977, Ethiopia was
demanding that the United States relinquish bases near the Red Sea,
and the Ogaden war had resumed. New initiatives, therefore, to
sustain Anglo-American strategic interests in Southern Africa
became top priority.

The initial reaction of the Patriotic Front (ZANU-ZAPU) and the
Frontline States to the Anglo-American proposals was scorn. Few of
the conditions had changed from the five points of the Kissinger
proposals. The major items of controversy of the document 'Rhodesia
— Proposals for a Settlement'[26] were the following:

1. Similar to the Kissinger proposals, the Anglo-American one
did not suggest how Smith would be convinced to step down, unless he
did it voluntarily: 'The two governments will take such steps as seem
to them appropriate to secure the transfer of power by Mr Smith . . . on
a day to be agreed.'

2. Similar to the Kissinger proposals, the Anglo-American plan
remained vague on the composition of the new army, seeming to
include the Rhodesian army as an equal force: the Commander in
Chief will command 'all armed forces which may be lawfully
operating' during the transition. On 1 September, Owen had said the
liberation forces would form the basis of the new army with elements
from the Rhodesian army, but this was not stated in the proposals.
Nyerere insisted on a written amendment calling for 'not only the
removal of the illegal Smith regime but also the dismantling of its
apparatus of repression in order to pave the way for the creation of
police and armed forces which would be responsible for the needs of
the people of Zimbabwe, and assure the orderly and effective transfer
of power.'[27] Owen and Young agreed, but the amendment was never
formally added and it was not shown to Smith when they met with him.
The Patriotic Front was clear about its position: 'The people of
Zimbabwe know that their independence shall come about and be
defended by their sons and daughters who have sacrificed lives and
sweated blood fighting in the ranks of the patriotic liberation forces.
Therefore, there can be no new army for an independent Zimbabwe

. . . It is only fair for us to be categorical on the question of the armed forces of the Rhodesian regime. They must be dismantled *in toto*. This includes the police.'[28] The composition of the army during the transition remained the fundamental barrier between Smith and the nationalists.

3. Reflecting the Geneva discussions, the plan called for the appointment of a British Resident Commissioner, where the Kissinger plan had left control during the transition in the hands of the white minority regime. The proposal was presented in terms of a 'return to legality' of British colonial rule and the granting of broad executive powers to the Resident Commissioner. But neither the Frontline States nor the Patriotic Front regarded the British administrator as 'neutral'. President Machel said in the United Nations on 3 October 1977 that the Resident Commissioner's powers are 'more concentrated than during the whole colonial period'. The Patriotic Front condemned his absolute power over the police, judicial system, civil service, and election process which would all still be under Rhodesian Front control: 'Whilst we believe that a Resident Commissioner is inevitable for the process of decolonisation, we cannot, however, agree to his assumption of absolute colonial powers . . . The installation of a Resident Commissioner does not introduce neutrality . . . By what faith can an election booth be regarded as "democratic, free and impartial" if it is surrounded at its four corners by Smith's henchmen, his policemen, his soldier, his District Commissioner, and his judge, supervised by a British colonial officer, all of whom combined yesterday in hanging hundreds of freedom fighters?'

4. The Anglo-American proposals did pledge in writing the election of parliament would be by one person-one vote. Yet Smith still hedged his definition of majority rule. On British television on 25 September 1977 he was asked whether he would now consider one man-one vote. He hesitated, 'Yes, with the provision that I would like to know what the alternative ideas are for preserving the kind of standards that I have referred to.' The Anglo-American proposals went a long way in preserving Smith's 'standards' through strong provisions for 'minority rights', as outlined in the draft constitution:[29]

    a. It insured one-fifth of the seats in parliament for minorities for at least the first eight years of independence.

    b. The Bill of Rights of the draft constitution provided for the protection of private property which the government could only expropriate on 'specific grounds of public interest' and then only with 'payment of adequate compensation'.

    c. The pensions of civil servants, who comprised 30 per cent of the white working population, were guaranteed.

    d. Provisions for land reform were left vague with the intent that only unused white land would be redistributed through purchase schemes (about 7.5 million acres of arable land).

    e. Free remittance abroad of pensions and payments for land and other property was guaranteed.

    f. Broad assurances of a continued capitalist economy were given, with a $1.5 billion Zimbabwe Development Fund to 'encourage commercial capital flows, especially in extractive, processing and manufacturing industries, supported as appropriate by national export credit and investment insurance agencies'.

Smith did not find the Anglo-American proposals exactly to his liking either. Feeling pressure from the Anglo-Americans that he should step down as leader of the Rhodesian Front (RF) so a new face could lead the RF during a transition, he called for a special election. On 31 August 1977 his party gained all 50 seats in parliament, and it reaffirmed 'good ol' Smithy.' In addition, Smith went to Lusaka to meet with President Kaunda about the transition. After the meeting Kaunda called for independence before majority rule, a line that had been fully rejected by the Patriotic Front and the Frontline States. This manoeuvre by Smith caused much tension in the Frontline and the Patriotic Front which will be analysed later. By November Smith rejected the Anglo-American proposals because he had made progress in establishing agreements with Muzorewa and Sithole for his 'broad-based government'. In September talks for an internal settlement had begun, but Muzorewa refused to attend because Smith had sent bombers to massacre over 1,000 people at refugee and military camps near Chimoio and Tembwe in Mozambique. Muzorewa said he was outraged at the 'slaughter of non-combatants'.

Malta I and II

David Owen asserted that the Chimoio attacks showed that the Smith government was 'simply not on its back' and took a wait-and-see attitude about the internal settlement talks. He did realise, however, that the attack and the talks for an internal settlement further divided the two sides and decided against trying for an all-parties conference about the Anglo-American proposals. The Patriotic Front refused to go to London because of Owen's statement, so he agreed instead to call a conference in Malta in February 1978. The Malta meeting was attended by Mugabe and Nkomo, Young and Owen, and the American Assistant Secretary of State for Africa, Richard Moose. Field Marshal Lord Carver, designated as the proposed Resident Commissioner, and Major-General Prem Chand, assigned as a UN representative, also attended. Both of them had travelled to Southern Africa trying to encourage negotiations among parties. Much agreement was reached at Malta, although Owen did not publicise it for fear of alienating Smith. The major points were the following:[30]

1. The Resident Commissioner would be required to act when a two-thirds vote in the Governing Council ruled except for matters of defence, internal security, external affairs, and operations of the proposed elections. The Council would have two members from each of the five delegations at Geneva (Smith – Rhodesian Front, Sithole – ZANU, Muzorewa – ANC, Nkomo – ZAPU, Mugabe – ZANU-PF);

2. The United Nations would help supervise elections;

3. Officials from Britain would be sent to fill the vacated posts of judges and senior civil servants who must resign, especially the Chief Justice, the Police Commissioner, and the Secretary to the Cabinet;

4. A limited amnesty would be offered to Rhodesian politicians, soldiers, judges and civil servants.

When Smith received the amendments to the Anglo-American proposals he immediately rejected them, for he now was sure he had an alternative and acceptable form of 'majority rule' in the internal settlement, the proposals for which were signed in Salisbury on 28 March 1978.

The discussion continued, however, in Dar es Salaam on 14-16 April, 1978. These 'Malta II' talks were attended by the same participants with the addition of US Secretary of State, Cyrus Vance. Further agreement was reached about the role of the UN and of the Resident Commissioner. The UN peace-keeping force would be important because the Rhodesian forces would be disarmed and stationed in barracks, and the air force would be grounded. The Resident Commissioner would have full executive powers but would be pledged to work with the Governing Council. The Patriotic Front now stated that it must play a major role in the Governing Council and that the internal parties (Smith, Muzorewa, Chirau, Sithole) be treated as one. Disagreement remained over whether the Rhodesian police force would be retained or only other 'acceptable' elements.[31]

The Anglo-American leaders agreed that much progress had been made and major hurdles had been overcome. Yet most of the Western press reported that the Patriotic Front remained inflexible. Robert Mugabe countered, 'The fact is the British, for their own reasons — perhaps afraid that an announcement that we have reached an agreement would prejudice their case vis-a-vis the so-called internal settlement agreement — have refrained from publicly telling the world that there has been a very wide measure of agreement, more than they have led the world to believe.'[32] After the Dar es Salaam conference, Owen and Young were to go to Salisbury to convince Smith to reciprocate with concessions of his own. When asked what they were going to do to encourage him to compromise, Young acknowledged that they were not intending to use any economic threats or political incentives to convince Smith.[33] In fact, Smith did not reciprocate until the Lancaster talks 16 months later. What happened instead was that the Anglo-Americans acquiesced to his latest 'internal settlement'.

Internal Settlement

The seeds of the internal settlement had been sown as far back as the Geneva Conference in 1976. The differences among the nationalists in the umbrella ANC had never been resolved, so at the end of 1976 ZANU and ZAPU came together to form the Patriotic Front (the details of which will be discussed in the next section). As the two increased their co-ordination, the other parties were moved to the periphery, especially because they did not have support from the guerrillas. The disintegration of the umbrella ANC and the formation of the Patriotic Front excluded two major leaders; Smith immediately enlisted their support. Several events made this 'marriage of convenience' possible.

As discussed earlier, Smith had changed somewhat the racial segregation of the constitution of Rhodesia and had amended the Land Tenure Act. These moves were calculated to make black partnership in his government more palatable to the Zimbabweans. Further, the escalated guerrilla war in 1977 and the negotiations for the Anglo-American proposals spurred Smith to look for Zimbabweans to bring into his government. Muzorewa and Sithole were

back in Rhodesia during the August elections from which Smith
received a white mandate. Smith told them they could engage in
politics as long as they renounced 'terrorist activities'. He was willing
to talk about sharing power with the African leaders. The talks had
been delayed by Muzorewa's reaction to the Chimoio and Tembwe
massacres. The conference began on 2 December 1977 and ended on
3 March 1978 with the signing of a new constitution. The talks
included Muzorewa, Sithole, head of the Council of Chiefs Chirau and
Smith, who described himself as one of four co-equals for the transition to the planned elections in January 1979. Yet the civil service,
police, and armed forces were to remain under white control. Sithole
stated that this settlement would end the guerrilla war: 'The guerrillas
have backed us as far as the internal talks go. Once we have made the
necessary arrangements we will go out and tell the guerrillas that what
we have been fighting for has now been achieved. The overwhelming
majority will support the settlement'. Muzorewa agreed, 'The
guerrillas will lay down their arms and support a government of the
people. The process of persuading them to return from the bush has
already begun.'[34]

It is important to look in some detail at the internal settlement to
comprehend what Smith was calling 'majority rule' and why the
Patriotic Front rejected it and fought on to Lancaster House, with
support from the Frontline. The settlement follows clearly Smith's
change in the definition of 'majority rule' with 'maintenance of high
standards' discussed earlier: whites were to retain veto power in both
the executive and legislature; the courts, army, police and bureaucracy were all to remain under white leadership; there were to be no
changes in white control of agriculture, mining and industry. From a
comparison of the major points with the Anglo-American proposals
(see pp. 68-71 and p. 74 of Chapter 3), it is clear why Smith tried this
neo-colonial solution before realities of the guerrilla war and of
international isolation forced him to go to Lancaster House.

The major points of the internal settlement are as follows:[35]

1. Majority Rule — one-person-one-vote was the agreed formula
for elections; yet this 'majority rule' was modified by three facts:
   a) the Patriotic Front was to be excluded from the election
      campaign, unless they renounced the guerrilla struggle;
   b) martial law would be enforced by the white army and police
      during the elections;
   c) political meetings had to be cleared by the government.

2. Separate voter rolls were maintained with the whites electing 28 of 100 seats to parliament for only 3 per cent of the population. Further, the 28 provided a possible veto to all legislation for ten years.

3. Land reform — Although the Land Tenure Act had been amended and then repealed, the new constitution reinstated its essence. Under rights of private property it proclaimed that no land could be alienated from the owner for five years after it was abandoned. However, if land was not put to use by 'reason of public disorder or any disaster' such time will be 'disregarded for the purpose of computing the period of five years' (section 124). In essence 50 per cent of the land would remain under control of 3 per cent of the population. Further, the executive and the legislature were given very limited powers of control over land, and even those powers were subject to veto in the white controlled courts. If the Land Tenure Act had continued in force, some of the control of the land would have passed to African members of the new government. Muzorewa stated while on tour in South Africa in July 1978 that '. . . farms and good lands must continue to remain in the hands of whites for our country to avoid facing hunger as other African countries which are now with only flags'.[36]

4. Executive powers — Appointment, promotion, dismissal of personnel in key executive positions were not under the control of the Prime Minister. The constitution reserved that executive power for five commissions and explicitly stated, 'In exercise of its functions under the Constitution, a Commission shall not be subject to the direction or control of any persons or authority'. (Section 109-4). Neither the parliament nor the executive would have jurisdiction over these autonomous bodies. The Commissions — Judicial Service, Police Service, Public Service, Defence Forces, Statutory Corporation — were to have three of their five members appointed by the President and the eligibility requirements were stringent enough to exclude all Africans. For example, members of the Public Service or Statutory Corporation Commissions must have been Secretary, Deputy Secretary or Under Secretary in the Ministry of Public Service for five years. Because of racial discrimination in education and appointments, no Zimbabwean would qualify for the positions. The requirements were a thin veil to cover racial control by appeal to 'merit'.

With this racially designed constitution and plans for an election carried out totally under his auspices, Smith was even less willing to negotiate with the Patriotic Front. He hoped, with Muzorewa and Sithole, that the new constitution would end the war. Still refusing to acknowledge the degree of support the Patriotic Front had, he expected the people to choose peace simply because they would have greater representation in the government.

While Smith was talking only with the internal settlement partici-pants, the hope and euphoria established by the Malta I and II talks in February and April 1978 were destroyed by the Anglo-American response to the Shaba invasion in May. President Mobutu's rule in Zaire had been challenged previously by organised guerrilla forces, but the 1978 Shaba uprising, the second in one year, showed signs that the guerrillas had support among the people.[37] Mobutu's Western supporters responded by flying in Belgian troops in American transport planes flown by American pilots. The foreign troops, by reports of the Western press, put down the uprising with 'massive repressive measures'. Further, the Western allies called for an 'all-African security force' to prevent 'foreign invasions of African territory'. The response of the Frontline States was best expressed by President Nyerere. Outraged by the audacious repression by the foreign troops and the arrogance of their overtly planning to use Africans to protect Western mineral interests, he lashed out:

> The OAU meets in Khartoum in July, but we are told that African freedom and its defence is being discussed in Paris and Brussels in June. Africa will fight against neo-colonialism as it has fought against Colonialism. And eventually it will win. Western bloc countries which try to resist the struggle against neo-colonialism need to recognise that it will not be African countries only which will suffer in the process . . .[38]

Shaba was the turning point for deterioration of relations for the next year. By June 1978, the United States Senate came within six votes of lifting sanctions in recognition of the March internal settlement with Muzorewa. In violation of sanctions, Smith was invited to the United States in November to explain how the proposed elections would work. In December, two American major-generals travelled to Rho-desia, South Africa, and Namibia to offer logistical advice to the white armies. This trip was in violation of the sanctions against Rhodesia and of the arms embargo against South Africa. By February 1979, the UN Security Council reported that the United States had supplied aircraft to Rhodesia since 1975, increasing by five times its combat capacity (see Chapter 5).

Two other major events also deflected attention from the negotiations. First, the American government turned its diplomatic attention to the revolution in Iran against the Shah. The crisis in Iran strengthened the hand of those in the American government who emphasised the Soviet threat to American interests (Brezinski); Ambassador Andrew Young was asked to resign for talking with a representative of the PLO. Conservative Senators (e.g., Jesse Helms) raised their voices even louder that the Rhodesian conflict was also a battle between East and West.

Second, in October 1978 Idi Amin's forces invaded thirty miles into northern Tanzania to the Kagera River, destroying cattle, sugar refineries, public buildings and killing many Tanzanian civilians. The Tanzanian People's Defence Forces were quickly mobilised, and President Nyerere vowed to fight until Amin's troops were removed from Tanzanian soil. As the Tanzanians defeated the disorganised Ugandan soldiers, they continued their advance, in co-ordinated operations with Uganda National Liberation Front (UNLF) opposition forces, all the way to Kampala and finally to the northern border of Uganda. The Amin regime was toppled by April 1979. President Samora Machel did not view the invasion of Amin as separate from the Southern African struggle:

> Imperialism thinks that the obstacle to their proposals on Zimbabwe is Tanzania. They think that President Nyerere is the one who blocks the proposals. They are conscious of the fact that Tanzanians and President Nyerere are involved with the Zimbabwean struggle as their own struggle . . . It is not an accident that imperialism is behind all this. The imperialists are responsible for the aggression against Tanzania. Uganda is simply an instrument used to divert attention and to open a new front.[39]

In August 1979, the Defence Ministers of the Frontline States, meeting to discuss Rhodesia's bombing of three ZAPU refugee camps in Zambia, noted that the timing of Amin's invasion of Tanzania 'coincided with the escalation of the acts of aggression by racialist minority regimes in Southern Africa against the Frontline States.'[40] The extent of international involvement in Amin's decision to invade Tanzania is not clear,[41] but the impact was to burden Tanzania with a huge deficit from the war, which the Western countries were slow to ameliorate through issuance of new loans (see Chapter 4). The debt was a serious new burden on the Tanzanian economy, which had not suffered much from the Zimbabwean war.

Events in Zaire and Uganda reduced the trust between the Frontline States and the Anglo-Americans that had been nurtured during the Malta talks. The Iranian revolution underlined dramatically the Cold War issue between the Soviets and the American government; some members in the US Congress opposed any discussion with the Zimbabwean nationalists who were armed by the Soviets (ZAPU), or for that matter, by the Chinese (ZANU). The serious negotiations were interrupted by these factors and by the progress of Smith's internal settlement.

After the constitution was signed legitimising the internal settlement, elections were held about a year later (17-20 April 1979), and Muzorewa became Prime Minister of Zimbabwe-Rhodesia on 28 May 1979. The internal settlement was exactly the kind of government that the Patriotic Front and Frontline States were fighting to prevent. It brought black faces into the Smith government, but left full executive power with the whites. Any changes in the economy were not discussed. Smith had his kind of majority rule: sufficient black faces to legitimise white control of the state and the economy. The new government pledged to redistribute land and more important, to end the war.

The election turnout was estimated at over 60 per cent of the Africans even though the Patriotic Front was excluded from the poll. The Front had pursued two tactics for the elections: leave the village to avoid voting if at all possible or vote if necessary to avoid injury. The Front did not really try to sabotage the elections because security was intense. In some areas the avoidance worked; in Chibuwe the Rhodesian government reported that more had voted than were on the census rolls. And in other districts (e.g., Buhera), less than 10 per cent of the voters turned out. Both sides declared their election strategies a success. Muzorewa considered he had a mandate from the people. The Patriotic Front called the whole campaign and election a fraud. Several international observers agreed with the Front; they reported massive intimidation by Rhodesian forces and white employers and declared that the elections were not free nor fair.[42] The real test of the election, however, was not the number of counted ballots. The test was the fact that the guerrilla war escalated, not abated, after Muzorewa came to power. The people voted more by their co-operation with the guerrillas than by marking an election ballot.

Unity Among The Nationalists

When the nationalists were released from Smith's jails, there was a twelve-year history of rivalry among them. Two armies were being trained, with no joint operations. The unity statement in Lusaka by the four liberation groups only intensified the rivalry. It was difficult to present a united front to Smith when there was little agreement about the role of the armed struggle.

Neither the African National Council (Muzorewa) nor Frolizi (Chikerema) had significant armed forces, for they had worked for majority rule through protests and petitions. A call for a ceasefire would not alter their strategy. Chikerema had been vice-president of ZAPU until the splinter group, Frolizi, was formed in 1971, ostensibly to heal the ZANU-ZAPU split. When the umbrella ANC was formed, Chikerema quickly worked to gain influence over Muzorewa, sharing Muzorewa's criticism of ZANU and ZAPU. The two continued to push for peaceful solutions to the crisis, entering talks for internal settlement with Smith.

ZANU and ZAPU, however, had been waging guerrilla war for several years, although they disagreed about tactics and the relative importance of the armed struggle. A ceasefire would circumscribe the core of their strategies — strategies approved only after failure of other alternatives and after much debate.

ZAPU, with a strong centralised command, had launched their armed struggle in 1967 in conjunction with the ANC (African National Congress) of South Africa in the north-west section of Rhodesia; the assaults were unsuccessful for they engaged the Rhodesian forces in conventional warfare and Rhodesian firepower was too strong for the guerrillas. (Subsequently, South Africa sent in troops to help patrol the Wankie area to block both ZAPU and ANC-South Africa infiltration.) ZAPU had conducted several incursions into Rhodesia across the Zambezi River from Zambia; few, if any, were successful.

The lack of success of ZAPU has various explanations, often depending on the ideological position of the analyst. First, the objective conditions were difficult. The Zambezi River was more of a barrier than a conduit. Ambush on the river was easy and frequently successful; many men and much material never reached the Rhodesian side of the river. Supply lines were more difficult to maintain across the river than ones that depended on long marches under the cover of foliage from Mozambique. Second, some analysts emphasise the military choice of ZAPU as a limitation to its success. Soviet tactics based on heavy artillery were not as adaptive to guerrilla war in Rhodesia as the Chinese tactics adopted by ZANU. Although ZAPU fighting caused dramatic effects during the war (such as the ability to shoot down two Viscounts), major strikes could not be sustained as readily as small-unit sabotage tactics. Third, others emphasise the political choices of ZAPU. ZANU, especially, was critical of the emphasis of Nkomo on building an international reputation, combined with a quick readiness to negotiate, first with the British (1960's) and later directly with Smith (1975-80). Most analysts agree that ZAPU did not mobilise the people as much as ZANU, even in its own zones of operation.[43] ZAPU did infiltrate many villages and even cities; presence of ZAPU cadres was essential for education of the people and for the successful armed incursions. Critics say the difference was the degree of mobilisation — from arming the populace to promoting political education, and offering medics for basic health care. The relative importance of these geographic, military, and political restraints varied throughout the war. And they were the sources of conflict with the other nationalist groups.

ZANU also began infiltrating Rhodesia from Zambia and ran into similar problems of ambush at the river crossings. At first they also directly engaged the Rhodesian forces, as in the battle of Sinoia on 28 April 1966, the officially designated start of the war. Frelimo first offered ZAPU passage into Rhodesia via a liberated corridor in Tete province, but the party was not able to escalate the war at that time because of internal problems. (Ironically, the debate was between Chikerema and Jason Moyo over fighting strategy.) So Frelimo made the offer to ZANU, and they gradually began operating through Tete from Tanzania. The decision was to make a fundamental difference to ZANU's operations. Operating with Frelimo, ZANU cadres learned Frelimo's well-developed strategy and tactics of building a political base among the people. The guerrillas were taught by Frelimo to be first political mobilisers and then skilled soldiers. The military tactics depended on the political mobilisation, for it was the villagers, not heavy artillery, that would ultimately protect them. The link between Frelimo and ZANU became strong as each aided the other in their struggles. By the end of the Zimbabwean war, Frelimo was sending its young soldiers, some who had not fought in the Mozambican liberation struggle, to fight alongside of ZANU in order to gain experience.

ZANU was formed when members broke away from ZAPU in 1963 over the question of the importance of armed struggle versus diplomatic negotiations.[44] With Chinese training in the camps in Tanzania and under Frelimo tutelage in the field, by 1974 ZANU was escalating the war. Most of the imprisoned leaders were strongly opposed to the ceasefire that the Frontline States had conceded for their release. Several leaders refused to honour it, while Sithole was willing to agree. The debate over the ceasefire, therefore, was integrally involved with a leadership struggle within ZANU.

In prison Sithole had been tried in 1969 for sending messages conspiring to assassinate Smith; his notes were passed through an agent of the Rhodesian intelligence. On the witness stand, Sithole renounced the use of force as a means to change the government. He had abrogated principles of ZANU before by acting unilaterally, and in publicly renouncing armed struggle as an option for ZANU the other imprisoned leaders decided he had gone too far. After his trial he was separated from the others, because he was declared a convicted criminal rather than a political prisoner. When he rejoined them in 1973 a meeting was held among the detained ZANU members to discuss his remark. He was denounced by the detained members of the Central Committee and was voted out of office by them on 1 November 1974.[45] Thus, when Smith agreed to allow the detained nationalist leaders to go to Lusaka for talks with the Frontline States on 8 November, the detained Central Committee members had not had time to inform ZANU military command in Lusaka (Dare re Chimurenga-DARE) of their actions. The ZANU group at Que Que Prison decided to send Robert Mugabe and Moton Malianga (ZANU Secretary for Youth) to represent ZANU at the Lusaka meeting; they did not send Sithole. The Frontline Presidents refused to accept Mugabe and Malianga, sent them back to Que Que and demanded that Sithole be sent to represent ZANU. The Presidents' response was not totally out of order for they interpreted the deposition of Sithole by only five in prison as a *coup d'etat*. Further, when they contacted the ZANU DARE about who should be representing ZANU, the DARE designated Sithole, because they had not heard of the events in Que Que. It was Sithole, not Mugabe, who was flown to Dar es Salaam for further consultations.

The change of ZANU leadership was only very slowly accepted by the Frontline Presidents. It was not until the Geneva Conference in October 1976 that Mugabe attained full support from the Frontline.

The first factor in their reluctance was the way in which Sithole was deposed. Second, after the rest of the ZANU leadership confirmed Mugabe, the Presidents were still not convinced that he, as a political leader with no guerrilla training, had the full support of ZANLA. Finally, the Chitepo murder (March-April 1975) disrupted ZANU's operations totally and made effective co-ordination among the leaders and with the guerrillas in Mozambique very difficult. In short, the Frontline States during 1975-76 were not promoting unity among the nationalists, but rather were a factor in the continuing disunity. This conflict between ZANU and the Frontline States exploded over the Chitepo affair.

Herbert Chitepo, the National Chairman of ZANU, was killed by a bomb planted in his car in Lusaka on 18 March 1975. The Zambian authorities immediately insinuated that the bomb was planted by factions within ZANU. At first, the accusation seemed probable, for the rebellion by young field commanders, led by Thomas Nhari in November-December 1974, had resulted in the death of about 60 ZANLA cadres. The rebel field commanders had killed several of their leaders at the Chifombo camp and tried to kidnap Tongogara and several other officials in Lusaka. ZANLA had increased its forces from 300 to 5,000 in two years because of emigration from Rhodesia.[46] The recruits were dispersed too widely in the field and supplies were insufficient and slow getting to the fronts. In addition, the Rhodesian army had removed villagers from their homes and settled them in 'protected villages.' Initially this tactic did disrupt the guerrillas' support base, and the Rhodesian army killed more in two months in October-November 1974 than in the previous two years 1972-74.[47] However when Chitepo was killed, the rebel commanders had been arrested and tried by a ZANU commission of inquiry at Chifombo resulting in the execution of some of the rebels; the guerrillas were once again under the leadership of the DARE. Chitepo was a member of the DARE and his leadership was popular with the guerrillas because he was espousing the continuation of the armed struggle and sending increased supplies to the front. After the unity agreement of December 1974, the OAU, at the request of the Frontline States, voted to give funds only to the umbrella ANC; therefore, funds for specifically ZANU supplies were short. Chitepo tried to remedy the situation; ZANU leaders visited Romania and China seeking greater arms aid.

ZANU received word that the Zambian authorities were planning

to arrest several cadres at Chitepo's funeral, so they dispersed the
leaders. Senior Commander Rex Nhongo went to Tanzania and did
not return to Zambia. However, other ZANLA members of the high
command, Josiah Tongogara, Mayor Urimbo, Joseph Chimurenga,
Josiah Tungamirai, Justin Chauke and Sarudzai Chinamaropa were
sent to Mozambique but Frelimo returned them to Zambia to testify
at the international commission of inquiry that Kaunda had set up.
Frelimo later said that they understood the commission would
conduct a serious investigation and would not have returned the
leaders if they had realised what would happen.[48] The hearings were
less than due process: forty-six of the fifty-seven men in prison were
not even called to testify even though the trial was to judge all of them.
Of the leaders only three of eighteen were allowed to testify. They
were not allowed to hear the case against them nor to cross-examine
their accusers. ZANU published a document condemning every
aspect of the proceedings and denying that Chitepo was killed by one
of their own. The evidence presented at the proceedings was scanty;
some written testimonies were given only after ZANU members were
beaten by Zambian police.[49] The international commission, comprised
of representatives from Botswana, Tanzania, Mozambique and ten
other African states, concluded that the death of Chitepo was the
result of ethnic feuding in ZANU, citing the previous field commanders'
uprising as background.[50] But ethnic divisions could not fully explain
that rebellion, for various ethnic groups were on both sides. They were
also fairly well represented in the DARE and the high command.

ZANU replied that the conflict was ideological: Chitepo was
adamantly for continuing the war and was against the Frontline
ceasefire. ZANU accused Kaunda of trying to stop their guerrilla war
to enforce the ceasefire so negotiations could proceed between Smith
and Nkomo.[51] In fact, the armed struggle was effectively blocked for
about one year, and Kaunda did encourage Nkomo to talk with Smith
several times in the next four years.

After independence, journalist David Martin was able to obtain
an oblique confession from Rhodesian security forces that they had
planted the bomb.[52] Yet the proceedings of the subsequent hearing
were entirely under Kaunda's auspices. ZANU interpreted the
Frontline agenda as peace at any price; Kaunda, tired of ZANU
dissension on Zambian soil and anxious for peace, wanted unity
among the nationalists and an attempt to give the ceasefire a chance.
And Kaunda did not act alone. The other Frontline Presidents were

convinced enough that ZANU's factional fighting was causing problems for the liberation struggle that there was no major protest from
them as members of the international commission. Nyerere closed the
ZANU office in Tanzania in May 1975. As stated above, Frelimo had
handed ZANU commanders over to the Zambian authorities and
participated in the commission. But later, an envoy carried a message
from Machel to Kaunda at Mulungushi asking for their release.

During 1975 the war among the different Angolan forces was
escalating. As stated earlier, Kaunda was openly supporting
UNITA, after pushing for a unity government. By the time of bitter
fighting among the Angolans, Nyerere and Machel were behind the
MPLA. Unity among the Frontline States, therefore, was not strong in
1975. The Chitepo affair occurred at a time when the other Frontline
Presidents would not or could not pressure Kaunda to be more lenient
with the ZANU leaders. Only when the Patriotic Front was formed
between ZANU and ZAPU, just before the Geneva Conference in
October 1976, did Nyerere and Machel demand the release of the
ZANU leaders.

Muzorewa, Sithole, Chikerema and Nkomo testified at the
commission's inquiry and they supported the view that Chitepo was
killed by ethnic factions in ZANU. Such a testimony, of course, served
their own purposes, and it also illustrates the intensity of the rivalry
among the nationalist groups.

The OAU Council of Ministers meeting was to be held just one
month after the Chitepo assassination in April 1975. The Frontline
States were working to have Sithole released from Smith's prison to
attend. Sithole had been rearrested because he allegedly was planning
another assassination plot against Smith. The Frontline States
demanded that South Africa obtain his release from Smith, and
Vorster did convince Smith to release Sithole. ZANU decided to try to
get Mugabe and Edgar Tekere (Deputy Secretary for Youth and
Culture) out of Rhodesia to attend the meeting. They were successfully smuggled out of Rhodesia into Mozambique where they stayed,
some saying they were organising in the guerrilla camps; others said
that Mozambique kept them restricted in Quelimane. In fact, both
opinions were correct. They began important organising among the
guerrillas in Mozambique; kept under close watch by Frelimo, they
were then restricted to Quelimane. Sithole went on to Dar es Salaam
and represented ZANU in the important OAU Council of Ministers
meeting which was formulating strategy for support of the nationalists.

In August Sithole represented ZANU at the Victoria Falls conference; Nkomo, Chikerema and Muzorewa were also there as part of the leadership of the umbrella ANC. Presidents Nyerere and Machel had already changed their minds about the necessity of armed struggle; they were formulating what became the dual policy of the Frontline States: negotiations with armed struggle. They let the Victoria Falls Conference plans continue because they preferred a negotiated settlement and because they wanted to support Kaunda in his manoeuvres for a peaceful settlement. But Nyerere and Machel were as certain as ZANU that the conference would not be a success and were already convinced of what Mao Zedong had stated about guerrilla war:

> The greater the political progress the more we can persevere in the war, and the more we persevere in the war, the greater the political progress. But fundamentally, everything depends on our perseverence in the War of Resistance.[53]

As discussed earlier, the Victoria Falls Conference ended in total impasse, with Smith more confident than ever because he had used the enforced ceasefire to position his troops in what had been the areas of greatest guerrilla infiltration, resulting in serious defeats of ZANLA forces.

Divisions within the umbrella ANC (UANC) were serious; Muzorewa kicked Nkomo out of the ANC for his willingness to negotiate alone with Smith. An internal and external ANC were formed. By this manoeuvre, Muzorewa started losing support among the Frontline Presidents. Nyerere reminded him that the ANC was not a party, let alone *his* party. It was a united front and ousting one leader destroyed the front; it was not simply the removal of one member of an integrated party.

By January 1976, members of both ZANU and ZAPU (especially Josiah Tongogara, who was in prison in Zambia, and Jason Moyo) understood that continued support from the Frontline States and a successful guerrilla struggle required some effort to form a joint military operation. Nyerere and Machel were willing to provide training camps and rear bases for the struggle but Machel stated that they must fight as a single army, not as two, if they were to use Mozambique as a rear base. In January 1976, therefore, the ZANLA and ZIPRA forces formed ZIPA, the Zimbabwe People's Army. The ZAPU military command met with ZANU leaders who were still in jail in Mpima, Zambia. In response, Nyerere agreed to open Nachingwea, once a training camp for Frelimo, to 5,000 recruits, half ZANLA and half ZIPRA. This was the first effort for military co-ordination under the support of the Frontline.

In June, Muzorewa went to the OAU Liberation Committee meeting and accused Nyerere of setting the guerrillas against him, for he had not been allowed in the camps. He called the recruits in Tanzanian camps 'Mbita's high command,' referring to the Tanzanian head of the OAU Liberation Committee, Major Hashim Mbita. Muzorewa had information that the two guerrilla forces were clashing at the camps. In fact, at Kingolwira and Mgagao in Tanzania, fighting had broken out with some deaths on both sides. By August most of the ZIPRA forces had returned to Lusaka; ZIPA became mainly ZANLA. The fighting was over loyalty to each group's leaders but also about the tactics of warfare. Tanzania had Chinese instructors in the camps, and their strategy conflicted with what ZIPRA had been taught by the Soviets.

With two ANC organisations and the split within ZIPA, the Frontline States called a conference in September 1976 in Dar es Salaam to try once again to unite the leaders. They argued for twelve hours and could not come to an agreement. Nkomo agreed to sign a unity statement with Muzorewa, Sithole, and Chikerema but not with ZIPA because he felt they were mainly ZANLA. Finally, the Frontline States declared that their support would go to the armed forces of ZIPA and that Mugabe and Nkomo had to work out the political leadership.[54] On 8 October 1976 the Patriotic Front was formed as a loose coalition between ZANU and ZAPU; it endured many conflicts and feuds until the independence of Zimbabwe in 1980.

Presidents Nyerere and Machel also prevailed upon Kaunda to release the detained ZANU leadership (16 October 1976) so they could attend the Geneva Conference which was the culmination of the Kissinger shuttles. The ZANU leadership flew to Geneva with Mugabe as their head; but Britain, with Ivor Richard to chair the meeting, complicated the discussions with Smith by following the suggestion of Nyerere to invite Sithole to attend. Nyerere was still trying to unite the nationalists in the hope that Smith could not compromise any. Muzorewa and Sithole participated in the discussions, but the new Patriotic Front clearly took the lead. (Confronted with this Patriotic Front unity, Smith did not see it as a defeat, but as an opportunity to co-opt the leaders who were now clearly being pushed to the sidelines: Muzorewa and Sithole.) With the political coalition between ZANU and ZAPU seemingly solved, new conflict emerged among the ZIPA forces, which were now mainly ZANLA stationed in camps in Mozambique. They refused to recognise the leadership of their newly released leaders.[55] President Machel called them to see him, told them that the attempted coup they were planning was illegal, and shipped them off to Geneva to observe the negotiations. The young commanders disagreed with any talks with Smith and criticised the others for the discussion. While the High Command was in jail in Zambia, they themselves had directed the camps for sixteen months and came to enjoy the power they had acquired. After Geneva, the ZANU leadership sent the young commanders back to Mozambique via other routes so Tongogara and Rex Nhongo, a ZIPA commander who recognised the leadership of the released ZANLA cammanders, could get back to the camps first to take command. This clash again delayed the resurgence of the armed struggle.

But the political coalition was surging ahead. On 9 January 1977 the Frontline States gave full recognition to the Patriotic Front as the sole representative of the Zimbabwean people. After repeated testimonies from the ZANLA commanders that Mugabe was their leader, the Frontline accepted his leadership over Sithole and recognised that neither Sithole nor Muzorewa had any troops with which to fight the necessary war. Smith had once again shown at Geneva that he would not compromise without the persuasion of the armed struggle. On 7 February 1977 the OAU Liberation Committee also gave its full recognition to the Patriotic Front, and the OAU Heads of State accorded recognition by July. These formal recognitions were essential, for it meant that OAU liberation funds would then be allocated to the Patriotic Front. The UANC was cut off. In the view of the majority of the international community, the Patriotic Front became the sole legitimate representative of the Zimbabwean people. A political united front was formed.

Military unity, however, was not achieved. By June 1977, ZANLA was able to escalate the war, but ZIPRA was still holding back. By March 1978, ZANLA was protecting territory it largely controlled, while ZIPRA was still trying hit and run sabotage. However, although ZANLA was taking the lead in waging the 'year of the people's storm,' or perhaps because of the war's escalation, conflict within ZANLA continued. In January 1978 Frelimo had to imprison three former members of the DARE (Henry Hamadziripi, Mukudzei Mudzi, Rugare Gumbo) and several supporters for plotting to seize power and join ZAPU. (When released in 1980, most joined Sithole although they had alleged unity with ZAPU).[56]

Only in May 1979 did the Patriotic Front sign a military unity document, forming a Joint Executive Committee with a Co-ordinating Council and a Defence Council.[57] But it remained a piece of paper. Joint operations amounted, at most, to joint co-ordination of a few attacks. This lack of military co-ordination was a major point of dispute with the Frontline States. President Nyerere said that he had heard of states with two political parties but never of one with two armies. At the Non-Aligned Conference in Havana in 1979, where the Patriotic Front received full support over the Smith-Muzorewa government, the Frontline again chastised the Patriotic Front for its inability to unite the military commands. They made the Patriotic Front cut its demand for total control of the transition security force of Rhodesia. They admonished the Patriotic Front that their demand to direct the combined Rhodesian and guerrilla forces during transition was unreasonable, given their inability to co-ordinate their own armies. This military dissension was a major test of the new state of Zimbabwe. One of the first tasks of the new government was to unite at least the ZANLA-ZIPRA forces at the same time that the enemy forces were integrated into the new army.

The political unity forged with the assistance of the Frontline was absolutely essential to the negotiated settlement, especially because Smith had succeeded in setting up an internal settlement with Muzorewa, Sithole and Chirau. With the Patriotic Front united, the Frontline States could argue that the internal settlement excluded those who were doing the fighting. If the Patriotic Front had split, Muzorewa might have succeeded in legitimising his power. However, the Frontline States quickly moved to obtain international recognition of the Patriotic Front as the legitimate representative of the Zimbabwean people. Their unity was crucial to the rejection of the Muzorewa internal settlement by the international community as no real change in power. Patriotic Front unity and their ability to sustain the war convinced the international community to reject the neo-colonial state of Zimbabwe-Rhodesia.

Notes

1. David Martin and Phyllis Johnson, *The Struggle for Zimbabwe* (London: Faber & Faber and Harare: Zimbabwe Publishing House, 1981), p. 17.
2. Colin Legum, *Southern Africa* (London: Rex Collings, 1975), p. 8.
3. For a full discussion of the role of Lonrho in the detente and of this document, see David Martin and Phyllis Johnson, op. cit., pp. 133-143.
4. Smith denied that South Africa was exerting any pressure on him. He said his regime and South Africa agreed that a settlement would 'bring about as much normality as possible in Southern Africa. There is no difference of opinion between us.' *Financial Mail* (Johannesburg), 15 November 1974. Yet he was letting leaders, with whom he had previously refused to sit around the same table, help decide the future of Zimbabwe.
5. Republic of Zambia, 'Dear Mr Vorster . . . Details of Exchanges between President Kaunda of Zambia and Prime Minister Vorster of South Africa' (Lusaka: Zambia Information Services, 23 April 1971).
6. Fifth Conference of Heads of State and Governments of East and Central Africa, Lusaka (April 1969).
7. Seventh Conference of the Heads of State and Governments of East and Central Africa, Mogadishu (18-20 October 1971).
8. Personal interview with Vernon Mwaanga, Lusaka, 5 June 1979.
9. Ninth Extraordinary Session of Council of Ministers, OAU, 'Declaration of Dar es Salaam on Southern Africa' (7-10 April 1975).
10. For the nationalists' reaction to the proposals, see ZAPU: Memorandum to Commonwealth Heads of States Conference on the Fearless proposals,' 7 January 1969, in Christopher Nyangoni and Gideon Nyandoro, eds., *Zimbabwe Independence Movements, Select Documents* (New York: Barnes & Noble, 1979), pp. 124-141.
    'African National Council: Why the ANC says No to the settlement proposals. Statement to the Pearce Commission in Salisbury,' 3 January 1972, Ibid., pp. 210-214.
    'Joshua Nkomo: memorandum on the settlement proposals submitted to the Pearce Commission,' February 1972, Ibid., pp. 215-223.
    'Frolizi: memorandum to the Liberation Committee of the Organisation of African Unity,' January 1972, Ibid., pp. 224-230.
11. Harry R. Strack, *Sanctions: The Case of Rhodesia* (Syracuse, N.Y.: Syracuse University Press, 1978), p. 28.
12. Sir Seretse Khama, Address to the Development Committee of the European Parliament, June 1977, quoted in Commonwealth Secretariat, *The Front-Line States: The Burden of the Liberation Struggle* (London: Commonwealth Secretariat 1979) p. 39.
13. Extensive accounts of the history of the Zimbabwean nationalist groups can be found in the following:
    John Day, *International Nationalism: The Extra-Territorial Relations of Southern*

Rhodesian African Nationalists (New York: Humanities Press, 1967).

Davis M'Gabe, 'The Beginnings of Guerrilla Warfare,' *Monthly Review* 20 (March 1969), pp. 39-47.

B. Mazoe, 'How Zimbabwean Liberation Groups Began,' *African Communist*, no. 69 (1977).

Abel Muzorewa, *Rise Up and Walk* (Nashville, Tennessee: Nabingdon, 1978).

Simbi Mubako, 'The Quest for Unity in the Zimbabwe Liberation Movement,' *Issue* 5, no. 21 (1975), pp. 7-17.

Maurice Nyagumbo, *With the People* (London: Allison and Busby, 1980).

Boniface Obichere, *Crisis in Zimbabwe* (Boulder: Westview, 1979).

Michael Raeburn, *Black Fire! Accounts of the Guerrilla War in Rhodesia* (London: Julian Friedman, 1978).

Nathan Shamuyarira, *Crisis in Rhodesia* (Nairobi: East African Publishing House, 1967).

Anthony R. Wilkinson, 'From Rhodesia to Zimbabwe,' in Basil Davidson, Joe Slovo and Anthony R. Wilkinson, eds., *Southern Africa: The New Politics of Revolution* (London, 1976).

S.E. Wilmer, *Zimbabwe Now* (London: Rex Collings, Ltd., 1972).

14. 'Zimbabwe Declaration of Unity,' Lusaka, 7 December 1974 in Christopher Nyangoni and Gideon Nyandoro, eds., op. cit., p. 295.

15. Julius Nyerere, President of the United Republic of Tanzania, 'Special Message to foreign envoys accredited to Tanzania' (8 June 1978).

16. Eddison Zvobgo, *Tanzania Daily News*, 5 October 1979.

17. *New York Times*, 14 May 1976.

18. Speech to South African Parliament, 28 January 1977.

19. See newspaper reports, 25-26 August 1975, in *Tanzania Daily News. Times of Zambia. The Rhodesia Herald.*

20. Reprinted in Lester A. Sobel, ed., *Rhodesia/Zimbabwe 1971-1977* (New York: Facts on File, 1978), pp. 91-92.

21. *Times of Zambia*, 27 September 1976.

22. David Martin and Phyllis Johnson, op. cit., p. xvii.

23. Interview of Samora Machel by Mozambican press quoted in *Tanzania Daily News*, 7 September 1980.

24. This interpretation was offered by Secretary of State Cyrus Vance at more than one press conference in 1979.

25. By September 1977, however, Minister for Development and Planning, Marcelino dos Santos, was in Peking for consultations, and Sweden was consulting Mozambique on defence. *Washington Post*, 21 February 1977.

26. 'Rhodesia: Proposals for a Settlement,' presented to Parliament by the Secretary of State for Foreign and Commonwealth Affairs (September 1977). Provisions cited directly from this document.

27. 'The Road to Zimbabwe: The Anglo-American Line,' *Washington Notes on Africa* (Washington Office on Africa, Fall 1977), p. 4.

Final Communique of Commonwealth Heads of Government, London 8-15 June 1977, *Africa Contemporary Record 1977-1978* (New York: Africana Publishing Co., 1979), pp. C44-C48. Statement to demand dismantling of Smith's forces during transition.

28. Zimbabwe Patriotic Front, 'Statement on British "Proposals for a Settlement" in Rhodesia,' 12 September 1977. Subsequent quotes from the Patriotic Front come from this document.

29. The draft constitution is part of the 'Proposals for a Settlement,' cited above in note 26.

30. *The Times* (London), 3 February 1978.
    The Observer (London), 5 February 1978.
    Press Release, Dar es Salaam, 26 March 1978.

31. *Tanzania Daily News*, 20 April 1978.

32. Ibid., 23 April 1978.

33. Personal interview, Dar es Salaam, 16 April 1978.

34. *Tanzania Daily News*, 4 March 1978.

35. 'Rhodesia: Draft Constitution of Zimbabwe Rhodesia,' 1979. All the quoted sections that follow are from the draft constitution.
    See also Committee on Foreign Relations, U.S. Senate, 'A Rhodesian Settlement? Analysis of Agreement signed by P.M. Ian Smith, Rev. N. Sithole, Bishop A. Muzorewa, and Senator J. Chirau, on 3 March 1978' (Washington, D.C.: U.S. Government Printing Office, June 1978).

36. *Uhuru* (Dar es Salaam), 22 March 1978.

37. 'Here We Go Again: Shaba II. Angola II? Washington Office on Africa, 20 May 1978.
    'Conflict in Zaire: Local Uprising or Global Issue?' *New York Times*, 2 June 1978.
    'The Battle for Zaire,' *International News*, 30 June 1978.

38. Julius Nyerere, 'Special Message,' op. cit.

39. *Tanzania Sunday News*, 12 November 1978.

40. *Tanzania Daily News*, 24 August 1979. Some of the OAU states did want to condemn Tanzania equally with Uganda for sending troops into another African country. The Frontline States strongly supported Tanzania's right to defend itself by striking at the source of the aggression. Later reports emphasised the internal strife within Uganda as the major impetus for Amin's aggression; he sent troops to war to hide the fact that his loyal forces were killing rebellious elements in his own army, and the soldiers loyal to him were encouraged to pillage Tanzania as their reward.

41. Tony Avirgan and Martha Honey, *The War in Uganda: The Legacy of Idi Amin* (Westport, CN: Lawrence Hill, 1982).

42. *Free and Fair? The 1979 Rhodesian Election: A report of Observers on Behalf of the British Parliamentary Human Rights Group* (London: Parliamentary Human Rights Group, May 1979).
    Claire Palley, 'The Rhodesian Election Campaign,' (London: Catholic Institute for International Relations, April 1979).
    U.S. Senate, *Congressional Record*, 15 May 1979, pp. S5562-S5589.

43. Colin Legum, ed., 'Rhodesia,' *Africa Contemporary Record 1977-78* (New York: Holmes & Meiers, 1979), p. B1037.
    Xan Smiley, 'Zimbabwe, Southern Africa and the Rise of Robert Mugabe.' *Foreign Affairs* (Summer 1980), p. 1064.

44. For a detailed account of the ZANU split from ZAPU, from the perspective of a ZANU member, see Nathan M. Shamuyarira, op. cit., pp. 173-193.

45. Leopold Takawira, ZANU Vice President, had rejected Sithole's 1969 stand, but died in 1970 in prison. Simon Muzenda and Eddison Zvobgo were no longer in prison: Malianga as chair did not vote. Mugabe — abstained; Tekere, Nkala and Nyagumbo — for; Sithole — against. See David Martin and Phyllis Johnson, op. cit., pp. 147-149.
46. ZANU, 'The Price of Détente,' p. 1. Verified by newspaper reports.
47. Simbi Mubako, 'Aspects of the Zimbabwe Liberation Movement 1966-76,' International Conference on Southern African History, Lesotho, August 1977, quoted in David Martin and Phyllis Johnson, op. cit., p. 167.
48. Personal interviews with Frelimo officials, April 1979.
49. 'My conclusions would indicate beyond doubt that the Accused 3 [Safat Kufamazuba] was a victim of unfair and improper conduct on the part of the police authorities . . . the statement in question is inadmissible in evidence.' Judge M.M. Moodley, Trial within a Trial Ruling, The People versus Joseph Siwela, Josiah Tongogara, Safat Kufamazuba, HP/67/1976, High Court for Zambia, Lusaka, 20 October 1976.
50. 'Report of the Special Commission on the Assassination of Herbert Wiltshire Chitepo,' Lusaka, March 1976.
51. Personal interviews with ZANU officials in Dar es Salaam, Tanzania and Maputo, Mozambique, March-April, 1979.
52. David Martin and Phyllis Johnson, op. cit., p. 190.
53. Mao Zedong, 'On Protracted War,' *Selected Works*, Vol. 2 (Peking: Foreign Language Press, 1975), p. 131.
54. David Martin and Phyllis Johnson, op. cit., p. 217.
55. 'ZIPA Denounces the Geneva Perfidy,' mimeo., 20 November 1976.
56. David Martin and Phyllis Johnson, op. cit., p. 275.
57. Dar es Salaam Agreement on 'Unity of the Patriotic Front,' mimeo., 9 April, 1979.

CHAPTER 3
The High Price Of Political Victory

A full analysis and explanation of the differences and tensions along the Frontline are the task of the rest of this book. The first section of this chapter, therefore, will simply outline the major pressure points to provide an overview of the complexity of the struggles. The tensions in the alliance, some of which almost broke the Frontline apart, followed similar tensions among the nationalist forces: the importance of armed struggle and the choice of one liberation leader over another. Zambia was at the centre of all the controversies. The second section discusses how the *legal* compromises accepted by the Patriotic Front at the Lancaster House negotiations were turned into an overwhelming *political* victory at the elections when the Zimbabweans were finally allowed to voice their opinion. Smith, until the very day of elections, still felt he 'knew our Africans'[1] and expected the Zimbabweans to vote for Muzorewa, or perhaps Nkomo, either of whom would then form a coalition government. The last section investigates the cost of supporting the Zimbabwean independence for each of the Frontline States. An assessment of the costs begins to explain some of their vacillations and underlines the high price for political victory.

Tensions Along The Frontline

Tensions among the Frontline States mainly centred around the role of Zambia. Frelimo leaders referred to Zambia as the 'weak link' in the Frontline chain.[2] Zambia was a weak link, not because it was so much worse off than the others, but because its economy was the most vulnerable to outside reprisals of the three states that did the most to sustain the armed struggle. Botswana, as will be analysed in subsequent chapters, had an economy fully linked into South Africa's. It was a member of the Frontline but was quite limited in the contributions it could make. When Mozambique closed the border to Rhodesia (3 March 1976), Seretse Khama said he would do the same.

He was convinced by Nyerere and Machel that such a move would seriously jeopardise the viability of the Botswanan economy and the Frontline would have more, not fewer, difficulties. If Botswana had had the means by which to withstand South African reprisals for its closing the border to Rhodesia, international sanctions against Rhodesia would have been much more successful. In addition, Botswana had no army with which to defend itself from 'hot pursuit' by Rhodesian forces against fleeing Zimbabweans in Botswanan territory. Botswana, therefore, offered bases for refugees, but immediately transferred to Zambia those who wanted guerrilla training.

Although Angola had rich mineral resources and a large army, it was also a lesser player among the five. First, the MPLA had to fight the South African invasion in its 'second war of liberation'. In March 1976 South Africa retreated but did not desist from its attacks. Supporting Jonas Savimbi in southern Angola and attacking SWAPO camps, South Africa invaded Angola many times. Between March 1976 and June 1979, they killed 1,383 and wounded 1,800 SWAPO cadres and Angolan citizens.[3] Angola's frontline faced Namibia.

The new Angolan MPLA government did provide some bases for training of ZIPRA, a fact which angered Nyerere because the Frontline States had agreed to train all the recruits, both ZIPRA and ZANLA, at joint camps in Tanzania. The MPLA was more supportive of ZAPU because of their historical contacts with the group, yet it also urged ZIPRA to share more of the fighting.

President Kaunda of Zambia was the only Frontline leader to have talks with South African and Rhodesian officials. Before the Frontline States were formed, Zambian officials had at least four talks with South African officials. On 9 August 1975, just before the Victoria Falls conference, Kaunda's envoy, Mark Chona, met in Pretoria with Rhodesian and South African government leaders. Although the Frontline States were co-ordinating activities, he did not fully inform his colleagues about the discussion. One explanation could be that his August talk was at the time that South Africa was preparing to invade Angola to support UNITA against the MPLA. Kaunda was also sympathetic to UNITA, had given them sanctuary in Zambia and permitted the American CIA to use the Zambian radio to broadcast pro-UNITA propaganda into Angola. After the South African initiatives failed to promote accord between the nationalists and Smith, Kaunda started talking directly with Smith. On 25 September 1977 Kaunda met with Smith as he made his first visit to

black Africa since UDI by flying to Lusaka. Kaunda reported he found
Smith very intelligent and personable; he mistook those character-
istics for willingness to compromise. By November 1977 Kaunda was
promoting independence before elections. Kaunda with Nkomo
changed their long-stated position for internationally supervised
elections before independence to calling for independence first.

The other Frontline Presidents responded very negatively.
Nyerere recalled, 'I broke off relations with Britain (1965) on the issue
of elections: No independence before majority rule — that's what we
all said. How can I turn around now and say to the British: 'Oh, forget
about elections — just hand over to the Patriotic Front?'[4] Joaquim
Chissano, Foreign Minister of Mozambique, agreed that Frelimo had
refused elections but explained that the Mozambican situation was
not comparable to Zimbabwe: 'We had beaten the Portuguese army.
We had also penetrated that army. We knew it would never fight us
again. We had only to maintain our demands; we knew they would
have to accept them. But the Patriotic Front has not beaten Smith.
They are imitating Frelimo's political tactics of 1975, without being in
a position to imitate them effectively. They should go back to
NIBMAR [No independence before majority rule]'[5]

Robert Mugabe responded by citing a secret poll taken by the
Americans in Rhodesian towns. The survey gave ZANU 35 percent of
the vote and ZAPU only 5 percent, with 26 percent to Muzorewa.[6]
ZANU definitely felt that the proposed change in the NIBMAR policy
was to put Nkomo in power by fiat because he would not win elections.

In response to the Kaunda manoeuvre, the other Frontline
Presidents called for the Patriotic Front to accept the Anglo-
American proposals as the basis for negotiation. After the Anglo-
Americans refused to put pressure on Smith to match the Patriotic
Front compromises, Kaunda brought Nkomo and Smith together
once more. Smith was interested in legitimising his internal settlement
with Muzorewa and Sithole by including Nkomo. In August 1978, the
Nigerian Commissioner for External Affairs, Brigadier Joseph Garba,
also agreed to a meeting between Smith and Nkomo, set up by
Kaunda; Mugabe was not included. Mugabe was later flown to Lagos
and informed of the first meeting; he was asked to attend a projected
second one. He refused and promptly informed the other Frontline
Presidents of Kaunda's latest promotion of direct talks between
Smith and Nkomo. Machel was angered that once again a unilateral
settlement was being attempted. He accused the collaborators of

trying to make the Rhodesian independence conflict look like a civil war.[7] Nyerere declared that the 14 August meeting was the real reply of the British and Americans to the Malta II accords. Instead of rejecting the internal settlement out of hand, they were encouraging Smith to co-opt Nkomo. Nyerere analysed that Smith was willing to abandon his puppets because he was feeling the pressure of the war.[8] Smith replied that Nkomo and Mugabe were prisoners of Nyerere.[9] Tension along the Frontline and within the Patriotic Front mounted. Smith also miscalculated, however, for the attempted meeting damaged his internal settlement. Muzorewa, Sithole and Chirau were also angry that he had tried to bring Nkomo into the scheme without consulting them.

During the same period, Nyerere chose to nationalise Lonrho, the giant conglomerate that operated in Zambia and Tanzania, as well as in Rhodesia and South Africa.[10] Roland (Tiny) R. Rowland, Chief Executive, facilitated talks between Smith and Kaunda; when Smith flew to Lusaka in October 1977 it was in a jet owned by Lonrho. Nyerere expelled Lonrho in June 1978, and the acquisition of Lonrho's assets became legal on 23 October 1978. Nyerere clearly stated that the timing of the nationalisation was in protest against Rowland's interference in the Zimbabwean liberation struggle.[11]

Two national interests of Tanzania coincided in the nationalisation of Lonrho. First, the Tanzanian government could take another step toward national control of important productive sectors. Not simply Lonrho assets, but its productive capacity would no longer be directed by foreign interests. Second, the nationalisation was one of the few economic messages Nyerere could send to Western interests that the Tanzanian government was serious about the liberation of Zimbabwe through negotiations with the Patriotic Front. He did not approve of Lonrho's, or any Western party's, interference by facilitating secret and unilateral talks outside Frontline auspices. It was Kaunda's turn to be furious. He reminded Nyerere that Rowland had been helpful to the liberation struggle in many ways, such as suing the oil companies that were violating international sanctions to provide Rhodesia with oil (and thereby avoiding the Lonrho pipeline from Beira to Salisbury which was supposed to have monopoly concessions for oil delivery). Nyerere persisted, and the Lonrho subsidiaries were fully nationalised with much less compensation than Rowland thought was fair. In response Rowland tried to convince the IMF and the World Bank to halt aid to Tanzania. A member of the

British Parliament Edward du Cann, and Lonrho director, tried to block any British aid to Tanzania until 'full compensation' was paid.[12]

The most serious challenge to Frontline solidarity was the Zambian government's decision to open its southern border on 6 October 1978. The severe crisis exploded when Kaunda announced he was opening the border to Rhodesia for the first time in five years. He stated that Zambia could not do without the fertiliser stalled in Mozambican ports; it would not arrive in time for planting and the maize crop would suffer. He had to ship the fertiliser through Rhodesia because it had been delayed in the Mozambican ports after Dar es Salaam could not handle it. Nyerere and Machel, therefore, were not consulted about the opening; in fact, they were blamed for the necessity. They flew to Lusaka to try to convince Kaunda of alternative plans to ship the fertiliser. He was cool to them and refused any alternative proposals. Nyerere returned home and released statistics on the Dar es Salaam port to disprove Kaunda's allegations. Mozambique published documents showing that fertiliser had been unloaded at Beira and sent to the Zambian border, but no Zambian trucks showed up to transport it.[13] If it was lying in the Mozambican ports, it was Zambian inefficiency, not Mozambican. Further shipments from Beira to the Zambian border would have blocked the rail line. *Tempo,* a Mozambican weekly magazine, called the border opening 'an important breach in the economic encirclement of Ian Smith's racist and illegal regime... Zambia's economic system which largely depends on international capital makes her the weak link in the economic encirclement of the racists and makes it vulnerable to imperialist pressure.'[14] The Mozambican government accused the United States of shipping its consignment of fertiliser to Zambia through Beira in an attempt to force the use of the Beira-Umtali line that had been closed by Mozambican enforcement of sanctions.

Clearly, Zambia's respect of international sanctions against Rhodesia was hurting Zambia more than Rhodesia.[15] By 1978 the Bingham Report published statistics documenting how the major oil corporations were violating sanctions. Arms were clearly still arriving in Salisbury (see Chapter 5). Although extremely important politically, Zambia's enforcement of sanctions was, therefore, of minor economic consequence to Rhodesia. The opening of the border was discussed at several cabinet and Central Committee meetings and Reuben Kamanga stated, 'During all these meetings we agreed that the only way we could save our agricultural industry was through the reopening of the southern route.' Kaunda emphasised the intensity of the need: '. . . if we had not done that, we could have collapsed as a nation; there is no doubt about that.'[16]

There was also concern that the border opening could be used by Smith to hold Zambia hostage. Smith could retaliate to guerrilla attacks by seizing Zambian supplies at any point along the route. Further, the rail line had been a major sabotage target for both forces. ZAPU and ZANU responded in different ways. Nkomo pledged his support to Kaunda: 'This affects our struggle because after all, the railway line is one of our targets. But we understand the problems facing Kaunda and we will do our best to see that the railway line is left alone.' The ZANU Central Committee stated that 'we would be the last to suggest that the political considerations of our own situation outweigh and thus take precedence over extreme economic necessities of Zambia'. But they echoed Machel and Nyerere by appealing to Kaunda to reconsider: 'We hope it is not too late to appeal to the good judgement of Zambia to review its decision and examine other possibilities which we hear do exist.'[17]

It is significant that the Frontline did not snap totally apart over this crisis. It was the most serious breach of the Frontline States' principle of consulting each other on policy issues about the liberation struggle. The Zambian government later tried to make amends by denying it had blamed Tanzanian and Mozambican port facilities; instead, it emphasised all the structural constraints on the economy for the necessity to open the border.[18] Those constraints are the topic of analysis in Chapter 4.

The overriding disagreement among the Frontline States was the choice of which nationalist leader to support. Kaunda preferred Nkomo to assume power. Although Nkomo received military aid from the Soviets, he was clearly the more moderate of the two leaders in the Patriotic Front. ZAPU was more strongly centralised under Nkomo's leadership and did not have as much factional dissonance as that which plagued ZANU. Finally, Nkomo seemed more willing to compromise to obtain a settlement than Mugabe. Several times Nkomo entered unilateral talks with Smith.

None of the Frontline States was quick to accept Mugabe's leadership because of the factional discord within ZANU. One interpretation could be that the Presidents were trying to be careful not to impose their choice on ZANU and so waited until the ZANU High Command was clear about its choice. Some ZANU members, however, felt that Frontline hesitancy, on the part of Nyerere especially, was an effort to block their own choice of a leader. They contend that Mugabe was clearly endorsed several times before the Frontline States accepted his leadership.[19] Mugabe was first selected by the imprisoned leaders in November 1974; he was reaffirmed by the guerrillas in the camps in Tanzania in 1975; and in the Mgagao Declaration, 43 officers stated that Mugabe was their spokesperson. It was not until the Geneva Conference in October 1976 that he represented ZANU with the full support of the Frontline States.

After the Patriotic Front was formed, Nyerere was one of the more outspoken against Nkomo's willingness to talk with Smith; he also criticised Nkomo for not sending his forces to fight more. Nyerere's demand throughout the Frontline involvement was consistent: unity of the nationalists to confront Smith more effectively both at the negotiating table and in battle. This goal was primary as he shifted his considerable power as Frontline Chairman in the OAU Liberation Committee behind the groups most willing to sustain an alliance. He was furious with ZANU when they argued against dissolving their party into the ANC. When the ANC fell apart, he pushed for other coalitions and supported ZIPA (the combined forces of ZANLA and ZIPRA in 1976) by providing training bases and funds. When the Patriotic Front was formed, he worked to maintain it; he supported Mugabe who was willing to sustain the Patriotic Front unit (in contrast to some of his commanders) and whose forces were building a base in the people. Finally, he was deeply disappointed when ZANU decided to run in the March 1980 elections as a separate party from ZAPU, rather than as a united Patriotic Front party.

Frelimo at first had close links with ZAPU because of their interaction and discussion overseas. Both were recognised (along with the MPLA, PAIGC, ANC, SWAPO and MOLINACO – National Liberation Movement of the Comoros) by the First International Conference of Solidarity with the fighting peoples of Southern Africa (Khartoum, 18-20 January 1969) as 'the sole official and legitimate authority of the respective countries'. ZANU was not so accredited by the fifty-four countries attending the conference sponsored by the Afro-Asian People's Solidarity Committee and the World Peace Council. However, when ZANU, not ZAPU, responded to Frelimo's suggestion to begin infiltrating troops through Tete, the historical affinity changed. As early as 1972 Machel was travelling to Kaunda and

Nyerere to convince them that it was ZANU who was doing the fighting. Very close links established by joint operations throughout the war made it easier for some of the key leaders in Frelimo to understand the factional discord within ZANU. Further, Frelimo also had to resolve serious conflicts within its ranks during its war of liberation against the Portuguese. Therefore, three times Frelimo moved quickly, at the request of ZANU High Command, to restrict the dissidents: October 1976 during the Geneva talks; the 18 January 1977 detention of 25 ZIPA leaders; January 1978 detention of the 'Unity Group'. All parties agree that ZANU needed Frelimo's subvention to fight the war: training in the mobilisation of the people and subsequent guerrilla warfare, territorial proximity to Rhodesia, sanctuaries for refugees and camps for guerrillas, food and clothing, weaponry. Even with this vital support, Frelimo did not direct ZANU nor did they always agree about strategy and tactics, but co-operation was sustained throughout the war.

President Machel joined President Nyerere in castigating Kaunda and Nkomo for their repeated attempts to talk unilaterally with Smith. Further, Machel had no patience with ZAPU for its lack of fighting. He tried several times to convince the Soviets to arm ZANU as well as ZAPU. He made appeals to Fidel Castro and President Mengitsu Haile Mariam of Ethiopia to approach the Soviets, especially when the Rhodesian air attacks increased. Soviet anti-aircraft artillery would have considerably increased the defence capability of the camps in Mozambique. In the end the only Soviet weapons which ZANU received were ones supplied by the Soviets to Mozambique; Frelimo gave them to ZANU.

Because of historical linkages from the early 1960's, mutual ties to the ANC of South Africa, and similar links to the Soviet Union, the MPLA in Angola was more supportive of Nkomo and ZAPU. The MPLA built its strength in the urban areas more than in the rural areas so was not as critical of ZAPU tactics as the other Frontline States. Because of its own struggles against South Africa, however, the MPLA did not often attend Frontline meetings and was not regularly involved in the tensions over the choice of leaders. President Khama of Botswana joined Nyerere's plea for unity and gave his voice of support to the groups that were trying to formulate united fronts. Because it was little involved in the war hostilities, Botswana, like Angola, participated only peripherally in the efforts to promote one leader over another. The major tensions were clearly among the principal participants: Zambia, Tanzania, Mozambique.

From Lancaster House To Harare

In 1977 the conflicts within the Patriotic Front had not seriously affected the war; mobilising was continuing at a very successful pace. Recruits were pouring into Mozambique and Botswana faster than they could be absorbed by ZANU and ZAPU. Even though the war was escalating, not abating as promised by Prime Minister Muzorewa, and even though political and economic decisions were clearly still in the hands of the white minority, the Western allies moved away from promoting the Anglo-American proposals to 'creeping recognition' of the Muzorewa regime. Margaret Thatcher came to power with an election promise that sanctions would be lifted for Zimbabwe-Rhodesia. The conservatives in the US Senate were pushing for US recognition of the regime. In a tour of the United States, Nkomo lashed out against such moves: 'You (US) talk as if you are the arbiter and judge of what happens in Zimbabwe. We have never suggested a form of government for the US. What right do you have to tell us how to run our government?'[20]

The response from the Frontline States, in co-ordination with Nigeria, was twofold. Nigeria — having blundered by promoting the secret Nkomo-Smith talks in August 1978 — now turned its economic power on Britain. In May 1979 it denied any contracts to British firms in Nigeria stating that bids from Britain would not be welcome until majority rule was achieved in Zimbabwe. In July the Nigerian government nationalised Shell-BP because BP was engaging, in swap arrangements with its North Sea and Nigerian oil, enabling it to sell oil to South Africa. To further deliver the message to Britain, the Nigerian government dumped £500 million (about $1.2 billion) on international currency markets.[21]

The Frontline States effectively mobilised international opinion against the Muzorewa-Smith government as illegitimate. Two days after Thatcher's election all the ambassadors from the British Commonwealth unanimously sent the Prime Minister a letter warning her against recognition of Muzorewa. At the Non-Aligned Conference in Colombo a strong statement was issued denying that there was majority rule in Zimbabwe-Rhodesia. The July OAU meeting in Liberia issued an even stronger statement; the Patriotic Front was given overwhelming support as the sole legitimate representative of the Zimbabwean people, with conservative African governments joining the vote. The Commonwealth Conference was held on 2-8 August 1979 in Lusaka. In spite of several incidents trying to sabotage Zambia's ability to host the conference, such as cutting all the telephone lines to all the major hotels, the agenda was set to discuss the Rhodesian question with Prime Minister Thatcher. Tanzania and Nigeria had threatened to leave the Commonwealth unless it demonstrated abhorrence of all forms of racist policy.[22] But in a well-planned speech, President Nyerere suggested there was a new reality in Rhodesia. Prime Minister Thatcher conceded. During informal meetings, the Commonwealth quickly convinced Thatcher to agree to call one more all-parties conference to negotiate majority rule. The pace toward negotiation moved so fast, in fact, that the Patriotic Front felt it had not been fully consulted. They agreed to go to London because the Frontline States had no strings attached to the negotiations.

Smith went to the Lancaster House conference in London in September 1979 well aware that he was losing the economic war. His own Combined Operations Commander, General Walls, had publicly stated that the war could not be won militarily. Rhodesian records later found by the independent Zimbabwean government analysed that the economy could not last more than six months. But the British and Smith went to Lancaster House hopeful that they would rescue the political war. They anticipated that the Patriotic Front would not compromise and would walk away from the conference; the Front could then be legitimately excluded because they would not negotiate in 'good faith'. The Patriotic Front attended with equal resolution to maintain the talks and not walk away. Josiah Tongogara, commander of ZANLA, summarised their purpose:

> To us, London is definitely our second front. What is meant by second front is that we have the home front, which is the front for physical confrontation, and then we have the London front, which we term a peaceful front. In the home front, whenever we go to the battle, you put on your uniform, get your kit bag and your gun. Now here in London you put on your suit and a tie and then you go and talk. So it's a peaceful front.[23]

At times maintaining the second front was very difficult, for it was clear to the Patriotic Front that the British and Rhodesian negotiators had met together and brought terms for negotiation already agreed upon. Machel accused Britain of using threats, pressure — not dialogue — to 'bestow credibility on members of the illegal regime'.[24] The Frontline Presidents agreed with the Patriotic Front's frustrations, but convinced them more than once to stay in London and keep talking.

Smith finally backed down from insisting that the whites retain parliamentary blocking power. The British would not accept the transition time of six months as the Front requested, but finally agreed to two months. The number of Commonwealth troops called to supervise transition and elections was increased (to 1,100 not to the 5,000 that the Front wanted). The number of assembly points for the Patriotic Front guerrillas to enter during the ceasefire was augmented to sixteen, with one in the very centre of the country, recognising the penetration by the guerrillas. In turn, the Patriotic Front accepted that the whites would be over-represented in parliament for seven years: 20 seats out of 100 for 3 per cent of the population. They agreed that the transitional forces would be treated equally, rather than turning over security immediately from the Rhodesian army to the guerrillas. They accepted full responsibility for pension payments to be freely remitted outside the country and for the public debt, estimated at $1.2 billion, plus the secret loans. And they very reluctantly accepted the principle that land confiscated by the state would be recompensed with funds that could be remitted outside the country free from taxes or deductions.

The land concession was the hardest to make, for land was the symbol of the whole struggle. Tongogara asserted, 'Anyone who joins the armed struggle, he's joining on the basis of land.' The Tribal Trust Lands (TTL's) had three and one-half times the population as the carrying capacity of the land. The 6,000 European farmers had 80 per cent of the good land (45 per cent of the total).[25] The Zimbabwean view was that the white settlers stole the land from the African population in the first place and pushed them into the TTL's. The whites replied that they had improved the land and made it more productive. The Lancaster House agreement permitted the acquisition of under-utilised land only for the promotion of public benefit and with adequate compensation. The key concepts of 'under-utilised', 'promotion of public benefit', and 'adequate compensation' were left undefined in the accords. It would only be clarified in the courts of the new nation. The Patriotic Front agreed to these provisions only after the United States and Britain once again verbally promised massive amounts of aid to help the new government pay compensation to the white farmers.

Lord Carrington, who presided at Lancaster, proved that the colonial power could arbitrate. Very tough issues were resolved, and the ceasefire went into effect on 21 December 1979. Lord Soames, Governor for the transition period, was much less successful at resolving conflict. But the difference was not due to their personalities nor their administrative skills. The British government had decided that negotiations were necessary to resolve the crisis, but it equally decided to support Muzorewa in the elections. Further, Soames had to act within the structure of the existing white state apparatus. The daily functioning of the state was still in the hands of the white Rhodesian minority. This fact was an obvious restraint on independent decisions, but Soames also used it as an excuse. Almost every day in many sectors, the British Governor, expressing few verbal reprimands, allowed the terms of the transition to be violated: (1) composition and use of the military, (2) movement of refugees, (3) control of propaganda, and (4) restriction of freedom of movement and of the press. These violations will be discussed in sequence.

At Lancaster the 'Kaunda Plan' that 'opposing armies should be frozen and accorded equal status' was accepted as a compromise. The Patriotic Front forces would no longer be considered illegal nor would they be in full command as they had earlier demanded. In spite of the short time given to notify their forces of the ceasefire (21 December to 4 January deadline) most of the Patriotic Front guerrillas entered the sixteen assembly points by the deadline. The Rhodesian army was to be restricted to their barracks unless called upon to maintain order, and the Patriotic Front forces could be equally summoned. In fact, the Rhodesian army and police had full control of security, not joint or 'equal' operations by both militaries. Muzorewa's auxiliary forces were allowed to move freely while Patriotic Front forces were guarded in their camps. Equal treatment of the opposing armies was never established.[26] Further, South Africa was supposed to withdraw its troops immediately; they withdrew about 300 from Beitbridge only after international protest. But a very large number, ZANU said thousands, remained in the country. In fact, the British admitted inviting more into the country to 'monitor the elections' in clear violation of the provision that the only foreign troops would be the Commonwealth observers.[27]

One reason for the transition time was to allow the over 300,000 Zimbabwean refugees to return home from Zambia, Mozambique, and Botswana to vote in the elections. In Mozambique where over

150,000 of the refugees were, only one entry point was established, several hundred miles from the large camps. The authorities in charge of processing the refugees let them only trickle in even at that one point, with the result that most of the refugees were disenfranchised. Political prisoners were also to be released before elections, but two months after the British took administrative control of Rhodesia, Amnesty International reported that 'torture is still standard procedure to elicit information from detainees who number 6,000 political prisoners and 2,000 martial law (curfew violators) detainees'.[28]

The state apparatus was also used to promote pro-Muzorewa propaganda. The print and television media continued to refer to Muzorewa as the Prime Minister and to refer to the guerrilla fighters as terrorists. Several tons of ZANU literature — posters and leaflets for the campaign — were seized at the airport, while Rhodesian air force planes were used to drop pro-Muzorewa leaflets on remote villages. All rallies in Salisbury were prohibited the last weekend before the elections because Muzorewa was holding a three-day 'fair' with free food, music, dance, and exhibits. In contrast, rallies were banned for ZANU in Victoria Province.

Lord Soames also selectively restricted the freedom of movement of the ZANU and ZAPU candidates while permitting the Muzorewa candidates and auxiliary forces to move freely. Soames delayed Mugabe's return to Salisbury for over a month, the final reason given that the arrival time conflicted with a Muzorewa rally. A plane, sent by the OAU to take Nkomo and Mugabe to the meeting in Addis Ababa, Ethiopia, was not allowed to land at the Salisbury airport. Soames banned Enos Nkala from campaigning for elections because his speeches were 'inflammatory'. Finally, there were two assassination attempts on Mugabe's life. He narrowly missed death in Fort Victoria, and his house was attacked. Because others were also attacked, ZANU candidates resorted to sleeping in different locations each night.[29]

This less than impartial administration of the transition to elections raised a cry of protest from the international community. As early as 10 January 1980 the Frontline States met with Mugabe and Nkomo and then issued a strong protest against the ceasefire violations. On 19 January, the Secretary-General of the Commonwealth, Shridath Ramphal, stated that the presence of South African troops in Rhodesia is a 'major violation' of the Lancaster agreement; he confirmed the ZANU-ZAPU fear that the Commonwealth monitoring force was too small to be effective and deplored the fact that Muzorewa's auxiliary forces were being used against the Patriotic Front forces.[30] A few days later, on 25 January, the OAU Liberation Committee called for the OAU Council of Ministers to meet two weeks early to study the situation in Rhodesia. They also mandated the Africa Group to call an emergency UN Security Council meeting for the same reasons. The new government in Uganda insisted that Soames be recalled, and Kenya stated it would remove its troops from the Commonwealth monitoring force if the South Africans remained in Rhodesia.[31]

At the February OAU Council of Ministers meeting, Foreign Minister of Mozambique, Joachim Chissano, called for the African nations to sever ties with Britain because of its gross violations of the Lancaster accords. Three of the Frontline States joined by three others — Angola, Mozambique, Tanzania, Congo (Brazzaville), Ethiopia, and Guinea-Bissau — called for collective African action against Britain. The final resolution voted on 19 February 1980 demanded the following: refugees to be returned immediately, release of political prisoners, confinement of Muzorewa's auxiliaries to bases, cessation of hostile propaganda against ZANU-ZAPU, and removal of South African troops from Rhodesia.

By the beginning of February the UN Security Council voted against the manner of British handling transition. They passed two resolutions — 469 and 463 — to demand that South African troops be removed from Rhodesian territory. The Nigerian ambassador expressed the views of the African Group in condemning the Soames administration:

> The withdrawal of one of two companies from Beit Bridge will not change anything. It is common knowledge that there are thousands and thousands of South African troops in the country in gross violation of the Lancaster House agreement . . . There are South African parachute battalions at Rutenga and Chirundu. There are South African air force personnel flying the Mirage jets, helicopters and light aircraft that the illegal regime acquired just before the Lancaster House agreement. All these must be expelled as no self-respecting African will accept a government installed on the suffrance of the South African armed forces.[32]

It was after the UN resolutions that Soames requested more South African aid: they sent 90 anti-mine vehicles to help transport

the ballot boxes to the election booths. On 13 February President
Nyerere cabled Secretary-General Kurt Waldheim to send an independent UN observer group to Rhodesia to monitor the British supervision of transition. Waldheim asked Soames' permission to send the
UN observers; Soames replied that it would be 'inappropriate' and
asked Waldheim to come and observe the elections instead. President
Nyerere recalled the Tanzanian High Commissioner, Amon Nsekela,
from London for 'consultations'.[33] The Tanzanian President was very
close to cutting off relations with Britain as he had done when Smith
had first declared UDI in 1965.

As Zimbabweans were preparing to go to the polls, President
Nyerere gave a press conference accusing the Thatcher government
of 'dishonesty, perfidiousness, and of prostituting the honour of
Britain':

> I want to make the position of Tanzania very clear, and I don't do
> this lightly. My country is a small, poor country. Just now it has
> immense economic problems. The British don't need Tanzania;
> it is conceivable that we need them. But we shall not accept a
> betrayal of our continent... We cannot accept a government in
> Rhodesia which is the result of collusion between British racists,
> Rhodesian racists and South African racists... Tanzania and the
> Frontline States have made it clear to Britain that they wanted
> the war in Rhodesia to end. Britain should, however, not
> misread that commitment to peace. It was not an acceptance of
> racism, and the war would be continued if Britain was bent on
> taking her partners for a ride... The Commonwealth decided to
> trust the British. And indeed we decided to persuade the leaders
> of the PF — both of them — to trust the British... Now I must
> say that the whole thing was a trick.[34]

The other Frontline States shared Nyerere's fear that the conditions of the campaign would prevail during the three-day election. But
Britain, having done everything in its power to set up Bishop
Muzorewa, enforced the stringent election requirements: the polling
proceeded with minimal intimidation or assault. Of the estimated
7 million Africans, 2.7 million voted, an estimated 80 per cent of those
eligible. (Full population statistics were not available because the
Rhodesian government systematically underestimated the African
population when censuses were taken.) President Nyerere stated that
'if Abel Muzorewa wins the elections, he is going to turn that country
into another bantustan. But we are willing to accept any outcome of a

free and fair election.'[35] The Commonwealth Observer Group concluded that the elections had provided 'an adequate and acceptable means of determining the wishes of the people in a democratic manner'.[36] ZANU was the only party of the nine that ran in the elections to accept the results before they were announced. Eddison Zvobgo stated, 'We will accept the results in advance. Under the circumstances of the war, it was as free and secret an election as it was possible to hold.'[37]

The results are now history: ZANU (PF) 57 seats, Patriotic Front (ZAPU) 20, and UANC 3. The victory was so overwhelming that the combined vote (70 per cent) of ZANU and ZAPU in the parliament would be sufficient to amend the constitution. ZANU had been confident that it had fully mobilised the people, yet not even the Frontline States fully shared their confidence. But the people were sufficiently mobilised to withstand intimidation and confusion during the campaign. In contrast to British or American elections, the results were not to be decided during the campaign; they had been decided during the war. The Zimbabwean people knew who had done the fighting to make Smith agree to internationally supervised elections; they knew who was providing health care in areas that the Rhodesian government could no longer enter; they knew who promised land. A few slogans dropped from aeroplanes, especially from the very planes that had days earlier been bombing them, would not change those realities.

The achievements of the Patriotic Front, supported by the Frontline States, are highlighted by juxtaposing the terms of the internal settlement that Muzorewa and Sithole accepted to those of Lancaster (see p. 74). The Patriotic victory was two-fold: a constitution that gave the majority-rule government political and economic control and an overwhelming election victory that abolished any chances for the minority white party to engage in destabilising political coalitions.

Close comparison of the Anglo-American proposals with the final Lancaster settlement encouraged critics to suggest that the Patriotic Front capitulated to the dominant powers. However, just one glance at the summary comparison of the settlement reveals that the Lancaster House settlement differs in all the major provisions from the Smith-Muzorewa internal settlement. Smith clearly relinquished political and economic control; his only hope was that the nationalists would have to form a coalition government with Muzorewa, at which

COMPARISON OF MAJOR PROVISIONS OF THREE SETTLEMENT PROPOSALS

	Anglo-American Proposals 1977–1979	Internal Settlement 1978–1979	Lancaster House 1979
Franchise	universal suffrage	'universal suffrage' with martial law PF not permitted in elections	universal suffrage
Election Authority	British Resident Commissioner; police, judiciary, bureaucracy under whites	Rhodesian government	British Governor Commonwealth observers and troops; police, judiciary, bureaucracy under whites
Army	vague promise of Rhodesian and guerrilla forces as equals	Rhodesian army	Rhodesian and guerrilla forces as equals
Land	adequate compensation; only unused redistributed; overseas remittances from land payments permitted	little redistribution; white courts retain veto over redistribution	adequate compensation; only unused redistributed; overseas remittances from land payments permitted
Minority Rights	whites reserved 20 seats in parliament for 8 years	whites: 28 seats for 10 years — a veto power	whites: 20 seats for 7 years — no veto power

point the 20 reserved white seats in parliament would become important. The British compromise at Lancaster from their Anglo-American proposals was in the terms of the transition to elections. The British Resident Commissioner and the Commonwealth troops were to keep check on the still functioning white bureaucracy, judiciary, and police. When Britain did not fulfil these agreements during the transition, the Frontline States repledged themselves to support the war.

The concessions that the Patriotic Front made over compensation for land were ameliorated by the overwhelming election victory. For example, the ZANU government, which needs no coalition to rule, can now define such important concepts as 'adequate compensation,' 'under-utilised,' and 'promotion of public benefit' for the transfer of land. Further, the terms and process of transformation of the army, police, and bureaucracy are now fully in the hands of the ZANU government. ZANU has the legal power to take control of the state and of the economy.

Costs Of The War

As the many approaches to Smith and the disagreements with the nationalists show, the Frontline States preferred negotiations to armed struggle. However, when faced with Smith's intransigence, supported to a degree by the Western powers (see Chapter 5), the Frontline States chose to assist the armed struggle of the nationalists. The choice was a serious one, taken by governments whose budgets could not provide basic necessities, such as water supply and sanitation, even without the cost of supporting the Zimbabwean nationalists. For most of the international community, to enforce sanctions simply meant a drop in trade which probably could be compensated for by increasing trade elsewhere. In contrast, sanctions against Rhodesia by the neighbouring states affected the survival of their major productive activities. As will be discussed in the next chapter, their economies were integrated through colonial trade and transport links; enforcing sanctions ripped the linkages apart, with adverse effects on the weaker economies. Further, offering the guerrillas sanctuary provided the better equipped Rhodesian army with a ready excuse to bomb and raid civilian villages and refugee camps.

It is impossible to quantify the total costs to the Frontline economies, for the war affected their overall political economies:

disrupting lives, exacerbating problems of development that were already acute, and on the positive side, providing opportunities for growth that would not have been pursued without the war disruptions. The direct costs of the war, for security and enforcement of sanctions, will be given only very approximate dollar value. The discussion will focus more on two impacts of the war: *development retarded* and *development diverted*. When alternative transport links were built, such as Tazara for Zambia, the cost is not totally negative for obvious benefits accrued to both Tanzania and Zambia with the new 1,000 mile railroad. For example, production for the market has increased along the railroad. Yet the countries might not have chosen to invest such massive funds in the project if it had not been the single transport line for Zambia after the closing of the Rhodesian border. If Rhodesia had been under majority rule, Zambia could have used the rail links to the south and would have had the freedom to choose among other urgent development programmes. The forced choice of the Tazara is an example of *diverted development*. In other cases, the costs of the war actually *retarded development*. Spending large amounts of government revenue for defence does not release funds for schools and health clinics. Expenditure for arms has a high opportunity cost for poor nations. The final cost of the war that will be discussed was the need to provide for refugees. Attempts were made to help the refugees grow their own food and be self-sufficient, and many were. Other countries helped share the cost, but the clear responsibility was on the border states.

Zambia was incurring high costs which retarded development before the formation of the Frontline States and that fact was one reason for its formation. The Zambian government was finding it difficult to be the major rear base for both guerrilla forces. At UDI in 1965, even before the outbreak of serious hostilities, Zambia's oil supply was reduced to a serious low of 14 days while the oil corporations had secretly agreed to build up Rhodesia's supply to 90 days. Smith, in fact, waited to declare UDI until the oil was in storage in Rhodesia. After exposure of five oil corporations' violations of sanctions in 1979, Kaunda filed suit against 17 Western oil corporations for damages ($1.9 billion) resulting from the breach of the 1962 agreement of the Federation of the Rhodesias and Nyasaland.[38] The ability of the transnational corporations to carry out this collaboration with Smith is just an indicator of the vulnerability of Zambia to its more powerful neighbour (see Chapter 4). The governments of

Zambia and Tanzania built the Tazama oil pipeline in 1972 from Dar es Salaam to Lusaka (contracted to an Italian firm for £16 million, approximately $44.8 million) which did not solve the problem but reduced the strangulation grip that Rhodesia had on the Zambian oil supply.

From Zambian independence in 1964 to 1977, defence expenditures doubled as percentages of total expenditures.[39] Such costs clearly retarded development. Rhodesian aggression grew in magnitude and boldness as the war continued. During the Lancaster House talks, many people were killed in Zambia; for example, in October 1979 ten bridges were downed in four days, bridges which provided Zambia's links to the sea.[40] The government had to put a 5 percent surtax on the salaries of government employees who earned over $190 per month to try to rebuild the bridges. The overall war damage to Zambia's infrastructure has not been calculated, but repairs and payments will continue for years to come.

The price of Zambia's closing the border to Rhodesia cannot be accurately calculated. The UN estimated that it was costing as much as $1,250 million per year (1973-1978) in terms of lost revenue and higher transport costs, for Zambia had to reroute 68 percent of the imports and 55 percent of the exports.[41] But that figure does not include such items as the need to resort to alternative sources, disruption in production because of transport breakdowns, etc. The Tazara railway was completed ahead of schedule in June 1975. Financed under the conditions of a long-term, low-interest loan, the railroad clearly was a vital link that sustained Zambia's ability to resist retaliation from Rhodesia. With the Tazara railroad and the Tanzam highway running parallel to it, 90 percent of Zambia's goods were being exported through Dar es Salaam, Tanzania.

The rail link to Dar es Salaam did not solve Zambia's problems. Although some argument could be made that the Tazara would promote development, it is generally assessed that the one rail link was insufficient to Zambia's needs. It did provide development opportunities in north-east Zambia but at a high cost of development diverted from other areas. Minimally available transport to the sea adversely affected the food production in Zambia. Needed fertilisers and seed were not reaching the farmers in time, mainly due to the overburdening of the transport lines. By October 1978 Zambia felt obliged to reopen the border to the south. The opening immediately relieved some of the delays, but did not cure the transport artery pressure. Rhodesia used its rail link to harass Zambia, often delaying goods and diverting cars. Fertiliser and seed imports were still a problem and production in June 1979 of maize, the staple crop, was only 50 percent of annual average yield and in 1980 only 40 percent.[42] The government could not raise producer prices to provide incentives for greater production because of the government debt. With the difficulty of getting fertiliser and seed, low prices for the production, and difficulty in obtaining transport for marketing, agricultural production dropped drastically in Zambia. Certainly, not all the problems of Zambian agricultural production were related to the war.[43] The war turned what were chronic blockages to increased production into shortages that threatened survival.

Copper had contributed as much as 90 percent to Zambia's foreign exchange. At the beginning of the Frontline States' talks in 1974 the price was indexed at 177 (1970: 100); by November 1975 it had dropped to 74.4. The current account of balance of payments was $77 million in surplus and dropped to a 1975 deficit of $611 million.[44] Few countries have suffered such a steep decline in revenues in twelve months. The Southern African conflict did not cause the decline in copper price, but certainly made it more difficult for Zambia to cope with the consequences. With the closing of the border, coking coal had to be imported from West Germany instead of Rhodesia. (Later Zambia's own sources were put into use.) Conversion was made from coal to heavy furnace oil. Further, the transport difficulties adversely affected efficiency as spare parts were late in arriving and copper bars stacked up at the rail heads. Higher transport costs added to costs of production at a time when the prices were so depressed. Such a drastic change in its foreign exchange liquidity had to be of concern to President Kaunda as he pressured the umbrella ANC and especially ZANU to negotiate with Smith and obey the ceasefire in 1975.

The costs incurred by Mozambique for the war against white minority control of Rhodesia were mainly in the category of retarded development; very little benefit was measurable, for the war added direct costs to the government without providing much in alternative revenue or production. Mozambique has a 1,000-mile coast line so its own trade could continue during the war, but under the Portuguese, the Mozambican economy was built to service the more industrialised neighbours of Rhodesia and South Africa. Beira and Maputo served as major outlets to the sea for both countries, and that linkage gave Mozambique an important pressure point against the Smith regime.

But not without cost to its own economy. Because the economy was service orientated as a legacy of 400 years of colonialism, Mozambique did not have ready alternatives to replace the loss of revenue from its transport services. When the border was closed in March 1976, rail traffic fell to 60 percent of normal. Estimates by the UN stated that revenue lost to transport was $106-132 million per year, which was approximately one-third of its foreign exchange earnings. Estimates for 1979 were that the cost of closure was $300 million, which almost equalled foreign exchange earnings. By July 1978 only $20 million of international aid had been provided in the previous 18 months.[45] In 1984 the Mozambican government estimated the total direct and indirect costs of sanctions against Rhodesia to be $556 million, which corresponded to more than two years of *total* exports from Mozambique.[46]

Such costs clearly retarded development projects. An estimated 13,000 jobs were lost from the reduction of rail and port traffic when the border was closed, although the government did delay the closure until some alternative employment could be found. The closure also made Mozambique even more dependent on revenue in the service sector from South Africa. However, the South African government did not simply stand by while Mozambique enforced sanctions against Rhodesia; the apartheid regime responded with severe economic retaliation. By the end of the war in 1979, South African trade through the port of Maputo was 61 percent of the 1973 level of traffic through the colonial Portuguese port. In 1980 Mozambican workers in South African mines had been cut to less than 40 percent of the 1975 total, leaving 70,000 Mozambicans unemployed. In addition, on 10 April 1978, the South Africans unilaterally ceased the sale of gold at the fixed price of 29.75 rand per ounce which had allowed the colonial Mozambican government to sell it at a much higher rate on the world market to finance the balance of payments deficit.[47] South African direct support of Rhodesia will be discussed later, but it is necessary to emphasise that it also used its economic power against Mozambique when that country was enforcing UN sanctions against Rhodesia. Honouring sanctions exacted a high price from the Mozambicans, a price they are still paying.

The sole benefit of the border closure might have been that the hardship underlined the necessity for the Mozambican people to transform their service economy to a productive one in order to gain economic stability. Yet it probably was not necessary to learn this lesson so dramatically, as Frelimo had already formulated those goals as part of its own policy.

The government estimated at the end of the war that Mozambique had suffered over 350 major attacks from Rhodesia with 1,335 Mozambicans killed (in addition to Zimbabwean refugees) and 1,538 injured. Over 50,000 Mozambicans were displaced by the war, and damage to the infrastructures was estimated at $50 million. Part of that damage was the bombing of oil tanks in Beira which cost about $3 million.[48] As with Zambia, the most serious damage came during the Lancaster talks when Rhodesia bombed important irrigation installations and bridges, disrupting the food production in Manica province, a major agricultural producer.

The damage to infrastructure such as the oil tanks and the irrigation system are costs of disrupted development. In a country having just finished its own war of liberation, food production is a priority. The Rhodesian war interfered greatly with Mozambique's ability to develop its agricultural potential. Two serious floods also caused great damage in 1977 and 1979. Projects of flood control take international co-operation as rivers do not respect boundaries, and Mozambique can only now begin to work with its neighbour Zimbabwe to control and utilise the vast water potential for agricultural production. At times during the war northwest Gaza was actually cut off from the rest of the country. Further, bombing of telecommunication posts disrupted communications between northern and southern Mozambique.

Response to these development needs was impaired because of the necessity to allocate much of the government revenue to defence. In 1976 and 1977 the government spent 20 percent of total expenditure on defence and by 1979 it had increased to almost 30 percent.[49] Procurement of weapons means that books and medicines cannot be purchased. The cost of supporting the war was very high for this poor and newly independent country to pay.

The war budget did not include the cost of sustaining several refugee camps which housed as many as 150,000 refugees by the end of the war. International aid did help, but Mozambique contributed greatly. The country was left with 95 percent illiteracy after the Portuguese left. The demand for top personnel to direct the army and to administer the refugee operations took skilled personnel away from development projects that Mozambique needed to pursue. A major cost of the war was this drain on trained personnel to find means of survival, rather than to plan imaginative development programmes.

The Botswanan government did not offer sanctuaries to guerrillas but found it had to establish its own defence forces because of unprovoked assaults from Rhodesia. Using the excuse of 'hot pursuit,' Rhodesian forces frequently raided Botswanan villages. Botswanan defence forces extracted $32 million over four years from the development budget, according to a UN estimate, and retarded development of other projects.[50]

The most obvious threat to Botswana's production capacity was the outbreak of foot and mouth disease in Rhodesia which spread to the Botswanan herds. By 1977, the Rhodesian government was not vaccinating animals in the rural areas. The disease spread rapidly and decimated many cattle in Botswana. Export of healthy animals was difficult because the buyers suspected the disease and did not want to chance buying contaminated meat. Foreign exchange earnings from Botswanan beef exports dropped off by one-third from 1977 to 1978.[51] In response, the government built a fence on the border with Rhodesia at an expense of $450,000.

From the closure of the Zambian border in 1973 until October 1977, the major road from South Africa to Zambia was used constantly by overweight trucks trying to get goods to land-locked Zambia. Botswanan officials estimated that a 30 gross ton truck cost the government $575 for each return trip for maintenance cost and reduced life of the road system. After that date, weight restrictions were put on the trucks and the use of rail to Francistown reduced the costs by 50 percent. These costs seem modest to a developed economy but were substantial to a country that achieved independence as one of the poorest in sub-Sahara Africa. As Khama stated to the European Parliament Development Committee: 'It has to be understood that it is our existence as a sovereign state which could be jeopardised if the international community applied conventional aid and project evaluation in our circumstances. Emergency life-line projects like the Botswana-Zambia road may not show a positive rate of return but are crucial for our economic survival.'[52]

Some of the costs of the war to Botswana could be counted as long-term benefits, for several projects were initiated to lessen somewhat its vulnerability to Rhodesian and South African forces. Botswana initiated 11 emergency programmes estimated at $56 million: the programmes included such necessities as an oil storage depot and the purchase of some of its own rolling stock, for Botswanan railway lines were totally owned and run by Rhodesia.[53]

Tanzania shared the cost of diverted development. Its role was not as important as a sanctuary to guerrillas or refugees, although it did help train most of the guerrillas. Its economic role was more to enable Zambia to survive the border closure. Between 1965 and 1975, Tanzania spent over $300 million on Zambian-related transport expenses. Over $180 million was Tanzania's share of the external debt to build the Tazara railway; $72 million contributed to building the Tanzam Highway and $48 million renovated the Dar es Salaam port so it could handle more traffic.[54] The Second Five Year Plan (1968-74) outlined the importance of the Tanzam Road to overall development:

i)   The construction of the Tan-Zam Highway overshadows all other development in the sector, particularly during the first three years of the Plan.

ii)   Because of the heavy impact of the Tan-Zam spending the level of spending on other communications projects will be less than would otherwise have been desirable.

iii)   The estimated cost of the Tan-Zam Highway is . . . slightly more than half the total allocated to roads in the Plan.

The completion of the road, however, did not end the economic and political difficulties. Zambian importers used the 'Great North Road' not only to ship from Dar es Salaam, but also from Kenya. Over-weight trucks, especially from Kenya, destroyed the roadbed, the greatest length of which was in Tanzania; it was highly expensive to keep the road in repair. The government imposed a 30-ton weight restriction which antagonised both Zambian and Kenyan shippers.[55] Finally, the emphasis of these links precluded the development of what might have been a priority under other circumstances. For instance, the southern part of Tanzania remains virtually cut off from the rest of the country during the rainy season, as long as six months in some years. Construction of dams and all-weather roads to this area were delayed because of the priority to keep Zambia alive.

At the height of hostility between Zambia and Tanzania over Zambia opening its border to the South, the Zambian officials accused Tanzania of making money on their monopoly of Zambian transport. The figures show that recurrent revenue was only slightly in excess of recurrent expenditures for some years and broke even in others.[56] Tanzania clearly was not as deprived of revenue as Zambia, but it did not benefit from Zambia's difficulties. The Dar es Salaam port gave Zambian goods top preference and provided free storage up to 14 days, a gesture unheard of in any other port in the world. The Dar es Salaam port simply had trouble handling all the traffic and was not efficient enough to avoid blockage of Zambian imports and exports. The port delays caused the shipping companies to add a surcharge on the shipments because the ships often had to wait two weeks in port before off-loading. In November 1977 the surcharges cost the government as much as $3 million for one year.[57]

The costs to Angola for the support of the Zimbabwean war has not been calculated, either by the United Nations agencies nor by the Commonwealth study cited above. Angola did offer two ZAPU training camps, but they were mainly financed by the Soviets. This aid was necessary because Angola's economy was devastated by its own war of liberation and the repeated invasions by South Africa. (See the next chapter.) Angola's frontline was mainly turned toward Namibia, not Zimbabwe.

Table I shows the United Nations High Commissioner for Refugees' (UNHCR) aid to Angola. However, the refugees were not from Rhodesia, but from Zaire and Namibia. (See Table II for the aggregate figures.) Of the total refugee population of 56,000 in 1979, 20,000 were Zaireans, 35,000 Namibians, and 1,000 South Africans. In 1980 the number of Zaireans declined, but there was an influx of more Namibians and South Africans seeking refuge.[58] Given the assault on its productive forces by South Africa and the increasing numbers of refugees from Namibia, it is surprising that the government of Angola offered any assistance to Zimbabwe. Further, when the training camps were in place, the Rhodesians bombed them. (See Chapter 4.) Angola suffered the least from the Zimbabwean war of the five Frontline States, but only because it carried almost the total burden as sanctuary for refugees and guerrillas from Namibia.

The figures from 1975 through 1979 in Table II illustrate the massive exodus of Zimbabweans and the increased burden on the Frontline as they rallied to support the armed struggle. All of the refugees enumerated for Mozambique are from Rhodesia, and Mozambique clearly carried the most cost. In 1978, 25,300 Zimbabweans arrived in Botswana, but 11,600 were immediately transferred to Zambia, reflecting the agreement that Botswana would transfer most to Zambia. In 1979, 96 percent of the refugees in Botswana were Zimbabwean, but the numbers were increasing from Namibia and South Africa.[59] Zambia received about 40,000 Zim-

TABLE I

UNHCR ALLOCATIONS FOR REFUGEE AID (US $ THOUSANDS)

	1974	1975	1976	1977	1978	1979	1980
Angola	. . .	136.2	3,931.5	14,556.0	4,109.6	5,113.8	6,185.8
Botswana	41.2	136.8	181.9	880.6	8.143.0	4,441.7	1,350.2
Mozambique	100.0	3,346.1	1,926.0	3,861.5	4,666.5	6,594.6	11,426.6
Tanzania	3,003.7	2,673.8	4,739.8	2,607.8	3,940.1	4,365.6	6,721.2
Zambia	564.3	464.0	660.7	1,864.4	2,802.8	6,613.0	7,129.1

. . . Not enumerated before independence from Portuguese colonial rule.

Source: High Commissioner for Refugees, United Nations, (UNHCR), *Report on UNHCR Activities,*
             annual in August to the General Assembly, 1975–1981.

TABLE II

TOTAL NUMBER OF REFUGEES IN EACH COUNTRY

	1974	1975	1976	1977	1978	1979	1980
Angola	...	...	220,000	250,000	141,000	56,000	73,000
Botswana	2,500	2,500	4,000	4,300	19,000	23,300	1,300
Mozambique	...	14,500	27,000	42,000	100,000	150,000	100
Tanzania	193,000	171,000	154,000	163,500	160,000	155,700	n.a.
Zambia	40,000	36,000	33,600	64,000	70,000	57,000	51,000

. . . Not enumerated before independence from Portuguese colonial rule.

n.a. Not available.

Source: High Commissioner for Refugees, United Nations, (UNHCR), *Report on UNHCR Activities,* annual in August to the General Assembly, 1975–1981.

babweans.[60] The vast numbers of refugees in Tanzania are from Rwanda and Burundi; Tanzania only hosted about 350 Zimbabweans.[61]

These refugee figures do not include those Zimbabweans officially in the armed forces of the liberation groups. All the countries had training camps except Botswana, so the number of Zimbabweans in the Frontline States would be much higher, especially for Tanzania, Mozambique and Zambia. These figures do not simply represent numbers of people to be fed and clothed. All the countries tried to provide adequate health care and education in the camps. The refugees worked hard to grow their own food and provide their own services, such as education, but supplies and trained personnel from the host country were necessary. As will be seen in the next chapter, the host nations were so underdeveloped that they could not provide adequate services for their own people, but still, they willingly aided the Zimbabweans.

The disruption of infrastructure and production within the Frontline States by the Zimbabwean war, as well as the cost of offering sanctuaries, explain somewhat their vacillation and tensions with the Zimbabwean nationalists. These direct costs from the war must also be put in context of their histories of dependence and underdevelopment, which will be analysed in the next chapter. Angola and Zambia are rated among the richer of the Third World countries, but such a listing derives from their raw mineral wealth, which is more an indicator of potential development. The other three, Tanzania, Botswana, and Mozambique, are considered the poorest of the poor. What needs explanation is not their poverty or even their obvious weaknesses in the Rhodesian conflict, but rather, their ability to endure the conflict at all. Yet they endured to back the Patriotic Front's demands for legal control of the state and of the economy. The explanations of this improbable outcome are the subject of the rest of this book.

Notes

1. Julie Frederikse, *None But Ourselves: Masses vs. Media in the Making of Zimbabwe* (Johannesburg: Ravan Press and Harare: Zimbabwe Publishing House, 1982), pp. 16-19.
2. *Tempo* (Maputo), 13 October 1979.

3. *Tanzania Daily News*, 1 and 4 November 1979.
4. Conor Cruise O'Brien, 'The End of White Rule?' *New York Review of Books* (7 March 1978), p. 25.
5. Ibid., p. 26.
6. Ibid.
7. *Tanzania Daily News*, 17 September 1978.
8. Ibid., 11 September 1978.
9. Ibid., 12 September 1978.
10. Suzanne Cronjé, Margaret Ling, and Gillian Cronjé, *The Lonrho Connections* (Encino, CA: Bellwether Books, 1976).
11. *Tanzania Daily News*, 3 June 1978.
12. Ibid., 8-11 November 1979. Tanzania paid £10 million for compensation which was half what Lonrho demanded but more than the original offer of £1.3 million by Tanzania. *African Business* (August 1983), p. 7.
13. *Tanzania Daily News*, 11-12 October 1978.
14. *Tempo* (Maputo), 13 October 1978.
15. State House, Republic of Zambia, 'Sequence of Events Leading to Decisions to Open Southern Railroad Route for Transportation of Fertiliser and Cotton', 6 October 1978.
16. *Times* of Zambia, 12 October 1978. According to some reports, the IMF was making the opening of the border a prerequisite for further loans.
17. Both ZANU and ZAPU responses are quoted in State House, Republic of Zambia, op. cit.
18. *Zambia Daily Mail*, 12 October 1978.
19. Personal interviews with ZANU leaders in Dar es Salaam and Maputo, March-April 1979.
20. Television interview, CBS, 19 May 1979.
21. At the Commonwealth Conference in Lusaka, British Foreign Secretary Lord Carrington told the Nigerian Commissioner of External Affairs, Henry Adefope that the nationalisation was a 'monstrous act.'
   Nicholas J. Spiliotes, 'Nigerian Foreign Policy and Southern Africa: A Choice for the West,' *Issue* 11, nos. 1-2 (Spring/Summer 1981), p. 45.
   See also, John S. Stremlau, 'The Fundamentals of Nigerian Foreign Policy', Ibid., pp. 46-50.
22. *Tanzania Daily News*, 9 August 1979.
   Extracts from Communique of the Meeting of Commonwealth Heads of Government, Lusaka, 1-7 August 1979, *Africa Contemporary Record 1979-1980* (New York: Africana Publishing Co., 1981), pp. C26-C29.
23. Interview of Josiah Tongogara by Alves Gomez of Mozambique Information Agency, reprinted in the *Guardian* (New York), 28 November 1979.
24. Mozambique Information Agency (AIM), *Bulletin* (October 1979), p. 8.
25. Roger Riddell, *From Rhodesia to Zimbabwe — The Land Question* (London: Catholic Institute for International Relations, 1978), pp. 5-7.
26. The official Commonwealth Observer Group protested to Lord Soames about a number of compaign irregularities, including deployment of Rhodesian troops against the guerrillas. The deployment was not denied by Soames; instead, he tried to justify it by citing infringements by the guerrillas. International observers

(200 from 30 countries) generally agreed that most of the violent infringements were committed by the Rhodesian forces and Muzorewa's auxiliaries.

27. *Tanzania Daily News*, 21-22 February 1980. The OAU sent a 5-person team to investigate presence of South African troops. See also footnote 33.

28. Ibid., 22 February 1980.

29. *Tanzania Sunday News*, 27 January 1980.

30. *Tanzania Daily News*, 20 January 1980.

31. Ibid., 15 and 25 January 1980.

32. Ambassador Usman Abubaker, Speech, United Nations Security Council, 30 January 1980, quoted in the *Guardian* (New York), 13 February 1980.

33. The 3,000 South African troops figure was given in *Tanzania Daily News*, 21 February 1980. *Africa News* (17 March 1980, p. 11) reported that the 'British admitted that South Africa sent troops to facilitate the elections'. Nyerere's policy reactions reported in *Tanzania Daily News*, 10, 17, 24 February 1980.

34. Ibid., 26 February 1980.

35. Ibid., 7 February 1980.

36. Ibid., 4 March 1980.

37. Ibid.

38. Ibid., 28 November 1979.

39. Commonwealth Secretariat, *The Front-Line States: The Burden of the Liberation Struggle* (London: Commonwealth Secretariat, 1979), p. 7.

40. *Tanzania Daily News*, 24 November 1979.

41. UN Economic and Social Council, *Assistance to Zambia: Report of the Secretary-General* (E/1978/114.5), 5 July 1978, Annex.

42. *Zambia Daily Mail*, 13 June 1979 and *Los Angeles Times*, 30 July 1980.

43. International Bank for Reconstruction and Development, *Basic Economic Report: Zambia*, 3 October 1977.

    Robert Klepper, 'Zambian Agricultural Structure and Performance', in Ben Turok, ed., *Development in Zambia* (London: Zed Press, 1979).

    P. Ollawa, *Rural Development Policies and Performance in Zambia* (The Hague: ISS Occasional Paper 59, 1977).

44. Commonwealth Secretariat, op. cit., p. 4.

    UN Economic and Social Council, *Assistance to Mozambique: Report of the Secretary General* (E/5812), 30 April 1976, p. 22.

    Gloria Jacobs, 'Mozambique: By 1990, Only Memories of Underdevelopment', *Southern Africa* 12, no. 9 (November-December 1979), p. 17.

45. United Nations General Assembly, Report of Economic and Social Council, *Assistance to Mozambique: Report of the Secretary General* (A/33/173), 12 July 1978, p. 27.

46. People's Republic of Mozambique, Economic Report, Maputo, January 1984, p. 30.

47. Ibid., pp. 30-31.

48. Martha Honey, 'Hopes for a Long Peace', *New African* (March 1980), pp. 21-22.

49. Gloria Jacobs, op. cit.

50. UN Economic and Social Council, *Assistance to Botswana: Report of Secretary General* (A/32/287, S/12421), 26 October 1977.

51. Government of Botswana, Department of Customs and Excise, reported in Economist Intelligence Unit, *Quarterly Economic Review, Southern Africa*, Annual Supplement (1980), p. 49.

52. Commonwealth Secretariat, op. cit., p. 53.
53. Ibid., p. 48.
54. Ibid., p. 20.
55. US Agency for International Development, *Development Needs and Opportunities for Co-operation in Southern Africa: Transport/Communication*, Annex B (March 1979), p. 330.
56. Commonwealth Secretariat, op. cit., p. 20.
57. Ibid., p. 21.
58. United Nations High Commissioner for Refugees, 'Report on Assistance Activities in 1979-1980 and Proposed Voluntary Funds Programmes and Budget for 1981', 14 August 1980 (A/AC. 96/577), p. 5.
59. Ibid., p. 10; Ibid., 14 August 1979 (A/AC.96/564), p. 4.
60. Ibid. (1980), p. 105.
61. Ibid.

CHAPTER 4
Dependence Of The Frontline Political Economies

The struggle for Zimbabwe was not an internal civil war. Because of the history of colonialism in Southern Africa, the conflict had international implications from the first mass demonstration for majority rule. Control over the state meant the ability to control the economy which had been dominated by British and South African capital since the end of the 19th century (see Chapter 5). However, foreign capital not only dominated the Rhodesian economy, but all of the Frontline States. Their political independence did not bring economic liberation; in fact, their analysis was that they could achieve economic liberation only with the independence of Rhodesia and South Africa.[1] The struggle in Zimbabwe, therefore, cannot be understood as an isolated political conflict. Not only Rhodesia, but also the economies of the politically independent Frontline States were dominated by foreign interests, mainly British and South African, but also American.

These economic linkages imposed real structural constraints on the Frontline economies, the form and extent of which will be discussed empirically in this chapter. The first two sections outline the basic theories of the origins and reproduction of dependence, which is then critiqued in the third section, both for its economic and political implications. Fourth, empirical analysis documents the dependence relations of each of the five on the advanced capitalist states. According to a set of dependence criteria, all of the Frontline States are economically dependent on Western capital. The final section concludes that the dependence theories help to designate constraints on the Frontline economies but cannot explain the causes or the political effects of those constraints. Caught at the level of analysis of the nation-states, the theories do not look at the domestic social formations. As will be discussed thoroughly in Chapters 6 and 7, it is these social formations, based in both pre-capitalist and capitalist production relations, which perpetuate dependence and also offer clues for its transformation.

Theories Of Dependence

With the emergence of monopoly capitalism, the specialisation of production and the international division of labour became more intensive. The dependence theorists have been helpful in specifying the effects of the dominance of monopoly capital (production and finance) in the world capitalist system; national capitals cannot be examined in isolation from this historical development.

According to Marx and Lenin, the historic role of capitalism is to develop the productive forces through the social organisation of the production process into large scale enterprises. This increased centralisation of production has two major effects on labour: it encourages the specialisation of labour which promotes greater efficiency and it facilitates the ability of labour to organise for higher wages and better working conditions. This labour demand, along with competition in the market place, encourages technological innovation. Thus, the forces of production are gradually developed through the specialisation of labour and technological innovation. According to the dependence theorists, in the development of capitalism under colonialism this progressive mission of capitalism was blocked. The forces of production in the colonial economy are made to serve the needs of the more advanced capitalist economies, not of internal development.[2] Summarising many similar definitions,[3] economic dependence can be described as a 'conditioning relation' whereby processes of capital accumulation and investment are contingent on external factors. As Fernando Henrique Cardoso and E. Faletto emphasise: 'From the economic point of view, a system is dependent when the accumulation and expansion of capital cannot find its essential dynamic component inside the system.'[4]

Because production in the colonies was directed to the needs of foreign capital, specialisation in production occurred. The subordinate economies were forced to specialise in the production of primary commodities in mining and agriculture. Peasants producing food crops were forced to produce cash crops for the export market if the colonial power could extract the surplus value from that labour. For example, peasants in Northern Mozambique had to produce cash crops to pay taxes to the Portuguese. The price they received for their marketed cotton was about one-tenth the price that Portuguese settlers received for the same grade of cotton. The Portuguese made huge profits by selling the cotton at much higher international market prices. Forced to grow cotton to pay taxes, the peasants had insufficient land and time for adequate food crop production. Their level of nutrition fell drastically. In other areas of Mozambique, the peasants were pushed off the land into unproductive areas with plots too small for even subsistence. This alienation from the land was one reason why males sought jobs as migrant labourers on the plantations or in the mines.[5] With intensive exploitation of the migrant labourers, from low wages and long hours, the plantations and mines produced cheap commodities for the factories of the colonial power. For many African countries, basic processing of these goods began only after independence. Their role as colonies was to supply raw material for the factories in Europe. Cotton, sisal, iron ore, copper, tea and coffee were all shipped unprocessed from Southern Africa to Britain and Portugal. The result of this lack of processing was to deprive the colonial economy of the spin-off effects. Processing of raw materials creates industries which provide jobs; it has a multiplier effect on the growth of capital as investment opportunities increase. With the specialisation of production, these spin-off benefits accrued mainly to the advanced capitalist countries.

Where competition on the international market was minimal, there was little incentive to improve the efficiency of production. In the Portuguese colonies, for example, a few companies were given land concessions and had oligopoly control of the market to purchase cash crops for export. One company could control the export of a product and was guaranteed a market in Portugal. For instance, simply three *latifundist* companies controlled 85 percent of Angola's coffee production and two controlled Mozambique's cotton production. There was no need, therefore, to be innovative; profits were insured. Where competition for international sales did exist, there was some development of the productive forces. In Southern Africa, this transformation occurred mainly in the mines to lower cost of extraction of the ores. The result is, therefore, that a country like Zambia has highly sophisticated technology in its copper mines while simple technology to provide readily accessible water is not available in most villages.

The specialisation of production also fostered the international division of labour. Literacy was not needed for production; it was even considered a political threat by those who wanted to obfuscate efforts by labour to organise. Illiteracy in Angola and Mozambique after 400 years of Portuguese colonialism was over 95 percent for both countries at the time of independence. This high rate was the result of not only of the relative poverty of the colonial regime but also of the Portuguese desire to control the labour force. The colonies became the suppliers of cheap and underskilled labour; advanced skills for agriculture and industry were not developed.

Surplus was extracted from the colonies to serve the needs of the colonial power, but from these few examples, it is clear that the pattern of colonial intervention in the development of the forces of production varied considerably according to different factors: the period of colonial exploitation, the natural resource base of the colony, the presence of settlers, the level of development of the productive forces when the colonial power gained hegemony, the relative success of organised resistance, the competitive position of the colonial power in the world market. Each case must be analysed historically to understand the perpetuation of the domination and exploitation. A brief analysis of the colonial intervention in each of the five Frontline States is presented in Chapters 6 and 7. What is important here is to outline the general pattern of underdevelopment which has maintained economic dependence of the Frontline States on advanced capitalism.

Perpetuation Of Dependence And Underdevelopment

Some theorists claim that this historical division of labour has prevented economic development into contemporary times. Others say that economic growth can occur in a dependent economy, but that it is partial and distorted.[6] The latter point out that sectors of dependent economies use highly sophisticated technology with labour skills equal to any in the advanced capitalist countries. Using a more dynamic analysis than most dependence theorists, Fernando Henrique Cardoso states that dependence and a structural dynamism of industrialisation are not incompatible, but are linked in practice. He characterises it as 'dependent development.'[7] Economic growth does occur; however, it can be distorted in several ways. First, the growth occurs in only one or two major sectors, such as the example of mining in Zambia. Even where technological innovation does occur, it remains in isolated sectors: producing mainly for export, such development has little impact on productive forces in other sectors. Thus a computer network for information processing might be available in a country still producing its major foreign exchange earner with a hoe.

Second, growth can occur with production diversifying away from primary products to manufacturing for import or export substitution.

Some spin-off effect is initiated as investment is made in other sectors. This growth, however, is not development, for it seriously underdevelops other sectors. Commercial farmers, highly mechanised and efficient, produce on large tracts of land taken from the peasant producers who are impoverished as a result. The difference from the development of advanced capitalism is that there are no jobs created in the urban areas for this 'surplus labour.' In addition, production for luxury consumption diverts limited productive forces from production for basic needs, such as low cost clothing, housing, or transport. The labour is 'not needed'; therefore, production does not provide for its basic needs to make a more efficient and healthy labour force. 'Dependent development' exacerbates the inequitable distribution of resources among factors of production. It is growth that benefits only a small segment of industry or of labour. The theorists agree that income distribution is especially inequitable during initial periods of accumulation; the history of the advanced capitalist countries attest to this relationship. However, they argue that these conditions are even worse in dependent capitalism. Labour, in general, is left unskilled. Technological innovation and machinery are only in isolated sectors. The conditions of work and the standard of living deteriorate for the vast majority. Finally, in Latin America or in Africa these conditions can continue for centuries.

   The first major reason why growth can occur in certain sectors of dependent economies without fostering development (improved technology, creation of jobs, etc.) in other sectors is that the transnational corporations can provide the forward linkages. Thus chrome is mined in one country, transferred to another for processing and to a third for production into capital goods. This total process can be controlled by one vertically integrated transnational corporation, although it involves three separate national economies. Growth occurs in the extractive sector of the mineral country while employment and revenue from processing occur in another. The multiplier effect of integrated production is denied to the primary commodity producer. As Samir Amin concludes:

> When iron ore of Lorraine is eventually worked out this may create a difficult reconversion problem for the region, but it will be able to overcome these difficulties, for an infrastructure has been formed on the basis of the mineral, which could be imported from elsewhere. But when the iron ore of Mauritania is worked out, that country will go back to the desert.[8]

Because so much has been written about the role of transnationals in perpetuating dependency in developing economies,[9] it is not necessary to elaborate the theories here. It is sufficient to point out that the transnationals are considered one of three major means of reproducing underdevelopment through dependence linkages of the post colonial state to industrialised countries. Controlling technology and the flow of capital, the transnationals can and have toppled governments that threaten their hegemony. As will be discussed thoroughly in Chapters 6 and 7, the five Frontline States have all taken major steps to reduce control of production by the transnational corporations in their economies. Mozambique and Tanzania have nationalised all major sectors of their economies and set conditions for foreign corporate investment. Angola, Botswana, and Zambia have intervened and required majority state ownership of important mines in an effort to delimit foreign control of this sector.

Trade relationships are a second major perpetrator of dependence. Because of the historical specialisation of production, advanced capitalist countries now export mainly manufactures, the prices of which keep rising relative to primary products, especially agricultural commodities. Even with greater production, therefore, it is difficult for primary commodity producers to purchase manufactures and capital goods for their own development needs. This deterioration in the terms of trade is historical over the long term. Only for brief periods has the price of certain commodities increased relative to manufactures. Only a few minerals deviate from this general trend of terms of trade deterioration (oil, uranium).

Table III shows the terms of trade by purchasing power for three important commodities produced by the Frontline States for the period of their struggle for the independence of Zimbabwe (1975-80). It indicates the amount of oil or of US dollars earned by the sale of one ton of copper, coffee or cotton on the international market. As the table shows, by the end of only five years, the purchasing power of the primary commodities, either in terms of oil or of dollars, has declined by almost 50 percent. Production would have had to *double* in *five years* simply to stay at the same level of foreign exchange earnings. Further, a market for that doubled production would have to be available to realise that revenue. However, if production does double and goods flood the international market, the prices could deteriorate further.

TABLE III

TERMS OF TRADE FOR SELECTED COMMODITIES

The following gives the purchasing power of one ton of the designated commodity for barrels of oil and for US dollars necessary to cover the debt service payments at prevailing rates.

	Oil *(barrels)*	*Foreign Exchange* *(US $)*
Copper (Zambia and Botswaha)		
1975	115.40	17,800
1980	58.38	9,482
1980 as % of 1975	51%	53%
Coffee (Angola and Tanzania)		
1975	147.52	22,754
1980	81.84	13,294
1980 as % of 1975	55%	58%
Cotton (Tanzania and Mozambique)		
1975	119.00	18,392
1980	59.16	9,609
1980 as % of 1975	50%	52%

Source: *South* (London) as reported in *Africa News*, 23 February 1981, p. 9.

Angola, unique among the Frontline States, has a stable source of high revenue for its primary commodity, oil. Zambia is more typical of the dependence linkages with its reliance on copper exports, the price of which fluctuates greatly. Copper has earned as much as 90 percent of Zambia's foreign exchange. Net revenue to the central government from copper exports, which was over $5 million in 1974 dropped to almost zero in 1977.[10] Because of depressed prices for the copper, to mines were consuming most of the foreign exchange they earned. Contrary to a developed economy, Zambia cannot quickly divert production to other sectors. What further distinguishes the advanced countries from the dependent ones is the diversification of their exports. If a price falls for one product, the advanced economy is probably exporting other products for which the price has risen. (The US is a major agricultural exporter, but also a major weapons exporter.) Thus, a single commodity producer is vulnerable to the deteriorating terms of trade for its export, which can drastically reduce revenue for development projects.

The third means to perpetuate dependence is through capital

transfers. To diversify beyond the single commodity, to increase manufactures for exports, more investment is needed. Yet capital is also necessary to provide much needed social services such as health care and literacy as well as for basic infrastructure, such as roads. It is difficult, therefore, to accumulate sufficient capital for productive investment. The countries turn to foreign sources of capital to supplement their investment capabilities. The capital provides relief in the short term, but often perpetuates dependence in the long term. Investment is most often in capital intensive projects which require further imports of machinery and technology to sustain. It arrives piece-meal, making it very difficult for the government to integrate the development projects, even if the will to do such is there. A project financed by the Bank of America may not be co-ordinated with a similar one financed by the World Bank (IBRD). Profits from increased production in one sector are often not realised because of blockages at another stage of processing or in transport or in marketing. Finally, foreign capital is expensive to use. Interest payments quickly accumulate and take huge percentages of the export earnings to pay. New loans simply become hedges on the old ones.

Dependence theorists, therefore, have specified indicators of unequal international economic relationships: transnational control of production, inequitable trade relations, foreign debt. They have shown the difficulty of transforming those relationships, which originated under colonialism, even after decades of political independence. Criticism of the theories, however, have emerged for several reasons.

Critiques Of Dependence Theories

Although dependence theory starts from the premise of the dominance of international capital, it does so at the level of analysis of the nation-state. Dependence theorists attacked neoclassical economic models for treating Third World economies as isolated entities, detached from their histories of colonialism and from their present subordination to international capital.[11] However, the dependence theorists, in turn, have kept their analysis at the level of exchange relations between countries. The critics say that the dominance of international monopoly capital should not be analysed in the sphere of circulation, such as trade relationships, capital, and technological

transfers. This sphere is simply a reflection of the primary relationships, the social relations of production.[12] The dominance of international monopoly capital must be analysed by its effects on the social
relations of production and on the forces of production — in short, the
mode of production within the dependent economies.[13] The subordinate role of developing economies in the sphere of circulation
simply signals the differences in the modes of production between the
developing and developed economies. Looking at exchanges between
nation-states corrects the problem of ignoring the historical and international context of a political economy, but it is an analysis of effects,
not causes. To change fundamentally dependence linkages, the differences between the modes of production must be transformed.[14]

Modes of production can be mixed, especially in the transitional
periods. Certainly, the capitalist mode of production dominates the
countries in question, both the developed and the developing. But the
five Frontline States have pre-capitalist modes of production as well.
The economies do not have fully proletarianised labour. In times of
crisis, some workers can go back to the villages and live off the land. If
necessary, wages that do not keep up with inflation can still be supplemented with produce from the family in the village. Production by
villagers for the commercial market is dominant, but villagers can and
do return to food production for the local market when market prices
for cash crops are not attractive enough to induce their labour; they
can resist government programmes in this way.

In contrast to the dependence theorists who say capital penetration under-developed the Third World economies, the critics say that
capitalism has not penetrated fully all sectors of the economy.[15] They
agree that there has been a long-term transfer of surplus away from
the periphery, but the under-development of the forces of production
is rooted in the dominant class's ability to intensify the exploitation of
labour by increasing the length of the working day (absolute surplus
value) and by reducing the cost of reproduction of labour (relative
surplus value). As stated earlier, in the leading capitalist countries,
the cost of labour was reduced by increasing the organic composition
of capital; worker productivity increased with the technological
innovation of machinery. As workers organised and demanded higher
wages, profits were maintained by increasing efficiency with technological innovation and by maintaining cheap mineral sources over-
seas.The pressure of free wage labour for higher wages and of the

competition for lowering prices are the impetus for capitalism to develop the forces of production.

The under-development of the forces of production in the colonies was the result of the lack of free labour and the relative lack of competition. The cost of labour was reduced not by improving its productivity, but by reducing the cost of reproduction of labour through lowering the levels of subsistence. During the colonial period, this was accomplished through forced labour and/or migrant labour:

> . . . the fact of forced labour in agriculture, either in pure form (slavery) or in correlation with peasant possession of subsist-ence plots, undermined the economies' ability to develop a free wage labour force for industry. ...it was the characteristic feature of the forced labour systems that their difficulties in developing the productivity of labour were more than counter-balanced by their success in reducing the costs of labour through reducing the subsistence of the work force.[16]

These critics of dependence assert that the extraction of absolute surplus labour continues after independence. Sometimes labour con-tinues to be forced, but more often it is done by political organising to extend the working day. How can one possibly extend the working day of a peasant who works from dawn to dusk? The extension is not in the total amount of time worked, but in the amount of time worked on commodities to be commercially marketed. For example, in Tanzania families are assigned one-acre plots upon which to grow cash crops for export, not just for local consumption. In that way, the village leaders can keep track of who is contributing adequately to export produc-tion. A neglected plot or one not up to par can be the subject of the next village meeting.

The critics of dependence theories agree that international capital is dominant. They strongly disagree that the fundamental expression of that dominance is in exchange relations. Instead, one should analyse the impact of the dominance by looking at the mode of production and the form of extraction of surplus. Class analysis is necessary, therefore, to understand the dynamic relations of produc-tion which specify the relations of exchange.

Another level of critique of dependence theories concerns their assumptions about the political expressions of dependence. Emerg-ing from economic theory, the first generalisations left the relation-ships between the economic and political unspecified; it was treated as unproblematic. The government of a dependent economy would do little to thwart the interests of dominant capital.[17] This perspective perhaps derives also from the fact that dependence theory evolved from analysis of the Latin American states. Indeed, there is much empirical evidence to show that dependent economies are often client states. However, some went so far as to assert that political independence made little difference; control by foreign capital remained complete in a weak and dependent economy.[18]

By the 1970s, theorists began to challenge this simple correlation between economic dependence and totally comprador states. With empirical data, Bill Warren made the case that political independence was relevant to the struggle for local control over the economy. Colin Leys, using Kenya as a case study, rejected the puppet regime interpretation to describe the developing capitalist state of Kenya. Using a Bonapartist explanation, he instead revealed the contradictions between foreign and domestic capital in the development of Kenya. Africanisation of the economy was not just window dressing of black faces for white ones, but set up real antagonisms between the different capitals. Nicola Swainson in her analysis of Kenya shows how national capital used the state to struggle against foreign domination. Control of the state apparatus was an important means for gaining control of the economy. According to these theorists, dependence linkages are real constraints and at times can severely limit the action of developing economies, but the relationship is not determinant.[19] A dependent economy does not dictate the form of the state nor its policies.

Because of these important criticisms, some theorists have discarded dependence theories altogether and others have tried to modify them to overcome the criticisms. The approach of this study is neither of these alternatives: it is rather to restrict the scope of dependency theories. This study focuses on international exchange relations as *descriptive* indicators of potential economic constraints, but departs from dependency theories to *analyse* the dynamic impact of such constraints.

The dependency theorists' important contribution to the field was to focus on the role of international capital in weak and developing economies. Although international capital influences domestic relations of production in every national economy, the influence is more important for the under-developed economies. As will be shown in the next section, large segments of the regular development budgets of the Frontline States are financed by foreign sources, either by loans and aid or by royalties and taxes on foreign investments.

Further, the argument here is that exchange relations are not so drastically divorced from relations of production as the critics assert. Exchange is, after all, production in circulation, and thus its analysis can be a good way to *begin* discussion of the forces and relations of production.[20] The deteriorating terms of trade relate directly to the fact that these economies remain primary product producers, instead of producing high technology manufactures. This distinction directs attention to different levels in the development of the forces of production for *further* analysis. In short, the deteriorating terms of trade are an indicator, not an explanatory variable. The critics are correct that explanation is found in analysing the relations of production.

This analysis of the Frontline States, therefore, begins with the exchange relations indicators of the dependence theorists because they describe the international economic context of the Zimbabwean liberation struggle. The indicators immediately reveal similarities among the five Frontline States in their dependence on Western capital for major financing; these similarities are important, for, as will be shown later, they are one basis of the alliance. The Frontline could identify with the demands of the Zimbabwean nationalists for full control of the state because of their own post-independence difficulties in ameliorating the international economic constraints of their economies. A state that could not take control of production (such as that set up under Muzorewa) could not be called sovereign. The exchange relations, however, also immediately reveal differences among the Frontline, which are as important as the similarities. To explain these differences, therefore, this study departs from the dependence theories and directs attention to class analysis and theories of relative state autonomy (Chapters 6 and 7). The international dependence linkages set the context for the Zimbabwean struggle, but only with analysis of the associated process of class formation in each of the five states will we begin to understand the outcome.

In summary, the argument is that it is important to *describe* the economic dependence of the Frontline States on Western capital to understand Frontline hesitations, vagaries, and even contradictions in foreign policy. But if such constraints were determinate, the Frontline States would not have been able to sustain their support for

the Zimbabwean nationalists. Therefore, this study departs from the
dependence theorists to *analyse* how the Frontline States were able
not only to endure, but to continue support for a Zimbabwean state
that could legally take control of production and for a government not
beholden to South Africa.

Frontline States' Economic Dependence

Indicators of dependence are many,[21] but all tend to focus on the
structure of domestic production and the concentration of economic
relations with a few states. First, analysis of domestic production
structures is used to determine the extent of diversification of the
economy. The less diversified from the colonial pattern of single commodity producer, the more vulnerable to international economic competition the economy is supposed to be. Second, concentration of
economic relations with a few states is an indicator of possible
economic dominance. If trade, aid, and capital investment are from a
few sources, then options for purchasing goods or for obtaining international finance are more limited. The dependence theorists point out
that this concentration is most restraining during crises when the
sources of capital (banks, government, international agencies) collaborate to deny any funds. Chile in 1973, when the US co-ordinated
economic retaliation against the Allende government by most of the
international organisations and banks, is often cited as the classic
example of the ability of the dominant powers to destabilise a
dependent economy. However, in many less dramatic cases, national
and international lending agencies have agreed that an economy is too
'high risk' to receive further funds, such as Jamaica, Peru, and
Tanzania after the war against Idi Amin.

This study will analyse the economic dependence of each of the
Frontline States according to the following criteria of the structure of
domestic production (1-3) and of concentration of external economic
relations (4-5):
  1. primary product production
  2. contribution of productive sectors to GDP
  3. external debt
  4. concentration of trading partners
  5. concentration of loan sources.
The criteria are not exhaustive, but are sufficient to delineate the
general pattern of the foreign economic relationships of the Frontline
States. They were chosen for maximum comparability among the

five. Because of the wars of national liberation in Mozambique and Angola, however, the data for them are necessarily less available. The governments themselves do not have complete data for the years of 1974 and 1975. In Mozambique and especially in Angola, the Portuguese settlers left precipitously, destroying or removing everything they could before departure, from typewriters and trucks to government files. The Angolan war of liberation disrupted the economy and severely limited availability of educated personnel for data collection and recording. Survival against South African aggression, not accurate trade statistics, was the priority. The limited data for Angola and Mozambique reflect these concrete political realities and perhaps are yet another indicator of Portuguese under-development of their colonies.

The political economies of each of the five states exhibit the general characteristic of underdeveloped primary commodity producers of minerals and cash crops. The Angolan and Zambian economies remain dominated by the highly developed mineral sector. The labour is skilled; the forces of production are modern. However, this sector remains quite divorced from the others which are not developed. When Zambian copper and cobalt prices fell, there were no other sectors in Zambia that could ameliorate the loss. Botswana is a new participant among the mineral producers, for its mines were just developed in the early 1970s. Even with the lessons learned from its neighbours, however, the government has not been very demanding of the foreign corporations investing in the minerals. To attract foreign investment to develop the mineral production, the government has given liberal terms to the corporations. The outflow of capital from expatriation of profits, dividends, and interest was $30.9 million in 1975 and $42 million in 1977. The latter figure represents 18 percent of the GDP per capital.[22] In addition, copper is exploited without processing; diamonds are cut overseas. The mineral wealth in all these economies, therefore, has not yet provided bases for other major industries.

Angola, of course, with its large quantities of oil has a great advantage over the other two. The price of oil was fairly stable and high for almost a decade. But it is now questionable whether even this unique energy product will permanently retain its relatively high price. The more fundamental consideration is whether the revenue from this high flyer is invested in diversification of other production. Angola produces almost all the oil in the Southern African region but refines only 4.4 percent of it. The Portuguese used the oil revenue to pay for their war against the Angolans. Unfortunately, the use of the oil revenue for arms continues in Angola. Because the MPLA government continues to support SWAPO in the struggle for Namibia, South Africa frequently attacks Angola. Therefore, much of Angola's foreign exchange is needed to buy arms and to pay the armed forces. (In 1983, President dos Santos estimated that the war had cost $10 billion since independence.) The political reality of the war has forced the Angolan government to delay the many development projects that are planned and which could diversify their production to reduce dependence on oil revenue.

Tanzania and Mozambique are even poorer than the others, for they have few major minerals under exploitation (e.g., gold and tin in Tanzania, coal in Mozambique). It is estimated that Mozambique has rich deposits of tantalite, necrolite, bauxite, and natural gas, but they are not yet fully explored let alone developed. Tanzania has few known minerals; oil has been discovered off the coast, but it is not yet determined if the quantity is enough to satisfy even its own needs. In 1979, it spent half of its export earnings for oil and imported less than in 1972 but paid ten times more.[23] The two remain, therefore, primary commodity producers of cash crops: cashews, cotton, coffee, sisal, sugar. The products are only partially processed in the country so the foreign exchange is dependent on price fluctuations in the London commodity markets. The terms of trade of some of the products have deteriorated since 1975, as was shown in Table III. In addition, the crops are vulnerable to severe climatic conditions. For example, the floods in 1977 and drought in 1979 affected cashew production in Mozambique.

Tables IV a-b compare the most important domestic exports for the five. They confirm that minerals and cash crops are the major foreign exchange earners and show the great variability in revenue from the commodities. The value of exports reflects both the quantity of the commodity produced and the price.

For Botswana, the value of meat exports fell in 1978 because of foot and mouth disease spreading from the Rhodesian herds. The foreign exchange earnings dropped because the EEC refused to import Botswana beef.[24] With the fence built to control the cattle, by 1979 the revenue had once again increased. Diamond and copper earnings increased with the opening of new mines. The substantial

TABLE IV-a
VALUE OF EXPORTS

BOTSWANA (MILLIONS PULA)

	1970	1974	1975	1976	1977	1978	1979
Meat	...	31.9	36.4	43.0	45.0	30.0	82.0
Diamonds	...	30.1	32.1	37.5	47.0	76.0	181.0
Copper/Nickel	...	8.2	22.0	51.8	40.0	50.0	61.0
Hides and Skins	...	1.7	1.6	3.3	...	...	...
Textiles	...	1.6	2.5	6.1	...	...	...

TANZANIA (MILLIONS SHILLINGS)

	1970	1974	1975	1976	1977	1978	1979
Coffee	312.0	375.1	483.0	1 281.8	1 870.3	1 303.0	1 211.0
Cotton	247.0	472.6	296.7	613.4	542.3	419.0	492.0
Sisal	134.0	463.3	302.4	239.7	227.7	218.0	258.0
Cashews	115.0	196.2	176.9	131.1	187.7	229.0	145.0
Tea	42.0	69.1	81.2	134.5	179.9	...	164.0

ZAMBIA (MILLIONS KWACHA)

	1970	1974	1975	1976	1977	1978	1979
Copper	681.4	838.5	472.0	688.6	645.9	597.7	900.7
Zinc	11.0	25.2	20.3	26.6	17.9	17.6	27.1
Cobalt	6.3	7.9	7.1	15.9	15.3	36.7	129.9
Tobacco	2.9	5.8	5.0	5.1	5.8	3.5	2.6
Maize	...	7.6	1.4	.5	3.5	7.8	...

Sources: USAID, *Development Needs and Opportunities for Co-operation in Southern Africa: Botswana*, March 1979, p. 155.
Economist Intelligence Unit, *Quarterly Economic Review, Southern Africa, Botswana*, 1980, p. 49 and 4th Q 1980, p. 24.
United Republic of Tanzania, *Economic Survey 1977–78*, p. 20; Bank of Tanzania, *Economic Survey* 1980.
Republic of Zambia, *Monthly Digest of Statistics*, January/March 1979, p. 22; January/March, 1981, p. 22.

... not available.

TABLE IV-b

VALUE OF MAIN COMMODITY EXPORTS ($ MILLION)

ANGOLA

	1973	1974	1975	1976	1977	1978	1979*
Oil	224	371	...	...	...	628	1 000
Coffee	206	247	154	149	254	224	249
Diamonds	80	62	...	...	...	100	142
Iron Ore	49	31	...	...	...	0	0

MOZAMBIQUE

	1973	1974	1975	1976	1977	1978	1979*
Cashews	35.1	43.4	34.9	37.2	50.8	53.0	45.0
Sugar	15.8	45.1	16.4	17.6	22.3	6.0	35.0
Timber	8.1	9.3	10.9	6.3	5.2	4.9	...
Shrimp	3.8	8.0	7.9	12.3	21.0	17.4	24.0
Tea	6.6	8.1	5.1	6.6	13.4	13.3	21.0
Cotton	31.9	24.0	12.5	17.6	9.5	14.2	23.0

. . . not available.

*estimates calculated from source given below (1979).

Sources: ANGOLA   1973 — Labour Research Association, *Economic Notes*, February 1976.

1974–1978 — Economist Intelligence Unit, Quarterly Economic Review, *Angola*, Annuals, 1979, pp. 14 and 16; 1980, p. 14.

1979 — Ibid., Annual 1981, pp. 8–9, 13.

MOZAMBIQUE Estastística de Comercio Externo, quoted in Mozambique Economic Survey, 'Foreign Trade', Maputo, 1977.

Ministerio do Comercio Externo, quoted in Business International, *Mozambique on the Road to Reconstruction and Development*, Briefing Paper, 24–27 Feb. 1980.

1979 — *African Economic Digest*, 27 August, 1982, p. 24.

increase in value of diamonds from 1978 and 1979 (76 million pula to 181 million) reflects both an increase in price and production.

For Tanzania the dramatic rise in coffee values to 1977 reflected a price rise, not a production rise. Sisal production had dropped steadily to 1979, until higher wages were paid to the field workers. The other three (cotton, cashews, tea) illustrate the variability in value of the export earnings which plagues development plans. Good years — when weather, production inputs, and international prices are all favourable — can be followed by precipitous drops in both production and prices. The dependent economy is vulnerable because it does not have diversity in export production; development plans are delayed.

The data for Zambia show the deterioration in price (and subsequently in production) of its major foreign exchange earner, copper. The decline from 1974-1975 was especially severe. By 1976 the price of cobalt had risen to offset partially the losses in copper. By 1978 the balance of payments deficit had improved from $800 to $400 million. Maize production increased to 1977, but by October 1978, maize was a crucial (net) import to prevent widespread hunger. The need for increased maize production was the major reason given for opening the border to Rhodesia in 1978; the government had to import fertiliser for the maize crop. By the end of the Zimbabwean war (1979), both cobalt and copper were once again major export earners for Zambia.

Table IV b reveals the effect of the wars of liberation on Angola and Mozambique's primary commodity production. The economies are not only dependent on primary commodities for export, but the wars disrupted that basic production. Data is not available for Angola's exports during the period of the 'second war of liberation'. Basic trends are known, however. For instance, iron ore production had not yet resumed even in 1983 because the major mines are in the south, the area of South Africa's invasions. Diamond production fell drastically during 1976-1978 to approximately 340-400 carats per year, and smuggling was widespread. By 1980 the export earnings had doubled over 1979 because of the increase in the price on the world market.[25] Coffee production also declined seriously because workers were not available to tend the trees on the plantations abandoned by the Portuguese. It was reported that the state had difficulty encouraging workers back to the farms, with a further delay in the resumption of production. Coffee export revenue did not fall as much as produc-

tion because the state exported its reserves. By 1980 coffee production had increased, but not to the pre-independence levels.[26]

The rise in price and production of oil has been the mainstay of the
Angolan economy during these extremely difficult times. The wars
did not affect the oil production which is in the north, and the Western
corporations (mainly Gulf Oil) are satisfied with the terms of their
contracts with the new state. In 1979 oil earned two-thirds of all
export earnings. After the Zimbabwean war (1980), Angola earned
$2 billion in oil revenue (80 percent of all export earnings).[27] In the
crisis situation of the new state, with destabilisation from South
Africa, this wealth clearly distinguishes Angola from other peripheral
capitalist economies. As stated above, however, the oil wealth has
only been able to help the new state survive; the revenue has not yet
been available for diversifying the economy to overcome 400 years of
Portuguese colonial underdevelopment. For example, in 1974 Angola
produced 90 percent of its domestic food needs; by 1980 it was
importing over 50 percent of its food consumption because of the war,
and only the oil wealth made this possible.[28]

Mozambique's export sector has no single commodity to guarantee
substantial export earnings. Sugar, timber, and cotton exports had
not gained their pre-1975 levels of export value. Aided by the Soviet
Union and East Germany, the fishing industry has grown, but at a
price of permission to the Soviets to do major trawling themselves.
Government officials complain that the waters are overfished. Cashew
exports increased drastically to 1978 because material incentives
(cloth, cooking oil, etc.) were offered to the peasants for care of the
trees and harvesting of the nuts. Tea production increased as state
farms were set up on the abandoned plantations. Export earnings
increased 34 percent in 1978 over 1977. By 1979 there was a 50 per
cent increase over 1978, in spite of Rhodesian assaults on the infrastructure.[29]

The three countries which have been independent since the
1960s have tried to diversify their economies away from this historical
primary commodity dominance, with little success. According to
Table V-a, agricultural production in Tanzania contributes about
50 percent to GDP. It is a smaller sector in Botswana because of the
increased importance of mining; agriculture still employs the vast
majority of the people. Neither has made much progress in
developing manufacturing. By 1980 manufacturing had actually
dropped for Botswana to only 4.5 percent of GDP. As long as

TABLE V-a

GROSS DOMESTIC PRODUCT AT FACTOR COST BY TYPE OF ECONOMIC ACTIVITY
(BY PERCENTAGES AT CURRENT PRICES)

	1967	1974	1975	1976	1977	1978	1979	1980
BOTSWANA								
Agriculture, Forestry	44.3%	33.7%	29.4%	24.4%	23.9%	20.2%	15.4%	11.9%
Mining	1.7	8.7	8.6	12.5	13.5	15.8	23.2	32.4
Manufacturing	8.7	5.5	7.4	7.7	8.1	6.9	8.5	4.5
Public Administration	18.6	9.8	11.9	13.4	15.4	14.8	14.5	10.2
Total GDP (Millions Pula)	41.3	184.9	208.5	269.8	310.8	354.2	505.7	670.9
TANZANIA								
Agriculture, Forestry, Fishing	42.6%	38.8%	41.2%	45.0%	50.2%	53.0%	51.8%	50.5%
Mining	2.9	.3	.6	.5	.5	.4	.5	.6
Manufacturing	8.5	10.0	10.4	11.3	10.4	9.9	10.3	10.0
Public Administration	11.0	12.7	13.0	11.7	10.1	9.4	10.0	10.3
Total GDP (Millions Shillings)	6,735	14,010	16,988	20,853	26,655	29,653	32,396	34,711
ZAMBIA								
Agriculture, Forestry, Fishing	13.8%	10.6%	13.1%	14.2%	16.0%	16.7%	14.3%	14.3%
Mining	32.1	32.9	13.6	17.8	11.7	12.1	18.4	17.0
Manufacturing	9.3	13.4	15.9	14.3	15.6	17.2	16.5	16.9
Public Administration	11.2	12.5	17.1	16.1	17.2	16.7	16.0	16.3
Total GDP (Millions Kwacha)	716.7	1872.9	1571.1	1923.5	2010.6	2291.0	2622.9	3027.2

Sources: USAID, *Development Needs and Opportunities for Co-operation in Southern Africa*, Botswana, March 1979, pp. 146–147;

Government of Botswana, *Statistical Bulletin* 7, no. 2, June 1982, p. 37.

Economist Intelligence Unit, *Quarterly Economic Review, Tanzania*, 1981, p. 6.

United Republic of Tanzania, *Economic Survey, 1977–78*, p. 10; *1981*, pp. 8–9.

IBRD, *Basic Economic Report, Zambia*, 3 October 1977, p. 184.

Republic of Zambia, *Monthly Digest of Statistics*, January/March 1979, p. 50.

TABLE V-b

MANUFACTURING AS PERCENT OF
GROSS DOMESTIC PRODUCT (GDP)
(AT CURRENT PRICES)

	1970	1973	1975	1977	1979
Angola	10.2%	18–10%	. . .	8.0%	22.0%
Mozambique	15.0	14.0	10.0	. . .	15.0

. . . not available

Sources: Economist Intelligence Unit, Quarterly Economic Review, *Angola,*
Mozambique, annuals, 1981.

1973 — Ann and Neva Seidman, *Outposts of Monopoly Capitalism*
(Westport, Conn.: Lawrence Hill, 1980), p. 238.

1979 — Centre for Strategic and International Studies, 'Background
Information on Angola', paper for Conference on Angola's
Economic Prospects, Washington, DC, 24 March 1982, n.p.

Botswana is in the customs union with South Africa, Botswanan
manufacturing will not be able to compete with its highly developed
neighbour. There is an 'infant industry' protection clause in the
customs union agreement, but the tariff structure would result in
creating national prices much higher than world prices.[30]

In spite of policies to increase local processing of the agricultural
products, manufacturing in Tanzania contributes only about 10 per
cent of GDP. Zambia is the only one which shows real growth in manufacturing production. Zambia's mining had been developed to serve
the industrial needs of Rhodesia and South Africa as illustrated by the
fact that total manufacturing was only 6 percent of GDP, and
domestic production provided less than one-third of the goods for the
local market at independence in 1964. Formulating plans to produce
more for the local market by increasing manufacturing from
1965-1976, the government did encourage the manufacturing sector
which grew a healthy 7.7 percent per annum.[31] Table V-a shows that
its share of GDP increased from 9.3 percent in 1967 to 17.2 percent
in 1978. This increase, however, was limited by the fact that it
was based on 'import substitution' and still depended heavily on the
import of machinery and spare parts for production. It was also capital
intensive and provided little employment. Finally, some of the
production replaced decentralised peasant production (such as brick

making) and created problems of distribution and of destroying income for the rural areas.

Tanzanian manufacturing was subordinate to Kenya during the colonial era. Its economy was directed to providing Kenya's nascent industries with raw materials.[32] After independence, the government tried to diversify. Because the country was poor with little skilled labour, most of the budget had first to be spent on infrastructure and administration. This expenditure on non-productive sectors is expected in the short-run, but the trend has continued for Tanzania. The government has not been able to direct expenditure to the productive sectors, although the Third Five Year Plan (1978-1983) still pledged this goal. (Industrial production was to receive 24 percent of total investment for a projected 9.3 percent growth.) From Table V-a, manufacturing as percent of GDP has increased little — 1967:8.5%; 1977:10.4%; 1980: 10%.

The contribution to GDP also reveals the large percentage that the non-productive sector of public administration contributes to GDP as a service. The large percentages as high as 15 percent (1977) for Botswana, 10 percent for Tanzania and 17 percent for Zambia reveal that important sectors of GDP are providing services, not goods. Manufacturers promote growth, with the spin-off effects. Services are a necessity but often stimulate an economy in ways that contribute to inflation. An underdeveloped economy needs to spend much on services for education and health. The balance between 'growth' and 'distribution' is a precarious one. The fairly large percentages of GDP for services do reflect these priorities for the governments. Yet growth in the productive sector is also important for improved quality of life and economic stability.

Detailed data on contribution to GDP by sector are not available for Angola and Mozambique. Table V-b does give approximate percent contribution of manufacturing to GDP for selected years. Angolan manufacturing had risen to 22 percent of GDP by 1979; Mozambique's manufacturing was 15 percent. This production is similar in structure, however, to the other three economies; it is mainly manufacturing for processing of agricultural production or partial processing of minerals. The mineral wealth within the Frontline has not been translated to diversification of production and development of manufacturing production. All five remain primary product producers.

   The diversification of production has not succeeded, but the states have also pledged to diversify their trading partners to reduce their vulnerability to outside political pressure. Tanzania has been the most explicit in asserting its independence from colonial trade linkages; the second Five Year Plan emphasised the need to 'diversify away from a few dominant overseas markets'. The goal of seeking out new trading partners was reiterated in subsequent annual plans and in President Nyerere's review of the economy a decade after independence. Tanzania has successfully diversified its trade links away from the ex-colonial power of·Britain. After independence exports in 1964 to Britain were 30 percent of all exports. Imports from Britain were 32 percent of all imports. By 1977 both had dropped to about 15 percent total exports and imports.[33]

   Tanzania states it has diversified its trade by increasing exchange with Scandinavia, and indeed, Table VI-a shows that imports from there increased from 2.6 percent in 1970 to 6.3 percent in 1977. But the majority of the trade volume diverted from Britain has been directed to other EEC countries and to the US. By 1979 these two were receiving 54.3 percent of the exports and providing Tanzania with 54.9 percent of its imports. Especially as the EEC often acts as a bloc, it is questionable that Tanzania has diversified its trade. Exchange with the Soviet bloc countries shows little variance for the seven years. Trade with the People's Republic of China fell considerably with the completion of the Tazara railroad. Although Tanzania has an explicit policy to increase trade with its neighbours and although the Tazara railroad links it with Zambia, trade with Zambia has not increased appreciably. In interviews, government officials stated that the two countries do have products to trade, but the implementation is slow as inertia preserves old patterns of trade, and internal economic constraints slow initiative for new directions.[34] Trade with Mozambique has increased; this new link since the independence of Mozambique in 1975 will be analysed in Chapter 8, for their permanent commission of co-operation is an example for future relations within the Southern African region.

   Zambia's first priority was not to reduce trade with the ex-colonial power but to pull away from reliance on South Africa which provided almost one-quarter of its imports in 1967 (23.6%). Table VI-b shows that they were still 17.3 percent in 1970 but reduced to 6.6 percent by 1978. Exports to South Africa were .1 percent in 1978.[35]

TABLE VI-a

TANZANIA — MAJOR TRADING PARTNERS BY PERCENT OF TOTAL IMPORTS AND EXPORTS

	1970		1974		1975		1976		1977		1978		1979	
	Imports	Exports	Imports	Exports	Imports	Exports	Imports	Exports	Imports	Exports	Imports	Exports	Imports	Exports
EEC*	45.1	36.8	29.8	36.8	33.7	35.8	44.2	30.2	47.1	47.6	52.5	49.7	50.7	49.1
USA	8.6	9.6	7.2	8.1	13.4	6.6	6.4	10.1	4.7	13.4	3.5	11.1	4.2	5.2
Soviet Bloc	1.8	2.0	1.6	6.3	2.1	3.4	.8	2.3	.5	2.5	1.1	3.8	.9	2.4
PR of China	13.7	3.5	11.6	3.5	11.0	4.4	7.4	3.0	2.5	3.3	3.7	2.8	3.7	.5
Mozambique	.0	.01	...	...	.0	.11	.10	.34	.38	.5	...	...	.2	3.1
Zambia	.8	7.0	1.2	1.4	.4	1.0	.5	.6	.4	1.2	...	...	.7	2.2
Scandinavia	2.6	2.5	3.1	2.4	5.9	4.1	7.0	2.9	6.3	2.2	...	...	...	...
Total Imports and Exports T. Shillings (Millions)	1,939.2	1,688.7	5,429.7	2,537.4	5,288.1	2,548.7	4,751.8	3,815.0	6,160.0	4,482.2	8,798.0	3,362.0	8,885.0	4,125.0

. . . not available

*Includes United Kingdom

Source: Calculated from East African Community, East African Customs and Excise Department, *Annual Trade Reports, 1970, 1974–1977;*
United Republic of Tanzania, *The Economic Survey, 1981,* pp. 23, 24, 29.

TABLE VI-b

ZAMBIA — MAJOR TRADING PARTNERS BY PERCENT OF TOTAL IMPORTS AND EXPORTS

	1970		1974		1975		1976		1977		1978		1979	
	Imports	Exports	Imports	Exports	Imports	Exports	Imports	Exports	Imports	Exports	Imports	Exports	Imports	Exports
EEC*	37.4	54.2	38.6	57.4	37.9	62.0	42.3	47.5	44.0	55.0	46.3	57.5	42.0	45.8
USA	9.7	.2	7.8	.6	12.5	.0	10.8	15.5	10.7	10.3	7.8	10.4	9.3	10.2
Soviet Bloc	1.2	.6	.5	.0	.4	.1	.4	.2	.3	.4	.7	1.1	.7	.9
PR of China	.6	4.8	4.5	2.4	2.9	2.5	1.9	2.5	1.2	3.2	1.3	3.1	.4	3.2
Mozambique**	. . .	. . .	.0	.1	.0	.0	.0	.1	.0	.0	.0	.0	. . .	. . .
Tanzania	1.5	.1	.7	.8	.2	.3	.2	.7	.3	.4	.2	.3	. . .	. . .
South Africa	17.3	1.2	7.6	.4	6.8	.3	7.5	.2	7.2	.3	6.6	.1	10.8	.4
Total Imports and Exports Kwacha (Millions)	340.7	715.0	506.6	905.1	597.6	521.0	536.7	751.9	536.7	708.5	992.8	686.8	597.8	1 091.0

. . . not available

* Includes United Kingdom

** .0 Represents negligible trade

Sources: Republic of Zambia, *Monthly Digest of Statistics*, January-March 1979, January-March 1981.
         Office of Permanent Secretary for Commerce, Industry and Foreign Trade, Special Communication, Lusaka, June 1979.
         Republic of Zambia, *Annual Statement of External Trade*, 1967.

TABLE VI-c

BOTSWANA — MAJOR TRADING PARTNERS BY PERCENT OF TOTAL IMPORTS AND EXPORTS

	1974		1975		1976		1977		1978		1979		1980	
	Imports	Exports	Imports	Exports	Imports	Exports	Imports	Exports	Imports	Exports	Imports	Exports	Imports	Exports
Europe	5.4	47.1	4.6	49.4	3.3	43.1	2.2	52.9	2.6	50.8	3.2	66.8	2.4	63.5
Northern and Southern America	4.0	10.5	2.4	21.6	2.0	34.0	1.7	26.8	2.0	27.6	1.3	17.3	3.0	21.0
South Africa	75.3	37.5	79.8	23.6	81.4	15.1	85.8	11.6	84.7	13.6	87.7	7.0	87.0	6.6
Other Africa	13.8	4.2	12.8	4.5	12.2	7.5	9.9	8.4	9.9	7.4	6.9	8.4	6.7	8.4
All Others	1.5	.6	.5	1.0	1.1	.3	.4	.3	.7	.6	.9	.5	.8	.5
Total (UA '000)	125,418	81,990	169,288	105,040	181,385	153,172	239,605	156,653	307,090	192,676	438,289	367,253	537,592	391,335

Sources: USAID, *Development Needs and Opportunities for Co-operation in Southern Africa, Botswana,* March 1979, p.156.
Republic of Botswana, *Statistical Bulletin,* 7, no. 2, June 1982, pp. 25–26.

TABLE VI-d
MOZAMBIQUE — MAJOR TRADING PARTNERS
BY PERCENT OF TOTAL IMPORTS AND EXPORTS*

	1973		1974		1976		1977		1978		1979	
	Imports	Exports	Imports	Exports	Imports	Exports	Imports	Exports	Imports	Exports	Imports	Exports
Europe	48.5	47.2	54.4	50.1	33.8	30.2	37.8	60.0**	31.7	66.1	19.1	47.2
USA	4.9	13.6	6.5	13.0	4.1	23.7	2.7	20.4	3.2	20.5	4.1	20.6
Centrally*** Planned Economies	.05	.04	...	...	...	...	1.1	.2	...	...	18.0	9.3
Portuguese Colonies	3.1	4.5	1.8	3.6	...	...	...	...	...	...	...	...
South Africa	14.7	9.4	19.5	10.9	15.3	7.7	...	...	...	...	...	...

... not available

* Mozambique neither publishes international trade statistics nor does it provide official balance of payments. statistics on a transaction basis. The data, therefore, are mainly based on trading partners' reports and on UN estimates.

** Very approximate correction of misreported UN calculation.

*** See separate source below.

Sources: 1973 — Estastistica de Comercio Externo, quoted in Mozambique Economic Survey, 'Foreign Trade', Maputo, 1977.
1974 — Institute Nacional de Estastistica, Boletin mensal de estastistica, Provence de Mozambique, December 1974, pp. 67–69.
1976 — Business International, Mozambique on the Road to Reconstruction and Development, Briefing Paper, Maputo, 24–27 February 1980 p. 37.
1977–79 — United Nations estimates based on partners' trade accounts, reported in Economist Intelligence Unit, Quarterly Economic Review, Mozambique, Annual, 1980, 1981.
Centrally Planned Economies — People's Republic of Mozambique, Economic Report, Maputo, January 1984, p. 46.

TABLE VI-e

ANGOLA — MAJOR TRADING PARTNERS BY PERCENT OF TOTAL IMPORTS AND EXPORTS

	1973*		1977*		1978		1979		1980	
	Imports	Exports	Imports	Exports	Imports	Exports	Imports	Exports	Imports	Exports
Europe	70.2	43.7	33.1	8.0	61.7	23.6	56.4	28.5	51.6	22.2
USA	9.8	38.5	5.6	34.0	3.6	49.7	5.6	21.4	7.1	31.8
Centrally Planned Economies	.0	.1	16.9	2.0	16.9	5.4	15.7	6.9	16.9	6.3

	1973*		1977*		1978		1979		1980	
	Imports	Exports	Imports	Exports	Imports	Exports	Imports	Exports	Imports	Exports
Africa	8.8	5.7	...	...	2.1	10.2	3.0	3.4	2.2	4.1
Latin America	1.0	1.1	...	...	5.5	8.0	9.8	35.1	10.8	28.9

... *not available*

* Figures for Africa for 1973 are only for Portuguese colonies.

** Figures for Democratic Republic of Germany not available.

Sources: 1973 and 1977 — Economist Intelligence Unit, *Quarterly Economic Review, Angola,* annual, 1980, pp. 12–13, 15. 1978–1980 — Banco Nacional de Angola, mimeo.

TABLE VI-f

DESTINATION OF MERCHANDISE EXPORTS* (% OF TOTAL)

Origin	1979			
	Industrial Market Economies	*Developing Countries*	*Centrally Planned Industrial Countries*	*Capital Surplus Oil Exporters*
Angola	33%	66%	0%	1%
Botswana	. . .	. . .	. . .	. . .
Mozambique	43	49	1	7
Tanzania	57	40	2	1
Zambia	82	18	0	0

. . . not available.

* Definition of merchandise exports includes the following: fuels, minerals, metals, food and live animals, beverages, tobacco, inedible crude materials, oils, fats, textiles, yarns, fabrics, clothing, machinery and transport equipment. See p. 186 of report for exact SITC divisions.

Source: World Bank, *World Development Report 1981*, Oxford University Press, 1981, p. 154.

Closing the border completely to Rhodesia in 1973, Zambia success-fully diverted trade from the south. When the border was opened, the trade figure increased for a short period until the independence of Zimbabwe. Now, of course, Zimbabwe can replace South Africa as its major supplier in the region.

Other attempts to redirect trade have not been so successful. The EEC remains the dominant partner both as a source of imports (42.0%) and for exports (45.8%) in 1979. If one included the USA with EEC, then Zambia's trade with the advanced capitalist market in 1979 is similar to Tanzania's: imports — 51.3% and exports — 56%. Trade with the Soviet bloc has remained virtually unchanged; the slight increase with the People's Republic of China reflects terms provided for by the Tazara rail project.

Data was not available for Botswana under the exactly same categories, but it is sufficient to reveal the trade pattern (Table VI-c). Botswana is a member of the South African Customs Union which is clearly reflected in the trade statistics. South Africa provides Botswana with about 85 percent of its imports and is a major customer for Botswana's exports. Aggregating Europe with South Africa, the two take 70-75 percent (1979, 1980) of all Botswana's exports. Clearly, Botswana has not been able to diversify its trade. Captured by the customs union, it remains heavily dependent on South Africa and the West for its markets.

Again, data from Angola and Mozambique are not exactly comparable. It is clear even with the sketchy data (Table VI-d) that Mozambique trades overwhelmingly with the West. In 1977 and 1978, Europe bought about two-thirds of all Mozambican exports and in 1979, almost 50 percent. If one adds the United States to the purchasers, the West bought the following percent of Mozambican exports: 1977 — 80.4%; 1978 – 86.6%; 1979 — 67.8%. Imports from the West were less but still impressive: 1977 — 40.5%; 1978 — 34.9%; 1979 — 23.2%. The import data reveals Mozambique's attempts to diversify its trading partners.

Angola, with its oil sold mainly to the United States, has even stronger trade links to the West. In 1973 exports to the West from Portuguese Angola were 82.2 percent (Table VI-e). After indepen-dence by 1978, it was still 73.3 dropping to 54 percent by 1980. The major purchasers are the United States, Japan and the United Kingdom. Imports show the same trend: 1973 — 80.0%; 1978 —

65.3%; 1980 — 58.7%. The largest suppliers are the United States, Portugal, West Germany, and France.[36] Angola, like Mozambique, is trying to diversify away from colonial linkages, but during the time of the Frontline struggle, both were dependent on the West for trade. These two Marxist-Leninist states are not captured by the Soviets. From these figures, it is obvious that they are very much open to trade with the West — and still dependent on it. Table VI-f gives a direct comparison of the states. The World Bank statistics show that Angola sent little or no merchandise exports to the centrally planned industrial states in 1979; Mozambique sent only 1 percent, (see definition on table). This table corroborates the findings of the individual country tables; trade by the Frontline States is principally with the West.

Because the structural transformations of the three economies of Botswana, Zambia, and Tanzania have not been possible, they face the too familiar pattern of periodic financial crisis. Zambia's foreign exchange crisis has been the longest, lasting from the copper price downturn in 1975, with only occasional relief in short-term price increases, until a longer term increment by the end of 1978. In 1978 Zambia had to take an IMF stabilisation loan with strict controls to help its foreign exchange position: copper production had fallen with the prices; transport costs due to the closing of the border with Rhodesia had increased drastically the price of imports; maize production was lower, and food had to be imported. It was the most severe financial crisis of the Frontline States, requiring drastic reduction in imports and consequently, in domestic consumption, a situation often linked with political instability (according to dependence analysts).

The first major foreign exchange crisis for Tanzania was in 1974 with a long drought that swept much of Africa. The cash crops were destroyed which seriously reduced foreign reserves. The second major crisis was worse, and its effects continue to plague the Tanzanian economy. The war against Idi Amin (October 1978) lasted several months with a further long-term security presence (until June 1981) in Uganda by Tanzanian forces. As stated earlier, the costs of the army, of support for Ugandan refugees, and of aid to the new Ugandan government, have been a heavy burden on Tanzanian foreign exchange. For the first time, Tanzania had to borrow heavily from commercial banks. The government appealed for $375 million for special aid to pay interest on the loans. The Western donors (Scandinavia included)

TABLE VII-a

BOTSWANA — PERCENTAGE OF OUTSTANDING PUBLIC DEBT BY MAJOR SOURCES

Source	1970	1973	1975	1976	1977
Advanced Capitalist Bloc	100.0%	98.2%	81.1%	98.5%	98.3%
Scandinavia*	0	1.7	18.8	1.4	1.6
Other**	0	.1	.1	.1	.1
Total (Millions of Pula)	.31	27.78	14.47	12.37	18.10

* Mainly Swedish International Development Agency.

** The Botswanan government has not disaggregated this category, but sources confirm there is no aid from socialist countries. See USCIA, *Communist Aid to Less Developed Countries of Free World*, August 1977, p. 11.

Source: Calculated from 'Government Operations' in USAID, *Development Needs and Opportunities for Co-operation in Southern Africa, Botswana*, March 1979, p. 151.

TABLE VII-b

TANZANIA — PERCENTAGE OF OUTSTANDING PUBLIC DEBT BY MAJOR SOURCES

Source*	1967	1970	1973	1975	1978****
Soviet Bloc	3.6%	3.5%	3.6%	2.6%	.9%
PR of China	19.3	41.7	34.3	30.5	31.0
Advanced Capitalist Bloc**	44.2	30.4	42.7	48.6	51.0
Scandinavia***	6.2	7.2	8.2	9.8	13.6
Multilateral Arab Funds	.0	.0	.7	.01	3.2
Zambia	.05	.0	.3	.2	.1
Other	26.6	17.2	10.1	8.5	.03
Total (Millions of $ US)	220.291	600.676	826.983	1,189.177	1,008.265

* Division of Sources reflects the ideology of the Tanzanian (and Zambian) government that views Soviet sources as different from PRC; IBRD sources as under control of advanced capitalist countries; Scandinavia as democratic socialist and distinct from advanced capitalism.

** Includes IBRD and IMF loans.

*** Denmark, Finland, Sweden — Norway not recorded.

**** To March 1978.

Sources: Calculated from IBRD, *Tanzania Basic Economic Report*, No. 1616 – TA, Main Report, December 1977. 1978 — Ministry for Finance & Planning, reported in *Tanzania Daily News*, 25 October 1978.

TABLE VII-c

ZAMBIA — PERCENTAGE OF OUTSTANDING PUBLIC DEBT BY MAJOR SOURCES

Source*	1970	1973	1975	1976
Soviet Bloc	19.0%	9.3%	6.1%	4.1%
PR of China	.0	23.7	33.3	39.4
Advanced Capitalist Bloc**	79.9	66.4	57.1	52.5
Scandinavia***	1.0	.6	1.5	2.1
Multilateral Arab Funds	.0	.0	.02	1.9
Total (Millions of $US)	185.069	475.755	609.659	827.523

* Division of Sources reflects the ideology of the Zambian (and Tanzanian) government that views Soviet sources as different from PRC; IBRD sources as under the control of advanced capitalist countries; Scandinavia as democratic socialist and distinct from advanced capitalism.

** Includes IBRD and IMF loans.

*** Denmark, Finland, Sweden — Norway not recorded.

Source: Republic of Zambia, *Financial Report for Year Ending 31 December 1976.*

waited until an IMF team evaluated the economy. The terms of the
IMF loan were so devastating to Tanzania's social welfare programmes that the government kicked the team out of the country. The
height of this feud was during the Lancaster House talks late
1979. Although they supported the end of Amin's regime, the
Western donors were leaving the burden of financing his removal to
Tanzania. The coincidence of the British manoeuvres at Lancaster
House and the IMF intransigence against Tanzania was noted by
many observers of Tanzanian politics. The government would have
been hard pressed to provide support for continuing guerrilla war in
Zimbabwe if the Lancaster discussions had broken down.

   Botswana has been in a situation unique of all the Frontline
States: 'Until 1976, Botswana's monetary and financial system was an
integral part of South Africa's. The South African rand was legal
tender in Botswana, the country's international reserves were incorporated into South Africa's, and there was little formal regulation of
Botswana's financial system'.[37] Since 1976, Botswana has been slowly
reducing this extraordinary economic dependence. Because of the
diamond exports, it has been able to maintain a balance of payments
surplus. But the economy's continuing vulnerability to outside factors
is illustrated by the following development budget plan. Even by
1979-1980, a full two-thirds of its development budget was financed
from the outside.

Development Budget[38]

	1976-77	1977-78	1978-79	1979-80
Percent from foreign sources	82.3	77.4	74.5	66.7

   Characteristic of dependence, these economies remain quite
vulnerable to outside forces: commodity price fluctuations, drought,
invasion. Access to foreign exchange through loans and grants
become crucial in these crises. Tables VII a-c show historically the
sources of this needed capital and are comparable for 1970, 1973, and
1975. The major donors remain the Western countries and the international monetary agencies dominated by them. To summarise the
three in a direct comparison, loans from the advanced capitalist
sources as a per cent of total loans are as follows:

	1970	1973	1975
Botswana	100.0%	98.2%	81.1%
Tanzania	30.4%	42.7%	48.6%
Zambia	79.9%	66.4%	57.1%

During the early formation of the Frontline States (1974-75), the three were very much in debt to the West. Exactly comparable statistics are not available for later years, but reports confirm that the pattern continues. From Table VII–a one can notice that Botswana was successful in obtaining more capital from the democratic socialist countries of Scandinavia for only 1975. The advanced capitalist sources (which includes South Africa) regain their overwhelming dominance in 1976 and 1977. The percent of loans from them in these years is 98.5 and 98.3 respectively. Botswana's reserve position improved considerably at the end of 1979 reaching a record high of $342 million, the result of a dramatic increase in exports, especially diamonds.[39] By the end of the decade, therefore, the newly exploited minerals were helping Botswana to reduce somewhat its dependence on foreign capital.

Although 65 percent of Tanzania's development budget was financed by foreign capital (1979),[40] the Tanzanian government argues that its dependence is less because it increased aid from Scandinavia, smaller powers willing to give grants instead of loans. Table VII-b shows that Scandinavia did increase its share of loans to Tanzania from 6.2 percent to 13.6 percent by 1978. Tanzania also asserts that capital financing is more in terms of grants than loans so the dependence is not as great as it appears. However, the United States remains a major contributor, and its terms for capital transfers have become more difficult. It is true that several countries, Britain included, totally wrote off Tanzania's debt to them in 1979, but the government certainly cannot rely on such good will in calculating development plans.[41] During the 1979 foreign exchange crisis, the government found it had overestimated food crop production and had to import it on an emergency basis. Western donors did respond quickly to this need.[42] The total disbursed foreign debt in 1979 was $1,095 million; the largest creditor was the World Bank followed by China (Tazara Railroad), Sweden, and the United Kingdom. The Third Five Year Plan (1978-1983), delayed two years by the balance of payment crisis, still projects that 62 percent of the expenditure will come from overseas.[43]

The IMF loan to Zambia in 1978 was crucial to ameliorating Zambia's crisis, and the other donors were mainly Western. Because of the disruption of the infrastructure and of production due to the Rhodesian war and the fall of copper prices, Zambia's total disbursed foreign debt rose to $1,558.6 million at the end of 1979. The debt service was 21 percent of exports. In 1980 the debt increased further to $4,770 million.[44] Once again the IMF helped the burden of the debt service with a loan in 1981, but the terms of the loan were stringent in curtailing the government's expenditure for social services. Zambia's debt, greatly exacerbated by the war, has increased its dependence on Western financial sources.

Even at the independence celebrations of Mozambique, President Samora Machel reminded the euphoric Mozambicans, '. . . it in no way diminishes the greatness of our struggle and of our people and country to have to acknowledge that the economic and financial situation is catastrophic'.[45] The country had been plundered, for Portugal squeezed what it could from the Mozambican economy to finance the ten-year war against Frelimo. The economy was further disrupted by the war in Rhodesia, as was enumerated in the last chapter. Appeals were made by the United Nations for special assistance; Table VIII shows the contributions. By 1979 the advanced capitalist states had provided $70.6 million or 24.7 percent of the total sanctions assistance. Scandinavia (50.5%) and the Arab states (23.2%) gave substantial amounts, but the socialist countries responded little (.3% of the total). In addition, the total amount pledged fell well short of the amount of lost revenue.

The sanctions assistance was a special fund, and aid to development programmes gives a more comprehensive picture of the aid pattern to Mozambique. Table IX shows contributions by foreign sources to the developing sectors for 1976-1977. In dollar amounts and in diversity of sectors aided, Scandinavia is the leading contributor. It gave $36.6 million versus $22.6 million of the second largest donor, the advanced capitalist bloc.[46] The Soviet bloc concentrated its capital transfer to the mining sector. Again, the West has provided most of the foreign revenue for Mozambique.

The current account deficit was the worst in 1977, reaching $200 million; the balance of payments deficit then improved. By 1979 the external debt was $100 million (and more if soft loans are added to it). Scandinavia remains the major donor; Brazil offered a $100 million line of credit in 1980. Britain and Italy extended a $300

TABLE VIII

SANCTIONS ASSISTANCE TO MOZAMBIQUE (MILLIONS OF $US)

Source	To 1977	Inclusive to 1979	Total	Percent of Total
Soviet Bloc	.8	.8	.8	.3%
PR of China	0	0	0	0%
Advanced Capitalist Bloc	52.8	70.6	70.6	24.7%
Scandinavia	15.1	144.5	144.5	50.5%
Arab League States	28.2	66.5	66.5	23.2%
Others	0	4.0	4.0	1.4%
Total from all donors			286.4	100.0%

Sources: Report of the Secretary-General to Economic and Social Council, *Assistance to Mozambique,* A/33/173, 12 July 1978, p. 24.

Economist Intelligence Unit, *Quarterly Economic Review: Mozambique,* Annual 1979, p. 33.

TABLE IX

MOZAMBIQUE: PROPORTION OF SELECTED DEVELOPMENT SECTORS FINANCED BY EACH EXTERNAL SOURCE, 1976–1977

Sector	Total Investment $ US Million	Advanced Capitalist Bloc	Scandinavia	Soviet Bloc	PRC	Arab Loan Fund
Agriculture and Rural Development	73.4	9.1%	38.6%	0%	0%	16.4%
Mines	3.9	0	49.0	42.0	0	0
Transport and Energy	88.9	8.7	2.7	0	0	0
Social Services*	52.5	15.5	7.6	0	0	0

* Includes education, health care, water.

Source: Calculated from Report of the Secretary-General to UN Economic and Social Council, *Assistance to Mozambique,* A/32/96, 9 June 1977, p. 17.

TABLE X

DEVELOPMENT ASSISTANCE — 1975–77 ANNUAL AVERAGES
(MILLIONS OF $US)

	Bilateral Industrial Market Economies*	Bilateral Industrial Centrally-Planned Economies**	Multilateral***
Angola	7.5	.7	9.4
Botswana	39.1	.0	9.1
Mozambique	37.2	19.7	19.2
Tanzania	234.7	17.0	64.8
Zambia	72.9	9.3	10.9

* Includes OECD, plus Iceland, Ireland, Luxembourg, Portugal and South Africa.

** Includes USSR, Eastern Europe, People's Republic of China.

*** Includes World Bank group, regional banks, EEC, UN institutions (not OPEC or COMECON).
Source: United Nations, *Statistical Yearbook*, 1979, pp. 881–884.

million loan in February 1981. Mozambique is also the major recipient of SADCC funds (see Chapter 8), receiving about $760 million of the pledges from the Western donors for improvement of its transport infrastructure in 1981.[47]

The Soviets have provided technicians and aid for development of vital sectors, and Bulgaria and East Germany are providing funds. However, aid from the socialist countries (including the People's Republic of China) has not come close to matching that from the West (see Table X). Soviet requests for permanent mooring of warships and for increased fishing rights have regularly been denied by the Mozambican government.

Angola, with its oil wealth, was not experiencing financial restrictions during the Frontline struggle for Zimbabwe. External debt in 1978 was only $57.4 million or 2.2 percent of its GDP.[48] The $100 million aid for agriculture and marine development extended by the Soviet bloc had hardly been tapped.[49] About 10,000 technicians from socialist allies (mainly Cuba) were in Angola, but many were paid their salaries by the Angolan government.[50] The United Nations estimated that Angola received annual average aid from the centrally-planned economies of only $.7 million for 1975-1977. (See Table X.) Annual average aid for the same period from the market economies was $7.5 million with another $9.4 million (annual average) from multilateral agencies.

By 1980, with the escalation of the war over Namibia, Angola was seeking more credit to finance development programmes. Sonangol (the state oil corporation) and Gulf Oil jointly received a $50 million Eurodollar loan for a gas injection project to increase output at Cabinda. In spite of the American government's hostility toward the MPLA government, the Export-Import Bank extended a $97 million loan. The United Nations responded to the increased war with $40 million aid extended over several years, and the FAO gave $50,000 in food aid in 1980.[51] The announcements of new aid programmes to Angola make it clear that the government has retained close links to the West and is considered a 'good risk' by capitalist financial criteria.[52] Vital support is provided by the socialist countries, but certainly not to the exclusion of the West. As the conservative Georgetown University's Center for Strategic and International Studies concluded in 1982, 'Despite Angola's close political and military relations with the USSR and Cuba, Luanda's key economic ties remain with the West. Western industrialised countries purchase the bulk of

Angola's exports and provide the financing, equipment and expertise for the economic reconstruction now in progress. Luanda is increasingly favouring greater co-operation with the United States, Western Europe and Japan.'[53]

According to the data describing the structures of the Frontline economies, therefore, all five remain underdeveloped. They are primary producers and dependent on a few commodities for export earnings. The volatile prices for the commodities on the world market (often with a downward trend) make it difficult for the governments to fulfil development plans. External aid to help overcome the colonial legacy of underdevelopment is mainly from the West.

These structural constraints on economic growth became the source of economic crisis as the countries engaged in support of the armed struggle for the liberation of Zimbabwe. Emergency aid for Mozambique and Zambia, the two states that paid the highest costs to be Frontline supporters, was mainly from the West. Tanzania also received emergency aid from the West to alleviate somewhat the cost of the war against Idi Amin. As the war escalates in Namibia, even wealthy Angola is now turning more to capital financing from the advanced capitalist states. According to the indicators of both trade and capital transfers, all five of the Frontline States were dependent on the West during the period of the Frontline struggle for Zimbabwe (1974-1980).

Summary

Economic dependence did constrain the political struggle for Zimbabwe in various ways. When Kaunda seized the moment after the Portuguese coup in 1974 to begin unilateral secret talks with South Africa over Rhodesia, the price of copper was falling drastically. This reduction in foreign exchange earnings made it more difficult for Zambia to sustain the Zimbabwean refugees. By October 1978, the Zambian economy was in such difficulty that the border was opened to the south. An economic necessity, according to the Zambian authorities, this action was a setback for the political unity of the Frontline and for the military goals of the Patriotic Front which had made the railroad a major sabotage target.

The economic constraints on Botswana drastically limited its role as a Frontline State and therefore weakened the alliance. If Botswana had been able to assert more economic autonomy from South Africa, the Rhodesian conflict would have been shorter. In contrast, the trade and investment dependence of Angola had little political effect for the Frontline during the Rhodesian crisis; this impact was to be realised only as the Namibian war escalated.

Problems of Tanzania emerged when it tried to finance the cost of the Idi Amin war through bank loans. There was no immediate impact of this difficulty on Frontline policy, but it would have made Tanzania's pledge to continue support for the guerrillas, if the British did not promote fair elections, very difficult to fulfil.

The structure of Mozambican underdevelopment and dependence limited its ability to help the refugees and guerrillas.United Nations aid was supportive, but it was insufficient, as was bilateral aid. It is clear that Mozambique sacrificed much in short-term development to support the Zimbabwean struggle. In spite of its economic dependence, the Mozambican government kept Zimbabwean political independence a priority.

Because their major trade partners and aid givers were also financing the Rhodesian army and aiding the Rhodesian economy to the final days of the war, the Frontline States sought alternative aid. Tanzania and Mozambique distinguish the social democratic countries of Scandinavia from the advanced capitalist states and accepted much aid from Norway, Denmark, and Sweden. Indeed, these states were consistent in condemning Rhodesia's minority rule and its aggression against the Frontline States. Zambia was able to reduce its economic linkages with the south, but that success made the economy further dependent on its advanced capitalist benefactors. The Botswanan economy is still captured by South Africa; in its attempts to reduce its dependence, it too turns more toward the West. Angola and Mozambique have both tried to diversify their external economic linkages by seeking trade and capital from the socialist countries. The socialist states have provided crucial military and economic support. Their aid for development and their trade linkages, however, remain subordinate to Western ties.

This economic dependence was used as leverage by the advanced capitalist powers of Britain, the United States, and South Africa against the Frontline States. As will be seen in the next chapter, all three made it economically possible for the Smith government to wage the war against the Zimbabwe nationalists as long as it did. Yet the Frontline attempts to diversify their international economic and political linkages in turn imposed constraints on Rhodesia's allies.

Notes

1. This interpretation was consistently and unanimously repeated by government officials in interviews in Tanzania, Mozambique, and Zambia. Denying that their view was simply rhetoric, each official was readily able to cite economic data to support his view.

2. Theotonio Dos Santos, 'The Structure of Dependence,' *American Economic Review* 60 (May 1970), p. 231.

3. See Philip J. O'Brien, 'A Critique of Latin American Theories of Dependence', in Ivor Oxall et al., eds., *Beyond the Sociology of Development* (London: Routledge and Kegan Paul, 1975), pp. 12-13.

4. F. Cardoso and E. Faletto, *Dependence and Development in Latin America* (Berkeley: University of California Press, 1979), p. xx.

5. Charles Van Onselin, *Chibaro* (London: Pluto Press, 1976).

6. For different views on the controversy, see the following:
   Samir Amin, *Unequal Development* (New York: Monthly Review, 1976).
   A. G. Frank, *Capitalism and Underdevelopment in Latin America* (Cambridge University Press, 1971).
   Osvaldo Sunkel, 'National Development Policy and External Dependence in Latin America', *Journal of Development Studies* 6, no. 1 (October 1969), pp. 23-47.
   Bill Warren, *Imperialism — Pioneer of Capitalism* (London: NLB, 1980).

7. For a good analysis of Cardoso's view relative to other dependent theorists, see Y.A. Kahl, *Modernization, Exploitation and Dependency in Latin America* (New Jersey: Transaction Books, 1976), pp. 135-136.

8. Samir Amin, op. cit., p. 229.

9. John H. Dunning, ed., *The Multinational Enterprise* (New York: Praeger, 1971).
   Peter Evans, *Dependent Development: The Alliance of Multinational, State and Local Capital in Brazil* (Princeton: Princeton University Press, 1979).
   Norman Girvan, *Corporate Imperialism: Conflict and Expropriation* (White Plains, N.Y.: Sharpe, 1976).
   Stephen Hymer, 'Is the Multinational Corporation Doomed?' *Innovation* 28 (1972), pp. 10-18.
   United Nations, Department of Economic and Social Affairs, *Multinational Corporations in World Development* (New York: United Nations, 1973).
   Theodore Moran, *Multinational Corporations and the Politics of Dependence* (Princeton, N.J.: Princeton University Press, 1974).

10. *The Financial Times* (London), 15 December, 1977.

11. This is often labelled as the ECLA model (Economic Commission for Latin America). The dependency theories arose in protest against development plans for Latin America that perpetuated large profits for US corporations at the expense of social services and of local control.

12. Henry Bernstein, 'Sociology of Underdevelopment vs. Sociology of Development?' in Henry Bernstein et al., eds., *Development Theory: Three Critical Essays* (London: Routledge and Kegan Paul, 1980).

Ernesto Laclau, 'Feudalism and Capitalism in Latin America', *New Left Review* 67 (May-June 1971), pp. 19-38.

Anne Phillips, 'The Concept of Development', *Review of African Political Economy* 8 (January-April 1977), pp. 7-21.

13. Robert Brenner, 'The Origins of Capitalist Development: A Critique of Neo-Smithian Marxism', *New Left Review* 104 (July-August 1977), pp. 25-92.

Lorraine Culley, 'Economic Development in Neo-Marxist Theory', in Barry Hindess, ed., *Sociological Theories of the Economy* (London: Macmillan, 1977).

John Weeks and Elizabeth Dore, 'International Exchange and the Causes of Backwardness', *Latin American Perspectives* 6, no. 2 (Spring 1979), pp. 62-91.

14. F. Cardoso, 'Dependency and Development in Latin America', *New Left Review* 74 (July-August 1972).

Norma Chinchilla and James Dietz, 'Toward a New Understanding of Development and Underdevelopment', *Latin American Perspectives* 8, nos. 3-4 (Summer and Fall 1981), pp. 143-146.

15. R. Fernandez and J. Ocampo, 'The Latin American Revolution: A Theory of Imperialism Not Dependency', *Latin American Perspectives* 1, no. 1 (Spring 1974), pp. 30-61.

Claude Meillassoux, 'From Reproduction to Production', *Economy and Society* 1, no. 1 (February 1972), pp. 93-105.

16. Robert Brenner, op. cit., pp. 84-85.

17. A. G. Frank, op. cit.

A critique of this review is in Thomas Angotti, 'The Political Implications of Dependency Theory', *Latin American Perspectives* 8, nos. 3-4 (Summer and Fall 1981), pp. 124-137.

18. This determinist view has been most consistently expressed by European revisionist communist parties, such as the French CP.

19. Bill Warren, op. cit.

Colin Leys, *Underdevelopment in Kenya, the Political Economy of Neo-Colonialism* (London: Heinemann, 1975).

Nicola Swainson, The Development of Corporate Capitalism in Kenya, 1918-1977 (Berkeley: University of California Press, 1980).

20. Appreciation to Joel Samoff for remarking this point to me (personal letter, 20 October 1982).

21. James A. Caporaso, 'Dependence, Dependency, and Power in the Global System: A Structural and Behavioural Analysis,' *International Organization* 32, no. 1 (Winter 1978), pp. 13-43.

Robert D. Duvall, 'Dependence and Dependencia Theory: Notes toward Precision of Concept and Argument', *International Organization* 32, no. 1 (Winter 1978), pp. 51-78.

S. Jackson et al., 'An Assessment of Empirical Research on Dependencia', *Latin American Research Review* 14, no. 3 (1979), pp. 7-29.

22. Bank of Botswana, *Annual Report, 1977*, pp. 8 and 20.

23. *Tanzania Daily News*, 2 September 1979.

24. Economist Intelligence Unit, *Quarterly Economic Review: Southern Africa, Botswana* (4th Quarter, 1980), p. 14.

25. Economist Intelligence Unit, Quarterly Economic Review, *Angola* (Annual, 1981),p. 13.
26. Ibid., p. 8.
27. Ibid., p. 9.
28. Economist Intelligence Unit, Quarterly Economic Review, *Angola* (2nd Quarter, 1981), p. 2.
   US Department of Agriculture, Economic Research Service, 'Angola's Agricultural Situation', mimeo. (Washington, D C., 23 March 1982), p. 1.
29. Based on United Nations estimates in Economist Intelligence Unit, Quarterly Economic Review, *Mozambique* (1st Quarter, 1981), p. 15.
30. Penelope Hartland-Thunberg, *Botswana: An African Growth Economy* (Boulder, Colorado: Westview, 1978), p. 61.
31. IBRD, *Basic Economic Report, Zambia* (3 October 1977).
32. E.A. Brett, *Colonialism and Underdevelopment in East Africa* (London: Heinemann, 1973).
   Justinian Rweyemamu, *Underdevelopment and Industrialization in Tanzania* (Nairobi: Oxford University Press, 1973).
33. East African Community, East African Customs and Excise Dept., *Annual Trade Reports*, 1964 and 1977.
34. Interviews with B. Nebwe, Permanent Secretary of Commerce, Industry and Foreign Trade, Republic of Zambia, 31 May 1979; W. Mwakimi and M. M. Kassaja, Ministry of Trade, Republic of Tanzania, 9 September 1978.
35. These figures indicate the trade the government prints. Government officials admit that the actual figures were higher from 'clandestine' trade.
36. Center for Strategic and International Studies, 'Background Information on Angola', paper presented for Conference on Angola's Economic Prospects (Washington, D.C., 24 March 1982), p. 5.
37. Hartland-Thunberg, op. cit., p. 55.
38. National Development Plan quoted in USAID, *Development Needs and Opportunities for Co-operation in Southern Africa: Botswana* (March 1979), pp. 110-111.
39. Economist Intelligence Unit, Quarterly Economic Review, *Southern Africa: Botswana* (1st Quarter, 1980), p. 23.
40. Economist Intelligence Unit, Quarterly Economic Review, *Tanzania* (Annual, 1980), p. 9.
41. Terms of capital transfers through 1975 are available in IBRD, *Tanzania: Basic Economic Report*, No. 1616 — TA Main Report (December 1977), p. 168.
42. Tanzania exported 70,000 tons of maize to Zambia and Mozambique because planners estimated a surplus. Five months later in February 1980, Tanzania requested 175,000 tons of cereals in emergency food assistance. Japan provided some food aid; the US gave a loan for Tanzania to purchase $5 million of rice. *Africa News*, 21 April 1980, pp. 4-5.
43. United Republic of Tanzania, *Third Five Year Plan for Economic and Social Development, General Perspectives*, Part I (1 July 1976 — 30 June 1981), p. 9.
44. Economist Intelligence Unit, Quarterly Economic Review.
44. Economist Intelligence Unit, Quarterly Economic Review, *Zambia* (Annual, 1981), p. 20.
45. *Africa* 82 (June 1978), p. 62.

46. Report of the Secretary General to UN Economic and Social Council, *Assistance to Mozambique* (9 June 1977, A/32/96), p. 17.

47. See Economist Intelligence Unit, Quarterly Economic Review, *Mozambique*, op. cit. for regular reports of aid and loans.

48. Economist Intelligence Unit, Quarterly Economic Review, *Angola* (Annual, 1981), p. 22.

49. Center for Strategic and International Studies, op. cit., p. 4.

50. Hard data on the cost of the Cuban technicians and military are difficult to verify. Angolan officials, however, regularly agree that the cost is high and is paid in foreign exchange. A 1983 estimate was $40 per day per soldier, more than $300 million per year for the 20,000-25,000 Cubans who were still in Angola to assist its defence against direct South African invasions and occupation. Statistics quoted from 'analysts' in *The Washington Post*, 1 October 1983.

51. Economist Intelligence Unit, Quarterly Economic Review, *Angola* (2nd Quarter, 1980), p. 6 and (2nd Quarter, 1981), p. 11.

52. See Economist Intelligence Unit, Quarterly Economic Review, *Angola*, op. cit., for regular reports of aid and loans. American corporations have spoken out in support of the 'business-like' and 'non-ideological' approach of Angolan officials to trade and investment.
'David Rockefeller cites Advantage to US of Normal Ties with Angola,' *The Washington Post*, 3 March 1982.
'Gulf Oil under Fire for Supporting Angola, *Africa News*, 22 March 1982.

53. Center for Strategic and International Studies, op. cit., p. 6.

CHAPTER 5

Across The Negotiating Table: Allies Of Rhodesia

Foreign capital has dominated Rhodesia since its inception. Rhodesia's position as a dependent capitalist state did not decline with industrialisation, for its impressive industrial growth was financed by foreign capital. The white settlers remained junior partners throughout their period of political rule. A full two-thirds of the present Zimbabwean productive capacity is owned by foreign capital.

Through the internationalisation of British capital from the end of the 19th century to the present, Rhodesia became fully integrated into the world capitalist system. After the Unilateral Declaration of Independence (UDI) in 1965, South Africa became an important second in trade and finance. By independence, it is estimated that South African investment had gained at least parity with Britain.[1] The United States has remained third. British and South African capital control 80 percent of the manufacturing production. Ninety percent of the mining sector is owned by the British, South Africans, and Americans in roughly equal shares.[2] Of the $1.75 billion of private investment in Rhodesia in 1979, only about one-sixth was of Rhodesian origin.[3] Economist Duncan Clarke has summarised this capital penetration as follows:

> It is hard to find a sub-Saharan African example comparable to the Zimbabwean case, in which the role of foreign investment has been so long established, as deeply integrated into the sectors producing the bulk of the output, so strongly inter-connected with local capital . . .[4]

At different times in the struggle for majority rule, the Frontline States and the Zimbabwean nationalists engaged in talks with the British, the South African, and the American governments. These diplomatic negotiations reflected the objective economic relations, for each of the three states was a major contributor to the Rhodesian economy. In order to understand the limitations and success of the

Frontline States, it is necessary to analyse the context of the international economy. The British and American governments supported the white minority regime throughout the struggle, although their support was delimited by the realities of their own economies. All three broke sanctions; only South Africa sent troops. These choices are not arbitrary nor accidental. They are made in the context of the total world capitalist system and must be analysed to be understood.

This chapter will delineate the important variables comprising the international political-economic context of the struggle. Not only the support for Rhodesia by the British, South Africans, and Americans, but also the constraints on the pursuit of their economic self-interests will be analysed. The success of the Frontline was integrally related to the crisis of advanced capitalism. In addition, the political limitations imposed by mobilisation of international opinion in favour of an independent and non-racist Zimbabwe will be discussed.

Great Britain As The Colonial Power

The British role in the Zimbabwean negotiations and in the administration of elections can be understood only through analysis of its economic stake in its colony. British capital had benefited greatly from white minority rule in Rhodesia. The story of British dominance in Rhodesia has been told; it presents a classic example of imperialism as it evolved from the 19th century to the present.[5] It is not necessary to repeat the historical detail, but a general outline of the international division of labour will help to explain the transition to majority rule.

White settlers arrived in Mashonaland with the hope of finding vast mineral resources similar to the ones discovered in South Africa. Deposits were found, although they were not as extensive as the rich mines on the Rand. A major problem for the settlers was to engage labour for the mines because both the Shona and the Ndebele were self-sufficient subsistence farmers with little need to acquire cash. Through a systematic policy of land alienation, often carried out by force, the white settlers were able to push enough Africans off the land to supply a cheap labour force to the mines. No longer subsistence peasants, they needed the wages to survive. Wages were suppressed by monopoly control in the region, by enforced migrant labour (contracts were only for 6 – 12 months), and by legislation to prohibit unions. In addition, through wage and political manipulation, the mine owners separated the white miners from the Africans. British imperialism in Rhodesia, therefore, was established to promote mineral exports, as cheaply as possible, to the mother country. Rhodesian chrome was supplied very cheaply, as a strategic mineral to the defence industries of the foreign powers.[6] Today gold remains a major foreign exchange earner.

Land alienated from the African peasants was consolidated and sold to white settlers. Producing on large tracts of the most fertile land, the settlers were able to grow vast quantities of agricultural products for export. As much as 50 percent of the agricultural production was exported. Land alienation was legitimised by the idea of 'racial parity'; Africans and settlers were to have equal amounts of land. By 1976, this division meant that individual European farmers (numbering 6,682) had access to 100 times more land than the individual African farmers (680,000).[7] And the size of the plots do not tell the whole story, for the white settlers had control of 90 percent of the fertile land (at most 50 percent of which was used).[8] Important agricultural sectors, such as sugar, citrus fruits, forestry, and ranching were all owned by foreign capital.[9] A major purchaser of the exported food was the mother country. Rhodesia provided Britain with agricultural as well as mineral commodities.

Rhodesia did not remain an exporter of only simple commodities. Growth in its manufacturing sector increased until it was second only to South Africa on the continent. In 1980 manufacturing was about 25 percent of GDP. Rhodesian industrialisation, however, was also dominated by foreign capital; only two of the ten largest industrial companies were Rhodesian, and they ranked fourth and seventh.[10] Foreign capital could further influence production by its dominance in retail marketing, finance (banks and investment houses), and insurance (operating through South African regional headquarters).

Although industrialisation has shown impressive growth, it is an example of 'distorted development' discussed in the previous chapter. African wages were a fraction of white wages for the same jobs. Skilled jobs were reserved for whites only. Illiteracy remained 70 percent among African adults, even with the advanced industrialisation. Health care was segregated and inferior for Africans, as was the housing. In a country that exported 50 percent of its agricultural production, most African children suffered from malnutrition. In certain areas (reported in Victoria Province and Macheke district), it was estimated that 90 percent of the children were malnourished.

Infant mortality was 1.7 percent for the whites, but estimates set it at 12 to 22 percent for Africans.[11] Incomplete social statistics for the African population is another indicator of the relative underdeveloped social conditions for the African workers.

Racism, made legal by the state, exacerbated the exploitation of African labour. Africans were relegated to the unskilled, unorganised, 'temporary labour' sector of the working class simply by the colour of their skin. Racial domination in Rhodesia was, therefore, essentially a class phenomenon. Rhodesian race relations, as in South Africa, 'can be characterised generally by the subordination of the African majority and the domination of Europeans or, alternatively, by a range of class-specific policies, such as mining compounds, land alienation, native reserves, pass laws, labour bureaux, influx control, migrant labour, and job reservations.'[12] Racial ideology justified exploitation of the African majority as they were labelled incompetent and incapable of creative innovation. To emphasise the class basis of racism does not deny that racism has a reciprocal impact on social relations. The strength of the ideology makes it an intervening variable, not a dependent one or a residual category.[13] Racism takes on a predominance of its own, not always linked directly back to class antagonisms. The emphasis here is that the racial prejudice is very much a product of capitalist development. It is profitable.[14] Regulating every aspect of the Africans' lives from birth in segregated villages to burial in segregated cemetaries, the racial state controlled the African workers, what they could produce, when and under what wage conditions. Economic growth occurred, but at the expense of Africans' health, education, and general livelihood. Only the minority benefited from the economic growth.

The racially segregated affluence was attractive to white settlers even after World War II, illustrated by the number of British citizens who emigrated to Rhodesia. Cheap land and a high standard of living were offered to the kinsfolk back home; from 1953 – 1960, immigration in Rhodesia from Britain increased by 40 percent.[15] By 1973 only 10 percent of all white Rhodesians were born in Rhodesia. Settler ties remained strong with Britain.

Great Britain As The Negotiator

In spite of the fact that Britain did not intervene in the formation of the racial state by the white settlers, either at the time of 'responsible government' in 1923 or at UDI in 1965, some supporters of majority rule saw the Crown as a mediating factor against the more conservative intransigence of the white Rhodesian government. The British government was viewed as more 'rational' or 'disinterested' than the white settlers or their transnational corporate supporters. It was theorised that the government promoted the overall class interests of the capitalists, not just of a fraction represented in the transnationals in Rhodesia. The government, therefore, should be able to take a longer view of economic self-interest: incorporating some of the Africans into the middle class of civil servants and professionals would increase their interest in the status quo. This theory, therefore, concluded that the British government would support the liberal fraction of capital against the racism of the white settlers.

When the rest of Africa was becoming independent in the 1960's, the Zimbabwean nationalists appealed to the British to support their cause against the settlers. With retrospect, most of the nationalists now say that they lost valuable time in the years they spent looking to Britain for deliverance. The numerous petitions and talks made in London only gave time for the business interests to expand and consolidate their control. Political delay was used for economic expansion.

Tanzania also looked to the British for reasoned and peaceful solution to the white minority rule in Rhodesia. President Nyerere was pleased that the British acquiesced to demands by Northern Rhodesia (Zambia) and Nyasaland (Malawi) for total autonomy from the Central African Federation (CAF). Zambia and Malawi became independent in 1964, seceding from the political hegemony of (Southern) Rhodesia. Tanzania and Zambia immediately co-ordinated their economic interaction in an effort to give Zambia at least some alternative to the economic hegemony of Rhodesia in the region.

President Nyerere, however, realised the loyalties of the British when Rhodesia declared UDI. He called for British intervention to stop the rebel regime and worked in the international organisations — the Commonwealth, United Nations, OAU — to isolate Britain. Nyerere broke diplomatic relations with Britain when the government refused to take action against the Rhodesian settlers.

The United Nations responded to UDI with international sanctions (SC 235) approved in 1968. Trade did decline, and certain sectors like tobacco export especially suffered. But the sanctions were only partially enforced, for the South Africans vowed to abrogate them.

Until 1975 when the Portuguese recognised the independence of their colonies, Mozambique also helped to provide goods to Rhodesia.

The British refused to intervene militarily against their kin in Rhodesia after UDI, but agreed to enforce economic sanctions. A major target of the United Nations was to stop the flow of oil, for Rhodesia had no sources of oil. Britain set up a naval blockade around the port of Beira, in Portuguese Mozambique. The transnational corporation Lonrho had built a pipeline from Beira to Salisbury and had monopoly control of the transport of oil. During ten years (1966 – 1975 — until the independence of Mozambique), Britain deployed 76 ships and over 24,000 men to enforce the blockade. While the blockade was paraded on the front pages of the international press, Shell/BP was shipping oil to Rhodesia from Maputo, a port further south, via South Africa. The two British corporations, along with the American Mobil and Caltex and the French Total, provided the oil necessary for all the needs of the Rhodesian regime.[16] During the investigations in 1979 which revealed this collaboration, it was learned that Prime Minister Harold Wilson knew as early as 1967 that the oil companies were supplying Rhodesia. Further, it appears that Rhodesia held off declaring its unilateral independence until a 90-day supply of oil was in Rhodesia in 1965; at the same time Zambia's supply was reduced by the oil companies to a critically low 13 days.[17] After 1971, Rhodesia did not ration oil to consumers. While protesting the actions of the white settlers, the British were in fact providing them the means by which to wage their war against the African people.

Britain offered two other vital means of support to the white minority government during its struggle for survival. First, Britain never required that subsidiaries in Rhodesia be cut off from investment funds. A major portion of the capital inflow was from British sources. The capital was important to the financing of the war economy. Second, Britain was the source of many of the personnel whose skills were crucial to the regime. The immigration figures quoted earlier revealed that most Rhodesians were recent arrivals in the country. As the war escalated, the manpower became even more important for the war machine. White males had to serve even up to the age of 50 years. Men who had been in the army were mobilised frequently in the reserves. The conscription seriously affected production in the economy as skilled personnel left the productive sectors to fight.[18] The shortage of white males to fight the war was exacerbated by increasing emigration from Rhodesia during the war; the Standard

Economic Bulletin reported that the net loss of the white population was 15,000–20,000 in 1979.[19] By not restricting the British emigration to Rhodesia, Britain provided the minority regime with another of its most vital resources.

Because of these various abrogations of the international sanctions, the economy had to adjust to restraints on trade, but there was no major economic decline from the sanctions. Income per capita grew about 5 percent per year from 1968 – 1974.[20] Total direct investment from transnational corporations was $1,000 million in 1965 and $1,525 million in 1974, a 38 percent increase during the 'sanctions'.[21] Further, much capital was mobilised locally because the Rhodesian government required transnational corporations (except South African ones) to retain their profits in the country through exchange controls. Transnational affiliates mobilised local funds with the aid of transnational banks, insurance firms, pension funds, and building societies. A comprehensive study by the Centre for African Studies, University of Eduardo Mondlane, documented that sanctions were not deleterious to the Rhodesian economy:

> . . . the imposition of sanctions did not seriously hamper economic development within Rhodesia. This is clearly indicated by the fact that, after some initial years of adjustment, from 1967 onwards up to 1974 the economy expanded rapidly . . . Manufacturing increased by 94 percent in *volume* in the period 1964 – 73. . . This expansion was based on processing primary output and import-replacing consumption output. Mining expanded by 200 percent in output from $53.5 million in 1965 to $165 million in 1974. . . Net capital inflow for the period 1965 – 73 equalled $174.6 m. with its highest level in 1973 at $51.3 million. Thus, the expansion in Rhodesia was the result of foreign capital and of further immigration which increased the settler community by another 25 percent.[22]

Analysing the pattern of foreign investment that survived sanctions, the *Social and Economic Survey*, conducted by the Patriotic Front under the auspices of the United Nations Conference on Trade and Development (UNCTAD), confirmed the conclusions of the Maputo study.[23]

The lack of progress in the bilateral talks between Britain and Rhodesia and the continuing buoyancy of the Rhodesian economy led Martin Loney to note the following:

. . . an examination of the negotiations between Britain and Rhodesia in 1966, 1968 and 1971 might lead an observer to the conclusion . . . that *it was Britain that was suffering the sanctions*. There is no more telling criticism of the strategy and technical implementation of sanctions than the fact that, as the years passed by, it was Britain and not Rhodesia which made the substantive concessions.[24] *[emphasis mine]*

The domestic economic conditions were an important context for British foreign policy. During the height of the Zimbabwean struggle, especially from 1973, there was a crisis in British capitalism. The balance of payments were in deficit; inflation was high and persistent. Productivity reached a historical low and never really recovered. As the Organisation for Economic Co-operation and Development (OECD) summarised in its economic survey of the United Kingdom:

After a long period of comparatively slow growth up to the early 1970's, the economy since 1974 seems to have entered a phase of approximate stagnation. The 1974/75 recession was deeper and the subsequent upswing was both shorter and weaker than the rest of the OECD area . . . GDP in 1980 will be about its 1973 level.[25]

These problems made the investment in Rhodesia look very attractive; cheap African labour created high profits. The corporations had an interest in staying in Rhodesia. But at the same time, they could not call upon the British government to defend those interests militarily. It would have been difficult for Britain to sustain the cost of a war. Economic links were not weakened, but they also were not protected by the British military. The best they could do was send a few mercenaries.

Only by 1974 did the Rhodesian GDP show no growth, and by 1978 there was a 7 percent decline. The Rhodesian dollar was devalued in October 1977 and again in April 1978. The decline in the GDP and the foreign exchange difficulties coincide with escalation of the guerrilla war. The cost of the war rose from $113 million in 1974 to $480 million in 1979.[26] By 1977 it consumed 40 per cent of government expenditure.[27] It was guerrilla war that disrupted the economy, not international sanctions. By 1979 a 'senior Rhodesian official' stated that the war cost $1.5 million per day and 'had virtually bankrupted the country.'[28]

Although the British government supported the white minority regime economically, it differed from its junior partner in the political strategy necessary to preserve the economic status quo. The primary question for Britain was how to preserve the control of production *and* political stability. War mobilises the peasants and radicalises them. The British goal was not to escalate the war but to find ways to end it with minimal changes in the relations of production. African faces in the government were not to be feared; it was social revolution that was to be thwarted. Britain's Foreign Secretary, Anthony Crosland, stated at a NATO Foreign Ministers' meeting in Brussels during the 1976 Geneva Conference between Smith and the nationalists that:

> if the British gave up hope, there would be no doubt over who would eventually win in the battlefield. But if the issue were settled on the battlefield it would seriously lessen the chance of *bringing about a moderate African regime in Rhodesia* and would *open the way for more radical solutions* and external intervention on the part of others . . . [29] [*emphasis mine*]

The major contrast between Britain as a colonial power and the white settlers reflected their different economic positions. The settlers did not want to relinquish political hegemony for fear of losing economic control as well. Their control of the state was vital to preserving their control of African labour and land. As guerrilla war escalated in Rhodesia, the British came to understand that their interests could only be maintained if political hegemony were relinquished.

An equally important reason for the restraint on British action was the successful political mobilisation of other African countries for majority rule. The Organisation of African Unity, urged on by the Frontline States, was firm in demanding the end to white minority rule. Britain's trade with the rest of Africa was more than double its trade with Rhodesia. Other African countries provided food and raw material to the ex-colonial power. Long before Nigeria nationalised British Petroleum in 1979, the threat of economic reprisals was a deterrant to military intervention in the Rhodesian conflict.

The Frontline States also succeeded in isolating Rhodesia politically. World opinion was mobilised against the injustices of racism. It was difficult for British corporations or the government to appear to be supporting the whites. Their participation in the economy had to be interpreted as a force for change. The flow of capital and personnel was to be a stabilising force while negotiations for 'peaceful' change were pursued. More direct aid for the whites had to be clandestine, such as the provision of oil.

Given these economic and political constraints, the pattern of

British support for their Rhodesian kin is more comprehensible. Looking for a political compromise that would not upset the economic status quo, the British government fully supported the Muzorewa government — until it did not stop the war. Further, the Frontline States were able to mobilise international support for the Patriotic Front's call for internationally supervised elections. Responding to the economic boycott by Nigeria and the international rejection of its Rhodesian policy, the Thatcher government embarked on the negotiations between Smith/Muzorewa and the Patriotic Front. But it was negotiation with threats. Both during the Lancaster talks and the transition to elections, British diplomats made it clear that Muzorewa was still preferred. In short, British collaboration with minority control of the police, army, media, and courts continued to the day of elections. The British were more willing than Smith to gamble in international elections, because they saw no clear alternative to ending the war; their direct intervention in the war was not feasible. The gamble was also accepted because Britain, and its American and South African allies, analysed that Muzorewa could win enough votes to force a coalition government. With previous experiences in Malaysia, Indonesia, Philippines, Vietnam, the Anglo-Americans did understand the mobilising potentials of guerrilla warfare. However, they seriously underestimated the extent of mobilisation accomplished by the Patriotic Front. The elections were lost to Muzorewa before the campaign began; monetary, political, and military support of Muzorewa during transition promoted his campaign but could not camouflage his record of collaboration with the white minority government.

Confident that Muzorewa could acquire a coalition government and aware of the international observations of the elections, the British Governor did regulate strict control of the balloting procedure, but the British gamble failed. Given an opportunity to cast a ballot without intimidation, the people voted their choice: the parties that had done the most fighting to end white minority rule.

The United States

A latecomer to Southern Africa, but one with increasing interest, is the United States. It entered the Rhodesian conflict via Angola. Or one could even say via the Middle East, for the United States government is still criticised by African leaders for bringing its disputes in other parts of the world to Southern Africa. The outside disputes tend to colour what the Americans see in Southern Africa, and the African leaders are constantly asking the United States government to understand Africa first and then see if it parallels Vietnam or Afghanistan.

The basis for this criticism originates in the American support of Portugal during the liberation struggle in its African colonies. Until the coup in Portugal in 1974, the United States provided military aid, equipment, and financial support to the Portuguese regime fighting the liberation forces in Angola, Guinea-Bissau, and Mozambique. The United States trained Portuguese at Fort Benning; it sold napalm left over from Vietnam; it provided planes and weapons through NATO, for Portugal was a member.

The reasons for this support are well-documented.[30] Only a short summary of the support is given here in order to analyse the 'lessons' that the US learned from Angola for Rhodesia. Of the three Portuguese colonies, the United States had the most economic interest in Angola. Gulf Oil explored and developed Angola's huge oil reserves. Its royalties alone, paid to Portugal, financed the war in Angola. American corporations were major shareowners in iron ore and diamond production. Thirty percent of Portuguese Angolan coffee was sold to the US. In Guinea-Bissau, Exxon was searching for off-shore oil, but there were no major American interests in the country. In Mozambique, there were very few corporations.

The major reason for US support of Portugal was not economic, but strategic. This is where the Middle East steps in. During the 1967 Israeli-Egyptian war, the United States used its base on the Azores to supply Israel. The Azores base had been leased to the United States by the Portuguese. It was the only feasible refuelling stop for the American planes, because European countries were politically sensitive to the Arab oil suppliers. The base was perceived as crucial to American support of any further Arab-Israeli conflict. Southern Africa, including Angola and Mozambique, also became more strategically important when the oil super tankers began going around the Cape instead of through the Suez Canal. Seventy-five percent of crude oil trade, and 44 percent of NATO's trade travelled around the Cape route. To have a NATO partner in the region was considered an advantage.

For these strategic and economic reasons, the United States supported the Portuguese until the very end of their colonial rule. It only offered a small retainer to one guerrilla leader, Holden Roberto, for a short while in the 1960's. Only very late in the liberation struggle did the United States step in with large sums of money and with mercenaries to back two of the liberation forces, the FNLA and UNITA. They were viewed as more supportive of American economic and strategic interests in Angola than the more radical and popular MPLA (People's Movement for the Liberation of Angola).

Secretary of State Henry Kissinger wanted to finance the FNLA and UNITA with much larger funds in 1975 so the new government would not fall to the MPLA as the Portuguese left. In December 1975 the US Congress, only eight months after the ignominious American retreat from Saigon, would have no further US involvement in nationalistic quagmires. They voted Kissinger down. By March 1976 the MPLA with Cuban support defeated the South Africans who had invaded 400 miles into Angolan territory in an effort to destroy the MPLA government. The American government saw this defeat as a major victory for the Soviet Union, not only in Angola but in all of Africa and in the Cold War. The United States remains the only government to refuse to recognise the MPLA government because there are 'too many' Cubans fighting with the MPLA to protect it from continuing invasions from South Africa.[31]

Kissinger joined the negotiations over Zimbabwe immediately after the MPLA had consolidated its rule in Angola. In April 1976, one month after the retreat of South Africa from Angolan territory, he started his first shuttle diplomacy on the African continent. He saw the conflict in Rhodesia as another opportunity for the Soviets to outmanoeuvre the United States in Southern Africa. Of first importance to the United States was the Soviet threat; the African appeal for majority rule must be answered in a way to weaken Soviet influence in Africa.

As stated in Chapter 2, in Lusaka on 27 April 1976 Kissinger suggested a plan for 'peaceful evolution' to majority rule which would encourage 'moderate leaders'. He said the United States was willing to pressure South Africa for change in apartheid if progress towards majority rule in Rhodesia could be made. He pledged American support to 'accelerate economic development in Southern Africa'. Through this development, the United States could increase its presence in southern Africa.[32] The intent of the Lusaka statement was further clarified in a press conference in September:

> We are facing a situation now in which a so-called armed struggle is already taking place in Rhodesia and is beginning in Namibia.

The history of these struggles is that they lead to escalating violence, drawing in more and more countries, and have the *danger of foreign intervention and the probability of the radicalisation of the whole continent of Africa*. For this reason, we want to provide a non-violent alternative to this prospect.[33] [*emphasis mine*]

As stated earlier, British Minister Crosland echoed the same theme in December in Brussels. The British and Americans were beginning to co-ordinate their Rhodesian policy. In fact, this joint policy was based on the American 'Tar Baby' option of 1969, formulated in the Nixon Administration with Kissinger's participation. National Security Study Memorandum No. 39 was the policy statement and 'Tar Baby' refers to option No. 2 which is quoted as follows:

Broader association with both black and white states in an effort to encourage moderation in the white states, to enlist the co-operation of the black states in reducing tensions and the likelihood of increasing cross-border violence, and to encourage improved relations among the States in the area.[34]

Political majority rule was morally correct, but economic majority rule threatened the economic status quo. Black faces in the government were acceptable so long as they did not try to take control of corporate domination of the Rhodesian economy. This neocolonial policy of one person-one vote with little change in the economic status quo was the policy consistently pursued by various American administrations throughout the Zimbabwean struggle.

President Carter initiated a Southern Africa policy review when he took office in 1977. By March he issued a Presidential Directive that did not sound much different from the Kissinger analysis: it asserted that spreading guerrilla warfare offered openings to the Soviet Union for increased influence.[35] The American goals remained the same: to preserve US strategic interests in the Southern African region, a stable 'non-communist' state was needed in Rhodesia.

The Presidential Directive revealed three differences in the tactics to achieve these goals. First, the Carter Administration rejected the arrogance of the Kissinger shuttle diplomacy and pledged to work with Britain for a resolution of the conflict. Second, South Africa would be asked to help with the negotiations but the United States would take 'visible steps' to reduce relations with South Africa unless changes were apparent in the apartheid system. Apartheid had shown its inherent instability with the June 1976 student demonstrations in Soweto quickly extending to workers and lasting to the end of the year. Verbal demands were the most intense at the beginning of the Carter Administration when the new human rights policy was at its apogee. Meeting with Foreign Minister Roelof Botha in Germany, Vice President Walter Mondale called for 'evident progress towards full political participation by all citizens of South Africa'. Botha replied, 'We're not prepared to accept any political system which must inevitably lead to our own destruction.'[36] President Carter, after the Mondale trip, did threaten South Africa that the United States would not use its Security Council veto to block oil sanctions and would remove American investment guarantees for South Africa. Neither threat was carried out.[37]

The third tactical change was that the Carter Administration made it clear that the Zimbabwean Development Fund, proposed by Kissinger to ease transition from white privilege to majority rule, would not be used just to 'buy the whites out'. It would be directed to Zimbabwean development.

By September 1976 the Kissinger-Crosland suggestions became incorporated into the Anglo-American proposals, presented by the Carter Administration and the British as a basis for negotiations to majority rule. As discussed in Chapter 2, they became the major diplomatic effort in the struggle.

Although the American government became directly involved in the Anglo-American negotiations for majority rule, it continued to abrogate international economic sanctions. Like the British, American corporations continued their operations in Rhodesia and even expanded their number; there were 54 subsidiaries in 1970 which had grown to 66 by 1976. The amount of investment was much less than British investment but it was in key sectors: chemicals, mining, fertilisers, electronics, and oil.

Union Carbide had $40-45 million invested in four subsidiaries. The corporation lobbied for the US Congress to lift sanctions on the importation of chrome from Rhodesia. Exaggerating the loss of a strategic mineral — there was a 20-year stock pile — and of jobs in the ferrochrome industry, Union Carbide gained executive and legislative support. (Union Carbide's former President, Kenneth Rush, was an adviser to the Nixon Administration at the time.) The United States imported chrome from 1971 – 1977). The Carter Administration did end this overt violation of international sanctions, which had previously been incorporated into American law. Hearings on the sanctions denied the previous Union Carbide argument about the loss of jobs:

... we do not believe that there is any validity to the argument that the Rhodesian sanctions will have any measurable effect on employment in the US. It does not affect our production of ferrochrome and would not deny supplies of chrome or ferro-chromium to the US so we cannot think that there would be any impact on employment.[38]

This reinstatement of sanctions did not, however, occur until there was a large smelting capacity to use lower quality ferrochrome, available from South Africa.[39]

Two of the five oil corporations importing oil to Rhodesia were American: Mobil and Caltex. In contrast to the British government investigation, the American Treasury Department only concluded, after several months of inquiry, that it could not rule on the case. Documents were not available because of the South African security restrictions on the publication of information about oil.[40] This sanctions violation, in contrast to chrome, was covert and continued throughout the war.

The strategic importance of Southern Africa had induced NATO to support the Portuguese in maintaining its colonial empire, but NATO support did not end with the fall of Portuguese colonialism. In 1973 NATO established contingency planning for outside the NATO boundaries, explicitly designating the super tanker oil routes as important defence concerns. NATO then co-ordinated activites with the South African military. The State Department responded:

We believe that the US and NATO must have an assured oil resupply to Europe in the event of hostilities. While the Department of State has had no actual role in the development of the SACLANT Plan, it has been aware of this effort and supports NATO contingency planning in principle as authorised by the Defence Planning Committee (of NATO).[41]

Rhodesia, as a part of this strategic Southern African region, received aircraft from the United States.[42] During the period of Rhodesian 'sanctions', Rockwell, Lockheed, and Boeing planes all found their way to Rhodesia. Rockwell's OV-10 spotter planes were being used by the Rhodesians. Twenty A1-60's made their way from Aermachi in Italy to South Africa to Rhodesia. Lockheed owns 20 per cent of Aermachi.[43] (In contrast to other goods, there was supposed to be an international arms embargo against South Africa: planes for military use would be part of this embargo.) In 1974 three Boeing

720's and eleven Bell helicopters were delivered to Rhodesia. Twenty Cessnas 337 also became part of the surveillance teams.[44] In December 1978 Major-General Richard Cooper and Milner Roberts toured South Africa, Rhodesia, and Namibia and proposed military advisers for the region.[45]

Capital, oil, and military equipment were all provided to Rhodesia during its war against liberation. A fourth form of support was personnel. Estimates vary, but from 1,000 to 3,000 Americans fought as mercenaries with the Rhodesian army. It is against US law either to recruit a mercenary or to be one.[46] Yet the Attorney-General never prosecuted these violators. Mercenaries were granted permanent resident status in Rhodesia as soon as they landed in Salisbury; technically, therefore, they were not mercenaries but Rhodesian 'citizens' fighting in the army. The US government, however, never took action against recruiters for Rhodesia. Advertising was done openly in the US for mercenaries to go to Rhodesia.[47] It has been documented that during the Angolan war US mercenaries were trained and sent to Angola by the CIA.[48] The inability of the government to prosecute mercenaries during the Rhodesian war raises speculation about the source of the recruitment.[49]

The ideological congruence between the American and the Rhodesian governments is best illustrated by the fact that the American government conducted several research studies during the conflict that assumed development would be directed by white settler skills and capital. From 1977-1979, the US Agency for International Development spent $1 million on the massive nine country and eleven sector reports for Southern Africa.[50] Except for the Namibian Institute, none of the liberation forces in Southern Africa was consulted about the studies which were centred on development plans for the total area. The US government simply conducted the study on such crucial items as transportation, refugees, and health without consulting the people whom they were studying. Several American scholars of Africa refused to participate in the studies.[51] They suggested that Southern Africans be consulted for the work; AID refused.

Ideological support for the white minority government was not only in official studies. The American press waged a campaign against the Zimbabwe nationalists whom they labelled as 'Marxist terrorists'. When six white missionaries were killed (possibly by Rhodesian troops disguised as guerrillas),[52] it hit the US front pages for days. The massacre of hundreds of African villagers by the white forces received sporadic attention. The press campaign was also directed against Mozambique. Other reports document how the American press in effect redefined the struggle for self-determination in Southern Africa in global Cold War terms.[53]

The US Congress prohibited any appropriated funds from going 'directly or indirectly' to 'Marxist African states' (Angola and Mozambique) in 1977 and tried to implement it again in 1978. It also directed the Administration to vote against Angola and Mozambique for entry into the international financial institutions, such as the World Bank and the IMF. But relief for flood victims in the Limpopo Valley in Mozambique was allocated (over $1 million). In 1978 and 1979, the United States also contributed about $6 million in food for the Zimbabwean refugees in Mozambique. Because Angola was not recognised by the United States, it received nothing. Americans were serious about a negotiated settlement for Rhodesia; the instability of the war threatened mineral supplies. They were concerned about Soviet and Chinese support for the guerrillas. Throughout the Anglo-American negotiations, however, the flow of capital, arms, and personnel was overwhelmingly to one side of the adversaries, the white minority. The food aid to Mozambique and Zimbabwean refugees was the only exception. The rhetoric in support of majority rule was given little material backing.

South Africa

In 1922 the white Rhodesians voted to remain separate from South Africa. Mainly of British origin, they wanted to protect themselves from Afrikaner nationalism. As a separate state they had the means to limit South African capital penetration. But South Africa has remained the dominant power in the region. Although the two economies did compete for labour for mines and agriculture, they became quite interlinked through trade, communication, and transport. Their dependent capitalist economies based on mining and agriculture and their racial division of labour created the same class interest for the rulers: industrial development based on racial discrimination isolated them by class and race from the majority of the people in Southern Africa.

The pragmatic response of South Africa to the Portuguese coup by promoting a negotiated settlement in Rhodesia must be analysed in the context of South Africa's role in the region. The gesture to convince Smith to negotiate with the Zimbabwean nationalists was in the context of South African support for Rhodesia: South Africa was the life-line for Rhodesia to fight sanctions and its major arms supplier. Mozambican President Samora Machel stated, 'South Africa supplied the oxygen that enabled the rebel regime to survive.'[54] As stated earlier, the regime never agreed to international sanctions and openly violated them, thereby providing the conduit for all other sanctions-breaking trade.

South African investment in Rhodesia was estimated at US$330 million for 1976 and $1.03 billion for 1979. This investment was concentrated in a very few transnational corporations such as Anglo-American, Johannesburg Consolidated Investments, and Messina Transvaal Development Corporation.[55] Anglo-American was by far the largest and controlled Rhodesian nickel, copper, and coal production as well as 70 percent of the total citrus fruit production. It was heavily involved in iron, steel, and ferrochrome and had extensive interests in sugar and forestry. It was the largest maize miller and food processor in the country.[56]

This capital investment in Rhodesia was supplemented by loans from South Africa to finance the war. The South African government provided badly needed funds as the Rhodesian GDP started to decline (1978: −3.9%; 1979: −.9%). The outstanding debt was about $300 million.[57] Although this capital transfer is not large (only 7 percent of the debt was external at independence), it was expedient to the war effort.

Co-ordination between South African and Rhodesian militaries was extensive. After the internal settlement which made Muzorewa a partner of Smith, Pieter W. Botha stated: 'South Africa, after consultation with the government of Zimbabwe-Rhodesia, has for some time now been looking to the protection of our interests as well as our vital lines of communication such as the rail links to Beit-bridge.'[58] In his work on the South African military, Richard Leonard has well documented the extent of the arms deliveries by South Africa to Rhodesia.[59] As one 'senior Rhodesian official' stated, South Africa gave all-out support to the Smith-Muzorewa government.[60]

By the time of the Lancaster House negotiations towards the end of 1979, South Africa had two battalions in Rhodesia under their own command at Fort Victoria.[61] The total number of South African troops was higher. Some served in the Rhodesian army, for one could serve without losing seniority after returning to the South African command. South African pilots were crucial to the war effort and flew many missions for the Rhodesians. According to some reports, South Africa sent 'a large number of "volunteer" pilots, gunners, and technicians together with a number of Alouette helicopters' to keep the counter-insurgency campaign operating.[62] Some were killed when Mozambique shot down their planes during raids into Mozambique. South African Mirage jets flew cover protection for the five Canberras that flew from Wankie to bomb ZIPRA forces in Angola; in addition, the planes had to stop for refuelling during the long mission and did so at Katimo Mulilo in South Africa.[63] The UN Unit Against Apartheid has fully documented South African violation of Angola's airspace.[64] These examples are simply suggestive of the co-ordination and support that South Africa offered the Rhodesian regime. As the guerrilla war escalated, South Africa contributed more personnel and equipment. They particularly increased their efforts after the internal settlement in March 1978 in order to sustain the Muzorewa/Smith axis.

Short of invading the country with the full force of the South African military, the South African regime provided essential economic, logistical, and military support to the Rhodesians. As the guerrilla war had more success, it was clear that South Africa would have to commit more and more military support. Bringing Muzorewa into power was an attempt to end the war by simply ignoring the popular support for the guerrillas. When it did not work, the British-American-South African governments supported the gamble for 'free and fair elections' including the Patriotic Front. One reason for their willingness to gamble was this ability of South Africa to intervene in support of Muzorewa. Both the military attacks against Zambia and Mozambique and the election campaign had intensive involvement by the South Africans. South Africa was a key actor in the strategy that military and campaign support would be sufficient to elect Muzorewa.

The major question that emerges is how could South Africa play this pivotal role in the support of Rhodesia when it had just been defeated militarily in Angola and had serious internal disruptions in 1976. Further, the government confronted its first major scandal in 1979 with the Muldergate exposures of misappropriation of the Ministry of Information funds. The buffer around the *laager* was smaller with the liberation of the Portuguese colonies; internal resistance was growing; and the government faced political and economic crises. How did South Africa muster the capacity for effective counter-revolutionary activity?

The answer can be found in the relations between South Africa and its Anglo-American allies. South Africa is strategically important to the Anglo-Americans; its supply of minerals and position along the Cape route make it vital to the defence of Western capital interests. The mineral dependence of the West has been played up by those who want to emphasise that the West cannot do without South Africa. For many of the minerals, there are alternative sources. Even so, the list of minerals, basic to the production of any advanced industrialised country, is impressive. Because the transnational corporations have gained high profits from cheap African labour and have, therefore, not fully developed other possible sources, radical cut-off of the supply from South Africa would require major readjustments in the Western economies.[65] Over 50 percent of the foreign investment in the $11 billion minerals industry is British; another 20 percent is American.[66]

Perhaps the most important British-American support for South Africa has been the build-up of its military-industrial complex through investment. Over 60 percent of the assets of banks in South Africa, about 90 percent of the oil refinery capacity, and 40 percent of the industrial capacity is directly owned by foreign capital, British and American being the most important by far. These linkages are well documented in many sources.[67] The point here is that with these interlocking economic and strategic interests, American and British capital do come to the aid of South Africa in time of crisis, for example, after Soweto. Production had already begun to decline before the uprisings, and they brought a further crisis of confidence. American capital bailed out the South Africans, just as British capital had after the Sharpeville massacre in 1960. Bank loans of several million dollars shored up the economy. The United States, while limiting aid to Mozambique and Angola for violation of 'human rights', secretly arranged a $464 million IMF loan for South Africa in 1977.[68]

The Americans and the British own almost 50 percent of the Anglo-American Corporation, one of the largest corporations in the world. It controls vast gold mines. The price of gold reached $840 per ounce in February 1980, reaping vast profits for the mines which only raised wages a few cents. For every $10 increase in the price of gold, it is estimated that the South African government receives about $242 million.[69]

The priority expenditure for these increased revenues has been defence spending, for external aggression and internal repression. South Africa has increased its defence budget threefold in the five years of Frontline State support for Zimbabwe from $933 million in

1974-1975 to $2.9 billion for 1979-1980. At the same time, the Defence Force almost doubled from 269,000 to 494,000.[70] The government is directly incorporating businesses into the security structure. One report stated that the Defence Force requested 'an undisclosed number of companies, including multinationals, to organise all-white military reserve units and store weapons and communications equipment at their own expense on company premises'.[71]

Britain and the United States, for the reasons discussed above, were constrained in their ability to intervene in Rhodesia. South Africa, on the other hand, contributed troops, weapons, and capital. Its capability was in part because of the willingness of the Anglo-Americans to loan and invest necessary capital during the economic crises in South Africa. The end of the Rhodesian conflict is too recent for documentation of the extent of American-British collaboration with South Africa for its military support of Rhodesia. But even without direct collaboration, South Africa would have found it much more difficult to offer the extensive support it did without the economic support it received from the Anglo-Americans.

Any thought by South African authorities for a full-scale invasion co-ordinated with a white Rhodesian coup was forestalled by the political acuity of Robert Mugabe. As the new Prime Minister, he did everything possible to assure the white minority that their interests would be respected. As Zimbabwe moves toward greater equity in the distribution of its resources, the state will come into greater conflict with these minority interests. As the internal strife escalates in South Africa, the apartheid regime will look for ways to 'preempt' guerrilla attacks. It is already staging such strikes against six (Angola, Botswana, Lesotho, Mozambique, Swaziland, Zimbabwe) of nine Southern African states in the Southern African Development Co-ordination Conference (see Chapter 8). For these reasons, there is no guarantee that South Africa will not invade Zimbabwe in the future.

The victory is not complete in Zimbabwe. The colonial political and economic legacy weighs heavily on the new state. There is a long struggle ahead for economic independence from the dominance of foreign capital. The struggle for political and economic transformations to give the people more control over their own lives is even longer. The key issue during the guerrilla struggle, land reform, is moving at a slow pace. More than five years after independence, banks, export-import trade, and basic industries remain controlled by the transnational corporations, while the 1983 IMF loan ($384.2 million) may provide further pressure to maintain the economic status quo by making it more 'efficient'. Further, endeavours for economic transformation might not succeed, because of external aggression. The next chapter analyses how the Frontline States, given their dependence on the powers that aided Rhodesia, were able to support this limited, but still consequential, victory of political independence for Zimbabwe.

Notes

1. Investment in Rhodesia by 'South African' firms is not entirely South African, however, for Anglo-American capital has fully penetrated the South African .economy. Many corporations with South African names are majority-owned by foreign capital. Colin Stoneman, ed., *Zimbabwe's Inheritance*, (London: Macmillan, 1981), p. 119.
2. Michael Bratton, 'Zimbabwe in the Making', *Southern Africa* (October, 1977), pp.6-8. Richard Carver, 'Frontline Plans Unified Strategy', *New African* (May, 1980).
3. René Lefort, 'Le Pouvoir au Zimbabwe', *Le Monde Diplomatique*, no. 314 (May 1980), p. 10.
4. John S. Saul, 'Zimbabwe: The Next Round', *Monthly Review* 32 (September 1980), p. 15.
5. Charles van Onselin, *Chibaro* (London: Pluto Press, 1976).
    Giovanni Arrighi, *The Political Economy of Rhodesia* (The Hague: Mouton, 1967).
    Robin Palmer, *Land and Racial Domination in Rhodesia* (Berkeley: University of California Press, London: Heinemann, 1977).
    Martin Loney, *Rhodesia: White Racism and Imperial Response* (Middlesex: Penguin, 1975).
6. The comparative prices of chrome from various sources reveal the desirability of Rhodesian chrome, the price of which was kept low by low wages to African miners.

Ferrochrome —	France	$1,356 per ton
	Japan	1,129 per ton
	South Africa	722 per ton
	Rhodesia	718 per ton
Chromite Ore —	USSR	$111 per ton
	Rhodesia	41 per ton

    Subcommittee on African Affairs, Committee on Foreign Relations, US Senate, 'Rhodesian Sanctions', (9-10 February 1977), pp. 74-75.
7. Roger Riddell, *From Rhodesia to Zimbabwe: The Land Question* (London: Catholic Institute for International Relations, 1978), p. 7.
8. Zimbabwe Information Group, *Bulletin*, nos. 5 and 6 (December, 1977-January 1978).

9. Duncan G. Clarke, *Foreign Companies and International Investment in Zimbabwe* (London: Catholic Institute for International Relations, March 1980), pp. 50-57.
10. René Lefort, op. cit., p. 10.
11. John Gilmurray, Roger Riddell, David Sanders, *From Rhodesia to Zimbabwe: The Struggle for Health* (London: Catholic Institute for International Relations, 1979), pp. 22-26.
12. Stanley B. Greenberg, *Race and State in Capitalist Development* (New Haven: Yale University Press, 1980), p. 406.
13. John S. Saul, 'The Dialectic of Class and Tribe', *The State and Revolution in Eastern Africa* (New York: Monthly Review Press, 1979), pp. 394 and 413.
14. In 1972, before the war seriously hurt the economy, after-tax earnings of 51 foreign manufacturing companies were $36.1 million, a 24.3 percent return on net asset values. Although net asset values are usually reported at a low level, the return on investment was considered excellent relative to other countries. D. G. Clarke, op. cit., p. 89.
15. University of Eduardo Mondlane, Centre for African Studies, 'Zimbabwe: Notes and Reflection on the Zimbabwe Situation', mimeo (Maputo, 1977), p. 4.
16. Lonrho filed a breach of contract for £100 million against the oil firms on 17 January 1978 stating they had violated Lonrho's rights over oil transport by avoiding the Beira-Salisbury pipeline to deliver oil.
17. Martin Bailey and Bernard Rivers, 'Rhodesia: Sanctions Breakers' Secrets Revealed', *New Statesman* (30 June 1978).
    Martin Bailey, *Oilgate: The Sanctions Scandal* (London: Coronet Books, 1979).
    The Bingham Report, *Report on the Supply of Petroleum and Petroleum Products to Rhodesia* (London: HMSO, 1978).
18. Reginald Cowper, Minister of Defence, had to resign in February 1977 after protests from the business community against conscripting men aged 38-50 years. *Daily Telegraph* (London), 14 February 1977.
19. Standard Bank of England, *Economic Bulletin* (November 1979). By 1979, British immigration into Rhodesia had largely stopped because of the war.
20. *New York Times* 15 January 1978.
21. Michael Bratton, op. cit., p. 7.
22. University of Eduardo Mondlane, op. cit., pp. 7-8.
23. This report became the basis for economic planning of the new government of Zimbabwe. Ibbo Mandaza, 'Imperialism, the Frontline States and the Zimbabwe Problem', paper presented at seminar, University of Dar es Salaam, 16 November 1979, p. 21.
24. Martin Loney, op. cit., p. 165.
25. OECD, *Economic Surveys: United Kingdom* (February 1980), p. 26.
26. René Lefort, op. cit., p. 10.
27. Economist Intelligence Unit, *Quarterly Economic Review: Rhodesia* (4th Quarter 1977), p. 3.
28. *New York Times* 28 April 1979.
29. Anthony Crosland quoted by John Saul, 1977, op. cit., p. 13.
30. 'Allies in Empire', *Africa Today* 17, no. 4 (July-August 1970).
    Mohamed A. El-Khawas, 'US Foreign Policy Towards Angola and Mozambique. 1960-1974', *Current Bibliography on African Affairs* 8, no. 3 (1975).
    René Lemarchand, ed., *American Policy in Southern Africa: The Stakes and the*

    Stance (Washington, D.C.: University Press of America, 1978).

    John Marcum, 'The Politics of Indifference: Portugal and Africa, A Case Study in American Foreign Policy', *Issue* 2, no. 3 (Fall 1972).

    William Minter, *Portuguese Africa and the West* (New York: Monthly Review, 1972).

31. This point is a major foreign policy debate within the US government. Some officials state that the only way to reduce the Cuban presence is to cease South African bombing of SWAPO camps and Angolan villages. South Africa bombs southern Angola to deter incursions by SWAPO, the liberation force fighting for independence, into Namibia. Other American officials insist that Cubans must leave immediately, no matter what threat South Africa poses. In the debate, the fact is rarely raised that the US has approximately 40,000 troops in South Korea — almost twice the number of Cubans in Angola — and does not claim that South Korea is not 'sovereign' because of the US presence. In addition, the American commander in Korea can command and deploy Korean troops, a power not permitted Cuban commanders by the MPLA.

32. James Turner and Sean Gervasi, 'The American Economic Future in Southern Africa', *Journal of Southern African Affairs* 3, no. 1 (1978), p. 87.

33. The Secretary of State, Press Conference, Bureau of Public Affairs, Department of State, Washington, D.C. (11 September 1976), p. 2.

34. Mohamed A. El-Khawas and Barry Cohen, eds., *NSSM 39 — The Kissinger Study of Southern Africa* (Westport, Connecticut: Lawrence Hill and Co., 1976), p. 84.

35. 'US Africa Policy 1980', *Africa News* (13 October 1980), p. 3.

36. Ibid.

37. David Martin and Phyllis Johnson, *The Struggle for Zimbabwe*, p. 270.

38. Julius L. Katz, Assistant Secretary for Economic and Business Affairs, Department of State, testimony for Subcommittee on African Affairs, Committee on Foreign Relations, US Senate, 'Rhodesian Sanctions',(9-10 February 1977), p. 75.

39. Subcommittee on Africa, Committee on International Relations, House of Representatives, 'The Rhodesian Sanctions Bill, H.R. 1746' (24 February 1977), p. 46.

40. Subcommittee on Africa, Committee on International Relations, House of Representatives, 'US Policy Toward Rhodesia' (8 June 1977), pp. 17-60. Ibid., 'Political Developments in Southern Rhodesia' (4 October 1977).

41. Donald Easum, Former Assistant Secretary of State for Africa, 'US Policy Toward Southern Africa', *Issue* 5, no. 3 (Fall 1975), p. 70.

42. A report prepared for the UN Security Council charged that NATO aircraft had been supplied to Rhodesia in large quantities since 1975, increasing five-fold the combat capacity of the Rhodesian Air Force. Sean Gervasi, 'Report on Clandestine Aircraft Transfers to Rhodesian Air Force 1976-78' (February 1979).

43. See a comprehensive list of 'Reported Arms Deliveries to Rhodesia', *Fire Force Exposed* (London: Anti-Apartheid Movement, 1979). Basic sources used for the list are as follows:

    International Peace Research Institute, *Arms Trade Registers* (annual).

    P. Lock and H. Wulf, *Register of Arms Production in Developing Countries* (Hamburg: Arbeitsgruppe Ruestung and Unterentwicklung, 1977).

    Sean Gervasi, 1979, op. cit.

    Western Massachusetts Association of Concerned African Scholars, eds., *US Military Involvement in Southern Africa* (Boston: South End Press, 1978).

44. *International Bulletin,* 14 March 1977.
    Tanzania Daily News, 18 December 1978.
45. *Facts and Reports,* 25 January 1979.
46. Relevant sections of the US Code are the following:
    US Section 959   (A) No enlistment, recruitment in foreign forces.
    958   No commission as officer in foreign forces.
    951   Recruitment is act of foreign agent.
47. Subcommittee on Africa, Committee on International Relations, House of Representatives, 'US Policy Toward Southern Africa' (3 March, 1977).
    When Congressman Charles Diggs asked directly how many Americans were fighting in Rhodesia, no reply whatsoever was given by the State Department, p. 50.
    Ibid., 'US Policy Toward Rhodesia' (8 June 1977), pp. 9-13.
    Michael Parks, 'Rhodesia Hires ex-GI's, Britons as Mercenaries', Baltimore *Sun* (20 May, 1976).
    Richard Lobban, 'American Mercenaries in Rhodesia', *Journal of Southern African Affairs* 3, no. 3 (July 1978).
48. John Stockwell, *In Search of Enemies* (New York: W.W. Norton and Co., 1978).
49. Report of a sworn statement by David Bufkin, a known mercenary recruiter, that the CIA supported his efforts for Rhodesia, *The Washington Post,* 26 December 1980.
50. USAID, *Development Needs and Opportunities for Co-operation in Southern Africa,* 1979.
51. Sean Gervasi, Ann Seidman, Immanuel Wallerstein, David Wiley, 'Why We Said No to AID', *Issue* 7, no. 4 (Winter 1977), pp. 35–37.
52. David Martin reports that Rhodesian security forces admitted, after the independence of Zimbabwe, that they did attack missions (with their faces blackened to discredit the guerrillas). David Martin and Phyllis Johnson, op. cit., pp. 281–282.
53. Michael Beaubien, 'Inadequate, Infrequent and Insufficient', *Southern Africa* (January 1980), pp. 7–9.
    'The Rhodesian Massacre', *New York Times,* 25 February 1977.
54. Samora Machel, Speech in Maputo, 14 February 1981, quoted in Mozambican Information Agency (AIM), *Bulletin,* no. 56 (March 1981), p. 3.
55. Duncan G. Clarke, op. cit., p. 133.
56. Ibid., pp. 66–69.
57. *Financial Times Survey* (London), 'Zimbabwe', 22 April 1980.
58. *Los Angeles Times,* 1 December 1979.
59. Richard Leonard, op. cit.
60. *New York Times,* 28 April 1979.
61. *Los Angeles Times,* 1 December 1979.
62. Richard Leonard, op. cit., p. 25.
63. *Africa,* no. 92 (April 1979).
64. Report of the International Mission of Inquiry, 'Acts of Aggression Perpetrated by South Africa against the People's Republic of Angola (June 1979–July 1980)', United Nations Centre against Apartheid, January, 1981.
65. Congressional Research Service, Library of Congress, *Imports of Minerals from South Africa by the US and OECD Countries,* prepared for Subcommittee on Africa, Foreign Relations Committee, US Senate, 1980. This document

concludes that the US has the capability to cope with the cutoff of minerals from South Africa if necessary.

Subcommittee on Mines and Mining, Committee on Interior and Insular Affairs, House of Representatives, 'Sub-Sahara, Africa: Its Role in Critical Mineral Needs of the Western World', 1980.

Michael Tanzer, *The Race for Resources: Continuing Struggles over Minerals and Fuels* (New York: Monthly Review, 1980).

Report of Study Commission on US Policy Toward Southern Africa (Rockefeller Report), *South Africa: Time Running Out* (Berkeley: University of California Press, 1981), pp. 318–322.

66. 'Southern Africa: Key to US Security', *New African* (May 1981), p. 44.

67. Simon Clarke, *Changing Patterns of International Investment in South Africa and the Divestment Campaign* (London: Anti-Apartheid Movement, 1978). This source gives excellent tables reproduced from South African government sources.

Ann Seidman and Neva S. Makgetla, *Outposts of Monopoly Capitalism* (Westport, CN: Lawrence Hill and Co., 1980) and personal communication with Ann Seidman, 12 May 1983.

Subcommittee on Africa, Committee on Foreign Affairs, House of Representatives, 'US Business Involvement in Southern Africa', Parts 1–3 (May–July 1971; September–December 1971; March–July 1973).

Dick Clark, Committee on Foreign Relations, US Senate, 'US Corporate Interests in South Africa' (January 1978).

68. For analysis of role of US capital after Soweto, see Simon Clarke, op. cit., pp. 16–21.

James Morrell and David Gisselquist, 'How the IMF Slipped $464 million to South Africa', Washington D.C.: Centre for International Policy, January 1978. An additional $1.1 billion loan from the IMF was awarded to South Africa in 1982.

69. *South* (September 1980), p. 69.

Vella Pillay, *The Role of Gold in the Economy of Apartheid South Africa* (New York: United Nations Centre against Apartheid, March 1981), p. 3.

70. Richard Leonard, op. cit., p. 13.

71. Jennifer Davis, 'The Roots of Total Strategy', *Southern Africa* (January–February 1981), pp. 10–12.

CHAPTER 6

Relative State Autonomy: Revolutionary Support For Zimbabwean Liberation

Introduction

During the period of colonial rule, foreign capital penetrated each of the Frontline States and became dominant in each political economy. Commodity exchange and capital financing are still predominantly from the West. Given the extent of control of Western capital in these economies, it is difficult to explain the degree of the political confrontation by these states toward the Western powers. To understand the ability of the Frontline States to support the independence of Zimbabwe, one must look at the social formations of the respective states. It must not be assumed that the dominant class runs each state; the relationship between the state and social classes must be investigated. In specific instances, under specific conditions, the state may act against certain interests of the dominant class. It is these instances and conditions which will be investigated in this and the next chapters. Each of the five states had different expressions of relative state autonomy, and these differences affected their roles in the Frontline. Using the theories of relative state autonomy, the two chapters analyse the ideological and material bases of the successful Frontline policy — and clarify the limitations on that success.

The diversity of the Frontline States seems to abrogate any idea of comparison among them. The five had very different colonial histories, different levels of development of their productive forces, and consequently, different relations of production. Some of these differences caused antagonisms within the Frontline. However, similarities in their social formations remain, and a comparison among the five will elucidate the reasons for the fundamental congruence of their policies for the liberation of Zimbabwe.

Each Frontline State experienced a long period of colonialism during which the colonial regime not only legalised white supremacy, but also succeeded in exacerbating ethnic differences among the Africans. As will be shown in the next sections, resistance to colonial repression was persistent; colonial rule did not penetrate certain areas in each of the five states until the 20th century because of this resistance. Yet it was not until the modern independence movements that the opposition united at a national level against the colonial administration. The post-World War II independence movements relied very much on the appeal to nationalism to unite the people across ethnic divisions, and this broad appeal was the first transformation necessary for the transition to political and economic independence. For example, Frelimo's goals were not just to oust the repressive Portuguese regime but also to transform social relations of production. Both those political and economic struggles required, first, a change in the dominant ideology. Frelimo stated that recruits arriving in the training camps in Tanzania came as members of a particular ethnic group . . . but they left as Mozambicans. This national perspective was the basis of unity and direction for the political-economic transformation. Further, the nationalist education did not only occur in the camps. With each guerrilla unit was a political commissar whose role in leading discussions about contradictions and antagonisms arising in the daily manoeuvres was considered as important as the role of the military commander. Finally, the war did not begin until two years of political education among the peasants had been completed.The MPLA similarly put political understanding as a priority over military training. For Botswana, Tanzania, and Zambia, three states which attained independence peacefully, national unity was equally important. Organising in various co-operative movements, associations, and unions, the movements were anti-colonial and anti-racist in promoting majority rule.

This nationalist appeal against external domination did not end with the raising of the flags of independence nor was it delimited by national boundaries. As stated in Chapter 2, Frelimo and the MPLA had long contact with ZANU and ZAPU when the liberation groups were all in exile. After achieving independence, Tanzania immediately aided Frelimo. The Botswanan leaders appealed to Britain for independence, as did Zambia, in order to remove themselves from white settlers' rule that extended from the Cape to the Copperbelt. These nationalist traditions have long and strong histories. The five Frontline States shared the perspective that struggle against racism did not end at their borders.

This ideological cohesion was tested during the second war of liberation in Angola, when Presidents Kaunda and Nyerere insisted on unity among the three parties to take power from the Portuguese. When the unity split open, Kaunda supported UNITA; Machel, and later Nyerere, backed the MPLA. It was also the year (1975) of great tension and serious obstruction of the armed struggle in Zimbabwe. When South Africa invaded Angola on the side of UNITA, that nationalist group lost all credibility for the Frontline. UNITA's mobilisation of peasants and its broad appeal were suspect from the moment they requested South African aid. The struggle against racism once again became the prime target, as the Frontline reaffirmed a majority government in Angola — or Zimbabwe — or Namibia — could not be beholden to South Africa to attain power. The majority government needed power to take legal control of the state and the economy. These basic goals were modest — but fundamental to the ideological cohesion in the struggle for Zimbabwe.

Their perspective was not simply altruistic. A strong national ideology provides unity and cohesion within each polity. Appealing to nationalism could unite the producers not only for independence but for economic development. The strength of the ideology is illustrated in Zambia and Tanzania: repeated appeals to the producers to work harder or to accept the inadequacy of consumer items were made in the name of the liberation stuggle. The populist appeal identified the enemy as external; only with the independence of Zimbabwe could disruptions in production or in the delivery of consumer goods cease.

During colonialism, indigenous industries were destroyed as emphasis was placed on agricultural and mineral production for export to the European factories. As several theorists have pointed out, the process of underdevelopment varied from colony to colony 'according to the vigour with which the colonial state was pressed to assist capitalists, according to timing of major expansions of commodity production, according to the extent to which pre-colonial social relations of production became embedded within the administrative apparatus of the colonial state'.[1] In spite of the differences, which will be discussed in the next sections, the underdevelopment of the productive forces left the post-colonial states with mixed modes of production. Foreign capital had penetrated the economies, but some peasant production remained at the subsistence level, *relatively* untouched by the capitalist market forces. The mixed modes of production provided important means for resistance against the dominance of foreign capital.

In addition to the mixed modes of production, none of the five states had an African national bourgeoisie at independence. Ownership of production and appropriation of capital (on a large scale) were reserved for the white settlers, foreign capital, and the colonial state. No African bourgeoisie was allowed to form. At independence, therefore, the state became the major means available for appropriation and accumulation of surplus. This role was expressed differently in each of the five Frontline States (some strengthened national capital, and others blocked its formation), but each of the five used the state to delimit the interests of foreign capital. Since independence each state has promoted state intervention in some major economic sectors to circumscribe control of production by both foreign capital and from fractions of small local capital (e.g., commercial traders). State intervention was viewed as a way to (1) co-ordinate the overall development of the productive forces, (2) increase production for local needs, and (3) direct the allocation of surplus. The independent states have tried to establish a broader base, not only of production, but also of the allocation of surplus. Each state has redirected surplus back to the producers by providing free health care, free education, better marketing facilities, and better water supplies. Food crop, instead of cash crop, production has been a priority for all five states. Therefore, each has increased state participation in agriculture with goals of increasing production, directing distribution, and subsidising staple food prices.

Other capitalist states in the periphery also intervene in the economy; indeed, one similarity of peripheral economies is the necessity to use the power of the state to direct and centralise development plans. What distinguishes the five Frontline States as a group is, first, that each state set priorities that were directed to improving the quality of life of their citizens. There is no Brazil — which had levels of economic growth that were termed a 'miracle' while infant mortality and malnutrition of the majority of the people increased — in the group. Second, each of the Frontline States has taken concrete steps within its own domestic economy to limit the hegemony of foreign capital within its borders. For some, the steps were nationalist and did not challenge the capitalist relations of production (Botswana, Tanzania, Zambia); for others, the steps were part of a revolutionary transformation to create socialism (Angola, Mozambique). These differences will be discussed fully in the next sections. But the point here is that in the group there is no Zaire or

Malawi or Bolivia which used state intervention simply to facilitate the penetration of foreign capital into the productive sectors of the economy. Finally, state interventions in the Frontline were variable in the success of attaining the goals (again, to be discussed shortly). During the time of the Frontline support for Zimbabwe, state intervention in all five was an attempt to *limit* hegemony of foreign capital and to *redistribute* surplus back to the producers. These two shared goals are significant. They distinguish the Frontline from other peripheral capitalist states.

It is suggested here that without these experiences in attempting to control foreign capital, based on their own anti-colonial struggles, the alliance would not have been possible. The support for the Zimbabweans to sustain their struggle for control of the state apparatuses grew out of the specific historical and material conditions of each of the Frontline States. Through their own struggles to transform their own post-colonial economies, the Frontline States could better ratify the goals of the Zimbabweans. Reciprocally, their historical experiences helped to inform and develop Zimbabwean nationalist goals.

This interaction is most fully expressed in the states' relation to South Africa. All five want to reduce the subordination of the Southern African regional economy to that of South Africa. In order to succeed they needed a free and independent Zimbabwe, which is central to the region not only geographically, but also economically. As the most industrialised state among them, with an agricultural surplus and extensive transport facilities, the Frontline States saw Zimbabwe as the lynchpin to their own struggle against both racism and dominance of foreign capital in the region.

These generalities remain vague and idealistic unless based on the historical specificities of each state, and one of the purposes here is to examine each political economy to analyse the complexities which the general comparisons tend to obscure. The following country sections will analyse the historical specificity of each state in order to understand whether relative autonomy was achieved by each. But first, it is necessary to clarify the theories of relative state autonomy.

Introduction To The Theories of Relative State Autonomy

Formulations about the position and role of the state in a social formation is one of the most underdeveloped theories of Marxism and is, therefore, highly controversial. Perhaps one of the reasons for the lack of attention to the state until recently is that Marx himself infrequently addressed the problem of the state. Engels contends that his relative neglect is not because the state is not important for analysis of relations of production but because attention needed to be first directed to the economy; Engels summarises as follows:

> If Barth alleges that we *altogether* deny that the political, etc., reflections of the economic movement in their turn exert any effect upon the movement itself, he is simply tilting at windmills. He should only look at Marx's *Eighteenth Brumaire* which deals almost exclusively with the *particular* part played by political struggles and events, of course within their *general* dependence upon economic conditions. Or *Kapital* . . . the section on the history of the bourgeoisie (Chapter XXIV). And why do we fight for the political dictatorship of the proletariat if political power is economically impotent? Force (that is, state power) is also an economic power.[2] [Emphasis and parentheses in original.]

Within the growing contemporary controversy about the role of the state, however, there are several fundamental bases of agreement. First, the capitalist mode of production is characterised by the separation of economic from political dominance in a particular social formation. With the feudal mode of production, political hegemony corresponded exactly with economic control of production; the lord of the manor not only provided land as a means of production but also security from outside invasions and adjudicatory authority to resolve disputes. Extraction of surplus was directly dependent on control over this coercive authority. In the capitalist mode of production, the relation between economic control and political hegemony is more obscure. A legal authority, separate from both the employer and the worker, is available for adjudication. According to Engels, the origins of the modern state are in the development of modes of production with antagonistic classes; the state, 'apparently standing above society', is to maintain the limits of order.[3] The means of production and the means of coercion are separate. This separation of economic control from political control gives the appearance of a neutral state, ready to resolve conflicts among classes. The appearance of neutrality is challenged by Marxist theorists as a mystification of the class base of the state.

A second agreement among Marxists is that the state is necessary to preserve the overall capitalist relations of production. It is the state that establishes the legal terms of contracts with free labour and the rights of property ownership. The state regulates labour as a commodity form and promotes the international transferability of another commodity, capital.[4] Marx and Engels were direct in affirming that the state emerges from class struggle and represents the dominant class. Most simply stated, '. . . the bourgeoisie has at last, since the establishment of Modern Industry and of the world-market, conquered for itself, in the modern representative State, exclusive political sway. The executive of the modern State is but a committee for managing the common affairs of the whole bourgeoisie'.[5] The state is not neutral, but serves the interests of the bourgeoisie in preserving the capitalist mode of production.

Marx is more careful in other statements, however, to show that the state is not a simple instrument of the dominant class. The oft-quoted aphorism given above does not summarise for all historical instances the relation of the dominant class with the state. The relations of production — the relations among classes — do influence the relationship between rulers and ruled, but the form that the state may take is problematic:

> It is always the direct relationship of the owners of the conditions of production to the direct producers . . . which reveals the innermost secret, the hidden basis of the entire social structure, and with it the political form of the relation of sovereignty and dependence. In short, the corresponding specific form of the state. This does not prevent the same economic basis — the same from the standpoint of its main conditions — due to innumerable different empirical circumstances, natural environment, racial relations, external historical influences, etc., from showing infinite variations and gradations in appearance, which can be ascertained only by analysis of the empirically given circumstances.[6]

The state reflects the relations of production, but several forms of a state may serve — be appropriate for — one mode of production. Different periods, different histories of national capital accumulation, will have different state forms. And this is where the controversy begins. Because the state is not simply an instrument of the class in control of production, the theoretical controversy is over specification of both (1) the conditions in which the state may have relative autonomy from the dominant class and (2) the circumstances which limit that autonomy.

Before entering the controversy over relative state autonomy, it is necessary to clarify first the meaning of the state. Engels, in discussing the origins of the state, distinguishes it from other social institutions by (1) the aggregation of its members on a territorial basis; (2) its monopoly as a 'public force' over the means of coercion; and (3) its public power of taxation and borrowing.[7] In *The 18th Brumaire of Louis Bonaparte*, Marx specifies the state institution as comprising the executive power, including the bureaucracy and the military. The neutralised parliament — immobilised by class feuding — left the executive free to promote its own policy, with the help of the bureaucracy and the military. The state is the civil and military bureaucracy, headed by an executive, in this case, Louis Bonaparte. In the *Civil War in France*, in an account of the history of state formation, the state organs also included the clergy and judiciary: 'The centralised state power, with its ubiquitous organs of standing army, police, bureaucracy, clergy, and judicature . . . originates from the days of absolute monarchy.'[8] In *State and Revolution*, Lenin emphasises the importance of the coercive institutions of the state machine: bureaucracy and military.[9] Depending on the historical instances, the parliament is included as part of the central state (p. 260) or is excluded (p. 271).

Poulantzas, who has perhaps done the most to spur the contemporary discussion over the state, tends to leave the definition of the concept rather vague; it is referred to variously as the 'political organisation of hegemony' or the 'condensation of a balance of forces'.[10] Other theorists define it simply as an organisation that cannot be reduced to class forces,[11] or as a set of apparatuses between and within which there are struggles.[12]

For this study, the definition will be based on those of Marx and Lenin for the modern state: the state comprises both the civil and the military bureaucracy and the government (mainly executive) which controls that bureaucracy.[13] For the states concerned, foreign policy formulation is the prerogative of the executive; the legislatures have only a weak power of review. This is not to say that the policy is made in a vacuum; especially in a war situation, the policy requires support from broad segments of the population. The definition simply designates the centralised political authority which is also the *locus* of power for foreign policy.

In order to avoid a reductionist conception of the state — as it is neither an instrument of dominant class forces nor an institution determined solely by economic structures — it is important to keep the state analytically separate from class forces. In that way, one can investigate where on the continuum a particular state operates — between autonomy from and service to the dominant class at a particular historical instance. The relation of the state to the class structure is not here treated as a given, but as a dynamic interaction that requires analysis.[14] As a structure which is constrained by economic relations, but which has a monopoly over the 'legitimate' means of force to preserve public order among conflicting classes, the state takes on a logic of its own. It is, therefore, necessary to demonstrate the class nature of the state for a specific social formation. For this study, a state is relatively autonomous when it acts against the perceived or actual interests of the dominant class.[15]

This *structural autonomy* is to be distinguished from *instrumental autonomy* which is freedom from direct demands (for or against specific policy formulations) by dominant interests or class fractions. Instrumental autonomy is not problematic for most theorists, for rarely does a state follow exactly each whim of the dominant class. It is the question of whether and under what conditions the state may actually *oppose* interests of the dominant class which is much debated. For this study, relative state autonomy refers to this structural autonomy — unless otherwise specified.

This definitional clarification does not close the debate, but rather specifies it. Bertell Ollman reminds us:

> What is important is to avoid the confusion that results from thinking that there is only one debate when there are really several . . . The widespread debate among Marxists over the relative autonomy of the state usually goes on at cross purposes because people involved do not sufficiently distinguish . . . whether the state is relatively autonomous from the ruling capitalist class, or from the economic requirements of capitalism, or from other alienated social relations, etc. As a matter of fact, there is a case to be made for relative autonomy within each of these perspectives . . .[16]

Bob Jessop also defines different kinds of autonomy.[17] As in most theoretical controversies, the debate begins with the definitions of the major concept(s). This definition of structural autonomy specifies a particular meaning so that the debate can focus more on the *conditions* for relative state autonomy, which can then be elaborated.

Finally, it is necessary to clarify the definition of dominant class.

Although the theorists differ in emphasis,[18] many agree with the perspective of this study that nation-states and their national class configurations cannot be analysed as isolated entities:

> The concreteness of the particular nation state and its economic form determination is to be explained in terms of the particular historic circumstances and preconditions under which the various total national capital develop. Of these factors a dominant role must be assigned to position within the world market context . . . [This concreteness] in turn played a decisive part in the determination of the particular pattern of development of the productive forces, of *class relations*, and last but not least, *the specific configuration of the state apparatus*, its functions and its perception of its function as much as its position in the context of class society.[19] [Emphasis mine.]

As argued in Chapter 4, the penetration of international capital is integral to state and class configuration in the periphery. Under colonialism, foreign capital could control the peripheral state by influencing the colonial office in the centre country. With political independence, direct political control is more difficult. Yet foreign capital is often integrated into the peripheral economy enough to become the dominant class or fraction thereof: 'Insofar as imperialist forces act, they operate within the class formation and cannot be conceptualised as the impersonal forces of the market; but rather they must be marked as part of the *internal* class alignments.'[20] The dominant class refers to those who own or control the means of production, and an important fraction of that class is often foreign capital.

Conditions Of Relative State Autonomy

The conditions in which a state may gain relative autonomy emerge from the dynamic nature of the capitalist mode of production. As stated earlier, the role of the capitalist state is to reproduce the *general* social relations of production. The state defends the interest of the dominant sectors as a whole, yet conflicts arise between the interests of specific capital and the general requirements of the total class:[21]

> The contradiction between the general social power into which capital develops, on the one hand, and the private power of the individual capitalists over these social conditions of production,

on the other, becomes ever more irreconcilable, and yet contains the solution of the problem, because it implies at the same time the transformation of the conditions of production into general, common, social, conditions.[22]

The state, in reproducing 'the general social power', tries to resolve the contradictions among specific capitals (but really only defers them to a later time). The individual capitals in competition with each other vary according to the development of the capitalist mode of production: monopoly vs. competitive capital, industry vs. agriculture, agribusiness vs. independent farming, craft industries vs. mass production industries.[23] Some theorists contend that these divergent interests, as different expressions of private control over production, could result in anarchy of competition without the state to regulate the general interest of capital over the dominated classes.[24] For example, Poulantzas has described the early days of fascism in Italy and Germany and the 'crisis of dictatorships' of Portugal, Spain, and Greece as specific historical instances of intensified competition among fractions of capital. This competition weakens the capitalist class in relation to the dominated classes, and the state gains relative autonomy.[25]

One general interest of capital is to maintain the reserve army of labour, and the state in advanced capitalist countries has assumed the role as guarantor of this reserve army.[26] Social services, paid for by the state, not by individual capital, are necessary for the reproduction of labour. Education and health subsidies are important costs born by the state. In addition. welfare, unemployment compensation, and retirement benefits help sustain the reserve army of the unemployed with maximum political stability.[27] These economic concessions, however, may have a negative effect for the dominant class or even eliminate a fraction of it. Some segments of the dominant class may be conscious of their long-term interests and tolerate or promote the state's role in social consumption.[28] Another condition of relative autonomy is the need for the state to make these economic concessions to the dominated classes, against specific interests of capital, in order to preserve the social conditions of capitalist production. The state cannot be a simple instrument of individual capital and at the same time fulfil its functions to reproduce the general social relations; Engels summarises as follows:

It is the interaction of two unequal forces; on the one hand, the economic movement, on the other, *the new political power, which strives for as much independence as possible*, and which having once been established, *is endowed with a movement of its own.*[29] [Emphasis mine.]

Relative state autonomy is most probable when the mode of production itself is in question. Marx attributed the rise of Louis Bonaparte as a strong executive to the inability of any one class to dominate. Capitalism was still weak in France, for production was still centred on the individual peasants; the capitalist class was divided between the new industrialists and the landed aristocracy; the workers had been defeated. In *The Origin of the Family, Private Property and the State*, Engels refers to periods when warring classes balance each other so that the state acquires a certain degree of independence. He cites the absolute monarchies of the 17th and 18th centuries, the Bonapartism of the First and Second Empires in France and the Bismarck regime in Germany.[30] Lenin adds the Kerensky government to the list.[31] When no one class can assert its hegemony over the state, it can take on a relative autonomy from the contending classes in determining the future structure of the social formation.

Today, in peripheral states, the mode of production may also be indeterminant because it is mixed. As stated earlier, the penetration of capital does not automatically end the pre-capitalist modes of production, for the transition to capitalism is dynamic. In most post-colonial states, capitalist modes of production are dominant, but pre-capitalist modes still exist. Some of the dominated classes still produce primarily in the pre-capitalist sector and therefore, are not as restrained by capitalist relations of production (e.g., no dependency on wage labour). They can use their subsistence base to resist the controls of capitalist relations. With these mixed modes of production, the structure of the social formation is less determinant, permitting greater autonomy to state initiative.

The mode of production may be in question because it is openly challenged by revolutionary forces. The state takes on an originative role and creates new social relations of production because the former ones are under attack and the nature of the new ones emerge from the political struggle. Zeitlin has emphasised the importance of the state in this transition: 'In every historical transition between modes of production, the effective deployment of state power is critical, but in none more than revolutionary transformations.'[32] Throughout Marx's writing, the political struggle takes on prime importance in the revolutionary transition in destroying the old relations of production and setting up the new ('. . . the overthrow of the existing ruling power and the dissolution of existing social relationships . . . is a political act.'[33]). For example, in Southern Africa, petty bourgeois elements allying with the subordinate classes have challenged openly the dominance of foreign capital protected by a white settler state. When the settlers are defeated, the mobilised, organised peasants/workers/petty bourgeoisie begin to transform the relations of production. Such a process is dynamic and gradual; the revolutionary transformation may not be successful for many reasons. During the process, however, the state gains relative autonomy from a fraction of the dominant class, foreign capital, which still maintains leverage over the economy.

The dominant class may also be weakened by a general crisis of capitalism, such as a depression or a major war. The current crisis of advanced capitalism, stagflation at home with lower production and high inflation, increases international competition among the capitalists. This competition has been expressed especially in the rivalry over cheap mineral resources and market outlets. Advanced capitalism is dependent on the minerals in peripheries such as Southern Africa; the peripheral states can use this competition to weaken foreign capitalist interests. Peripheral states can take advantage of the crisis in capitalism to pursue their own interests.[34] In response to this competition and to the challenges from national classes, foreign capital becomes willing to enter partnerships with peripheral states to minimise the cost of investment. Returns on investment and even control of production are negotiated by commitment from the host state to build infrastructure and supply a stable labour force. Bringing the post-colonial states into partnership reduces the costs to foreign capital but also restrains its dominance. In addition, the advanced capitalist state is restrained by fiscal crises from acting to protect overseas capital investment. Direct intervention, or policing investments abroad, is used only as a last resort because of cost and possible political instability at home. This process allows the state in the periphery to gain relative autonomy.

When both the national bourgeoisie and the working class are relatively weak and immature, the capitalist state may adopt the aims of industrialisation as its own: 'The autonomised state provides the conditions for the necessary modernisation of society when no extant class is capable of carrying out this imperative under its own political power.'[35] The state promotes national economic development to serve its own needs. Under Bonaparte the state promoted modernisation, in part, for its own aggrandisement, through military aggression. Economic development may also increase the resource base of the state. The weak bourgeoisie is content to concede the modernising role to the state as long as private profits are left alone. The relatively autonomous Bismarckian state in Germany promoted this type of modernisation from the top. This policy, however, quickly delimits state autonomy, for an industrialising state can increase the strength and size of the bourgeoisie which will quickly try to assert its dominance. The bourgeoisie is able to assert its interests over the landed aristocracy and/or merchant capital to gain its place as the dominant and ruling class.

Finally, the state serves its own interests by managing the concessions to the working class. Aiding in the reproduction of labour (education, health care, etc.) sustains the capitalist mode of production, but also promotes the legitimacy of the state. The strength of the state depends not only on its economic power in relation to other states, but also on internal political stability. The economic concessions render labour more acquiescent and promote political stability. In addition, in response to agitation by subordinate classes, the state commands resources to try to coopt segments of the opposition. They may be incorporated into the state committees or employment even into lower levels of management of the corporations. Political concessions such as universal suffrage or local government control enhance the economic concessions.[36]

The economic and political resources do not destroy the class struggle, however. Class struggles clearly influence the form a state takes, from democratic republican to authoritarian. Each social investment conceded by the state is a victory for the subordinate classes, even if they do not succeed in changing the economic structures.

The state may try to assert its own interests, such as guaranteeing stability or maintaining its tax base with 'full employment' policies, by allying with the dominated classes.[37] In this way, the state gains a power base to use against the dominant class. But this challenge would probably be quite temporary, or more probable, occur when the state is in transition. This challenge would tend to coalesce the dominant class which would then assert its control over the state.[38] In an alliance with the subordinate classes, the state would have to move to modify the social relations of production, and it is these structural constraints which most seriously limit relative state autonomy. In a revolutionary transition, however, the state can try to use its new power base in the dominated class as a means to challenge lingering control by fractions of capital over the economy. Relative state autonomy would be transitional, for either the capitalist class would unite to impede economic transformation or the revolution would succeed and a new dominant class would emerge to take control of production and of the state.

There are, therefore, several historical instances when the state may strive for relative autonomy. Yet such a tendency does not occur in a vacuum nor is it without limitation. Conditions appropriate for relative autonomy do not mean that the state will act, and a state asserting its autonomy will not necessarily succeed. Analytical separation of the state from the dominant class, affirming that it has a logic of its own, designates a possibility, not an automatic outcome. It is equally important, therefore, to assess the limitations on relative state autonomy.

Limitations Of State Autonomy

It may be fairly easy for a state to exercise instrumental autonomy, that is, to refuse to follow every whim and fancy of the dominant class. Members of the dominant class do not necessarily capture the personnel positions of a state, so obvious differences of style, procedure, and process will occur. The important, and severe, constraint on relative state autonomy is structural. Since the state exists to reproduce the mode of production, it must sustain capitalist relations of production. The state attempts to facilitate the accumulation process, to provide stability for private investment and profitability. If a state impedes or blocks the private appropriation of surplus from the social production, the dominant class will move against the state. One condition of relative autonomy is a dominant class that is impotent by internal competition among fractions, but a quick way for the state to unite the feuding fractions is to attack their general interests through appropriating surplus and through blocking opportunities for investment. Promotion of a revolutionary transformation of production relations is an extreme against which the dominant class will fight. But lesser actions which hinder the smooth functioning of the capitalist mode of production could also unite the dominant class.[39] The threshold of tolerance of the dominant class to react against structural change will vary with the historical circumstances — such as the level of development of the production forces, organisational strength of the dominated classes, and presence of struggle by other groups (ethnic, religious, etc.).

The power of the dominant class is the ultimate dependence of the state on resources produced by the mode of production that the dominant class controls. The state may try to compete with the dominant class in appropriating resources, directing resources to strengthen the autonomy of the state. Ultimately, however, it is the dominant class that controls the productive forces that create surplus. The state may exercise control of the coercive forces, but the dominant class controls the resources which provide revenue for the state (and its militaries). The dominant class may decide to export capital, to avoid or manipulate taxation, and/or to discourage entry of foreign capital.

A less drastic limitation on relative state autonomy is the requirement that the various institutions of the state must not be divided against themselves. A balance of class forces is not automatically reflected in the state apparatuses. The military, for instance, may remain the instrument of the landed aristocracy while the civil bureaucracy is not captured by one class. Such a lack of cohesion within the state apparatuses would restrict the ability of the state to act autonomously from dominant class interests.

The theories of relative state autonomy, therefore, direct attention to the importance of the state in the social formation. The state is not treated as an abstraction appended to a mode of production. The state may be captured by the dominant class or possibly, a site for struggle against fractions of that class to preserve the general interest of capital. In short, control of the state is worth fighting for, although it does not guarantee control of the forces of production. The limitations on state autonomy are consequential, as the pervasiveness and severity of neocolonialism attest. But control of the state can be decisive in the class struggle. This theoretical emphasis reflects the political reality of the periphery. None of the Frontline States had command over its own relations of production before achieving political independence. The Frontline did not demand economic independence as a precondition to political independence of Zimbabwe. Rather, the political independence affords an important base from which struggle over relations of production *may* occur.

This brief theoretical overview reveals how problematic are the conditions of relative state autonomy . . . and shows also how the theory needs elaboration. In this study the conditions which could promote and delimit relative state autonomy for each of the Frontline States will be analysed. Further, this analysis will help to elaborate the theory of relative state autonomy, for the case study reveals other conditions, not discussed above, in which relative autonomy from the dominant class may be asserted. The analysis uses the theory in a consciously critical way, in order to assess its limitations. The theory helps us to understand the Frontline States, but the study also elaborates the theory.

Each of the following country sections is organised according to a three-part outline. First, a very brief overview of colonial history sets the context for the emergence of alliances among classes after independence. Second, this background on the class formations facilitates understanding of the role of the state (given the class alliances). The central question asks for what classes or class fractions does the state act? Third, we can then evaluate to what extent the state was able to gain relative autonomy from the dominant class. Each section ends, therefore, with an analysis of how relative state autonomy influenced the state's participation in the Frontline.

Mozambique: Revolutionary Support For Zimbabwean Liberation

Colonial Political Economy

The Portuguese first viewed their coastal colonies (1505) as docking areas for ships on the way to India. As merchant capitalists they soon promoted trade with the interior for ivory, slaves, and gold. But this wealth from merchant capital was not invested in productive forces, for Portugal's vast empire and nascent industrial production came under British control early in the 18th century. British capital penetrated the Portuguese economy, setting up patterns of exchange of British manufactures (e.g. textiles) for Portuguese agricultural products (e.g., wine).[40] Portugal was even required to buy all its ships from Britain. The Portuguese economy remained predominantly based on peasant agriculture and tenant farming on large plantations. Famine was not infrequent.

Many Portuguese emigrated to the colonies, but mostly to Brazil. Various schemes — the first in 1849 and the last in 1961 — planning vast new settlements of Portuguese families in Angola were not successful;[41] Mozambique attracted even fewer settlers. Plans for development of the African colonies were continually frustrated by insufficient capital investment, either from the government or from private Portuguese businessmen. It was not until very late, when Antonio Salazar took power in Portugal (1928) and established the *Nuovo Estados*, that a concerted effort was made to promote Portuguese investment in the African colonies.[42]

The Portuguese African colonies were shaped by this relative underdevelopment of their colonial master. In spite of many attempts by the government to encourage Portuguese capital to invest in Mozambique, foreign capital dominated even from the 17th century. The government allocated land in the Zambesi river valley to those who agreed to develop it; these new *prazos* were then ruled as private fiefdoms whose owners had full control over life and death of anyone within the area. Because of resistance from the Africans and the unwillingness of the landholders to develop the area, the *prazo* system collapsed by the mid-19th century.[43] By the end of the century, large tracts of land were given to concessionary companies (e.g., Mozambique Co., 1888; Zambesi Co., 1892), mostly financed by British, French and German capital to develop the area. Since they were also mainly speculative in purpose, they reinvested little of their high profits back into the region. These profits were from payments (1) for the export of African labour to Rhodesian and South African mines and to cocoa plantations on Sao Thomé; (2) from heavy taxes; or (3) from forced labour if the taxes were not paid. Local production that did occur was for cash crops of rubber and coconut and later of sisal and sugar.[44]

High taxes and forced labour drove many Mozambicans to seek jobs in the South African mines; they could earn wages 300 percent higher than from Portuguese employ and could pay off the taxes with their cash earnings.[45] From a 1901 agreement, South African mining companies, owned by British capital, had many recruiting stations in Mozambique from which they contracted male labour for a period of 12–18 months. In that year, more than 50,000 Mozambicans worked in the South African gold mines, and almost as many were in Rhodesia.[46] Written into the contracts was the requirement that each worker would be repatriated after the term was completed; the labour had to be migrant. The wages were given to the Portuguese government in gold; the Portuguese then sold the gold on the international market and paid the Mozambican miners in escudos. The Portuguese, therefore, had a major source of foreign exchange in the migrant labour system; it worked in partnership with the South African mines, providing Mozambicans for contract labour.

A further source of foreign exchange was to provide another service to South Africa; the railway system and the port of Lourenco Marques (Maputo) were developed to serve the mines on the South African Rand. Fees for port and rail services were paid to the Portuguese government for use of these facilities, but initial financing was by foreign capital (mainly British). In the capital city of Lourenco Marques, foreign capital also financed the electrical system, trolly system and the first modern wharves. In 1900 only 27 percent of the investments in the city were of Portuguese origin.[47] By the end of the 19th century, therefore, Mozambique derived much of its revenue as a service economy to British capital in South Africa.

After Salazar took power, he refused to renew the concessionary companies' contracts in Mozambique. At the same time a new decree (1930) renewed the requirement for Africans to work for private Portuguese firms or for the colonial state for six months of the year. The programme also tried to increase the output of sugar, sisal, and copra from the plantations in central and northern Mozambique.[48] Peasants on their own land were forced to grow cotton (1926) and rice (1942) to supply the metropole. Rural African labour was, therefore, either exported to the mines, engaged in forced labour for the state or on the plantations, or required to grow cash crops on its own land. The enforcement of these provisions left little time for food crop production, resulting in the systematic malnourishing of much of the peasant population.[49] The few Africans in the towns (94 percent of the population was rural at independence) were relegated to the most menial jobs: maids and servants, labourers, cleaners, cooks, watchmen, etc. Class and race clearly coincided in the urban areas as the Africans were given the low-paying jobs, even if illiterate Portuguese arrivals had fewer skills than the Africans. By the 1960's, white workers, even if unskilled, earned twenty times as much as African workers, and mulattoes earned fourteen times as much.[50]

Competition for cheap African labour among the concessionary companies, plantations, and state (road construction and public works, etc.) resulted in conscripted labour of the most able-bodied men, women, and even children. By the 1950's, therefore, the enforced services to the colonial rulers by the Africans could be summarised as follows:[51]

1. contract labour (1878 — date of original state policy)

   a. miners outside Mozambique: contract labour was hired for 12-18 months at wages relatively higher than those in Mozambique, but at the price of serious disruption of family life.

   b. plantation labour: sometimes travel from the home village would be several days' journey so separation of families was also a problem here. Contracts could be simply harvesting crops or could extend for a whole growing season. To reduce costs, labour was usually sent home during the off-seasons.

2. forced cultivation (1938): peasants on their own land would be required to grow cotton or rice and would be paid one-tenth of the price European farmers were paid for the same grade and quantity of cotton and rice.

3. urban wage labour (1878): wages were so low in the urban areas that few Mozambicans chose to migrate to the cities. Wage labour was locked into menial jobs. Only very few even became clerks assigned to minor desk jobs. Most were messengers and cleaners.

4. forced labour (chibalo): originally the decree (1899) set the limit for six months at very low wages, but the time could be increased (and was) for minor infringements of the above three labour relationships — if one broke a contract or did not grow sufficient cash crops, etc.

5. prison labour: work conditions were often the same as above, for prison labour was loaned out to plantation owners or business firms, but labour was totally unpaid.

The Africans who collaborated with the Portuguese to enforce the above labour patterns were Portuguese-appointed 'chiefs' (*regulos*) and *sipais,* a type of militia who scoured villages and fields for the 'non-producing' African or the labour contract defectors. These Africans benefited immensely from their increased power . . . but their numbers remained very few. Other relatively privileged Africans were those who worked in the mines. Although subjected to the oppression of apartheid in South Africa, the miners were able to buy modest improvements to their homes or a few consumer items (e.g., radio; anyone who could afford a bicycle was considered wealthy).[52] But these few benefits depended on the family's ability to provide their own subsistence throughout the year by agricultural production. In years of drought or other economic problems, the miners' wages became simply a hedge against starvation. In short, only a very few

Africans were able to live much beyond subsistence; there was no national bourgeoisie among the Africans. Only a few obtained enough education to become *assimilados* (less than one percent by 1960), a privileged distinction given to Africans who could speak and read rudimentary Portuguese, gave up their 'tribal ways', and were employed in the capitalist economy. The very small numbers of *assimilados* belies the myth that the Portuguese were non-racist and treated the Africans as 'equals'.[53]

Traditional status divisions did remain important, especially in areas where the Portuguese supported the chiefs in return for tax collection or labour recruitment. Traditional ethnic divisions were also reinforced by colonial rule. To maintain control, the Portuguese emphasised the ethnic divisions and promoted them. From the first penetration into the interior, the Portuguese would ally with certain ethnic groups in order to conquer others; they exacerbated traditional hostilities among the Africans.

Given the different forms of labour exploitation, based on a racial doctrine which blocked Africans from sharing the profits of their labour, the colonies were very lucrative for Portugal and its settlers. In the 1960's alienation of the land intensified; by independence (1975), 0.2 percent of the population controlled 50 percent of the cultivable land in Mozambique[54] Africans who did grow cash crops received lower prices for the same quality and quantity of a product. The forced cash crop production provided immediate profits to the merchants who bought, for instance, cotton at two cents a bale and immediately resold it at twenty cents.[55] Samora Machel, the President of independent Mozambique, stated that his political education was not from 'reading Marx and Engels. But from seeing my father forced to grow cotton and going with him to the market where he was to sell it at a lower price — much lower than the white Portuguese grower.'[56] Although the economy remained mainly a service economy to South Africa and Rhodesia, the colonies became very profitable to Portugal, through land alienation, forced labour, suppressed prices to African cash crop producers: 'It is the surplus of the balance of payments of the overseas provinces which as a rule have more than re-established equilibrium in the payments of the escudo area and have made for the regular increase of the country's gold and foreign exchange holdings.'[57] Yet such receipts were rarely re-invested in Mozambique, as state and private businesses exported capital as quickly as it was accumulated. The economy remained a dependent service economy, a legacy for the new government to transform.

The State and Class Struggle in Mozambique

There is a long tradition of resistance to the humiliating disruption of family life and the systematic impoverishment of the Africans through the Portuguese colonial policy.[58] Portugal did not give independence to its colonies after World War II, avowing instead that the colonies were integral to Portugal as 'overseas provinces' not colonies. As stated above, to maintain control, the Portuguese emphasised the ethnic divisions and promoted them. In the early part of the liberation struggle, some leaders tried to take advantage of the successes and to limit the benefits to their own group. By 1962, however, the united Front for the Liberation of Mozambique (Frelimo) was formed from the National Democratic Union of Mozambique (UDENAMO), Mozambique African National Union (MANU), and the African Union of Independent Mozambique (UNAMI).

The peasants in the north became the motivating force for the armed struggle which was launched in 1964. Retaining access to productive land, they were relatively self-sufficient and could sustain the guerrillas as areas were liberated from the forced cash crop demands of the Portuguese. They joined Frelimo in large numbers to remove labour on plantations and/or the demand for cash crops from their area. 'Rich' peasants who hired wage labourers were a very small group. Middle and poor peasants were the base of the liberation struggle.[59]

Although a fairly high proportion of the population was in wage labour (20 percent), most were migrant labourers supported by peasant production.[60] Only a very few Mozambicans were proletarianised (category of 'urban wage labour' above). Some of the urban workers did stage important strikes during the liberation struggle; some were members of the urban underground of Frelimo.[61] Many of the proletariat, however, joined the organising efforts of Frelimo only after the armed struggle. After independence, they were mobilised into dynamising groups at the work place to obtain political education and organising skills to help them take command of production. The new state of Mozambique is based, therefore, on an alliance of the peasants/proletariat.

In the 1950's, the formation of a small group of African clerks and technicians (e.g., in hospitals) was tolerated by the Portuguese. Some of this new petty bourgeoisie became leaders of the revolution. Amilcar Cabral underlined the revolutionary consciousness of such a group based on the fact that they experienced every day the inequities and humiliations of colonial rule. He called this segment a 'revolutionary bourgeoisie'.[62] John Saul further analyses their emergence as a revolutionary force:

> ... a different kind of dialectic at work is [in] Mozambique, where one wing of the petty-bourgeois leadership did move to crystallise active and class-conscious peasant involvement in the liberation struggle, and in the process found itself embedded in a developing popular movement, whose ideology and organisation came in turn to *evoke from that leadership an ever firmer commitment to the revolutionary project* . . . [This role] emerged both from a fierce struggle within the petty bourgeoisie over the form that political mobilisation, economic reconstruction and military activity should take and *from the growing presence of the subordinate classes within the liberation movement.*[63] [Emphasis mine.]

As Saul states, the struggle was fierce over major issues of liberation. Two such political skirmishes are now famous in Frelimo history as examples of vital lessons of the revolution.[64] One militant, Lazaro Nkavandame, helped to set up co-operative stores in Cabo Delgado (a province in the north) in order to free the peasants from the Portuguese-controlled market and to provide basic commodities. Supplies were carried in from Tanzania by the peasants or brought from their own production. But the peasants protested: he was using their labour to enrich himself. They knew well African *sipais* and *regulos* and now, given the chance, other Africans were exploiting them in the same manner as the Portuguese.

Another leader, Mateus Gwenjere, taught at the Frelimo secondary school in Dar es Salaam. He advised the students to apply for advanced studies overseas and encouraged them to protest the Frelimo decision that students would spend their summer vacations back with the people in the liberated zones; the students subsequently complained that their education and skills were too important for Frelimo to lose as war casualties. A major struggle in the party occurred over the role of the new petty bourgeoisie in the war and the party. The conclusion was that division between mental and manual labour was not to be tolerated; those who were receiving an education owed their newly-acquired skills to the struggle of the peasants and must return as soon as possible to support that struggle.

After Frelimo's first President Eduardo Mondlane's assassina-

tion by letter bomb on 3 February 1969, the tension among the
Frelimo leadership over promoting economic and intellectual elites
intensified. Frelimo Vice-President Uriah Simango, Nkavandame and
others insisted that the political and military struggle be separated.
Taking a militarist viewpoint, they were against popularising the
struggle, for a mass-based movement would leave no room for their
stepping into positions of privilege and power. This manoeuvre for
neo-colonial independence was defeated. As Marcelino dos Santos
stated: 'The unfolding of the struggle itself . . . revealed a number of
contradictions which became particularly evident from the moment
our guerrillas had established liberated zones . . . Not only did we have
to continue the fight against colonialism, to destroy the repressive
forces, but we also had to start building and producing and creating
wealth. It is precisely from that moment that there appeared the
fundamental contradiction which existed — not in the Mozambican
population, but within the governing leadership of FRELIMO.'[65] It was
the mobilised peasants — involved in full-scale armed struggle — who
were to make decisions and enforce them. Frelimo policy promoted
education for all, but petty bourgeois attitudes of individualism,
elitism, and equivocation ('liberalism') were not to be tolerated; such
attitudes continue exploitation. Neither the war nor the ultimate
economic independence could be won without a mobilised peasantry.
Equally important, the petty bourgeoisie must be fully integrated into
the national, collective ideology as well as mobilised for any or all
tasks.[66]

Many similar political struggles were worked out in village
meetings, called *reunioes*; in the liberated areas, Frelimo encouraged
the peasants to take part in the decision-making concerning production, war, schools, marketing. Mass participation in all aspects of
decision-making formed the basis of the new political structures.

Class struggle was not the only area of conflict within Frelimo.
The same group that wanted to replace the privileges of the white
settlers with those for a new black bourgeoisie also promoted a
nationalism with racist overtones. They were anti-mulatto and anti-
white. Others asserted that exploitation is colour-blind; individuals of
all races try to exploit their own people. Because exploitation is
colour-blind, so is liberation; anyone, whose behaviour follows the
principles of self-criticism, collective production, collective decisions,
and full participation in work of all kinds, is integral to the liberation
struggle.

These practical lessons of war were crucial to a majority segment of the Mozambican society: the women. They entered the struggle as carriers of water and supplies for the guerrillas from Tanzania to Mozambique. When their supply columns came under Portuguese fire, they demanded the right to carry guns to protect themselves.[67] A struggle in the party soon resulted in training women's brigades. Other women took the lead in going to villages and speaking to the people, organising them to support Frelimo. The impact of these women leaders was profound on the village women; the war was not simply to fight the Portuguese, but also to challenge traditions which had silenced them into acquiescence.

These brief examples reveal the three aspects of change that Frelimo promoted in order to transform colonialism: ideology, structures, behaviour.[68] The ideology, worked out over long discussions over several years, clarified the nature of the struggle. In the training camps and in the villages, Frelimo leaders led long discussions about the definition of the enemy and the goals of the struggle.[69] The ideology promoted nationalism over ethnicity, co-operation over individualism; it required discipline, self-criticism. The goal was not limited to ousting the Portuguese; the goal also included ending traditional forms of exploitation. Nationalism did not mean perpetuating traditions which oppressed certain segments of society (e.g., women). The structures that provided mass participation in the liberated areas were continued under the new state. The village meetings, the co-operatives, the people's stores, and the people's courts were to transform the colonial structures of repression. One description summarises these transformations well: 'In contrast to the famous conception which sees the guerrilla fighter operating among the people as fish in water, one could say that Frelimo was the kind of fish which transformed the water it swam in.'[70]

The political ideology along with the political structures which greatly increased mass participation were to be the means for changing behaviour. Emphasis on changed behaviour referred to many areas of daily life. The goals were to promote co-operation and respect for the collective decisions. Others were to be judged by their behaviour, not their words, nor their skin colour nor their membership in a family of chiefs. Those who were leaders had to be the most disciplined and the most willing to serve in the unpleasant or difficult tasks. This peasant/worker/petty bourgeoisie alliance liberated over one-quarter of the country before the coup in Lisbon (April 1974) ended the war.

Radical transformation of the colonial state apparatus was the first priority as political structures were built to facilitate peasant/ worker participation both in political and economic decisions. The initial political innovation was the dynamising groups used most prevalently in the areas that had not been liberated before independence, to mobilise the peasants and workers to step in and take control of areas of administration, production, supervision, and adjudication that the Portuguese were abandoning in their precipitous flight from the independent country. (The settlers fled in panic and destroyed equipment and vehicles they could not take with them.) The dynamising groups offered political education to Mozambicans — who had been taught no other lesson than brutalised inferiority by the colonials — that they could begin to control their own futures.[71] Dynamising groups provided an essential organising transition from colonial oppression to political and economic representation.

Gradually, both People's Courts and People's Assemblies were established in the villages and at the national level. Leaders are now elected directly in the villages; representatives form assemblies at district, provincial and national levels.[72] Further, most villages are forming the mass popular organisations, such as the Organisation of Mozambican Women (OMM) and the Organisation of Mozambican Youth (OJM). The organisations are to raise political consciousness and to encourage participation in transforming social relations. For instance, OMM encourages women to overcome the sexual division of labour and join co-operatives that have traditionally been 'men's work'. It co-ordinates with Frelimo to sanction men who discriminate against women.

Among these multiple political structures, the party is supreme. One must be elected into the party. Party cells are being organised in the work place and in the neighbourhoods, for they replace the dynamising groups as the responsible authority in a locale. But the multiple structures in Mozambique do not allow initiative to be the monopoly of the party. As stated at the Third Party Congress: 'The democratic mass organisations are the most perfect connecting link between the Party and the People. The mass organisations are a great school where the consciousness of millions of workers — men and women, old, young *continuadores* — is developed.'[73] Non-party members have many opportunities to join in the task of directing production, setting priorities, and allocating surplus.

At independence most of the Portuguese left Mozambique virtually overnight. Abandoned plantations and large tracts of land have been transformed into state farms. Abandoned factories were nationalised and workers' production councils set up. But private factories and farmers did not have their capital expropriated if they produced according to the directives of the state: minimum wages were set; sexual and racial division of labour were outlawed; basic services such as sick leave had to be provided.

In the rural areas both state farms and communal villages were stated priorities. Members of communal villages have a voice in decisions about production and the distribution of surplus. Co-operative production occurs in the fields, in crafts, and in small husbandry. At state farms and in the factories, workers' production councils are to be active in decisions about the production process. These economic structures for participation have had the expected political problems of collective decision-making, but also severe structural problems, such as the lack of equipment or raw materials to carry out the task, or lack of skills to make informed decisions or to implement them. Mistakes are made; struggle occurs over a group or person trying to usurp the decision-making power.[74]

Transformation of the economy has just begun. It is still a service economy oriented to foreign exchange earnings from South Africa: Frelimo decided costs of severing those links were much more severe than costs of closing the border to Rhodesian traffic during the Zimbabwean war. The government is soliciting foreign capital, but it now enters Mozambique on Mozambican terms: deposits of rich minerals, good port facilities, and improved transport systems are offered in exchange for Mozambican conditions of production including limited expatriation of profits, training of nationals, labour-intensive technology and the use of local materials.

Further, the government is learning from mistakes in the transitional process. At independence distribution of goods was a major problem because many who had controlled commerce and the transport system left the country. Merchants who remained in the rural areas often charged three times the official price for goods.[75] The state intervened to run retail outlets (*Lojas de Povo*) and warehouses and encouraged the formation of consumer co-operatives. But the state-controlled people's stores proved highly inefficient because of the lack of skilled management and little transport. Corruption and hoarding increased. By 1979 the People's Assembly called for merchants to take over petty commerce.[76] In March 1980, President Machel said the state should not be involved in the sale of toothpaste and invited 10,000 Mozambicans in neighbouring states to return to enter the commercial sector.

In the process of transforming the state structure to eradicate the colonial state apparatus, new political conflicts emerged. The Third Party Congress (February 1977) addressed the question of defining the enemy. The Congress acknowledged a partial transformation of the state apparatus in the pro-socialist direction, but also the creation of new positions of power for a rising petty bourgeoisie.[77] As analysed by Frelimo, the problem was one of popular versus national democracy. The goal was to promote popular democracy — not to encourage leaders who are followed by passive masses or who lack confidence in the revolutionary capacity of the people (an error they felt Nkrumah had made).[78] The Third Party Congress called for the revitalisation of organisations to maintain the mass base: mass organisations, production councils, reformulation of the dynamising groups. But these decisions to further people's power floundered because they were not implemented.

As the war in Zimbabwe ended, further internal dislocations erupted. In the civil bureaucracy some of the new and retained civil servants continued to protect old hierarchies and privileges.[79] In 1981 contradictions within the security forces and police were exposed.[80] In the production councils in the factories, confusion and indecision were expressed over the role of the production councils in relation to the party cells and the administration. An 'offensive' was declared by President Machel, calling for a strengthening of the party in relation to the state apparatus. Conclusions from the offensive were that the party was too weak to fulfil functions of guiding and mobilising the people.[81]

As the process of change precipitates internal contradictions, individuals and groups move to take advantage of a hesitation, a mistake, or a power vacuum in a factory, in the fields, or within the state apparatus. The campaign against elements in the bureaucracy and military reveals the threat of those who move to challenge the new state. And this is where we have to put the Mozambican state back into the international economic context. The fraction of the dominant class which has lost the most from the anti-colonial struggle — foreign, including Portuguese, capital — still has economic leverage to take advantage of the internal contradictions. It was mentioned that the greatest limitation on relative state autonomy was structural; if the state moves to appropriate surplus of the dominant class or to limit opportunities for investment, the dominant class will unite to curtail the state's autonomy.

Elements of the dominant class in Mozambique have resorted to economic sabotage and fraud to defeat the transformation of social relations. Fraud in the expatriation of capital required the state to change its currency — voiding the value of the expatriated notes. Several Portuguese managers who remained to work in independent Mozambique subsequently took vacations (and sometimes state cars and office files) and never returned. Nationalisation of several corporations was necessary because of corruption and sabotage of production (Sena Sugar, Vdreira Glass Co., Boro Coconut plantation, etc.). The government ordered a whole new fleet of fishing vessels from a Portuguese businessman, paid in advance; he left the country and the ships were never delivered. One Western country sent a whole shipment of materials for the clothing industry; opened at the factory, the crates were full of rocks and shredded material.[82] The list of sabotage is long.

As discussed in Chapter 3, Mozambican territory was bombed several times during the Zimbabwean war — not just guerrilla camps, but refugee camps and Mozambican villages. Even now after the war, external sabotage continues as Mozambican mercenaries, financed by South African and Portuguese capital, attack unarmed civilians in several areas of Mozambique.[83] In short, this fraction of the dominant class has resorted to armed resistance to the structural changes in the Mozambican state and economy.

Basis of Relative State Autonomy

Given these fundamental internal problems and external assaults, how did Mozambique sustain its support for the Zimbabwean struggle? It must first be reiterated that the Zimbabwean struggle was not viewed as separate from the Mozambican struggle. To pursue fully the goals of the new Mozambican state, Zimbabwe had to be free of white minority rule. Mozambique's economy was tied to Rhodesia and South Africa as major sources for its foreign exchange. The goal of an independent Zimbabwe was not simply economic; in fact, it was more ideological and political. First, as shown above, the party and the people of Mozambique are anti-racist; they knew that struggle well and wanted to help the Zimbabweans overcome their racial oppression. Second, they agreed with the Zimbabwean nationalists that fighting a war that kills brothers and sisters is counterproductive unless full control of the state is possible. The goal is not only a change in the government, but also in the economy. Third, as many previously independent African states have shown, reducing dependence on colonial linkages is quite difficult if a state tries to act alone. An independent Zimbabwe would strengthen Mozambique's efforts to overcome neo-colonialism.

In striving to transform the mode of production, the Mozambican state gained some relative autonomy from the dominant class. The changes began with a fundamental transformation of the colonial state apparatus which served that class so well. The state moved in to take over when Portuguese and foreign capital fled. When the elements of the dominant class tried to regain its hegemony, the new state could resist because it represented the petty bourgeoisie/peasant/worker alliance. Progressive elements of the petty bourgeoisie that stayed in the new state recognised that its past success and future were bound with the workers/peasants, not the capitalists.

At no point in the Zimbabwean war was it certain that Mozambique could sustain the support. The fact that it has resisted even armed opposition from fractions of the dominant class is evidence that the state has gained relative autonomy by allying with the classes that were moving from a position of subordination to one of hegemony. Workers and peasants are not yet in control of production. Mozambicans would be the first to say they are a long way from achieving socialism. The transition to socialism is long and full of contradictions, especially for poor countries with a long history of colonial dominance. No one can predict if Mozambique will attain socialist relations of production. What is important is that the newly independent state is trying to turn economic and political control over to the producers. By the Fourth Party Congress in April 1983, Frelimo reaffirmed its roots in the peasants and former guerrillas. Discussions were carried on for a whole year before the Congress — and lively debate and criticism raged throughout the Congress sessions. The Central Committee doubled in size and the new members were peasants and former guerrillas. Party leaders were sent to the rural areas, leaving their Volvos behind in Maputo. Pledges were made to support communal production over the highly centralised state farms.[84] This process of open debate and criticism is important in the transition to build a people's democracy in a socialist economy.

Another element in achieving some relative state autonomy was that Mozambique was able to acquire support and resources from the socialist countries. Not only weapons to defend themselves, but crucial economic support was given by the socialist allies. The theories of relative state autonomy do address this possibility: the state can gain autonomy from the dominant class if alternative sources of revenue and expertise are available. Sometimes those alternative sources can come from within — from the dominated classes. Sometimes they come from without, from sources not allied with the dominant class.

Mozambique had both the alternative sources: production by the newly mobilised workers and peasants and from socialist allies outside. Aid for the military came from the German Democratic Republic, Hungary, People's Republic of China, Democratic People's Republic of Korea, Romania, and the USSR.[85] The Soviets provided arms to Frelimo and technical aid for dams and the fishing industry. Romania and China aided in textile production and in the ports. Mozambique is still economically dependent on South African and Western capital, but it has diversified somewhat its economic relationships, not only to the Soviets and East Europe, but also to China. These alternative sources of funding and technical aid were crucial during the crisis of the Zimbabwean war, for they moderated the control of the dominant class during the crisis.

The crucial basis of state autonomy for Mozambique to continue its role in the Frontline States was the process of revolutionary transformation of the state apparatus. The Mozambican state attained relative autonomy from the dominant class of white settlers and foreign capital as it came more under the control of the petty bourgeoisie/workers/peasant alliance. The transformation of the social relations is far from complete, and that struggle continues in Mozambique. These internal changes, however, provided a base from which to support Zimbabwean independence. Reciprocally the independence of Zimbabwe alters the regional economic-political status quo and provides alternatives to the present pattern of South African dominance over the Mozambican economy. The relative state autonomy facilitated participation in the Frontline; the success of the Frontline encourages internal transformations in Mozambique.

Angola: A Frontline State Besieged

Colonial Political Economy

Southern Mozambique was a labour reserve area for South Africa, but virtually all of Angola became a 'labour reserve' for centuries of its colonial history. Established early by mercantile capital, the slave trade dominated the Angolan economy from the 16th to the mid-19th centuries. The colonial government was involved in slaving as a major source of revenue. The white settlers were even allowed to pay taxes with slaves. Most of the Angolan slaves, however, were shipped to Brazil, for the Portuguese were more interested in developing Brazil, which they decided had potential for greater profits.[86] Depopulation estimates of Angola through the slave trade are as high as 4 million people — the most able-bodied young men and women.[87]

Domestic slavery was officially abolished in 1878, but legalised forced labour perpetuated conditions of work which differed little from slave labour. Forced labour for work on road construction or on private farms or in the fishing industry became legal for 'vagrants', defined by the state as almost any African engaged in subsistence agriculture. For example, under the slavery laws there were only about 600 slaves registered in the south in 1858; by 1913, under forced labour, over 10,000 Africans in the same area were producing cotton and rubber for a booming overseas market.[88] Owners of production did not have to pay wages high enough for subsistence of the labour force; paid barely enough to cover taxes, the workers and their families remained dependent on subsistence peasant agriculture for basic survival. In addition, forced labour, not abolished until 1961, further depopulated Angola as whole communities migrated to avoid the total disruption of their lifestyles. Many went to the Congo and some even travelled far into Botswana. From 1937-1946 it was estimated that one million Africans emigrated from all three Portuguese territories; [89] UN statistics for 1954 estimate that 500,000 Angolans were living outside the territory.[90] Such persistent depopulation has resulted in a population density averaging only five persons per square kilometre in Angola. Although there are important urban areas, the political and economic integration of the sparsely populated countryside remains an unresolved problem.

As in Mozambique, the Portuguese remained in the coastal areas or in small enclaves near the coast for centuries. They relied on

African traders for goods from the interior (ivory, wax, etc.). Most Portuguese settled in Brazil, and only 9,000 were in Angola as late as 1900 (.20% of the population). In 1940 they were one percent of the population and only in the 1960's did the percentage rise to 5.[91] Settlement projects for the interior were few and usually unsuccessful after a few years. Portuguese who were brought to Angola to become settler farmers soon migrated back to the coastal towns. When penetration of the interior became a serious endeavour in the 1880's, the Portuguese had to fight many wars and many African peoples were not 'pacified' until the 1920's.[92] For example, the Dembo people in a mountainous area only 150 km from the capital and port city of Luanda were not conquered until the 1920's (and became an early base of the liberation struggle in the 1960's).[93]

Because of the late penetration and sparse settlement, trade was the major economic activity of the early settler communities. As in Mozambique, merchant capital did not develop into productive capital in Angola until well into the 20th century. Most of the settlers were military men or administrators.[94] In southern Angola a rubber and cotton boom from the 1890's increased the number of settlers, but only temporarily until World War I.[95]

Productive capital investment was finally encouraged by the building of the Benguela (1929) and Mossamedes (1923) railroads. Copper mines were exploited; diamonds were discovered in 1912. And by the mid-1920's concessionary companies, similar to those in Mozambique, had large tracts of land on which to grow cotton and tobacco with forced labour.[96] These productive attempts were cut short by the depression. In addition, the *Estado Novo* established by Antonio Salazar required that the colonies pay for themselves; the state would not provide infrastructure or subsidies for investment.[97] Portugal, as a weak and underdeveloped colonial power, was not able to underwrite investment for development of the resources or provision of services (education especially) to the colonies. Foreign capital was restricted by law (capital for diamond mining and for the railroads were the only exceptions) in order to reduce competition from stronger British capital. Only in the early 1960's, after the guerrilla war broke out, did the Portuguese invite foreign investments to Angola in an effort to increase exploitation of the mineral resources. As the United Nations noted:

> It is significant that Portugal's policy of increasing the volume of foreign investment in the areas under its administration coincides

exactly with the start of the national liberation movements in Africa. The aim of this deliberate policy was, as experience has shown, to gain financial, material and other support from the foreign interests, which should then help Portugal in future exploitation of the natural and human resources and in repression of the growing political aspirations of the population in the areas administered by Portugal.[98]

Portugal greatly intensified its exploitation of the colonies, both economically and politically, after World War II. Land was confiscated from the Angolan peasants much more intensively than in previous decades. Moreover, peasants who kept their land were forced to grow more cash crops to pay very high taxes; the prices they received for the crops were also considerably lower than for the white settlers. By the 1960's foreign corporations were allowed to invest to exploit the rich mineral resources. Iron ore, copper, diamonds, manganese, and tin became major foreign exchange earners. Gulf Oil Corporation started drilling in 1968.[99] But the Angolan people did not benefit from this exploitation. Royalties from the corporations were handed over to the Portuguese government. Wages remained low and labour conditions were poor. Health and educational services were non-existent in many areas.

The (1) alienation of land in the 1950's, (2) the intensive exploitation of labour through forced labour and inequitable market prices for cash crops, and (3) the inadequate or total lack of services from the colonial power resulted in the outbreak of armed resistance to the intolerable conditions. In 1961 armed struggle was launched and by 1966 it was supported by a broad base of classes among the Africans against the Portuguese. The British, Americans, and South Africans supported Portugal until the coup in Lisbon in April 1974. It is not necessary to relate the details of the armed struggle here, for there are excellent accounts available.[100] It is important to note, however, that the revolution was supported by a broad front of peasants, workers, and petty bourgeoisie, yet not all united in one party, as will be discussed later.

The State and Class Struggle in Angola

The depopulation of the land and the inability of the Portuguese to take full control of Angola meant that the land was not as alienated from the Angolan peasant farmers as from those in Mozambique. The economy remained a peasant, subsistence economy. As Clarence

Smith has argued: 'Increased articulation with the capitalist mode of production modified but did not alter the basic relations of production within the peasant economy. Neither private ownership of the means of production nor the development of a class of labourers permanently separated from the means of production occurred'.[101] The survival of the peasant economy offered a strong base for the guerrilla warfare. With peasant production intact, the people could offer refuge and food to the guerrillas. In border areas, where the presence of the Portuguese was particularly low, the villages offered internal sanctuaries to the guerrillas. At the time of the war a small proportion of the peasantry could accumulate capital through cash crops. They grew maize, coffee, and cotton on 2–10 hectares, mainly with family labour, and were most important in the coffee producing North.[102]

By the 1960's many peasants were forced to work for agricultural concessionary companies or mines because of land shortages, taxation, and debt. (This situation was especially true of the central highlands.) Most of these marginal peasants remained 'semi-proletariat' on the mines and on the concessions, for the owners preferred migrant labour to avoid contribution to the reproduction of labour. A proletariat, dependent fully on wages to support the family, did not really form until the late 1950's in the growing towns. Consequently, most workers still maintained close contacts with their home villages, and their ethnic affiliations remained strong. A few Africans were taxi drivers or skilled artisans, but they remained poor, and subject to daily humiliation from their Portuguese clients.[103] In a few areas, like Luanda and Benguela, the workers were important and strongly organised as a base for early mobilisation for the revolution. For Angola in general, however, their numbers remained very small.

African traders who served as middlemen to the interior for the Portuguese, established a petty bourgeoisie in Angola which was stronger than in other southern African countries. There were a few opportunities for the traders to invest their surplus in productive investment, but they did control the interior commercial sectors. Only a very few Africans entered the 'new petty bourgeoisie' as office clerks and administrators, for literacy among the Africans remained about two percent. The administrative petty bourgeoisie was elite. Because the petty bourgeoisie is by nature economically insecure, it split apart during the time of crisis (as in most other modern revolutionary struggles).[104] Some joined the revolution, for the same reasons as discussed in the section on Mozambique. They became part of the vanguard of the revolution in alliance with the peasants and workers.[105] Others, however, wanted to gain private control of the commercial sectors and simply replace the Portuguese with their own control of the market. A third group is nationalist and appealed to the peasantry but with racial overtones of black solidarity, a predictable response to the virulent racism of the white petty bourgeoisie. These internal class antagonisms remain part of the struggle in Angola.

During Portuguese colonialism, but especially during the war, the Portuguese exacerbated the ethnic divisions within Angola. These divisions became one basis for the conflict among the three liberation groups fighting for independence from colonialism (FNLA, MPLA, UNITA),[106] but ethnicity alone cannot explain the irreconcilable hostility. All three groups had active memberships from more than one ethnic group. Nor does a rigid class analysis work. It is true that the FNLA in the north had more support from businessmen, petty bourgeoisie, chiefs, and cash-cropping farmers, all of whom wanted a larger share of the capital pie, but the FNLA also had a peasant following. The MPLA was started by petty bourgeois intellectuals, but gained a solid base in the workers in the cities and had a variable relationship with the peasantry (depending on the period of the war.)[107] UNITA was more rural orientated and had a large peasant following, but they varied from cash croppers to semi-proletarian. Further differences among the three liberation groups involved the form the leadership took, from the personalised and autocratic command of Holden Roberto to the more populist approach of Jonas Sávimbi. Finally, the goals varied. The FNLA was fighting for political independence, without much discussion about economic transformation. The MPLA and UNITA had programmes for political and economic independence from colonial rule, but varied considerably in their tactics. Savimbi, putting power before principles, was willing to use Portuguese aid to fight the MPLA; he collaborated with the Portuguese against the MPLA forces.[108] As the war for independence became the 'second war for liberation', Savimbi accepted aid from South Africa to fight the MPLA and the Cubans. With that step, Savimbi lost credibility with the Frontline and other African leaders, in spite of UNITA programmes for co-operative farming and land redistribution. The 'civil war' in Angola raised the same questions as the Zimbabwean independence struggle. Disagreements among the three groups were over the degree of state control of production after political independence and whether a group indebted to South Africa should come to power. The MPLA won both victories: a state that could legally take control of production and one that was not beholden to apartheid for gaining power.

Efforts to take economic control of production and to transform the relations of production are a process not completed when the flag is raised at independence. For Angola, a major deterrent to the transformation has been the continued aggression of South Africa. The Angolan military had to retrain from a guerrilla force to a conventional one; precious resources have been spent on arms and equipment. Frequent invasions from South Africa into southern Angola disrupted transportation and vital productive sectors. Angola, with a sparse population and much fertile land, was importing 90 percent of its food needs by 1981, due to the war with South Africa and a severe drought in the south.[109]

Because of these fundamental disruptions in the economic production and distribution, the class and ethnic (African vs. *mestico*) struggles have not diminished. The subsistence and cash-cropping peasants need distribution of seed, fertiliser, and marketing facilities; production levels are sensitive to producer prices. Coffee production fell drastically because of abandoned plantations, but also because workers initially refused to return to do the picking.

The struggle among industrial workers continues; they have the right and opportunity for consultation and participation at their workplace through the *Comissao Sindical de Empresa*. But the CSE's are under central control, and strikes are forbidden. There is a long struggle ahead before workers do take charge.[110] But these workers have historically been a strong force in the MPLA; industrial workers are continuing to challenge tendencies toward bureaucratisation and demobilisation.

One segment of the petty bourgeoisie is trying to take over the state apparatus in order to promote its own private accumulation.[111] Some authors have written the state off as controlled by the autocratic state managers; most observers say that the struggle is very much alive.[112]

No one in Angola speaks yet of workers' control, but major changes have been made. Abandoned land has become state farms; co-operatives are encouraged, with mixed success. The large scale livestock production has been a success, and workers' participation in the decisions about production turned around the drastic fall in coffee production.[113]

As in Mozambique, the mass organisations are also a means to mobilise and educate the peasants/workers. The mass organisations provide opportunities for participation in policy decisions and implementation concerning the constituencies they serve (women, youth). Through participation in daily activities of the mass organisations, members learn the goals and ideals of the party. The Central Committee Report to the MPLA Congress of December 1977 explains as follows: 'The mass organisations are unity bodies which, leading and organising the broad masses of the people, constitute the main vehicles for the transmission of the Party policies to the whole people, and they are the guarantee of the *participation of the masses in the study, discussion and implementation of Party policy in all sectors of activity.'* [Emphasis mine][114]

The MPLA has been able to forge an alliance of workers, peasants, and petty bourgeoisie who are struggling to turn political and economic control over to the people; the goals are similar to those of Frelimo. But the conditions impeding progress are more severe, and those conditions also breed fundamental opposition within the alliance. The war for independence caused many internal disruptions. Virtually all the herds were killed. The South Africans burned every bridge as they crossed during their 500 mile retreat in 1975. Ninety percent of the white settlers left. Vehicles were disabled. Factories were sabotaged. In short, when food production did begin, there were little facilities to get it to market, few personnel to plan and coordinate supply with demand. Spare parts were not available, and skilled personnel to do the repairs were not trained.

These internal dislocations were compounded by the war against South African invasions of Angolan territory. The iron ore production, a major foreign exchange earner, was not back in operation even in 1983, because the deposits are located in the south, the area of operation of the South African army. As stated earlier, fifty percent of the budget was spent on defence by 1979.[115] The Cuban forces (originally at 40,000 and down to 10,000 by October 1981 and up again to 15,000 in January 1982 because of South African invasions) are paid in full by the Angolan government,[116] as are most of the foreign technicians, school teachers, and health workers. In addition, massive numbers of displaced Angolans have fled their land to other areas in Angola because of the fighting, and thousands of Namibian refugees have sought asylum in camps in Angola.

Basis of Relative State Autonomy

Given this history of underdevelopment and the continued state of war in southern Angola, how could Angola have supported the Frontline States for Zimbabwe? First, as stated in earlier chapters, the role of Angola as a Frontline State to Zimbabwe was limited. It did not join the Frontline until March 1976 after the end of the 'second war of liberation'. Angola provided a couple of training camps for ZAPU, but did not need to help much with material aid, for ZAPU was receiving arms and supplies from the Soviet Union. (However, Rhodesian forces with the help of South Africa did bomb the ZAPU camps in Angola.) Angola's direct support of the Zimbabwean struggle was mainly ideological. Its defeat (with Cuban help) of the South African army gave important encouragement to the Zimbabwean nationalists in their struggle against white minority rule. Angola also helped the Frontline mobilise international diplomatic support for the Zimbabwean nationalists.

Angola's frontline is really turned more towards Namibia than towards Zimbabwe. With its independence, Angola immediately offered sanctuaries to Namibian refugees and camps for SWAPO (South West Africa People's Organisation) guerrillas. This logistic and material support enabled SWAPO to step up its armed struggle against South African rule in Namibia. It was this 'second front' for South Africa which indirectly helped the Zimbabwean nationalists. As shown in Chapter 5, South Africa gave substantial support to the Rhodesian regime, but held back from full mobilisation for Rhodesia. A major reason for such a limitation was that South Africa was fully involved in northern Namibia, with as many as 70,000 troops engaged there by 1980.[117] The South African regime, in short, saw Namibia as a priority and would have had difficulties in sustaining full mobilisation on two fronts. The Frontline States organised to support the Zimbabwean nationalists, but they did not see the Namibian struggle as separate from Zimbabwe. At present, Zimbabwe has joined the Frontline to direct attention and support to Namibian independence. Angola's priority in aiding SWAPO, therefore, was part of the Frontline strategy, and it served a clear purpose by engaging South Africa in a major war of counter-insurgency. Such a choice limited Angola's direct role in the struggle for Zimbabwe.

The question remains: how could Angola sustain its role as a Frontline State to support Zimbabwe and Namibia in spite of South Africa's heavy retaliation against SWAPO camps and Angolan villages? The first part of the answer is found in the relationship of foreign capital to Angolan resources. Angola's vast mineral wealth is a source of financial independence for the new state; Angola is underdeveloped but not poor, for the state has intervened to take control of ownership of the mines and of the oil wells. Although contracts were rewritten to establish terms more acceptable to the Angolan state, the transnational corporations have found the conditions profitable enough for them to remain.

Because of this mineral wealth, Angola has benefited from divisions among the foreign capitalists. During the 'second war of liberation', the MPLA defended the Gulf Oil Cabinda enclave from FLEC and FNLA who were armed by the US, France, and Zaire. Gulf Oil turned its royalties over to the MPLA with one exception in December 1975, when the US government required by law that they be put in escrow. Throughout the period of the Frontline States' support for Zimbabwe, the American government refused to recognise the sovereignty of the new state, while Gulf and other American corporations, satisfied with the conditions of business, supported the Angolan government. This division between the US capitalist state and individual capitalists is one reason for Angola's relative autonomy. As stated earlier, one condition for relative state autonomy results from individual capitals conflicting with what is perceived to be the general interest of capital. The American government refuses to recognise the new government of Angola, referring to it as a surrogate of Cuban and Soviet rule. The new state is a threat to the status quo of capitalist social formations in Southern Africa. The Angolan attempts to transform the relations of production are viewed as contradictory to the interests of advanced capitalism: profit for the short-term for individual corporations is not as important as protecting capitalist relations of production inside Angola as well as in the strategic area of South Africa, The American government has tried to isolate Angola in the world community; it has not discouraged South African armed aggression against Angola.

The corporate interpretation is that even a socialist state needs technology. They assert that the transition to socialism is long; and until the forces of production are developed, even a socialist state will be willing to pay an agreeable price for advanced technology. The corporations (Gulf Oil, Chase Manhattan Bank) have actually lobbied very strongly against US intervention in Angola and for the normalisation of relations.[118] This antagonism between the American state, trying to preserve the dominance of the capitalist social formation, and the individual capitalists' interests moderates the ability of the American state to intervene economically or politically in Angola. These restraints afford the Angolan state more autonomy in relation to these fractions of the dominant class.

The mineral wealth alone does not promote relative state autonomy; neither does the nationalisation of mineral production or of the major productive sectors. For other states, minerals in the hands of a dominant minority even with nationalisation have not deterred state autonomy. For example, Zambia's difficulties, in spite of its vast copper wealth, will be discussed in the next chapter. In Angola, however, to prevent local capital interests from simply replacing foreign capital, the Angolan state is beginning the long road to the transformation of the relations of production. The Angolan state is not waiting until the end of the war to increase workers' participation. Their interpretation is that such policies must be implemented *especially* because of the crisis. Only if the workers/ peasants are mobilised for production and participation can the crisis be overcome. As in Mozambique, the state can assert its relative autonomy against the dominant class, be they foreign or domestic capitalist interests. It tries to serve the interests of the dominated classes — not to preserve the capitalist mode of production but to transform into socialist relations. Such a political and economic base in the workers/peasants gives it crucial leverage against capital interests — in so far as those interests can continue to profit from the rich mineral deposits.

Finally, relative state autonomy has been increased by the ability of the state to seek alternative sources of support. As indicated in Chapter 4, Angola is fully integrated into the West, not the East. Western capital is invested in its major productive sectors. But the Soviets do offer alternative sources for trade and for technical advice. They are a vital source of military aid to deter the overthrow of the MPLA government.[119] Cuban combat troops were invited to Angola only after South Africa invaded in August 1975. The Angolan government recognises the important role of the Cubans and Soviets, for such assistance has been essential against armed intervention by South Africa.[120] The fact that the repressive state apparatus is not dependent on resources from dominant capitalist interests gives the state some relative autonomy from those interests.

As stated earlier, armed intervention is used only as a last resort by the dominant class to protect its interests. Not yet fully successful in taking control of production, Angolans have, nevertheless, succeeded in withstanding direct reprisals from capitalist interests who desire to maintain the dominant capitalist social formation in the Southern African region. Angola sustained its Frontline role and increased its relative state autonomy when Zambia and Mozambique were the border states most involved in the Zimbabwean conflict. Indeᵖendence of that central and pivotal state has released resources which are now turning to the southern Frontline facing Namibia. Angola is now the arena of the conflict, a position which intensifies both internal contradictions and external antagonisms. Yet Angolan leaders affirm that their economic struggle and the struggle for Namibia are one: the Angolan people will only gain full control of their productive sectors with the liberation of Namibia.[121] The independence of Zimbabwe was the necessary first step in that goal.

Notes

1. John Lonsdale, 'State and Social Processes in Africa', mimeo, paper presented at African Studies Association, Annual Meeting 21 October 1981, p. 48.
    See also Bill Warren, *Imperialism — Pioneer of Capitalism* (London: New Left Books, 1980), pp. 162–171.
    Robert Brenner, The Origins of Capitalist Development: A Critique of Neo-Smithian Marxism', *New Left Review* 104 (July–August, 1977), pp. 67–68.
2. Frederick Engels and Karl Marx, 'Engels to Conrad Schmidt in Berlin', *Selected Works*, Vol. 3 (Moscow: Progress, 1970), p. 494.
3. Frederick Engels, *The Origin of the Family, Private Property and the State* (New York: International Publishers, 1972), p. 229.
4. Hal Draper, *Karl Marx's Theory of Revolution*, Vol. 1 (New York: Monthly Review Press, 1977), pp. 256–258.
    Barry Hindess, 'Concept of Class in Marxist Theory and Marxist Politics', in Jon Bloomfield, ed., *Class, Hegemony and Party* (London: Lawrence and Wishart, 1977), p. 105.
    Nicos Poulantzas, *Classes in Contemporary Capitalism* (London: NLB, 1975), p. 78.
    Suzanne de Brunhoff, *The State, Capital and Economic Policy* (London: Pluto, 1978).
    Claus Offe, 'The Theory of the Capitalist State and Problem of Policy Formation', mimeo 1974, quoted in David A. Gold, *et al*, 'Recent

Developments in Marxist Theories of the Capitalist State', *Monthly Review* 27, No. 6 (November 1975), p. 39.

5. Karl Marx and Frederick Engels, 'Manifesto of the Communist Party', *Selected Works*, Vol. 1 (Moscow: Progress Publishers), 1969, p. 110.

6. Karl Marx, *Capital*, Vol. 3 (Moscow: Progress Publishers, 1959), pp. 791–792.

7. Engels, *Origins*, op. cit., pp. 229–230.

8. Karl Marx, 'The Civil War in France', in Marx and Engels, *Selected Works*, Vol. 2, op. cit., p. 217.

9. V.I. Lenin, 'State and Revolution', in *Selected Works*, Vol 2 (Moscow: Progress Publishers, 1963), pp. 243, 254–55, 258.

10. Nicos Poulantzas, *Political Power and Social Classes* (London: NLB, 1973), pp. 283, 287–88.

11. Theda Skocpol, *State and Social Revolutions* (Cambridge, Cambridge University Press, 1979), p. 33.

12. Harold Wolpe, 'Towards an Analysis of the South African State', *International Journal of Sociology and Law*, No. 8 (1980), pp. 399–421.

13. Critics will complain that this definition is too 'institutional', that the state is a site, a relationship, a process. The argument here is that definitions of the state which leave it as a 'condensation', 'site', or 'process', etc. are vague and indeterminant and do not inform theory. The usefulness of theory depends on its ability to explain empirical relations. In investigating the Frontline States, how does one analyse five 'sites'? A condensation does not exercise power. For a discussion of this problem, see Fred Block, 'Beyond Relative Autonomy: State Managers as Historical Subjects', *Socialist Register*, 1980, reprinted in *New Political Science*, No. 7 (Fall 1981), p. 35.

14. Theda Skocpol and Ellen Kay Trimberger, 'Revolutions and the World-Historical Development of Capitalism', in Barbara Hockey Kaplan, ed., *Social Change in the Capitalist World Economy* (Beverley Hills: Sage, 1978), pp. 128–129. Ralph Miliband, *Marxism and Politics* (Oxford: Oxford University Press, 1977), p. 67.

15. This definition of relative state autonomy does not preclude the possibility of the state having autonomy from the class struggle. The suggestion here is that the best indicator of the state's ability to be 'above' class struggle is its acting independently of the interests of the dominant class.

16. Bertell Ollman, 'Thesis on the Capitalist State', *Monthly Review* 34, No. 7 (December 1982), p. 44.

17. Bob Jessop, *The Capitalist State* (New York: New York University Press, 1982), pp. 182–183.

18. Michael Burawoy, 'State and Social Revolution in Southern Africa', *Kapitalistate*, No. 9 (Fall 1981), p. 117.

Nicos Poulantzas, 'The Internationalisation of Capital and the Nation State', *Classes in Contemporary Capitalism* (London: NLB, 1975).

Theda Skocpol and Ellen Kay Trimberger, op. cit., pp 131–135.

Kees van der Pijl, 'Class Formation at the International Level', *Capital and Class*, No. 9 (Autumn 1979), p. 1.

Mike Williams, 'The Theory of the Capitalist State(s)', *Capital and Class*, No. 9 (Autumn 1979), pp. 68–69.

Gabriel Palma, 'Dependency: A Formal Theory of Underdevelopment or a

Methodology for the Analysis of Concrete Situations of Underdevelopment?' *World Development* 6, 1978, p. 910.

19. Claudia von Braunmuhl, 'On the Analysis of the Bourgeois Nation State within the World Market Context', in John Holloway and Sol Picciotto, eds., *State and Capital* (London: Edward Arnold, 1978), p. 167.

20. James Petras, *Critical Perspectives of Imperialism and Social Class in the Third World* (New York: Monthly Review, 1978), p. 37. See also p. 55.

    See also: Colin Leys, *Underdevelopment in Kenya* (Berkeley: University of California Press, 1974), p. 206.

    Harry Goulbourne, 'The Problem of the State in Backward Capitalist Societies', *Africa Development* 6, No. 1 (1981), p. 49.

    Nicola Swainson, *The Development of Corporate Capitalism in Kenya* (Berkeley: University of California Press, 1980), p. 16.

21. Robert H. Davies, *Capital, State and White Labour in South Africa 1900-1960*, Atlantic Highlands (New York: Humanities Press, 1979), p. 27.

    Stanley Greenberg, *Race and State in Capitalist Development* (New Haven: Yale University Press, 1980), p. 390.

    Bharat Patankar and Gail Omvedt, 'The Bourgeois State in Post-Colonial Formations', *Insurgent Sociologist* 2, No. 4 (Spring 1980), p. 27.

    Ralph Miliband, op. cit., p. 88.

22. Karl Marx, *Capital*, op. cit., p. 264.

23. Maurice Zeitlin, ed., *Classes, Class Conflict and the State* (New York: Winthrop, 1980), p. 8.

24. John Holloway and Sol Picciotto, op. cit. This dilemma of capitalism is emphasised in the 'state derivation' theories.

25. Nicos Poulantzas, *Fascism and Dictatorship* (London: NLB, 1974). *The Crisis of the Dictatorships: Portugal, Spain and Greece* (London, NLB, 1976).

26. W. Zeimann and M. Lanzendorfer, 'The State in Peripheral Societies', *Socialist Register* (1977), p. 149.

27. Robert H. Davies, op. cit., pp. 30 -31.

    David Yaffe, 'The Marxian Theory of Crisis, Capital, and the State', *Economy and Society* 2, No. 2 (May 1973), pp. 186-232.

    A. Gamble and R. Walton, 'The British State and the Inflation Crisis', *CSE Bulletin* (Autumn 1973).

    Alan Wolfe, *The Limits of Legitimacy* (New York: Free Press, 1977).

28. James O'Connor, *Fiscal Crisis of the State* (New York: St. Martin's Press 1973), pp. 64-178.

29. Frederick Engels and Karl Marx, 'Letter to Conrad Schmidt', op. cit., p. 491.

30. Frederick Engels, *Origins*, op. cit., p. 231.

31. V. I. Lenin, op. cit., p. 246.

32. Maurice Zeitlin, op. cit., pp. 21-22.

33. T. B. Bottomore and M. Rubel, ed., *Karl Marx: Selected Writings in Sociology and Social Philosophy* (New York: McGraw Hill Book Co., 1956), p. 238.

34. The impact of the crisis of capitalism is dialectic. The crisis can and does hurt the peripheral economies. They lose markets; terms of trade deteriorate. However, there are advantages for the peripheral states in the crisis if they can avail themselves of them. The ability to take advantage of the crisis varies with the

resource base and the development of the forces of production. See Immanuel Wallerstein, 'The Rise and Future Demise of the World Capitalist System: Concepts for Comparative Analysis', *Comparative Studies in Society and History* 16, No. 4, pp. 406-407.

35. Hal Draper, op. cit., p. 408.
36. Jessop reminds us that Poulantzas abandoned his original argument that only 'classes and fractions of the power bloc can have privileged seats of power within the state apparatus . . . instead he suggests that the dominated classes can eventually secure real centres of power in the capitalist state itself'. Bob Jessop, op. cit., p. 185.
37. Fred Block, 'Marxist Theories of the State in World System Analysis', in Barbara Hockey Kaplan, ed., op. cit., pp. 32-33.
38. Nora Hamilton, *Mexico: The Limits of State Autonomy* (Princeton: Princeton University Press, 1982), p. 10.
39. Ibid., pp. 10-12.
   Erik Olin Wright, *Class, Crisis and the State* (London: NLB, 1978), pp. 15-16, 19-21.
40. William Minter, *Imperial Network and External Dependency: The Case of Angola* (Beverly Hills: Sage, 1972), p. 8.
41. Gerald Bender, *Angola Under the Portuguese: The Myth and the Reality* (Berkeley: University of California Press, 1978), pp. 58, 77, 107-188.
   James Duffy, *Portuguese Africa* (Cambridge, Mass: Harvard University Press, 1959), p. 98.
42. Douglas L. Wheeler, *Republican Portugal* (Madison: University of Wisconsin Press, 1978), pp. 217-219, 249.
   A. Smith, 'Antonio Salazar and the Reversal of Portuguese Colonial Policy', *Journal of African History* 15, No. 4 (1974), pp. 653-667.
43. Allen Isaacman, *Mozambique: The Africanization of a European Institution: The Zambezi Prazos, 1750-1902* (Madison: University of Wisconsin Press, 1972).
   S. Ishemo, *Some Aspects of the Economy and Society of the Zambezi Basin in the Nineteenth Century and Early Twentieth Centuries* (London: Institute of Commonwealth Studies), 1978.
   Carlos Serra, 'Prazos e companhias en Zambezia', *Tempo* (Maputo) No. 582, (6 December 1981), pp. 30-36.
   M.D.D. Newitt, *Portuguese Settlement on the Zambezi: Exploration, Land Tenure and Colonial Rule in East Africa* (Harlow: Longman, 1973).
44. J. Head, 'Sena Sugar Estates and Migrant Labour' (University of Edinburgh: Centre of African Studies, 1978).
   B. Neil-Tomlinson, 'The Nyassa Chartered Company, 1892-1928', *Journal of African History* 18, No. 1 (1977).
   Leroy Vail, 'Mozambique's Chartered Companies: The Rule of the Feeble', *Journal of African History* 13, No. 3 (1976), pp. 389-416.
45. Allen and Barbara Isaacman, *Mozambique in the Twentieth Century* (Boulder: Westview Press and Harare: Zimbabwe Publishing House, 1984), p. 33.
46. Centro de Estudos Africanos, Universidade Eduardo Mondlane, *The Mozambican Miner* (Maputo: 1977), p. 25.
47. Allen and Barbara Isaacman, 1984, op. cit., p. 4.

48. Douglas L. Wheeler, op. cit., pp. 249, 312.
    Leroy Vail and Landig White, *Colonialism and Capitalism in Mozambique* (Minneapolis: University of Minnesota, 1980).
49. Barbara Isaacman and June Stephan, *Mozambique: Women, the Law and Agrarian Reform* (Addis Ababa: Economic Commission for Africa, United Nations, 1980), ATRCW/SDD/RESOL/80, pp. 10-11.
50. Eduardo Mondlane, *The Struggle for Mozambique* (Harmondsworth, England: Penguin, 1969), p. 44.
51. Adapted from Eduardo Mondlane, ibid., pp. 91-93.
52. Centro de Estudos Africanos, op. cit., pp. 23, 66, 174.
53. Gerald Bender, op. cit., pp. 3-18, 103, 151.
    Allen Isaacman, *A Luta Continua* (Binghamton, NY: Fernand Braudel Center, 1978), pp. 9-10.
    F. J. Hammond, 'Race Attitudes and Policies in Portuguese Africa in the 19th and 20th Centuries', *Race* 9, No. 2 (1977), pp. 205-216.
    Eduardo Mondlane, 'Race Relations and Portuguese Colonial Policy, with special reference to Mozambique', *Objective Justice* 1, No. 1 (1969), pp. 14-19.
54. Marc Wuyts, 'Peasants and Rural Economy in Mozambique', paper presented at Universidade Eduardo Mondlane seminar, August 1978, p. 34.
55. Allen Isaacman, 1984, op. cit., p. 24.
    Eduardo Mondlane, 1969, op. cit., 85–87.
56. George Houser and Herb Shore, *Mozambique: Dream the Size of Freedom* (New York: Africa Fund, 1975), p. 44.
57. Xavier Pintado, 'Structure and Growth of the Portuguese Economy', (Geneva: EFTA, 1964), quoted in Eduardo de Sousa Ferreira, *Portuguese Colonialism from South Africa to Europe* (Freiburg: Aktion Drittee Weit, 1972), p. 234.
58. Allen Isaacman, *The Tradition of Resistance in Mozambique: The Zambesi Valley 1850-1921* (Berkeley: University of California Press, 1976).
    Reginald Coupland, *East Africa and Its Invaders* (Oxford University Press, 1938), pp. 51-52, 60-63.
    E. A. Friedland, 'Mozambican Nationalist Resistance 1920-49', *Civilisations* 27, Nos. 3/4 (1977), pp. 332-344.
59. Centro de Estudos Africanos, op. cit., pp. 107-108.
    John Saul, 'African Peasants and Revolutionary Change', *Review of African Political Economy* 1, No. 1 (1974), pp. 41-68.
60. Centro de Estudos Africanos, op. cit., p. 4.
61. Ronald Chilcote, 'Mozambique: African Nationalist Response to Portuguese Imperialism and Underdevelopment', in C. Potholm and R. Dale, *Southern Africa in Perspective* (New York: Free Press, 1974), p. 189.
62. Amilcar Cabral, *Revolution in Guinea* (New York: Monthly Review; 1969), pp. 62-63.
63. John Saul, *The State and Revolution in Eastern Africa* (New York: Monthly Review, 1979), pp. 9-10.
64. 'Press Statement on Lazaro Nkavandame', *Mozambique Revolution* No. 38 (March-April 1969), pp. 10-11.
    M. A. Samuels, 'The Frelimo School System', *Africa Today*, No. 3 (1971), pp. 69-73.

Samora Machel, 'Education in the Revolution', *Mozambique Revolution*, No. 57 (1973), pp. 20-24.

65. Eduardo Mondlane, *The Struggle for Mozambique*, reprinted by London: Zed Press, 1983, p. xxviii.

66. For discussion of these ideological goals, see Samora Machel, *Sowing the Seeds of Revolution* (London: Committee for Freedom in Mozambique, Angola and Guinea, 1975). John Saul, 1979, op. cit., pp. 46-52.

67. Personal Interviews conducted by Allen and Barbara Isaacman: Juliana Lais, Hirondiera Tonias, Marcelina Joaquim at Base Central, Mozambique, 25 April 1979. I was present and have notes of interviews. Tapes on file at OMM Archives. See also 'Mozambique Women in the Revolution' (Oakland: Liberation Support Movement, 1977), pp. 9-11.

Samora Machel, 'Women's Liberation is essential for the revolution', *African Communist*, No. 61 (1975), pp. 37-51.

Frelimo, 'First Conference of Mozambique Women', *Mozambique Revolution*, No. 54 (1973), pp. 22-24.

68. Personal Interviews, Tosé Alves Gomez, 14 April 1979: Aquino de Bragança, 18 April 1979.

Samora Machel, *Mozambique: Revolution or Reaction?* (Richmond, B.C.: Liberation Support Movement, 1975).

69. David and Marina Ottaway, *Afrocommunism* (New York: Holmes and Meier, 1981). According to the Ottaways, Frelimo had very little division between the military and political officials — less than other African liberation movements.

70. Nucleo da Oficina de Historia, Centro de Estudos Africanos, Universidade Eduardo Mondlane, 'Frelimo from Front to Party: Revolutionary Transformations', paper presented at University of Minnesota African Studies Council, 25 May 1983, p. 11.

71. Allen Isaacman, 1978, op. cit., pp. 24, 36, 42.

Carol Collins, 'Mozambique: Dynamising the People', *Issue* 8, No, 1 (1978), pp. 12-16.

72. Leo Casey, 'The Development of Frelimo Praxis', mimeo, December 1974. For discussion of elections to People's Assemblies, see:

Anon., 'Elections in Mozambique – The Reality of Liberty', *African Communist* 74, No. 3 (1978), pp. 60-74.

Anon., 'Mozambique Elections', *People's Power* 10 (1977), pp. 10-14.

Iain Christie, 'A Celebration Bigger than Independence...', *Africa*, January 1978, pp. 50-52.

For a history of the People's Courts, see:

Barbara and Allen Isaacman, 'A Socialist Legal System in the Making: Mozambique before and after Independence', *Politics of Informal Justice* Vol. 2 (New York: Academic Press, 1982), pp. 281-323.

73. Frelimo, 'The Third Party Congress of Frelimo', mimeo, Maputo, 1977.

74. Peter Sketchley, *Casting New Molds* (San Francisco: Institute for Food and Development, 1980).

Anon., 'Workers Control in Mozambique', *People's Power*, No. 11 (1977), pp. 21-29.

75. *Noticias,* 12 August 1977 and *Tempo* 348 (1977) quoted in Allen Isaacman, 1984, op. cit., p. 27.

76. Ibid., p. 28.

77. Nucleo da Oficina de Historia, op. cit., pp. 14-15.
   James Mittelman, 'State Power in Mozambique', *Issue* 8, No. 1 (1978), pp.4-11.
       — *Underdevelopment and the Transition to Socialism: Mozambique and Tanzania* (New York: Academic Press, 1981), pp. 81-102.
   P. Janke, *Marxist Statecraft in Africa – What Future?* (London: Institute for Conflict Studies, 1978).
   William Minter, 'Charting a Socialist Course: Frelimo Third Party Congress', *Southern Africa* 10, No. 3 (1977), pp. 2-4.

78. Nucleo da Oficina de Historia, op. cit., p. 15.

79. Samora Machel, Speech presented in Maputo on 18 March 1980, Mozambique Information Agency (AIM), Supplement to Bulletin 45.

80. Samora Machel, 'Garanter a Paz Tranquilidade e Seguranca', *Tempo*, No. 579, (15 November 1981), pp. 22-41.

81. Bertil Egero, 'Mozambique before the Second Phase of Socialist Development', *Review of African Political Economy*, No. 25 (September-December 1982), pp. 83-91.

82. Personal visit to Eden Clothing Factory, 20 April 1979. Purchase order and shredded cloth were shown to us.
   'How the Enemy Acts: A Case of Economic Sabotage', *People's Power*, No. 12 (1978), pp. 46-50.

83. Washington Notes on Africa, 'The Destabilization of Southern Africa', Winter 1981, pp. 1-5.
   Sean Gervasi, 'South Africa's Terrorist Army', *Southern Africa* 26, No. 5 (December 1982), pp. 5-10.
   Barbara and Allen Isaacman, 'The People's Counter Offensive', Ibid., pp. 10-12.

84. 'Fourth Congress of the Frelimo Party', Mozambique Information Agency, No. 82 (26-30 April 1983).

85. Personal interview, Tosé Alves Gomez, 14 April, 1979.
   William Minter, 'Major Themes in Mozambican Foreign Relations, 1975-1977', *Issue* 8, No. 1 (Spring 1978), p. 44-49.

86. For detailed analyses of the slave trade and its economic and political impact, see:
   Herbert S. Klein, 'The Trade in African Slaves to Rio de Janeiro (1795-1811)', *Journal of African History* 10, No. 4 (1969), pp. 533-549.
       — 'The Portuguese Slave Trade from Angola in the Eighteenth Century', *Journal of Economic History* 32, No. 4 (1972), pp. 894-918.
       — *The Middle Passage: Studies in the Atlantic Slave Trade* (Princeton: Princeton University Press, 1977).
   Joseph C. Miller, 'The Slave Trade in Congo and Angola', in Martin L. Kilson and Robert I. Rotberg, eds., *The African Diaspora: Interpretative Essays* (Cambridge, Mass: Harvard University Press, 1976).
       — 'Some aspects of the Commercial Organization of Slaving at Luanda, Angola, 1760-1830' in Jan S. Hogendorn and Henry A. Gemery, eds. *The Uncommon Market: Essays in the Economic History of the Trans-Atlantic Slave Trade* (New York: Academic Press, 1979).

87. James Duffy, *Portugal in Africa* (Harmondsworth: Penguin Books, 1962), p. 72.
88. W. G. Clarence-Smith, *Slaves, Peasants and Capitalists in Southern Angola, 1840-1926* (Cambridge: Cambridge University Press, 1979).
89. Henrique Galvao, Portuguese inspector-general of the colonies, quoted by Basil Davidson, *In the Eye of the Storm: Angola's People* (Garden City, NY: Doubleday, 1973), p. 136.
90. United Nations, Report of the Subcommittee on the Situation in Angola (A/4978), 1962, p. 38, quoted in Gerald J. Bender, op. cit., p. 142.
91. Gerald J. Bender, Ibid., p. 20.
       — and P. Yoder, 'Whites in Angola on the Eve of Independence; the Politics of Numbers', *Africa Today* 21, No. 4 (1974), pp. 23-37.
92. For accounts of African resistance to Portuguese rule, see:
    Ronald Chilcote, ed., *Protest and Resistance in Angola and Brazil* (Berkeley: University of California Press, 1972).
    Lawrence Henderson, *Angola: Five Centuries of Conflict* (Ithaca: Cornell University Press, 1979).
    René Pélisser, 'Campagnes militaires au Sud-Angola (1855-1915)', *Cahiers d'Etudes Africaines* 9, No. 1 (1969). A chronology of the military campaigns against the Africans.
93. Mark Roth and Allison Herrick, *Angola: A Country Study* (Washington, DC: American University Press, 1979), p. 38. Basil Davidson, op. cit., p. 135.
94. For accounts of nineteenth century Angola, see:
    Jill Dias, 'Black Chiefs, White Traders, and Colonial Policy near the Kwanza: Kabuku Kambilo and the Portuguese, 1873-96', *Journal of African History* 42, No. 2 (1976), pp. 276-290.
    David Birmingham, *Trade and Conflict in Angola* (Oxford: Clarendon, 1966).
    W. G. Clarence Smith and Richard Moorsom, 'Underdevelopment and Class Formation in Ovamboland, 1845-1915', *Journal of African History* 16, No. 3 (1975), pp. 365-382.
    Douglas Wheeler and René Pélissier, *Angola* (New York: Praeger, 1971).
95. See Gerald Bender, op. cit., pp. 59-132, for a concise and insightful account of Portuguese settlement schemes.
96. Carlos Rocha Dilolwa, *Contribuiçao a Historia Economica de Angola*, n.p., (1978), pp. 24-27.
97. William Minter, 1972, op. cit., pp. 30-32.
98. United Nations, Report of Subcommittee 1, 1965, quoted in Eduardo de Sousa Ferreira, 1972, op. cit., p. 45.
99. Americo Boavida, *Angola: Five Centuries of Portuguese Exploitation* (Richmond, B.C.: LSM Press, 1972), pp. 91-99.
100. Mario de Andrade and Marc Ollivier, *The War in Angola: A Socio-Economic Study* (Dar es Salaam: Tanzania Publishing House, 1976).
    Gerald Bender, op. cit.
    Basil Davidson, op. cit.
    Lawrence Henderson, op. cit.
    John Marcum, *The Angolan Revolution, Vol. 1: The Anatomy of an Explosion (1950-62)* (Cambridge, Mass: MIT Press, 1969).
    The Angolan Revolution, Vol. II: Exile Politics and Guerrilla Warfare (Cambridge, Mass: MIT Press, 1978).

Jonas Savimbi, *Angola, a resistência em busca de uma nova nação* (Lisboa: Edição da Agencia Portuguesa de Revistas, 1979).

John Stockwell, *In Search of Enemies: A CIA Story* (New York: W. W. Norton, 1978).

Douglas Wheeler and René Pélissier, op. cit.

101. W.G. Clarence-Smith, op. cit., p. 71.

102. African cash croppers had not produced for export until the 1920's and then were cut off by the depression. Their export production did not recover until the 1950's.

Henrique Lopes Guerra, *Angola, estrutura económica e class sociais* (Lisboa: Ediçoes 70, 1979), quoted in WG. Clarence-Smith, 'Class Structure and Class Struggles in Angola in the 1970's', *Journal of Southern African Studies* 7, No. 1 (October 1980), p. 111.

103. Franz-William Heimer, *The Decolonization Conflict in Angola, 1974-76, an essay in political sociology* (Geneva: Institut Universitaire de Hautes Etudes Internationales, International Studies in Contemporary Africa Series, 2, 1979), p. 74.

104. W.G. Clarence-Smith, op. cit., p. 113.

105. These discussions of the petty bourgeoisie and of the class composition of liberation groups which follows are based on Henrique Lopes Guerra, Franz-Wilhelm Heimer cited above and on the following:

Claude Gabriel, *Angola: le tournant Africain?* (Paris, Editions la Breche, 1978).

Debate on Angola, *Review of African Political Economy* 14 (January-April, 1979), pp. 107-110; Nos. 15-16 (May-December 1979), pp. 148-153; No. 19 (September-December 1980), pp. 6-7 and pp. 69-76.

106. FNLA – National Front for the Liberation of Angola; MPLA – People's Movement for the Liberation of Angola; UNITA – National Union for the Total Independence of Angola. Authors who emphasise most the ethnic 'tripolarity' of the three movements are:

Colin Legum and Tony Hodges, *After Angola: The War over Southern Africa* (London: Rex Collings, 1976).

John Marcum, op. cit.

— 'Lessons of Angola', *Foreign Affairs* 54, No. 3 (April 1976), pp. 407-425.

107. See Basil Davidson, 'Angola: A Success that Changes History', *Race and Class* 18, No. 1 (1976), pp. 23-37.

Clarence-Smith, 1980, op. cit., pp. 117-118.

Claude Gabriel, op. cit., pp. 224-230 for a critical view of relationship between MPLA and the workers.

108. *Afrique-Asie*, 8 July 1974; extract in *Review of African Political Economy* No. 5 (January-April 1976).

109. Economist Intelligence Unit, Quarterly Economic Review, Annual Supplement, *Angola*, 1981, p. 80.

110. Paul Fauvet, 'In Defence of the MPLA and the Angolan Revolution', *Review of African Political Economy*, 15/16 (May-December, 1979), pp. 148-152.

Agostinho Neto, 'On People's Power', *Tanzania Daily News*, 23 December 1977; an interview that assesses the mistakes made in the organs of 'people's power' that led to the coup attempt by Nito Alves and suggests changes being made by the party to correct them.

David Coetzee, 'Angola's Internal Struggle', *New African*, September 1980, pp. 11-17.

111. The Nito Alves coup attempt tried unsuccessfully to inflame the workers' grievances against the state. See Paul Fauvet, 'The Rise and Fall of Nito Alves', *Review of African Political Economy*, No. 9 (May -August 1978), pp. 88-104.

112. Claude Gabriel, op. cit., for the argument that autocratic state managers are in control. *Review of African Political Economy*, Debates, op. cit., for the argument that the class struggle continues.

113. Jennifer Davis, 'Report on a Visit to Angola', mimeo, March 1981. Economist Intelligence Unit, *Angola*, op. cit., p. 8.

114. Paul Fauvet, op. cit., p. 151.

115. Economist Intelligence Unit, *Angola*, op. cit., p. 14.

116. Gerald Bender, 'Why Optimism about a Namibian Settlement?'*New York Times*, 8 January 1982.

117. 'The Shooting War', *Southern Africa* 14, No. 1 (January/February 1981), p. 15.

118. 'Companies Resisting US Foreign Policy', *New York Times*, 27 July 1981.

119. Arthur J. Klinghoffer, *The Angolan War: A Study in Soviet Policy in the Third World* (Boulder: Westview Press, 1980).

120. Gerald Bender, 'Comment: Past, Present and Future Perspectives of Cuba in Action', *Cuban Studies* 10, No. 2 (July 1980), pp. 44-54.

121. Mendes de Carvalho, speech and interview, Los Angeles, 14 April 1980.

CHAPTER 7

Limitations To State Autonomy: Populist Support For Zimbabwean Liberation

Setting up programmes for the transition to socialism, the states in Mozambique and Angola have initiated basic structural changes in their economies. Challenging capitalist relations of production, the goal is to socialise the means of production by mobilising the producers to take control of production. Only initial steps have been taken toward this goal, for the transition toward socialism is a process. Yet these conditions form the very basis of state autonomy from the dominant capitalist class, and this relative autonomy facilitated their roles as Frontline States. For the other three Frontline States — Botswana, Tanzania, Zambia — the challenge to the capitalist class is not fundamental; it is more to limit the excesses of capitalism than to transform radically the relations of production. Yet the theories of relative state autonomy hypothesise that peripheral capitalist states can, under certain conditions, assert autonomy from the dominant class. This chapter will analyse each of the three political economies to investigate whether conditions for relative autonomy existed and what impact it might have had to promote the Frontline challenge to dominant interests in the region. The sections follow the same outline as for Mozambique and Angola: first, a brief overview of colonial political economy, second, an analysis of the state and class formations, and third, a discussion of relative state autonomy and its impact on Frontline policy.

Botswana: Humanitarian Support For Zimbabwean Liberation

Colonial Political Economy

Botswana became part of the line of march of British capital as it penetrated into the interior to the Southern and Northern Rhodesias. Few settlers stopped in Botswana, for there was little water, and at

214

that time, no known mineral deposits. Capital investment and settlers were more attracted to the rich mineral resources in the north. Britain only reluctantly took administrative control of the territory, primarily to protect the route to the northern mineral fields from three threats: advancing Boer farmers in the south, Portuguese in the east, and Germans in the west. Never wanting more than administrative rights over the area, the British did less to develop Bechuanaland (Botswana) than any of its other colonies.[1]

Before colonial rule was established in 1880, the Batswana produced rich fields of grain and owned large herds of cattle. By careful migration of the cattle and regulation of planting, an ecological balance was established that supported the whole community; no one went hungry.[2] As settlers established themselves in the areas around Botswana, however, the available grazing lands became more and more restricted. Whole communities moved into Botswana to escape control by the Boers. (As stated in the section on Angola, some even migrated from Angola to escape forced labour by the Portuguese.) In taking full control away from the British South African Company in 1895,[3] the British colonial government established the present borders of Botswana which left two-thirds of the Batswana under control of South Africa.

Because of the reduction in grazing and arable land resulting from the influx of whole communities, men from Botswana began to migrate to the South African mines in search of work as early as the 1880's.[4] Historically, therefore, Botswana has been a labour reserve area for South Africa since the nineteenth century, similar to Mozambique. By 1930, 5,000 Botswanan men were working in the mines and the number doubled every five years.[5] Estimates vary but show that a very high proportion of the adult male population worked in the mines (as high as 20–25 percent at any one time by the mid-1970's). Jack Parson calls this labour sector the 'peasantariat': the migrant workers must go to the mines to supplement the household incomes with their wages. At the same time, the worker is not fully proletarianised because he works on a contract basis far below subsistence wages. Two sources of income, marginal farming and meagre wages, are necessary for subsistence.[6] Parson also suggests that the creation of the peasantariat was within the context of ethnic political relations, thus mystifying the class relations: 'The mass of household/family-based subsistence producers in a tributary system faced with additional cash requirements was forced to send one or more members into available wage employment . . . But the process through which this happened . . . was conducted through existing tributary political relations . . .'[7] Labour for the mines was recruited through the ethnic group leaders; in addition, the migrants' families had to subsist on their own production. The migrant workers did not identify as working class, for they were not fully divorced from the land nor from the traditional ethnic provision of social welfare.

The tributary system might have alleviated some of the worst exigencies of migratory labour, by providing for the rural family in times of crisis, but it also revealed a pre-capitalist stratification of society based on cattle. Land was communally owned, for everyone had access rights. Stratification of society, however, was based on ownership and access to cattle; the traditional leaders were distinguished economically by the size of their herds, cared for by the labour of the less wealthy in the society. The communal land ownership limited the degree of stratification, for land could not be enclosed nor could one claim exclusive rights to boreholes. As will be discussed shortly, however, the wealthier cattle owners were able to translate this traditional power into increased economic wealth through the vehicle of the newly independent state.

Contemporary Political Economy

Labour migration did not cease with political independence (1966). According to a 1974 survey, 91 percent of the farms still did not produce enough food for self-sufficiency because of inadequate land and insufficient draught animals. The number of migrant workers reached a peak of 40,000 by 1978.[8] Only by the 1980's did Botswana begin to reduce its labour export to South Africa, mainly because South African policy changed to favour its own labour on the mines. By 1981 only 20,000 Batswana were on the mines.[9] (As noted earlier, Mozambique had chosen to begin reducing its labour export in 1975; later, South Africa reduced employment of labour from the Frontline States by mechanisation, using gold profits of the mid-1970's, and by hiring labour from the bantustans.)

The major reason for the increased migration to the South African mines until very recently is not simply South African willingness to hire more labour. Several government surveys in the early 1970's reveal that the percentage of impoverished peasantry was quite high. The Rural Income Distribution Survey, in addition to revealing the lack of food self-sufficiency, pointed out that 45 percent of the families fell below the poverty datum line.[10] An FAO survey in 1973 showed that 33 percent of the male heads of household had no cattle and 22 percent did no planting. Because of the migration of men (61.4 percent in the 20–29 age bracket were absent), the poverty was particularly severe for the female heads of household: 76 percent had no cattle and 49 percent did no planting.[11] Some income could be received from the husband's wage in the mines, but all surveys agree that it was insufficient even for subsistence. What is more likely the case is that increasing concentration of cattle and arable land into the hands of the wealthier pushed more men off to the mines, leaving the rural female heads of household in dire poverty, without draught animals for ploughing and without access to sufficient water.[12]

Migration has not only increased to the mines but also to the urban areas. The National Development Plan in 1976 called the rate of urbanisation one of the highest in Africa and admitted that it was above the normal pace expected under development schemes. Urbanisation was 15 percent in 1978.[13] By 1981, urbanisation increased even more with the drastic reduction in migrant labour to the South African mines. Some of the labour could be employed by the expanding mineral production in Botswana. In general, urban workers are paid less than on the mines and have few skills to offer for entry into government offices. The government has planned work projects to increase employment, but the problem is far from resolved and could be politically explosive. Labour unions are controlled by the state, and in the past labour unrest has been quickly crushed by the state.[14]

A few farmers have avoided the general rural impoverishment by gaining access to plough and oxen for planting, by acquiring some cattle, and hence forming a stratum of middle peasants. Many of these are in the Pupil Farmers Scheme; although they number little over 8 percent of the landholders, they harvest 26 percent of the main cereal crops.[15]

The government has leased or sold land to farmers; there are now about 400 freehold farms operated by 300 farmers.[16] Some of the farmers are mixed agricultural crop producers and herders; others in the west are solely for ranching. Receiving services from the government, the freehold farms are large and prosperous and represent an important source of wealth among the Batswana.

Another segment of the dominant class are the wealthy ranchers, most of whom do not engage in crop production. Many of them are top leaders in the government, and they use their position in the state apparatus to promote their own reproduction. Their position of influence and relatively higher salaries are used not to enter private business but to purchase cattle. The state has subsidised cattle production and has engaged in primitive accumulation through the consolidation of grazing land.[17] The state regulated access to boreholes and opened the Kalahari sandveld to grazing. By 1979 some *individuals* were wealthy enough to qualify for a fenced leasehold ranch with the ownership of 400 cattle, required by the *Tribal* Grazing Land Policy. The increased concentration of cattle ownership is best expressed by the fact that 0.4 percent of all rural households own 13 percent of the national total of cattle.[18] The Tribal Grazing Land Policy (1975) was to be a major attempt at land reform, but critics assert that its real purpose was to protect the general interests of the dominant commercial cattle-herders: 'The TGLP was directed primarily to checking the dangerously self-destructive aspects of commercialisation, and amounted to a systematic intervention by the state to secure the long term conditions of capital accumulation over competitive short-term self interest.'[19] Communal grazing land was retained for small farmers, but there continued to be peasantariat resistance to the TGLP.[20]

The alliance of foreign capital with the colonial state had blocked the development of commercial farms and retarded the development of ranching. In 1924 South Africa put a weight requirement on cattle from Botswana which effectively blocked most imports. Improved husbandry techniques gradually increased the quality of Botswanan cattle, but the marketing remained dependent on South Africa. By 1955 an abattoir had been built in Lobatse and Botswana could begin to ship beef to Europe. Finally, the EEC through the Lomé Convention made an exception to permit entry of Botswanan beef to the EEC. Now beef processing is 80 percent of the total agricultural output, while the average annual crop production is only two-thirds of required needs. (This figure is for a good year; drought in 1982 reduced crop production to one-sixth of need.)[21]

Until the 1950's when the abattoir was built, the major foreign exchange earner for the Protectorate was taxes and fees on the migrant mine workers; labour was the major export. After the 1950's beef also became the major export, with periods of downturns, such as in 1977–78 when foot and mouth disease spread from the untended Rhodesian herds into Botswana. By the early 1970's major strains of

minerals, especially diamonds, were discovered, and mineral production is now the major foreign exchange earner. In 1973–74
budgeted government expenditures could increase by 57 percent
because of the increased revenue from mineral production.[22]

The minerals are mined by foreign capital; Anglo-American
Corporation (South Africa) works one coal, one copper, one nickel and
three diamond mines. Production is capital intensive with few forward
or backward linkages to create employment opportunities. The state
provided the infrastructure for the mines and intervenes little in
production. The copper-nickel complex is only 15 percent owned by
the government (the rest by American Metal Climax Corporation and
Anglo-American). However, in 1975 the government negotiated to
take control of the most valuable mineral, diamonds. It changed its
ownership in the diamond mines from 15 to 50 percent and now
receives 65–70 percent of the profits from DeBeers which still
controls the marketing. But this government partnership in diamond
mining is an exception. In 1977 the permitted outflow of profits,
dividends, and interests amounted to 18 percent of the GDP per
capita. [23] The policy for expatriation of capital remains a major
incentive for foreign capital; corporations are also given a tax holiday
if they agree to train Batswana personnel. Botswana, more than any of
the other Frontline States, encourages and aids foreign capital
investment. It has no control over the processing or marketing of its
minerals. As a peripheral capitalist state, the government interferes
little with foreign private production in the mines.

In Botswana, during the time of the Frontline struggle for
Zimbabwe, there was no relative state autonomy. The dominant class
— composed of foreign capital, the large cattle ranchers, the free-hold
farmers, and the petty bourgoisie in the state apparatus (who were
aspiring to become large cattle owners) — used the state to its
advantage. It is not known how many individuals are at once large
cattle ranchers, free-hold farmers, and government bureaucrats, but
the overlap of the three groups is considerable. The opening of the
copper-nickel and diamond mines accelerated capitalist penetration
and class stratification, to create this emerging 'national' bourgeoisie.
During the 1970's, the three groups were united in their efforts to
attract foreign capital to finance the increasing demands made on the
state as well as to use the state to build a national capitalist base. As
stated earlier, the struggle is to preserve the general interests of this
dominant group, as the state facilitates increased private accumulation.

Some restrictions have been put on foreign capital, but they are minimal, reflecting the weakness of the very nascent national bourgeoisie and its insufficient capital to enter the mining sector. The state encourages foreign capital to develop the resources, while keeping close watch over the operations. Because the state has intervened mainly to regulate capital (rationalisation of private cattle grazing and overseeing of the mines) rather than to be a partner in investment, Botswana is more clearly a capitalist economy than any of the other Frontline States.

With the growing concentration of land and cattle under the auspices of the state, the political stability and the low level of class struggle in Botswana are surprising. The stability of the multi-party political system is based on several factors. First, migrant workers are more difficult to organise than proletariat. Not home most of the time, they are not easily mobilised or organised to present their interests.[24] The peasantry has no independent or self-sufficient base for production on which to centre their political organisation.

As important as the fragmentation of the producers, however, is the spectacular growth of the Botswanan economy. The benefits of the growth have been distributed widely enough to raise the standard of living of most of the people. Over 90 percent of school age children have access to schools.[25] From 1973 to 1977, real agricultural output increased greatly, resulting in a growth of household incomes of the poorer families that was higher than for the richer ones.[26] Economic growth has also expanded the opportunity for jobs in the government. As one study concludes, '. . . the BDP (Botswana Democratic Party) government has been able to spend its way out of political trouble; popular expectations have been low and results high'.[27]

Limitations to Relative State Autonomy

It is important to point out that the government leaders of Botswana fully supported the ideological stance of the Frontline States. Their own independence in 1966 symbolised the rejection of apartheid and racism; Britain had agreed not to incorporate the territory into South Africa unless the inhabitants consented, and the Batswana refused incorporation. Clear policy against racialism was part of the new government's programme. Economically integrated into South Africa, the government rejected any part of the apartheid ideology. When Ian Smith proclaimed UDI, therefore, the Botswanan leaders wanted to invoke at least partial sanctions against Rhodesia.

Not able to close the railway through Botswana because it was the only major route to the sea, the government did divert some trade and banned oil, arms, and military personnel from going through its territory to Rhodesia. The government stopped all flights to Bulawayo, Rhodesia. It refused to consider bids from Rhodesian firms for Botswanan government contracts.[28] Knowing apartheid well but having escaped bantustanisation of their own lands, the leaders were very supportive of the Zimbabwean struggle.

The role of Botswana in the Frontline States, however, does reflect the dependence of the economy on foreign capital and the lack of relative state autonomy from the dominant class. The Botswanan government was quite constrained in any overt support for the armed struggle. The government agreed to provide sanctuary for refugees, but would not harbour guerrillas. Anyone crossing into Botswana for refuge was flown out immediately to Zambia if he/she wanted to link up with the guerrilla forces. The government supported the Frontline resolutions for continuing the armed struggle, but could offer little economic support to the policy. In short, it played a humanitarian role. The government provided basic camps for Zimbabwean refugees which were supported materially and politically by international relief organisations.[29] Even for this humanitarian role, however, Botswana was bombed and had its own citizens killed by Rhodesians who would enter Botswanan territory in hot pursuit of 'guerrillas'. (See Chapter 3.)

The lack of relative state autonomy is evident in the fact that none of Botswana's Frontline policies acted against the interests of national fractions of the dominant class. The slight moves away from South African economic hegemony benefited the domestic fraction of the dominant class: the cattle ranchers did not want to be dependent on one market; establishment of the central bank would facilitate formation of a coherant national policy for monetary problems such as inflation. The pull away from South Africa benefited the formation of the nascent national bourgeoisie. Further, reduction of dependency on South Africa has not meant reduction of influence of foreign capital in general. Other sources of Western capital (see Chapter 4) have become alternatives to apartheid capital. In Botswana, foreign capital is still part of the dominant class and there is still antagonism with other fractions of national capital within that class.

Although Botswanan participation in the Frontline States was quite limited, its willingness to participate at all coincides with important economic and political choices that were made. The political choice was to loosen the ties somewhat with South Africa. Realising that economic independence was a long way off, the government moved to change somewhat the status quo. In 1969 a new customs union agreement was written which gave slightly more favourable terms to Botswana. (It was amended slightly in 1976 to modify revenue from duties.)[30] In 1974 Botswana made the commitment to buy out Rhodesian Railways which owned and ran the central line through Botswana. (The first rolling stock arrived in 1978.) As stated earlier, the government renegotiated the contract with De Beers in 1975 to take greater control of the diamond mining sector. It pulled out of the rand area and created its own currency, the pula, and a central Bank of Botswana to regulate monetary policy.[31] The Botswanan Development Corporation took part ownership in fourteen companies from hotels to manufacturing. Botswana joined the African-Caribbean-Pacific (ACP) countries in the Lomé Convention and received a share of the European market for beef sales, reducing greatly dependency on the South African market. By 1979 exports to South Africa had fallen to less than one-tenth of the total exports because minerals were a greater share in exports and were marketed outside the region.[32] These steps are not indicative of economic independence; Botswana remains very dependent on South Africa. But the degree of integration has been reduced; economic alternatives in the form of beef and mineral sales loosened the ties somewhat. The economic steps underwrote the political support of the Frontline States, and reciprocally, the political goals of the Frontline encouraged the economic steps.

With any serious threats from South Africa or Rhodesia, the Botswanan government would have had to retreat from the Frontline. But its stance was very important ideologically. With Botswana as a 'Frontline' State, Rhodesia was surrounded by forces hostile to white minority rule. To have such a weak and dependent state proclaim itself against white minority rule had an important ideological impact on the world community.

The leaders clearly shared the Frontline States' goal of helping to liberate Zimbabwe so its own economy could eventually have greater independence from South Africa. As will be seen in the next chapter, Botswanan Presidents Khama and Masire were instrumental in forming economic co-operation in Southern Africa to reduce the hegemony of South Africa in the region.[33] Botswana's economic independence will only come with the liberation of South Africa from white minority rule, but a neighbour like Zimbabwe will reduce the linkages to South Africa. Alternative markets for beef can open up in the region; alternative sources of goods to import are available. An independent Zimbabwe, especially with regional economic co-ordination, could loosen the grip of South Africa.

Tanzania: Populist Support For Zimbabwean Liberation

Colonial Political Economy

The slave trade under the influence of the Oman Sultanate on the island of Zanzibar ravaged Tanzanian territory during the 19th century. Slaves were sent from Tanzania to Arab states, as were ivory and gold. The slave market was not closed down in Zanzibar until 1873, and slavery was only halted in 1919. In 1890 an Anglo-German agreement divided East and Central Africa, the Germans were given Tanganyika as a sphere of influence.[34] Serious colonial penetration began shortly thereafter, but many of the ethnic groups, rejecting the imperialist decision, fought a series of wars against colonial occupation. Therefore, Tanzania (like the other Frontline States) was among the last of the African areas to be penetrated by colonial capital and to have the colonial power take effective control of the territory.

Germany lost its colonial claim after World War I; therefore, Tanzania became a League of Nations mandated territory to Britain whose settlers had already established extensive agricultural production in Kenya. As Angolan resources were diverted to Brazil, so the British diverted Tanzanian resources to Kenya after World War I.[35] Some German and British settlers did arrive in Tanzania, but not the large numbers of settlers that were in the neighbouring territories of Mozambique and Kenya. (The Germans expropriated 2 million acres, but by 1938 under the British, only a total of 9,345 German and British settlers were there.)[36] The settlers set up sisal plantations, mainly in the east-central part of the country, and established rubber and coffee plantations in the north. Plans were made to bring more white settlers, but the plans were never fulfilled as full British attention turned to Kenya.

The southern part of Tanzania became a labour reserve area for the plantations. The Germans tried to use forced labour, but resistance was strong; the Maji-Maji rebellion of 1905-6, during which an estimated 120,000 lost their lives, was in part a response to the forced labour. High colonial taxes were set to require Tanzanians to work for cash wages.

By the 1930's the northern part with fertile land became the enclave for peasant farming of cash crops for export: cotton, coffee, and tea.[37] Although parts of the north were occupied by white settlers, African peasants were encouraged to grow cash crops for export through a system of taxation that required cash payment. As in the Portuguese colonies, they received little in return for their marketed cash crops. Regulation of African farming under the British began as early as the 1920's, and had become widespread by the 1930's;[38] however, these Tanzanian peasant farmers remained in control of their land and were able to live above subsistence levels, even under colonial rule.

The southern area remains underdeveloped and is still a labour reserve area for the rest of the country. The central and northern sisal plantations remain, but now are under state control. Agricultural workers on the estates receive among the lowest wages of any labour in Tanzania. The north is still relatively the most productive area with, consequently, the greatest wealth. State policy after independence has been to try to ameliorate these regional economic inequities; the various rural programmes from *ujamaa* through villagisation and decentralisation promote this goal. (It is interesting to note, however, the *ujamaa* production was never tried in the wealthier areas of the north where individual peasant production remains the norm.)[39]

A further regional economic difference is important, for it has political expression today. Tanzania was perhaps fortunate in not having to overcome the economic and political hegemony of white settlers that Zambia, Mozambique and Angola confronted, but at the same time, Tanzania's economy was clearly set subordinate to Kenya's. The contradictions of this relative subordination to Kenya and resulting underdevelopment fully emerged during the efforts to establish an East African Economic Community.[40] When the Kenyan government rejected the industrial allocation agreement proposed at Kampala, the Tanzanian government protested that it was one of many examples of how old colonial patterns were being reinforced, not transformed. Finally, after Idi Amin came to power in Uganda and Mozambique gained independence, Tanzania began looking south for its economic liaisons. During the period under discussion, 1975–1980, the state was clearly directing its economic attention to its southern neighbours. Its participation as a Frontline State was not so much an expression of existing economic ties with southern neighbours, but more one of aspiration to greater economic exchange and co-ordinated development with them.

The State and Class Struggle in Tanzania

As a populist, President Nyerere insists that Tanzania has few if any class divisions: '. . . we in Tanzania have stopped, and reversed, a national drift towards the growth of a class society, based on ever-increasing inequality and the exploitation of the majority for the benefit of a few'.[41] This myth endures because, relative to other African states, class divisions in Tanzania have not had much political expression. In the colonial period peasant lands remained relatively small, but so did the number of settler plantations. Independent peasant production, not plantation production, was the basis of the economy. Some peasants were wealthy enough to hire labour and began to differentiate their interests from the smaller peasants. But the 1961 independence struggle was waged by a broad front of peasants, commercial traders, small factory owners, large farmers, artisans, shopkeepers, and civil servants.[42] In 1967, following the Arusha Declaration, the state intervened to limit the surplus accumulation of the most prosperous Tanzanians: the merchants. State marketing boards were established. The mining and industrial interests under foreign control were modest but were put under state partnership. Few areas were left open for investment of surplus as key sectors were nationalised: banks, insurance, housing, wholesale marketing, energy, and basic commodity production such as textiles and fertilisers.[43] In 1964 private contributions to total investment was 72 percent; by 1975 it was only 36 percent.[44]

Consequently, civil servants and party officials now have the greatest opportunity for accumulation of surplus through the state. (See Shivji, Saul, and Samoff for different interpretations of the bureaucracy.)[45] Their base salaries are modest, even low by Kenyan, Nigerian or Ivory Coast standards. But this basic salary is greatly increased by access to privileges: liberal personal use of state cars and land rovers, paid 'vacations' by frequent business trips within Tanzania and regular fully paid trips to foreign countries. Accumulation results in additional houses and access to, not ownership of, additional land for agricultural production. A few are able to invest in trucks and buses for transport services. In short, outlets for private investment are not extensive by any standard and are quite limited in the productive sectors. Investment in productive activities is mainly in agricultural production; one acquires access to land and hires wage labour to grow cash crops. But again, there are no large landowners in Tanzania; lease rights to use land measure plots in 100's of hectares, not 1,000's.[46]

Critics explain that these limitations on accumulation are simply a result of necessity; the forces of production are so underdeveloped that large savings and investment are not possible. 'Wealth' is relative. However, capitalists are not measured by the size of their bank accounts, but rather by their relation to the means of production. The state owns the major means of production. Further, there are structural restraints on the *private* expropriation of surplus (in contrast to Zambia; see the next section). Tanzanians cannot enter corporate jobs in the private sector while serving in government or party positions. They are constrained from speculation in real estate for private gain. They cannot purchase large tracts of land. In short, major productive sectors which create capital are closed to private control. As an economic crisis deepened in the 1980's — from debts as a result of the Idi Amin war, agricultural dislocations, and deterioration of the terms of trade (see Chapter 4) — more goods were exported to increase foreign exchange earnings, making many commodities scarce for local consumption. With this scarcity of goods, corruption increased, benefiting the state bureaucrats and traders. The government has not been able to prevent accumulation through corruption, but corruption was not extensive until the post-Amin war crisis. By 1982, the government estimated that 15 per cent of the marketed goods were through *magendo* (black market), and the proportion was growing.[47] At the time of the Rhodesian war, it was not extensive by any standards, and that war is only a minor factor in its subsequent spread. As shown in Chapter 3, the cost of supporting the Zimbabwean nationalists did stretch Tanzania's development funds for infrastructure, but most economic analysts cite other factors as causes of the economic hardships: oil price increases, cost of the Amin war, decline in peasant production, inefficient marketing procedures, and recurrent drought. [48]

To summarise, those in control of the state in Tanzania do control production through the state apparatus. They do have access to surplus created by the producers. This surplus is translated into private consumption (of cars, vacations, trips, etc.), but is not easily translated into reinvestment in the private sector. Therefore, by their relationship to the means of production, those in charge of the state apparatus form a fraction of the dominant class. If one adds further criterion of private expropriation of social production, however, that fraction is not fully capitalist. This distinction is significant for understanding the seemingly contradictory policies.

The Tanzanian state not only requires majority ownership in foreign-financed enterprises (a requirement which does not bother the transnational corporations because the state helps to carry the cost of initial investment and of building infrastructure — see the following section on Zambia), it also limits the ability of foreign capital to co-opt fractions of the class that direct the state apparatus. Tanzanian state managers have their fortunes tied to the state, not to one segment of production within the economy. The state acts, therefore, on behalf of the total class interests. Class self-interest is served by promoting the overall viability of the state, not one industrial corner of the economy.

It is this situation which has caused much controversy among analysts of Tanzania. The economy has been called both 'state capitalist' and 'socialist' and described as a total failure versus one that has successfully redistributed resources.[49] These different perspectives result from selective emphases on different sectors and indicators.[50] The restriction on private expropriation of social production are real, yet there are rich farmers and traders, relative to the peasantry, who exert a greater influence on state policy. At times, the state has allied with the workers/peasants against this national bourgeoisie in formation, such as the nationalisation of the marketing boards. Further, the government controls prices and taxes luxury goods heavily; it prevents totally or restricts the import of many goods for luxury consumption. (Many consumer items which are made in Tanzania — textiles, shoes, etc. — have severe import restrictions on items of foreign origin, but also items which are not produced in Tanzania and are labelled a luxury are strictly controlled.) The government, therefore, has circumscribed both private accumulation and consumption.

It has also, however, aided the wealthier farmers and traders against the middle and poor peasants.[51] For example, since 1974, in alliance with the wealthier farmers against the peasantry, the financial sector of the government has welcomed aid (especially from the World Bank) that is directed to the 'successful' farmer, and the Tanzania Rural Development Bank favours them in the granting of loans.[52]

These incentives/restrictions for the dominant class can occur in the same period, such as promoting production of crops through producer price incentives but also maintaining restrictions on the private expropriation of surplus (through taxes) and luxury consumption (houses, cars, etc.). These wealthy farmers and traders, therefore, influence the state, but do not capture it. Wealthy farmers and traders need the state to receive production inputs such as fertiliser, machinery, loans, etc., but they are critical of policies which limit their investment and consumption decisions. They need state control to protect them from foreign capital but fight against state limitation of their accumulation, by influence in the party or the bureaucracy (which in many local areas was hard to distinguish because personnel carry both party and administrative titles in this period of 1974-1980).[53]

Most analysts agree that *ujamaa* has been a failure and that direction of the peasants from above has increased. They are not mobilised as in Mozambique, and local control often remains on paper.[54] The villagisation programme has been described benignly as bringing the agricultural producers together for more collective production and allocation of services, while it has also been described critically as simply a means to enhance state control over the exploited. Allocation of services has increased — and so has state control. (In some areas it was reported that individual families are allocated one acre for their responsibility in 'communal' production as a means to monitor who is contributing time.) As noted in Chapter 4, agricultural production dropped in the late 1970's — due first to dislocations by the villagisation programme, and then due to peasant resistance to low producer prices and marketing inefficiency and corruption. Peasants had turned to smuggling or returned to subsistence production.[55]

It is also true, however, that the general quality of life in the rural areas increased from independence to 1980. Limits on the private expropriation of surplus facilitates the ability of the Tanzanian state to reallocate surplus back to the subordinate classes. Universal primary education was achieved in 1978, two years ahead of schedule: enrolment for the secondary schools (1975: 2 percent enrolment, one of the lowest in Africa) and for the university was kept down in an attempt to spread basic education and literacy among all the people. Adult literacy rose from 33 percent in 1967 to 73 percent in 1978. (Literacy rate in Kenya is 40 percent and only 10 percent in

Senegal.)[56] The health priority is preventive medicine for the rural sectors. For example, the programme to provide maternal-child health care to every village is being pursued. Life expectancy has risen from 37 to 51 years (1961-81) and infant mortality has fallen from 175 to 140 per 1,000.[57] Progress has been made in providing drinking water to the villages. These services greatly increased after the aggregation of individual families into village communities. (Between 1969 and 1976 the proportion of peasants in communities rose from 15 percent to 70 percent.)[58] Because of explicit priority given to food production, acreage under food crops rose consistently from 1970 to the drought of 1981. Although drought has seriously lowered productivity several times (most severely in 1974-75 and 1980-81), the country could be self-sufficient in food production in years of average rainfall.

The government subsidised producer prices to raise them while keeping prices for basic commodities low. But return on production is still low for the peasants, and consumer goods very frequently are simply unavailable in the rural areas. The state, therefore, does extract surplus from peasant production, but not without the return of social services to the rural areas. The realities of the peasants can be expressed in this seeming contradiction: they are exploited; they struggle against that . . . and their quality of life is much improved.

The role of foreign capital was analysed extensively in Chapter 4, so it is only necessary to highlight its relationship to the other classes here. As shown earlier, foreign capital (both grants and loans) looms large in the Tanzanian budget. By its relative size, technological predominance, and its crucial support in times of crisis, its economic importance cannot be ignored by the state managers. Yet those who represent foreign capitalist interests cannot run the state. At times the state allies with foreign capital against the peasantry, but at other times it moves against foreign capital.

Private capital must conform to state control of profits, of expatriation of capital, and of use of foreign exchange (import licences). Sometimes national control is exercised as much for ideological as for economic reasons, as in the case of nationalising Lonrho to signal to the Western powers the government's displeasure over the attempt by Smith to split the nationalists (1978). Because the national bourgeoisie in formation (traders, rich farmers, parastatal managers) is so weak and small, it tends to co-operate more with foreign capital than to compete. Large farmers, traders, and parastatal managers need foreign input of expertise and capital to survive; more important, they support the idea that the profit motive is the best way to pull the Tanzanian economy out of the doldrums.[59] The state managers sometimes join this alliance and sometimes move against it. For example, in no fewer than six studies in the Andrew Coulson volume on parastatals (*African Socialism in Practice*), the state managers used foreign aid more to expand their own spheres of influence than to promote 'self-reliance'. In two case studies, they did move to limit the excesses of transnational corporations.[60] The basic ideological disagreement is not that material incentives are needed to increase production, but that uncontrolled profits will increase the inequities even more, by promoting growth in certain sectors only. They are agreed that agricultural surplus must provide the capital for industrial development; but they frequently disagree over how to do it. The disagreement is basic — over the degree of private or collective production, the percentage of profit left to individuals, organisation of the work force, etc.

Workers, a very small proportion of the population, are strictly controlled by the state trade unions. Strikes are restricted by the government. As former Finance Minister Edwin Mtei lamented, 'go-slow' procedures are almost the norm.[61] In addition, the workers are on the defensive ideologically. The government has declared that wages cannot be very much higher than income of the peasant producers. Workers' demands for higher wages to meet inflation are countered with the argument that wages must be kept in line with peasant income.[62] Wages were raised in 1980 in response to inflation, but the point is that the government initiates the decision, not unions threatening a strike. (An illustration of this power is that until recently the leader of the one national labour union has also been the Minister of Labour.) Because of the discontent of the workers and for structural reasons (shortages of raw materials, spare parts), workers' output declined by 50 percent from 1970–1980.[63]

These class differences not only reflect economic struggles, but involve conflicts over political control also. Villagisation did not give local control to the peasants, but rather has bureaucratised decision-making. As one agricultural scheme replaced another, villagers were left to insert a few details. The state managers protected their position through promoting the ethos of planning and expertise over mobilisation: failures called for more expertise and planning for co-ordination.[64] Complaints and economic resistance did reach the central government which responded to specific abuses; for example, some of the villagers were forced to move before a harvest was reaped, or over-zealous administrators burned some houses down to get people to move to the villages. Compensation was paid to rectify the abuses. In the general elections of 1980, fifty MP's were removed from parliament by the electorate in a broad-based expression of discontent. By 1981, several government ministers and parastatal managers who had abused their power were removed. The political system is open enough for complaints to be heard, but that process is not the same as mobilisation of the people to take control of production and of political decisions.

In Tanzania there is no revolutionary transformation of the relations of production. At the same time, however, the state is based in the subordinate classes more than Botswana or Zambia. The state has intervened to control foreign capital and to limit private accumulation. Fundamental social services are provided and significant gains have been made in reducing the inequities among groups. For example, from 1969 to 1976, the disparity in purchasing power of public sector salaries/wages went from 50:1 to about 8:1.[65] (In Mozambique in 1982, it was still 20:1.)

This populist approach to social relations — redistributing some services and income back to the dominated class without relinquishing control — was also expressed in the nationalist appeal for support of the liberation struggle in Zimbabwe. The united people of Tanzania would sustain the Zimbabwean struggle. Villagers gave the little available cash they had to liberation funds. For example, 1974 was declared the 'year of liberation' and over $1 million was donated by gifts from villagers and workers to the liberation struggles in Southern Africa. The nationalist appeal for solidarity was made in pragmatic terms: Tanzanian 'self-reliance' from dominant foreign capital could only come with regional co-operation among independent states.[66] In a speech at the University of Ibadan, Nigeria, in 1976 President Nyerere explained:

> The reality of neo-colonialism quickly becomes obvious to a new African government which tries to act on economic matters in the interest of national development. . . Indeed, it often discovers that there is no such thing as a national economy at all. Instead, there exist in its land various economic jurisdictions which are directed at external needs and which are run in the interest of external powers.[67]

The Tanzanian state has intervened to assume the role of accumulation and its response to the crisis of accumulation at the end of the 1970's was to strengthen the state institutions. Planning and technical expertise, guided by the central state institutions, were the choices made to alleviate the problems. But the role of accumulation is not the only one the state must play: the Tanzanian state has been especially successful in its task of legitimation.[68] Although there have been crises of accumulation, there has been little challenge to the legitimacy of the state. The Tanzanian state is perhaps exceptional on the African continent for the strength and longevity of its dominant ideologies: self-reliance, rural development, and anti-racism. These general ideological goals have remained broad enough to survive modification in interpretation, or even may have been strengthened by the new interpretations.[69] For example, 'self-reliance' now is often articulated in terms of regional co-operation, not in terms of a single state; in the villages it does not mean family self-reliance, but rather self-reliance of different collectives . . . schools, production co-operatives, marketing co-operatives. With its own economic problems and with trying to help its neighbours, Zambia and Mozambique the difficulties made it poignantly clear that 'self-reliance' does not mean isolation but rather regional co-operation; the prospects for regional co-ordination are discussed in Chapter 8. The point here is that the Zimbabwean nationalist struggle was immediately integral to the Tanzanian ideology. It took little explaining to the people to legitimise Tanzania's participation; it was simply a continuation of the dominant ideology and current policies: an anti-racist struggle for independence from colonial rule which would eventually help the self-reliant development of the region. Probably because the cost was not overly high for the Tanzanian economy, there was little debate that support for the Zimbabwean nationalists must be sustained. The national response was an effort to increase production in order to give material support to the Zimbabweans. The legitimacy of Tanzanian support of the Zimbabwean struggle, therefore, facilitated the accumulation role of the state. Consequently, the problems of the costs of the war were greatly outweighed by benefits accrued from the legitimacy of the struggle. A broad nationalist appeal united all classes of Tanzanians to fight the lingering vestiges of racism in the region.

Limitations To Relative Autonomy

To play what can be contradictory roles (accumulation vs. legitimacy), the Tanzanian state variously allied with different classes. As stated earlier, it sometimes allied with foreign capital against the producers, but then would nationalise foreign production, both for reasons of accumulation and of legitimacy. Many authors have described these shifting alliances, but few have tried to explain the process. The thesis here is that the shifting class alliances is an attempt by the state to achieve its relative autonomy in order to fulfill its contradictory roles. The structural role of the state is to maintain the overall interests of the dominant class, but to do that, the state must promote not only accumulation but also sustain legitimacy. If specific interests of capital run counter to general interests of the dominant class, the state may curtail that specific interest (e.g., Lonrho).

The Tanzanian state's relative autonomy from the dominant class was possible because of several conditions. First, Tanzania has nationalised all major productive sectors and has curtailed drastically private expropriation of surplus. Private capital is welcome in Tanzania only under stringent conditions set by the state. Second, the state took advantage of rivalry among the advanced capitalist states and bargained with them for capital financing. When the British would not invest in a development project, the Swedish government or West Germans were offered the job . . . and they would take it. Third, the state could turn to the socialist countries as alternative sources of capital, but preferred to do so only in crisis. China agreed to build the Tazara railroad between Dar es Salaam and Kapiri Mposhi to provide an alternative route to the sea for landlocked Zambia; but China was approached for the job only after the World Bank, the United States, and Britain had refused the project as economically unfeasible.

Yet this basis for structural autonomy is quite limited in Tanzania. As discussed earlier, although the state has a base in the dominated class, they are not mobilised. Villagisation and decentralisation have increased bureaucratic control of the peasants. In addition, in contrast to Mozambique and Angola, the appeal for sources of funding separate from international capital has been only in times of crisis. As shown in Chapter 4, the overwhelming source of finance for development projects is the advanced capitalist states.

Structural limitations to relative state autonomy became acutely apparent, not in the Frontline struggle, but in the war against Idi

Amin. At first, the populist base offered strong support for the war; the invasion by Amin united fully all the Tanzanians. But the cost of the war ($500 million) was extraordinary to such a poor country, and after the fighting terminated, contradictions among the classes became more exposed. Consumer prices were high for staples that were rarely available. Producer prices remained low. Peasants increased their smuggling of coffee and cotton to Kenya. The workers responded with the 'go-slows', as wages could not provide subsistence in the inflationary economy. As stated earlier, in the elections towards the end of 1980, fifty former MP's lost their seats. The President made several changes in the cabinet. Under the burden of the war costs, the class struggle has intensified in Tanzania.

These structural limitations to state autonomy have not curtailed the ability of the Tanzanian state to assert instrumental autonomy — to demonstrate remarkable freedom from direct pressure for policy changes from fractions of the dominant class. The example is the ability of Tanzania to withstand demands by the IMF to fulfil preconditions for a loan. Tanzania is unique in the world (of periphery capitalist states) for holding out so long against IMF controls (over four years). Late in 1979 the IMF ordered strict curtailment of government spending as a precondition for a loan to help pay for the cost of the war against Idi Amin. The Tanzanian government refused the loan, stating that it could not cut state expenditures. The majority of the expenditures was for hard-earned social services like health care and education for the peasants. Further, foreign exchange was not used for luxury consumer items but for spare parts and transport equipment, items necessary to increase production.[70] Even when it became clear by 1982 that major capital infusions were necessary, the 1982 National Economic Survival Programme was formulated to include the $50 million per year loan for the next five years from the World Bank, but not the $500 million three-year loan from the IMF.[71] The IMF package still had too stringent controls in what the Tanzanian leaders considered essential expenditures. This decision represents a refusal to reduce drastically the income of the producers for the short run; it contests the logic of capitalist development that during financial crises state expenditures must be reduced no matter what the expenditures are for. Other sources of capital are being sought, both internally and externally. And the state continues to fulfil its role in the redistribution of revenue for social services.

The Tanzanian state also asserted instrumental autonomy in

nationalising Lonrho, not so much against its performance in Tanzania as against its role in the Rhodesian conflict. This economic confrontation (Lonrho tried several times for retaliation) underscored Tanzania's political position in the Frontline struggle.

The proposition here is that Tanzania obtained some relative autonomy by its serious curtailment of private expropriation of surplus. That structural autonomy, however, lessened as the Idi Amin war heightened internal contradictions. The structural antonomy, however, did facilitate the ability of the Tanzanian state to assert instrumental autonomy, not just in an occasional disagreement with fractions of the dominant class, but in major arenas of class struggle. For example, the ability of Tanzania to hold out against the IMF epitomised the ideological and economic conflict with international capital.

More important to this study, Tanzania's policies in the Frontline States reflected the strengths and weaknesses of this instrumental autonomy, After some hesitancy in 1975, President Nyerere fully supported the armed struggle. Aware of the limitations of the Frontline alliance, however, he promoted a pragmatic policy of willingness to negotiate while conducting the armed struggle. Several times he insisted that the Zimbabwean nationalists go to the conference table when they saw no possible compromise. He was more than once accused by the guerrillas of blocking their military advances. He adamantly criticised the inability of the guerrilla forces to merge into one army. He knew it was a weakness that Smith and his Western supporters would try to take full advantage of, for one of Smith's major tactics throughout the struggle was to try to establish an internal settlement with one of the liberation groups while isolating the guerrillas. Finally, Nyerere led the Frontline States' insistence that the Lancaster House talks should occur. Tanzania was suffering from the cost of the war with Amin; Zambia had opened its route to the south; Mozambique and Angola were suffering extensive damage from attacks by Rhodesian and South African forces. Therefore, pressure was intense on ZANU and ZAPU to go to Lancaster House and to accept the restrictive constitution that Britain offered to set up an independent Zimbabwe. However, when Britain blatantly violated many cease-fire agreements during the transition to elections (January-March 1980), Nyerere announced that Tanzania would support a renewed armed struggle.[72]

Tanzania's leadership in the Frontline States is best explained by the ability of the state to exercise instrumental autonomy against fractions of the dominant class. The state could withstand threats and direct retaliation from international capital against its policies as leader of the Frontline. This limited independence is based on the structural autonomy Tanzania had gained by curtailing private accumulation by the dominant class, which gave the state considerable legitimacy with the dominated classes. The state was able to play its contradictory roles — in the short term — of assuring accumulation but maintaining legitimacy. When the Amin war set up a crisis of accumulation, the state moved to take even more surplus from the producers and thereby initiated a crisis in legitimacy. The class struggle in Tanzania intensified.

Zambia: The Vagaries Of State Capitalist Support For Zimbabwean Liberation

Colonial Political Economy

The penetration of capital into Zambia was similar to that of Rhodesia (Zimbabwe) in that the British South Africa Company, in its unremitting search for minerals, signed a treaty in 1890 with Lewanika, King of the Lozi (Barotse), for mining concessions; that treaty was similar to the one the company had extracted from Lobengula of the Ndebele. By the 1920's, the company was mining rich copper sulphide ores in Zambia. The penetration of capital in Zambia, however, differed from the colonising of Rhodesia in two important ways. First, Zambia (then a territory called 'Northern Rhodesia') never had many settlers; second, agricultural production in Zambia was directed to serve the needs of the more numerous and dominant white settlers in (Southern) Rhodesia and South Africa and to feed the miners on the Copperbelt.[73] Africans were forced off the land or taxed so that they had to seek wages in the mines.[74] A railway route was built (1906) to link the Katangese copper mines to the south. With the additional discovery of Zambian ores, large white settler farms lined up along the route so that marketing would be easy: north to the copper mines and south to the larger settler communities. Today, the copper mines still dominate the economy, and most of the commercial farmers are still producing along this line of rail.

Zambia's position subordinate to Southern Rhodesia was formalised in 1953 by the creation of the Central African Federation of Northern Rhodesia (Zambia), Southern Rhodesia (Zimbabwe) and

Nyasaland (Malawi). The Federation was established to provide a larger base for capital formation. Northern Rhodesia and Nyasaland supplied labour and capital for the industrial development of Southern Rhodesia. In addition, although the settlers were few compared to its southern neighbours, Africans in Northern Rhodesia were not treated any better than in Southern Rhodesia. Controlling productive capital and the administration of the territory, the whites made it clear what place the Africans were to take — economically, politically and socially.

By 1962, in a broad nationalist front for the independence of Zambia, Africans refused subordination to both racial and political domination of the white settlers, and they rejected the economic domination of Southern Rhodesia. At independence in 1964, the British South Africa Company ceded its rights to the collection of Zambia's mineral royalties, and the transfer of capital from Zambia to Rhodesia ceased.[75] Yet the legacy was clear; the mining sector, owned by South African, British and American capital, dominated the economy with few linkages to other areas of the domestic production. The national economy provided only one third of the manufactures to the local market. Manufacturing contribution to GDP was only 6 per cent (see Chapter 4).

Class Struggle and the State in Zambia

In 1965, a year after Zambian independence, Rhodesia unilaterally declared independence (UDI) for white minority control of the state and the economy. The new Zambian government moved quickly to try to implement partial sanctions against the illegal regime, and by 1972 it had completely closed its border between the two states. The 80-year orientation of Zambia's economy to Rhodesia was drastically curtailed.

At independence no attempt was made to change the relations of production; foreign capital remained dominant (as discussed in Chapter 4). However, state intervention in the economy did increase gradually, as a pragmatic response to overcome the neglect of the economy under colonialism. The state had intervened to reduce the abuses of foreign capital control while promoting the reinvestment of surplus for development of the Zambian economy. Control of the state was a means by which to provide some fruits of independence to the Zambian people. Using revenue from copper, the government could reinvest in production and the infrastructure. The explicit goal was to reduce the inequality among productive sectors and in the distribution of income.

Four years after independence (Mulungushi Reforms, 1968), the government reserved small businesses for Zambian citizens and moved to take over larger commercial enterprises itself.[76] The government entered partnership with Zambian citizens in retail and wholesale trading, building material industries, and transport.[77] In August 1969 the government took 51 percent ownership of the vital copper mines (Matero Reforms) and in 1970 this policy extended a 51 percent state share to most large corporations still under private ownership and to a monopoly of all insurance. By 1975 one could no longer talk of 'regulated' private enterprise, for all major sectors of the economy (except the banks) were under state ownership and land reforms were announced.[78] The state had acquired the ability to increase surplus production, to accumulate surplus, and to redistribute it. As Turok points out, the state not only increased its role in accumulation, but also in legitimation.[79] The government redistributed surplus to expand services, such as health care and education. Loans were made available to small businesses, and some cooperative efforts at farming were set up.[80] The state's role in the economy greatly increased employment, and prices of basic commodities were kept low by subsidies. Until the economic crises of the mid-1970's, the fruits of independence were many as attempts were made to provide essential services to all of the population. The state increased its role in accumulation, but redistributed the surplus by providing basic services and employment. Therefore, it also increased its legitimacy.

The state intervention, however, did have an urban bias. Urban migration increased as jobs opened up in the cities because of Zambianisation, and the government did not discourage squatter settlements because the new residents were very supportive of the ruling United National Independence Party (UNIP).[81] Only about 5 percent of government expenditure was directed to agriculture,[82] while food subsidies were provided to keep food prices low for the urban masses, who comprised about 50 percent of the total population, one of the highest levels of urbanisation in Africa. One result of the urban bias has been an increase in the urban-rural wage differential since independence;[83] however, with the economic crises, the standard of living has now also declined in the urban areas. The gap between urban and rural wages, however, remains enough to encourage migration from the rural areas. A second result has been the increasing difficulty for national agricultural production to feed the people. For example, by 1979 maize production had dropped to half of that necessary to feed the population.[84] Only about 1,000 commercial farmers (white and African) grow about 60 percent of the marketed goods. Some emergent farmers have been able to grow a small surplus for the market, but the vast majority of the farmers remain small, subsistence farmers. They are not usually eligible for loans; without much animal, tool, or capital resources, these farmers find it difficult to increase their production. Part of the difficulty is the transport problem caused by the war, but a more fundamental factor is the urban bias of the government policy. The peasants are differentiated by their production levels and by ethnicity. Several researchers have reported that rural agricultural schemes have increased rural differentiation, helping further the more advantaged.[85] Therefore, the peasants have not been able to come together to challenge the urban bias in the programme.

The commercial farmers are few, but they comprise one sector of the ruling class. In contrast to the peasantry, they have expressed awarenes of their class interests.[86] They do organise politically to influence policy; in 1978 for example, the commercial farmers pressured President Kaunda to open the border with Rhodesia so fertiliser would arrive in time to plant their crops. In general, they opposed the enforcement of sanctions against Rhodesia, because their production dropped as the agricultural inputs such as fertiliser and spare parts for machines became less available with the border closure.

Although the state has intervened in the economy, the social relations have remained capitalist, with private appropriation fully accepted. The parastatal operations have given opportunities for Zambian petty bourgeoisie to learn managerial skills. After experience in the parastatals or on the boards, many then enter the private sector, hired directly by the corporations. Although it is illegal to be on the government and corporate payrolls at the same time, there is a regular flow of personnel between the two sectors.[87] Zambians can use their position and experience in the parastatals to set themselves up in the private sector as a manager, a consultant, or even as an investor. In the private sector, Zambians can accumulate capital for further investment. Several theorists have called this intersection between the two sectors state capitalism.[88] Those who are in charge of parastatals and who accumulate in the private sectors are referred to as a national bourgeoisie in formation. Ownership is by the state, but this class is able to appropriate surplus through the state apparatus. This form of state capitalism is characterised by the predominance of the state in a profit-motivated economy with an underdeveloped national bourgeoisie.[89]

This national bourgeoisie is weak and nascent so while it is dependent on foreign capital, it must also struggle to prevent foreign capital taking complete control. It is also dependent on the state but struggles against it. In the first instance, the national bourgeoisie in formation challenges the domination of specific foreign capital interests in an effort to preserve its own position in the reproduction of the social formation. If surplus leaves the country, investment for growth is limited. As summarised by Peter Evans in analysing Brazil's state capitalism:

> The support of the state is an essential element in (the local bourgeoisie's) defence against multinational corporations. They need a strong state.[90]

Profits, as the motivating force for production, must be restricted when individual profit acquisition threatens the economy in general. One example of this antagonism is directly related to the Frontline struggle: Zambia sued 17 Western oil companies for breach of contract after they reduced Zambia's oil supply to 13 days in order to provide Rhodesia with a 90-day supply just before UDI. This action was just one in a long history of actions which have sanctioned transnational corporations in order to support liberation from white minority rule.[91] The national bourgeoisie in formation is not a client to (comprador) international capital, but tries to delimit its control.

In the second instance, the national bourgeoisie has been both aided and restricted by the state. State intervention in most of the major sectors permitted Zambians to take over foreign firms, but also to enter into partnerships with the government. The government provides finance for infrastructure, sets priorities for imports which can favour certain enterprises, circumscribes labour union activities, and often sets up a monopoly marketing position. The state has clearly aided its private partners by underwriting their activities. Yet the state has also limited the activities of private individuals. The Leadership Code prohibits working for a private corporation while on the government payroll.[92] There is an informal limit for any Zambian enterprise to gross annual profits of K500,000 (approx. $375,000). Freehold tenure over state land has been eliminated. The nascent national bourgeoisie depends very much on the state, but then is very impatient when state policies are at variance with its immediate goals. It has succeeded in blocking some parts of national policy, such as socialist changes called for in the Matero Reforms or upholding the Leadership Code. In several domestic issues, the national bourgeoisie opposition has changed state policy.[93]

This class fraction was also at odds with the state over the Southern African policy. The border closure disrupted production plans because of the transport blockages. The closure might have provided the opportunity for local capital to expand at the expense of Rhodesian firms; however, foreign exchange shortages and transport shortages were too severe for local capital to take advantage of the reduced competition. Further, an independent and stable Zimbabwe would present even greater competition to Zambian capital. National-istic, this class fraction supported majority rule in Rhodesia; however, as the cost of such a policy rose drastically, both nationally and individually, it vociferously pushed for compromise and a quicker settlement.[94]

Its members saw their class position threatened by the possible collapse of the economy. Their views were expressed in ideological terms: why should Zambians suffer so much when the guerrillas were not? They criticised the 'minimal fighting' done by ZAPU guerrillas. Playing on chauvinism, they said that Zambia must protect itself first and let the guerrillas take care of themselves.

Part of the reason for the urban bias in government policy and toward subsidy of consumer goods was the strength of the mine workers, both as labourers in a crucial sector of the economy and as well-organised union members. The Zambian government 'perceived the mine workers as both an economic and political threat to the stability of the country'.[95] They supported state policy into the 1970's, having gained a 22 percent wage increase in 1968.[96] But as the economy entered the crisis period of the mid-1970's, the mine workers were considered a possible base for serious opposition to the government. In addition to the transport disruption caused by the war, copper prices plummeted on the international market. Two mines, Kalengwa and Luanshya, were actually closed because they were no longer profitable to mine. Short-term relief only came with an IMF loan in May of 1978 which was directed to the mines to keep them open and to preserve 160,000 jobs.[97] The government has succeeded so far in its balancing act with the workers: offering carrots and then coming down hard with a stick. Organised labour does have a political history and was a force that had to be reconciled. Every effort was made to keep workers on the job, even at the cost of net loss to the mines or the parastatals. Prices of basic commodities were subsidised by the government. At the same time, organised resistance by labour was dealt with swiftly. Having merged all the separate unions into a national congress controlled by the state, strikes in 'vital' industries were then strictly regulated by state laws. 'Vital' included anything from construction to copper to electricity to transport; the vast majority of the workers were therefore constrained. When a seven-day strike broke out on Tazara railway, the management, which was the government, fired 51 workers outright. The union was not consulted about the action.[98]

After the end of the Rhodesian war, the long-simmering opposition on the Copperbelt became a political threat to the government. President Kaunda moved with a stick and imprisoned the main leaders before they were able to extend their base of support and gain sufficient legitimacy to overthrow the government.[99] The struggle has not yet ended, however. As James Petras has warned, state capitalism can redistribute surplus to benefit the workers, but ultimately, surplus accumulation for the dominant classes comes from the workers:

> The national-state capitalist class directs and controls the process of capital accumulation but at the expense of the labour force — concentrating capital in its own hands. The state-capitalist regime attempts to redefine the terms of dependency and to contain labour demands to favour nationalist capitalist accumulation.[100]

Opposition to Zambia's role as a Frontline State was expressed by the national bourgeoisie in formation in parliamentary disputes: Kaunda even refused to seat 23 MP's in parliament. In the presidential elections of 1978, the Supreme Court ruled that Kaunda's principal opposition, Simon Kapwepwe, was not qualified to run for election. The opposition tried to show its strength by encouraging people to abstain from voting or to vote 'no' for Kaunda. However, there was a large turnout of 70 percent and Kaunda received 80 percent of the vote.[101] (But for the southern belt of constituencies, bordering Rhodesia, the vote was more than 50 percent against Kaunda.) There were two important reasons for the strong support. First, the party had realised the serious decline in its organisation and mobilisation of the people and had to decide to use the election as a new initiative for participation. (Although sometimes the mobilisation appeared to be more like coerced participation.) Second, there was no real alternative to Kaunda and UNIP. The opposition could not unite across class or ethnic lines. The war was escalating, not decreasing, and stability at home was a first priority in order to search for alternatives. Perhaps the secret talks between Nkomo and Smith in Lusaka in August 1978 and the border opening in October, just before the elections in December, were sufficient indications to the discontented that Kaunda was seeking compromises in the Rhodesian struggle in order to rescue the Zambian economy.

Opposition was also expressed by the fact that Rhodesian commandos could enter Zambia with impunity. They would fly or drive in, strike at a guerrilla house or base, and leave. The many raids were bringing the war home to Zambians whose fields were bombed or friends were killed.[102] In April 1979 several Rhodesians drove into the middle of Lusaka and riddled ZAPU leader Nkomo's house with bullets, only a couple of blocks from a main Zambian army garrison. Then the commandos drove across town and bombed Africa House where several liberation groups had their offices. No one was caught. The inability or unwillingness of the government to react to such incursions on Zambian sovereignty has not been fully explained. To accomplish such raids, the Rhodesians had to have help from Zambian citizens. Although many white farmers are related to white Rhodesians and had sent their children to Rhodesian schools, only one was convicted for hiding arms for Rhodesian commandos. The government was careful to prosecute the guilty, but made much effort to prohibit propaganda that would generalise such behaviour to all white Zambians. Opposition crossed race and class lines because no group was left unaffected by the war. Reactions to rally support or to demand compromise varied with the specific circumstances. The opposition was serious but the government was not isolated; many continued their pledge to sacrifice for Zimbabwean independence.

Limitations to Relative State Autonomy

The various opposing classes and antagonisms within classes help to explain Zambia's ability to remain a Frontline State as well as the serious limitations to that role. The ruling class was weak and fractionated (foreign capital, parastatal managers, private entrepreneurs, and commercial farmers).[103] The peasantry did not express a single class interest. The urban workers (parastatal and private) were dependent on the state and benefited from its policies. The mine workers were appeased somewhat through the maintenance of their employment. These competing interests enabled the government to use sanctions when necessary against the opposition — either against striking workers or in neutralising electoral opposition.

The state was not challenging capitalist relations of production, but rather promoting the general interests of national capital for a Zimbabwe that could take control of production and begin to challenge South African dominance in the region. Those in charge of the Zambian state represented what they perceived to be the general interests of the social formation: in order to remove external structural constraints on Zambian development, Zimbabwe must be independent under majority rule. Zimbabwe would offer competition to Zambian manufacturing, but government officials saw the removal of economic blockages more crucial to Zambia's economy. Essential trade and transport would open up.[104] The Zambian leaders were not promoting the socialist leanings of Robert Mugabe and ZANU. As seen in previous chapters, a moderate government with a capitalist economy in Zimbabwe was acceptable. However, the moderate government must be based on majority rule and not be a puppet to South Africa. The political objectives were clear. Zambians had also been colonised by white minority settlers. Zambians not only understood, but shared the Zimbabweans' moral outrage against exploitation of the masses for the benefit of a small colonial enclave. The experiences were too similar for Zambia not to respond to their neighbours. The long-term economic considerations were central, but the political and ideological struggle against racism and colonialism sustained the economic battle.

If one measured Zambia's decision to remain a Frontline State in cost-benefit terms, there would be little explanation of how it continued: the short-run economic costs were severe and totally disrupted the economy. But the ruling party also promotes the ideology of Humanism, and material assets are not the only measure of benefits. Independence was not only to improve the quality of life for Zambians, but also to reassert their dignity and affirm their culture. The Zambian pledge to 'Humanism' has often been reduced to slogans to obscure exploitive relations. But it is also an ideological force in social relations; it is used to mediate and moderate excesses of domination expressed in ethnic, racial, or colonial terms. It is this ideology which separates Zambia from Malawi, not so much the economic differences (as is now evident in that Malawi has joined the Southern African regional co-ordination to try to solve jointly their similar economic constraints; see the next chapter). The Malawian government has no ideology, such as *ujamaa* in Tanzania or Humanism in Zambia. There is no political expression to moderate the drive for private accumulation. Ignoring racism in Rhodesia and South Africa is interpreted as simply a pragmatic response to the realities of the region. In Zambia, this economic 'pragmatism' was moderated by the appeal for racial justice. Full stomachs were basic, but so was social equality for the Africans.

With a divided ruling class and a political base (even though precarious) in the subordinated classes, the state was able to assert relative autonomy. No one class dominated it. The arguments by Shaw and Eriksen that the Zambian government's foreign policy reflects the interests of the nascent bourgeoisie have not been empirically validated.[105] Shaw states: '. . . we cannot understand the development and foreign policies of an African state such as Zambia without reference to its political economy. Moreover, its political economy is largely determined by the interests of the ruling class; this class will continue to define the state *until challenged by internal and/or international opposition.*'[106] [emphasis mine]. This study argues that Frontline participation by Zambia cannot be explained as simply a reflection of ruling class interests. As early as 1966, Harry Nkumbula of the African National Congress of Zambia was complaining that Zambia's stand against UDI was 'committing economic suicide'.[107] At the end of 1978 Simon Kapwepwe was still echoing the same sentiments. However, support for majority rule in Zimbabwe continued, not without serious vacillations, and always at high short-term cost to the Zambian economy. The state was able to gain relative autonomy from the dominant class to sustain its role in the Frontline.

The conditions of relative autonomy were several. First, as the theory of relative state autonomy suggests, the weakness and divisions within the dominant class were important. Foreign capital is one fraction of this class, and still retains economic power, especially in the strategic sector of the copper mines. But its power has been somewhat circumscribed by the state taking partnership in the mines.

Investment, employment, and export of capital decisions are now shared with the government. The partnership does not alter Zambian economic vulnerability to foreign capital, but it also does not give foreign capital a totally free hand. The nascent national bourgeoisie was too small and weak and divided to impose its policy. They did complain, set up opposition in the campaigns, lobby, and resort occasionally to circumvention by corruption. But the national bourgeoisie could not take command of the policy because they were weak economically, and they were divided over the interpretation of their interests. Being a Frontline State did have long-term economic and political advantages: it was consistent with the preservation and growth of a nationally controlled economy. Therefore, although the cost was high for the national bourgeoisie, they did obtain some benefits from the policy. As discussed earlier, national capital was often at odds with foreign capital. This struggle within the dominant class granted the state more autonomy.

A second basis for the relative autonomy was that the state had some support from the subordinated classes. In fulfilling its role in legitimation, the state had redistributed surplus back to the workers. Workers greatly benefited with higher wages, education, health care, and subsidised food. Segments of the workers and elements in the party supported a Marxist interpretation of the directions in which the economy should move, and the independence of Zimbabwe was a crucial step. This faction was not strong, but the fact that it existed within the party and at times was protected by President Kaunda are significant. The state enjoyed, therefore, legitimacy among the dominated classes which increased its relative autonomy from the dominant class.

As in Tanzania, this limited structural autonomy did facilitate Zambia's ability to resist direct pressure from fractions of the dominant class (instrumental autonomy). The government welcomed funds from the Chinese for the Tazara Railroad after Western sources refused. Kaunda defended many times the right of ZAPU to receive arms from the Soviets and criticised the West for supplying Smith. At the end of the war, after the humiliation of the commando raids, the government announced it was accepting arms from the Soviet Union itself in order to better defend its borders. Although the resource base of the state is still mainly Western, the ability to turn to socialist alternatives in times of crisis (the need for emergency transport or arms) demonstrates the state's policy autonomy from the foreign capital fraction of the dominant class.

Relative state autonomy from the dominant class was possible, but it was relative. The most serious limitation on autonomous action was obviously structural. As the war escalated, Zambia's economy was not only enduring hardships; its viability was in question. In 1978, the IMF agreed to loan $390 million to the besieged economy, but only with the enforcement of its strict restrictions. Food subsidies were curtailed, and government services cut. Imports were reduced. The IMF demands increased the hardships, but the government perceived them necessary for economic survival. By the end of 1979, the disruption of transport had taken a serious toll on Zambian manufacturing, food, and copper production. The structural constraints were severe.

In addition, the states of the dominant foreign powers did directly exercise their economic power against Zambia on several occasions. South Africa's reduction of the supply of Zambian oil prior to UDI was one example. Western refusal to build the Tazara railroad because it was 'not economically feasible' was another. Zambia opened the border to Rhodesia in October 1978 to receive vital fertiliser in time for planting. President Samora Machel raised the question as to why the US had sent the fertiliser so late to one of the ports least able to service Zambia. Finally, Rhodesia bombed Zambia from 1976 onward, but only verbal protests came from the Anglo-Americans. However, the fact that Rhodesia did not bomb vital transport lines until the Lancaster House talks were under way at the end of 1979 demonstrates Rhodesia's relative restraint in the use of armed force as a last resort (encouraged, perhaps, by the fact that such bombing would have hurt corporate interests in Zambia, many of which were also in Rhodesia, such as Anglo-American). Bombing of the vital infrastructure was a last ditch effort as a show of force to gain more favourable terms in the negotiations.

Limitations on state autonomy also developed in relation to internal class formations. As local capital developed, the nascent national bourgeoisie grew stronger and was able to influence state policy to its benefit. Lack of sufficient pressure from the subordinate classes allowed this class to turn state power to their own advantage. These actions were couched in nationalistic terms. The increasing strength of Zambia's national bourgeoisie limited the state's relative autonomy, but did not destroy it. Zambian policy continued to pursue interests not entirely compatible with the local bourgeoisie.

The conditions of state autonomy in Zambia and the severe limitations on these conditions were evident in its Frontline policy. Its policy was the most volatile of the five. Bending to shifting pressures, Zambia took actions without consulting the others. These vicissitudes were discussed in Chapters 2 and 3. The important policy divergences from the Frontline are briefly summarised here as a reminder. The most serious conflict between a Frontline State and the guerrilla forces was between Zambia and ZANU over the Herbert Chitepo affair. The ZANU leaders still state that Zambia delayed their guerrilla actions for a full year by incarcerating their leaders. Several times during the Frontline negotiations, Kaunda urged Nkomo (ZAPU) to talk with Ian Smith. Nkomo conducted negotiations with Smith, separate from Mugabe (ZANU). The border opening to the south caused much friction because Zambia did not consult Mozambique or Tanzania of its intentions. Both Presidents Machel and Nyerere felt that consultation for such a drastic action should have been fundamental to Frontline unity. Zambia was the weak link in the Frontline encirclement of Rhodesia . . . but mainly because it did so much to support the Zimbabwean nationalists. Botswana could afford to be more consistent in its policy because its participation was so limited. The vicissitudes of Zambian policy are not surprising. Its perseverence as a Frontline State is. Zambian ideology against racism was central to the policy, and its limited autonomy from the dominant class made it possible to sustain the ideology.

Zambia's role in the Frontline was vital to the success of Zimbabwe. Even as a peripheral capitalist state, Zambia contributed greatly to the struggle against white Rhodesian representation of foreign capital in the area. Zambia's struggle was nationalist and anti-imperialist. It was not a struggle to transform the relations of production, but to limit the abuses of private expropriation by foreign capital in Zimbabwe, and by association, in Zambia.

Conclusion

Despite their historical dependence on foreign capital, the Frontline States have been able to challenge foreign interests in the Southern African region and to support the Zimbabwean struggle for independence. The similarities among the Frontline States, as outlined in the first section of Chapter 6, are the basis of the fundamental congruence of their policies in support of Zimbabwe.

Yet the Frontline actions can only be understood in the context of an analysis of each of their social formations. The roles and policies varied according to their internal social relations, which in turn promoted differences in relative state autonomy. A strict instrumental view of direct capitalist control of the states would not be able to explain the ability of the Frontline to endure; only in Botswana could we say that the dominant class has maintained control of the state. In the others, for the different reasons discussed above, conditions were present for limited state autonomy. Finally, the different conditions of relative autonomy help to explain the disagreements within the Frontline. The Mozambican economy was under assault as drastically as the Zambian, so an economistic account could not explain their differences in policy. The theories of relative state autonomy of the two states help to explain the different abilities of Zambia and Mozambique (and the other three) to sustain the struggle.

The theories of relative state autonomy improve our ability to explain the complexity of the Frontline States' policies. They reinsert the political back into overly economistic Marxist explanations of state action. They challenge the dependence theorists' assumption that the dominant class is the only determinant of state policy. The theories of relative state autonomy situate the state within the class formation, but do not assume that it is captured by any one class.

This analysis, however, raises two serious questions about the theories, one from within the theoretical formulation and one which questions the formulation itself. The theories of relative state autonomy do not consider seriously enough the possibility of alternative power bases for the state, outside the dominant class. They tend to ignore the possibility of support for the state from socialist states. Especially in a mixed mode of production, when capitalist relations of production are not the sole form of relations, sources of revenue and of support could be obtained outside the dominant capitalist class. Even Zambia was able to receive aid for arms from socialist countries when the fractions of Western capital were not willing to supply them; the Tazara railroad is another example. The structural constraint that the state's revenue is ultimately based in production controlled by the dominant class is somewhat ameliorated by socialist alternatives in the contemporary international scene. The socialist alternative is not automatic, but the theories should allow for the possibility of its influence.

Although the theories bring the state back into analysis of

political action, they still seem to ignore or underestimate the role of ideology. The state, to legitimise the mode of production, must sustain the ideology. The dominant ideology is that of the ruling class, but individual interests of that class variously act contrary to it. The state, in contrast, must promote it. For example, legitimacy of accumulation by Zambia's dominant class depended on the consistent struggle against racism. Zambianisation was the economic expression of 'Humanism', and it was the basis for the birth of the national bourgeoisie. The state could not then simply ignore the same struggle for human rights in an adjacent nation. Legitimacy took precedence over the accumulation which might have occurred if the state collaborated with Rhodesia. Theories of relative state autonomy do not explain that one basis of the state's relative autonomy is its role not only to sustain the general interests of capital; it is also to sustain the ideology which explains and legitimises those general intersts. In cases like the struggle for Zimbabwe, the anti-racist ideology must be separated analytically from the interests of the dominant class in order to analyse how it may become a powerful force *for* the state in the class struggle.

The political independence of Zimbabwe has not defeated imperialism in the Southern African region. Historical economic patterns are not eradicated overnight. The Frontline States agreed, however, that this political step was necessary before the economic struggle of the region could be confronted. The next chapter analyses their move to extend the struggle from political to economic independence.

Notes

1. Christopher Colclough and Stephen McCarthy, *The Political Economy of Botswana: A Study of Growth and Distribution* (Oxford: Oxford University Press, 1980), p. 12.
2. Food and Agriculture Organisation, United Nations, 'Botswana', *Apartheid* 126, nos. 7/8 (1978), p. 14.
3. Dr L.S. Jameson, one of Cecil Rhodes' right-hand men, decided to launch his raid against the Transvaal from Bechuanaland (Botswana). The total debacle of the expedition caused the British government to curtail activities of the British South African Co. and to increase the government role in the Protectorate. See Elizabeth Pakenham, *Jameson's Raid* (London: Weidenfeld and Nicholson,

1960), and summary of event in Richard Vengroff, *Botswana: Rural Development in the Shadow of Apartheid* (London: Associated University Presses, 1977), p. 26.

4. According to Jack Parson, there were several ways in which the Batswana were pushed into 'non-discretionary participation in the market': 1) rinderpest epidemic which decimated the herds (1896); 2) drawing of ethnic boundaries which restricted grazing (1899); 3) high taxation; 4) discrimination against Botswanan cattle in marketing. Jack Parson 'Theory and Reality in the Periphery: The State in Contemporary Botswana', paper presented at American Political Science Association annual meeting, 2–5 September 1982, p. 11.

5. Colclough and McCarthy, op. cit. See their discussion of migrant labour statistics, pp. 253–57. They point out that official statistics of labour contracts underestimate considerably the real numbers of workers, because many cross the border and find work in 'illegal' and 'unofficial' ways. For example, they estimate that 70,000 were in Botswana in 1977, not 40,000 in 1978, although the latter is the official count.

6. Jack D. Parson, 'The Political Economy of Botswana: A Case in the Study of Politics and Social Change in Post-Colonial Societies', University of Sussex, Ph.D. thesis, 1979, pp. 196–198.

7. Jack Parson, 1982, op. cit., p. 13.

8. FAO, op. cit., p. 15.

9. Jack Foisie, 'Botswana: Success in Black Africa', *Los Angeles Times*, 1 September 1981.

10. Government of Botswana, 'Rural Income Distribution Survey, 1974/75', June 1976, quoted in Lionel Cliffe and Richard Moorsom, 'Rural Class Formation and Ecological Collapse in Botswana', *Review of African Political Economy*, nos. 15–16 (May–December 1979), p. 41. For further statistics see USAID, *Development Needs and Opportunities for Co-operation in Southern Africa: Botswana* (March 1979), pp. 31–42.

11. Food and Agriculture Organisation, United Nations, 'A Study of Constraints on Agricultural Development in the Republic of Botswana' (Rome: 1974), Tables B1. 3–1.8.

12. Although traditionally men care for cattle while women do virtually all the crop and small livestock production, government extension services for crop production have been exclusively for men, ignoring the female heads of households.
See Carol A. Bond, 'Women's Involvement in Agriculture in Botswana' (Gaborone: Ministry of Agriculture, 1976).
Carol Kerven, Report on Tsamaya Village, Northeast District (Gaborone: Rural Sociology Unit, Rural Sociology Report, Ministry of Agriculture, Series No. 1, 1976).

13. Christopher Colclough and Steven McCarthy, op. cit., p. 3.

14. Jack Parson, 1979, op. cit., p. 350.

15. Lionel Cliffe and Richard Moorsom, op. cit., pp. 39–40.

16. Penelope Hartland-Thunberg, *Botswana: An African Growth Economy* (Boulder, Colorado: Westview Press, 1978), pp. 39–40.

17. Jack Parson, 1979, op. cit., p. 3.

18. Lionel Cliffe and Richard Moorsom, op. cit., pp. 37–39. Parson gives the figure that 8 percent of the herders own 40 percent of the cattle (1979), p. 5.

19. Lionel Cliffe and Roger Moorsom, op. cit., p. 50.
20. Jack Parson, 1982, op. cit., p. 20.
21. Economist Intelligence Unit, Quarterly Economic Review, Annual Supplement, *Southern African — Botswana* (1980), p. 44. *African Business* (June 1982), p. 71.
22. Richard Vengroff, op. cit., p. 19.
23. Bank of Botswana, *Annual Report* (Gaborone, 1977), pp. 8, 10.
24. For a thorough discussion of the political stability, see John D. Holm, 'Liberal Democracy and Rural Development in Botswana', *African Studies Review* 25, no. 1 (March 1982), pp. 83–102.
25. Jack Foisie, op. cit.
26. Christopher Colclough and Stephen McCarthy, op. cit., p. 195.
27. Christopher Stevens and John Speed, 'Multipartyism in Africa: The Case of Botswana Revisited', *African Affairs*, 76, n. 304 (July 1977), p. 386.
28. James H. Polhemus, 'The Impact of Zimbabwean Independence on Regional International Relations: Towards Congruence between Economics and Politics in the Southern African Subsystem', paper presented at the International Studies Association, Cincinnati, Ohio, 24–27 March 1982, p. 23.
29. See A. Van Egmond, 'Report on the Status of Refugees in Botswana, Lesotho and Swaziland with Guidelines for US Assistance', Robert R. Nathan Assocs. for USAID (20 April 1977).
30. For a critique of the previous union, see Government of Botswana, 'Transitional Plan for Social and Economic Development', (Gaborone, 1968), pp. 10–12. The new agreement is in Government of Botswana, *Government Gazette* 7, no. 64 (12 December 1969). For a discussion of the changes see Richard Dale, 'Botswana', C. Potholm and R. Dale, eds., *Southern Africa in Perspective* (New York: Macmillan, 1972), pp. 114–116.
31. For a discussion of the beneficial effects from creation of an independent monetary system, see Charles Harvey, 'Botswana's Monetary Independence — Real or Imagined?' IDS *Bulletin* (Sussex) 11, no. 4 (September 1980), pp. 40–44.
32. 'Botswana, South Africa's Vulnerable Neighbour', *Christian Science Monitor,* 10 June 1981.
33. Seretse Khama is considered the founder of SADCC by some observers.
34. Roy G. Willis, 'The Fipa', in Andrew Roberts, ed. *Tanzania Before 1900* (Nairobi: East African Publishing House, 1968), p. 92.
35. Justinian Rweyemamu, *Underdevelopment and Industrialisation in Tanzania* (Nairobi: Oxford University Press, 1973), pp. 116–120.
36. E.A. Brett, *Colonialism and Underdevelopment in East Africa* (London: Heinemann, 1973), p. 221.
37. Commercial production of agriculture began before the arrival of the Europeans, in response to the Arab trade. J. Iliffe, 'The Age of Improvement and Differentiation', in I. Kimambo and A. Temu, eds., *History of Tanzania* (Nairobi: East African Publishing House, 1969), p. 134. For the most comprehensive view of pre-colonial economies, see Helge Kjekshus, *Ecology, Control and Economic Development in East African History* (London: Heinemann, 1977).
38. Lionel Cliffe, 'Nationalism and the Reaction to Enforced Agricultural Change in Tanganyika during the Colonial Period', in L. Cliffe and J. Saul, eds., *Socialism in Tanzania* (Nairobi: East African Publishing House, 1972), pp. 17–20.

39. G.R. Mboya, 'The Feasibility of Ujamaa Villages in Kilimanjaro', in J.H. Proctor, *Building Ujamaa Villages in Tanzania* (Dar es Salaam: Tanzania Publishing House, 1975), pp. 64–68.

40. D. Wadada Nabudere, 'The Politics of East African Federation 1958–1965', Paper presented at University of Dar es Salaam seminar, 1 December 1978.

   K.S. Kim, 'Appraisal of the East African Economics Integration Scheme', in K.S. Kim, R.B. Mabele and M.J. Schultheis, eds., *Papers on the Political Economy of Tanzania* (London: Heinemann, 1979), pp. 181–188.

   Ann Seidman, *Comparative Development Strategies in East Africa* (Nairobi: East African Publishing House, 1972), pp. 289–291.

41. Julius K. Nyerere, *The Arusha Declaration — Ten Years After* (Dar es Salaam: Government Printer, 1977), p. 2.

42. John Iliffe, op. cit.

   John Lonsdale, 'Some Origins of Nationalism in East Africa', *Journal of African History* 9, no. 1 (1968), pp. 131–136.

43. S.S. Mushi, 'Indigenisation of the Economy in an Underdeveloped Country: The Tanzanian Experience', paper presented at Universities of East Africa Conference, 1976, pp. 21–23.

44. Andrew Coulson, 'Decentralisation and the Government Budget' (Dar es Salaam: Economic Research Bulletin, October 1975), p. 6.

45. Issa Shivji, *Class Struggles in Tanzania* (Dar es Salaam: Tanzania Publishing House, 1975).

   John Saul, *The State and Revolution in Eastern Africa* (New York: Monthly Review Press, 1979), pp. 167–199, pp. 339–349.

   Joel Samoff, 'Bureaucrats, Politicians, and Power in Tanzania: The Institutional Context of Class Struggle', African Studies Association, Los Angeles, 1979.

46. J. Boesen, B.S. Madsen, and T. Moody, *Ujamaa: Socialism from Above* (Uppsala: Scandinavian Institute of African Studies, 1977), p. 28.

   Michaela von Freyhold, *Ujamaa Villages in Tanzania — Analysis of a Social Experiment* (New York: Monthly Review Press, 1979), p. 64.

47. Tony Avirgan, 'Organising for Economic Survival', *Africa News*, 15 February 1982, p. 4.

48. R.H. Green, D.G. Rwegasira, B. Van Arkadie, *Economic Shocks and National Policy Making: Tanzania in the 1970's* (Hague: Institute of Social Studies, 1980), pp. 102–119.

49. For the two extremes of the argument that socialism has failed vs. succeeded in Tanzania, see

   Michael F. Lofchie, 'Agrarian Crisis and Economic Liberalisation in Tanzania', *The Journal of Modern African Studies* 16, no. 3 (September 1978).

   Reginald H. Green, *Toward Socialism and Self Reliance: Tanzania's Striving for Sustained Transition Projected* (Uppsala: Scandinavian Institute of African Studies, 1977).

   Those who advocate growth over distribution are as follows:

   Joel D. Barkin, 'Comparing Politics and Public Policy in Kenya and Tanzania' in J. Barkin, J. Okumu, eds. *Politics and Public Policy in Kenya and Tanzania* (New York: Praeger, 1979).

Reuben R. Matango, 'The Role of Agencies for Rural Development in Tanzania', in Andrew Coulson, ed., *African Socialism in Practice: The Tanzanian Experience* (Nottingham: Spokesman, 1979).

For an overview of criticisms see:

Richard Blue and James Weaver, *A Critical Assessment of the Tanzanian Model of Development* (Washington, D.C.: USAID Development Studies Programme, 1977).

P.F. Nursey-Bray, 'Tanzania: The Development Debate', *African Affairs* 79, no. 314 (January 1980), pp. 55–78.

Cranford Pratt, 'Tanzania: The Development Debate — A Comment', Ibid. (July 1980), pp. 343–347.

50. As Bertell Ollman has reminded us, apparently contradictory views of the state can be equally correct: 'representing as they do different tendencies inside the state relation. Dialectic truth does not fit together like the pieces of a puzzle, but allows for the kind of multiple onesidedness and apparent contradictoriness that results from studying any subject from perspectives associated with its different aspects.' Bertell Ollman, 'Thesis on the Capitalist State', *Monthly Review* 34, no. 7 (December 1982), p. 43.

Joel Samoff reminds us that contradictory views also arise when different researchers use different paradigms for analysis, resulting in quite different conclusions about the complexities of the state. Joel Samoff, 'On Class Paradigms and African Politics', *Africa Today* 29, no. 2 (1982), pp. 41–50.

51. For a discussion of the different strata of peasantry in Tanzania, see Michaela von Freyhold, op. cit., pp. 63–65. She discusses class antagonisms among the 'kulaks, middle, and marginal peasants', but also shows that they are 'not [yet] divided by class struggle'.

52. For a full discussion of capitalist criteria for domestic bank loans, see James H. Mittelman, *Underdevelopment and the Transition to Socialism — Mozambique and Tanzania* (New York: Academic Press, 1981), pp. 192–194, 216–224.

53. Ibid, pp. 201–202.

Joel Samoff, 'Crisis and Socialism in Tanzania', *Journal of Modern African Studies* 19, No. 2 (1981), p. 302.

S. S. Mushi, 'Decentralisation of Tanzania and Popular Participation', paper presented at the University of Dar es Salaam, 12 July 1977.

54. J. Boesen *et al.*, op. cit.

Justice Maeda, 'Popular Participation, Control and Development', Ph.D. Thesis, Yale University, 1976.

Michaela von Freyhold, op. cit.

55. As an example, it is estimated that only 10–25 per cent of the annual maize crop (the basic staple) passes through the official markets. The rest is consumed locally or traded illegally. Philip Raikes, 'Agrarian Crises and Economic Liberalisation in Tanzania: A Comment', *Journal of Modern African Studies* 16, no. 3 (September 1978), p. 314.

56. United Republic of Tanzania, *Economic Survey 1977–78* (Dar es Salaam, Government Printer, 1978), pp. 108–115.

'Tanzania, Which Way?' *New African* (February 1981), p. 30.

57. Ibid.

58. Amon J. Nsekela, 'Nationalism and Social Engineering in Tanzania', *Africa* 81 (May 1978), p. 72.
59. James Mittelman, op. cit., pp. 203–204, 228.
    Idrian Resnick, *The Long Transition: Building Socialism in Tanzania* (New York: Monthly Review Press, 1981), pp. 138–147, pp. 174–175.
60. Andrew Coulson, ed., op. cit.
61. Jean-Pierre Langellier, 'Tanzania's Socialist Choice: Peasant Power', *The Manchester Guardian*, 9 November 1980, p. 14.
62. Henry Mapolu, 'The Organisation and Participation of Workers', in Kim, Mabele, Schultheis, op. cit., pp. 272–77.
    — ed., *Workers and Management* (Dar es Salaam: Tanzania Publishing House, 1976).
    Paschal Mihyo, 'The Struggle for Workers' Control in Tanzania', *Review of African Political Economy*, no. 4 (November 1975), pp. 62–84.
    Pius Msekwa, 'The Quest for Workers' Participation', in *Labour in Tanzania* (Dar es Salaam: Tanzania Publishing House, 1977), pp. 68–85.
63. Jean-Pierre Langellier, op. cit., p. 14.
64. Joel Samoff (1979), op. cit., pp. 16–19.
65. Amon J. Nsekela, op. cit., p. 72.
66. S.S. Mushi, 'Tanzania Foreign Relations and the Policies of Non-Alignment, Socialism and Self-Reliance', in S.S. Mushi and K. Mathews, eds., *Foreign Policy of Tanzania 1961–1981: A. Reader* (Dar es Salaam: Tanzania Publishing House, 1981), pp. 34–66.
    Okwudiba Nnoli, *Self Reliance and Foreign Policy in Tanzania* (New York: NOK Publications, 1978).
67. Speech at University of Ibadan, Nigeria, November 1976, quoted in D.W. Nabudere, 'Imperialism, the National Question and the National Liberation Struggle', *New Outlook* (Dar es Salaam) 5, (September/October 1977), p. 21.
68. For discussions of the role of the bureaucracy and of the party sustaining legitimacy for the state, see:
    Joel Samoff, 1979, op. cit., pp. 19–22.
    Idrian Resnick, op. cit., pp. 94–96.
69. One nationalist appeal that has been discredited is *ujamaa*, a populist appeal for all to work together which could not stand the test of practice. In contrast to 'self reliance' or 'rural development', *ujamaa* was proposed as a specific policy for co-operative agricultural production. But it was never articulated in coherent organisational terms; it was proclaimed for everything from co-operatives with a small clique of entrepreneurs taking the profit to genuine attempts at collective farming under collective decision-making.
70. *Tanzania Daily News*, 9 March 1980.
71. Tony Avirgan, op. cit., pp. 2–3.
72. *Tanzania Daily News*, 26 February 1980.
73. Werner Biermann, 'The Development of Underdevelopment: The Historical Perspective', in Ben Turok, ed., *Development in Zambia* (London: Zed Press, 1979), p. 131.
74. Michael Burawoy, *The Colour of Class on the Copper Mines: From African Advancement to Zambianisation*, Zambian Papers No. 7 (Lusaka: Institute for African Studies, University of Zambia, 1972).

E.A.G. Robinson, 'The Economic Problem', in *Modern Industry and the African: An Enquiry into the effect of the Copper Mines of Central Africa upon Native Society*, 2nd ed. (London: Frank Cass, 1967), p. 187.

75. Carolyn Baylies and Nora Hamilton, 'The State in Peripheral Societies: Mexico and Zambia', mimeo (1981), p. 23.
76. Anthony Martin, *Minding their own Business: Zambia's Struggle Against Western Control* (Harmondsworth, England: Penguin, 1975), p. 267.
77. Richard Sklar, *Corporate Power in an African State: The Political Impact of Multi-National Mining Companies in Zambia* (Berkeley: University of California Press, 1975), p. 210.
78. Kenneth Kaunda, 'The Watershed', An Address to the National Council of UNIP, Mulungushi Hall, Lusaka, 30 June 1975.
79. Ben Turok, 'The Penalties of Zambia's Mixed Economy', in Turok, ed., op. cit., p. 75.
80. C.S. Lombard and A.H.C. Tweedie, *Agriculture in Zambia Since Independence* (Lusaka: Neczam, 1974), pp. 65–67.
81. W.J. Cowie, 'Rural Development in an Urbanised Mining Economy: Zambia', *Rural Africana*, nos. 4–5 (Spring-Fall 1979), p. 55.
82. Republic of Zambia, 'Financial Report for the years ending 1972–1976', Lusaka, quoted in Robert Klepper, 'Zambian Agricultural Structure and Performance', in Turok, op. cit., p. 147.
83. Doris Dodge, *Agricultural Policy and Performance in Zambia: History, Prospects and Proposals for Change* (Los Angeles: University of California, Institute of International Studies, 1977), p. 137.
The average Zambian farmer's purchasing power had declined by one third from 1964–1972 while the average urban worker's purchasing power was higher by two thirds.
84. *Zambia Daily Mail*, 13 June 1979.
85. Robert S. Bates, *Rural Responses to Industrialisation: A Study of Village Zambia* (New Haven: Yale University Press, 1976), Chapters 10–11.
Robert Klepper, op. cit., p. 148.
C.S. Lombard and A.H.C. Tweedie, op. cit., pp. 52–70.
P. Ollawa, *Rural Development Policies and Performance in Zambia* (The Hague: ISS Occasional Paper, 59, 1977).
William Tordoff, ed. *Administration in Zambia* (Manchester: University Press, 1980), p. 33.
86. Carolyn Baylies, 'Emergence of Indigenous Capitalist Agriculture: The Case of Southern Province, Zambia', *Rural Africana*, nos. 4–5 (Spring-Fall 1979), pp. 74–76.
87. Richard Sklar, op. cit., p. 200.
'Of 46 former or current personnel ... who could be identified as having business interests, almost three-fourths became involved in their private enterprises during the period in which they held parastatal positions.' M. Szeftel, 'Political Conflict, Spoils and Class Formation in Zambia', Ph.D. thesis, University of Manchester, 1978, p. 59, quoted in William Tordoff, op. cit., p. 31.
88. Douglas G. Anglin and Timothy Shaw, *Zambia's Foreign Policy: Studies in Diplomacy and Dependence* (Boulder, Colorado: Westview, 1979), pp. 394-399.

Carolyn Baylies and Nora Hamilton, op. cit.

S. Johns, 'State Capitalism in Zambia: The Evolution of the Parastatal Sector', San Francisco, African Studies Association, 1975.

89. Ben Turok, 'State Capitalism: The Role of Parastatals', paper presented at University of Zambia seminar, 1980, p. 1.

90. Peter Evans, *Dependent Development: The Alliance of Multinational, State and Local Capital in Brazil (Princeton: Princeton University Press, 1979), p. 270.*

91. Richard Sklar, op. cit., pp. 134-178.

92. Kenneth Kaunda, 'The Leadership Code and Responsibilities of the Leadership in the Creation of a new Social Order', speech to UNIP National Council, 2 December 1972 (Lusaka: Government Printer, 1973).

93. Richard Sklar, op. cit., pp. 455-457.

94. Kren Eriksen, 'Zambia: Class Formation and Detente', *Review of African Political Economy*, no. 9 (May-August 1978), pp. 12-13.

95. Michael Burawoy, op. cit., p. 77.

96. Buroway describes them as a labour aristocracy with an average income twice the national average for other Zambian employees. See Michael Burawoy, 'Another Look at the Mineworker', *African Social Research*, no. 14 (December 1972), pp. 276-280.

97. *Times of Zambia*, 8 May 1978.

98. *Tanzania Daily News*, 17 April, 1979.

99. *Africa News*, 10 November 1980; 9 February 1981.

100. James Petras, 'State Capitalism and the Third World', *Development and Change* 8 (1977), p. 12.

101. *Tanzania Daily News*, 16 December, 1978.

102. Press reports are numerous. For one summary, see 'Zambia: A History of Attacks from the South', *New African*, April 1981, p. 53.
    Tanzania Daily News, 8 and 13 March 1978; 25 August 1978; During Lancaster talks (late 1979), the raids were weekly.

103. William Tordoff, op. cit., pp. 32-33.
    Richard Sklar, op. cit., pp. 201 and 206.
    Ben Turok, 1979, op. cit., pp. 83-84.

104. Dominic Mulaisho, Economic Adviser to the President, personal interview, Lusaka, 5 June 1979.

105. Douglas Anglin and Timothy Shaw, op. cit., p. 398.
    Kren Eriksen, op. cit.

106. Douglas Anglin and Timothy Shaw, Ibid.

107. A long quote of Nkumbula's speech in the National Assembly is cited in William Tordoff and Robert Molteno, 'Parliament', in William Tordoff, ed., *Politics in Zambia* (Berkeley: University of California Press, 1974), p. 204.

CHAPTER 8

Legacy Of The Frontline: Southern African Development Co-ordination Conference (SADCC)

The cease-fire and elections for an independent Zimbabwe did not end the battle, for political success requires an economic base to survive. The new Zimbabwean government did fulfil the short-term goals of the Zimbabwean nationalists and the Frontline States: a state that could legally take control of production and a government that was not beholden to South Africa for attaining power. But these goals are only the means to the more important objective of economic liberation. Anglo-American and South African capital are still dominant in Zimbabwe, and the question remains whether production can now be turned not simply to create profit but to provide for the basic needs of the Zimbabwean people. Sir Seretse Khama expressed the view of the Frontline States at their Arusha conference on economic co-operation in July 1979 as follows: 'Many countries in the region have already won their political independence but their colonial past ensured that they continued to depend on others for economic survival. This economic dependence has in many ways made our political independence somewhat meaningless, particularly when one takes into account the fact that some of the countries on which some of us depend for economic survival do not share the human ideals on which our own societies are founded.'[1]

Nationalism and anti-colonialism are powerful ideologies that unite people against minority rule, but they leave the infrastructures intact — infrastructures which are integrated into the world capitalist system. Such integration has advantages: technology to resolve production problems is available, and the international market provides outlets for national production. However, the disadvantages are perhaps greater than the advantages. As an ex-colony, the new state is a junior partner, with an economy specialised to fulfil outside demand, not local needs. Production of manufactures is restrained because of small investment surpluses and low skill levels. When manufactures are exported, they cannot compete by price or quality on the world market.

Regional Basis Of National Development

In the 1960's during the nationalist drive for independence, African leaders often assumed that national development by each individual country would proceed after independence. (There were notable exceptions to this general approach, i.e., Nkrumah and Nyerere.[2] It is significant that Nyerere, now Chairman of the Frontline States, wanted to delay independence for Tanzania until Uganda and Kenya achieved independence, so all could strengthen their economic interaction.) 'National development' was given further legitimacy by traditional theorists who relied on the national economy as the unit of analysis. And more radical theorists (e.g., neo-Marxists) accepted the same unit of analysis, often simply changing the terminology (e.g., social formation for national economy).

An independent state that could legally take control of national production was a basic requisite, but it became clear that economic independence was extremely difficult to achieve alone. Tanzania and Zambia have the longest experience of the five in the Frontline in trying to assert national control over production with minimal success. Once again we return to the necessity of analysing the international context of national development. Integration into an international economic system with class divisions that cross national boundaries seriously delimits the effects of state action on the national economy. If only one part of the production process is domestic, then it is difficult to regulate that production; the fulfilment of national plans are restrained by this international division of labour. Inadequate technological knowledge and skills are part of the cycle of inadequate production, insufficient surplus for reinvestment and foreign exchange crises. Further, national capital for national development is rarely 'national'.

The question for newly independent states is how to overcome this underdevelopment without losing access to necessary technology and skills. Some dependence theorists[3] were emphatic that the new state must pull out of the world capitalist system: only by severing established economic relations would the country be forced to find domestic solutions to technological problems, train personnel in

appropriate technology and gradually become self-sufficient in production of basic necessities. This path was tried by the People's
Republic of China (PRC) and became the prototype for 'autocentric'
development. But no other country has followed that path, and the
People's Republic of China has now specified serious problems with
it. Most states simply could not take that approach because they do
not possess the vast natural or human resources of the PRC. In fact,
theorists now question whether any development could really be
'autocentric'.[4]

A second alternative proposed was to reduce the dislocations of
leaving the capitalist market by turning to the socialist countries more
fully. Trade, capital, and technology could be made available by the
advanced economies that are centrally planned. The success of Cuba
in promoting literacy, educating technical personnel, and providing
housing is cited to validate this approach. However, Cuba had no
choice but to rely on the socialist alternatives because of the
American-enforced embargo. And the problems with this alternative
are obvious. The technology may be as inappropriate for the
developing country as that from the capitalist economies. With crucial
needs for capital and skills, the new state could find itself trading its
colonial dependence for dependence on another power. Limiting
markets and sources of supply makes the economy more vulnerable to
short-term trends and fluctuations. Further, although the socialist
states are willing to help, their wealth is considerably less than the
advanced capitalist countries, and they are often less able to help. In
Southern Africa, government officials often complain that capital is
less available from the socialist countries, and loan terms are more
stringent.[5]

The policy alternative chosen by Zimbabwe and the Frontline
States is neither of the above. During the Zimbabwean struggle, the
Frontline States talked of coming together economically to enhance
their strengths and to attack their weaknesses on a regional basis. In
July 1974, before the Frontline was officially formed, Kaunda
proposed an economic transcontinental belt from Dar es Salaam to
Maputo on the Indian Ocean to Luanda on the Atlantic. During the
Frontline States' negotiations in support of majority rule in Zim-
babwe, the five states concluded many bilateral economic agreements
with each other. From the continual co-operation of the Frontline
States over Zimbabwe and the implementation of the bilateral agreements, the idea for regional co-operation to promote national

development evolved.[6] The political co-operation of the Frontline imparted economic lessons. The interlocking of the economies was made poignantly clear by Rhodesian bombing attacks on Zambia and Mozambique. Downed bridges in Zambia meant not only less food and fertiliser for the Zambian people but also less rail traffic revenue and jobs for Tanzanians and Mozambicans. The goal was to change their basis of unity from mutual poverty and exploitation to more positive aspirations of improving the quality of life in Southern Africa:

Underdevelopment, exploitation, crisis and conflict in Southern Africa will be overcome through economic liberation. The welfare of the people of Southern Africa and the development of its economies require co-ordinated regional action. The Frontline States believe that we in Southern Africa have the right to ask and to receive practical co-operation in our struggle for reconstruction, development and genuine interdependence . . . The dignity and welfare of the people of Southern Africa demand economic liberation and the Frontline States will struggle toward that goal.[7]

Regional co-ordination reduces some of the structural problems of underdevelopment. Mineral wealth can be shared for regional industries; manufacturing has a wider market for sales; skills can be pooled for regional research and development. Co-operation can greatly ameliorate the problems in the underdeveloped forces of production, as technology and skills are shared across national boundaries. Further, regional planning can rationalise the building of infrastructures and production units for a larger market.

Regional co-ordination, however, does not resolve the problems of the international division of labour. Regional economic units offer great advantages to the already dominant sectors that can take advantage of the greater transport and communication efficiency. Often regional economic unions have found that their agreements simply facilitated the penetration of large and more powerful foreign capital. In addition, benefits from regional co-ordination can accrue to a small class in one nation or another. In others, the benefits might be more equitably distributed. These differences in class structure among the individual states will be reflected in the policy priorities. For example, Malawi has chosen to build showpiece development projects — with South African capital — such as a new airport and a whole new capital city to attract the tourist trade, a means of earning foreign exchange. But the benefits of this foreign exchange earner may accrue mainly to the wealthy few, both Malawian and South African. In contrast, Mozambique has not designated its tourist industry as a priority because of limited benefits for the whole economy; capital and energy need to be used first to feed the people. Regional co-operation does not require reconciliation of these two national choices, but the choices illustrate the differences and conflict in approach to development problems, a conflict which reflects the different class bases of the state. As will be discussed more later, regional co-operation may, in fact, exacerbate the differences in the social relations of production among the countries. Further, these differences are more serious than the problems of the under-developed forces of production, because they do not have ready technical solutions. The social relations conflict raises fundamental political questions which must be answered as the new roads and bridges are being built. If not resolved, political roadblocks will render the new linkages useless. In order to analyse these problems further, it is first necessary to delineate the potential for develop-ment of the Southern African region and to investigate the Southern African Development Co-ordination Conference's programme for regional co-operation.

Potential Wealth Of The Region

The potential wealth of Southern Africa is vast, and not even fully explored. With 60 million people in 5 million square kilometres of land, the combined GDP is $20 billion (excluding South Africa) even at the present level of underdevelopment. In general, the area is not overpopulated. (Lesotho is overpopulated, and some would say Malawi is.) On the contrary, the restraint to development in most of the region is insufficient population, such as Angola where the popula-tion is only 5 persons per square km. Although good arable land is scarce in some regions — Lesotho is losing 1 percent per year of its arable land to erosion[8] — there is more than sufficient land for several of the countries to be food exporters. Only Zimbabwe and Malawi are consistent food exporters; Zimbabwe exported 238,017 tons of maize in 1981, only one year after the war. Even during the severe drought in 1982, it was able to trade food. Zimbabwe is helping its neighbours with food aid, but long-term solutions are required to fulfil the potential in both food and cash crop production. Production for export from the region exists already for numerous agricultural products, but could be increased substantially for coffee, sisal, tea, cotton, tobacco, sugar, wool, wood pulp, beef, leather, maize, wheat, and cashews. The goal is to shift some of that export to partners in the region, as an alternative to competition in the international market.

TABLE XI

NET INSTALLED CAPACITY OF ELECTRIC GENERATING PLANTS, 1980 (1000 KILOWATT HOURS)

	Total Electricity	Hydroelectric
Angola	600	400
Botswana	0	0
Malawi	106	67
Mozambique	1800	1520
Tanzania	258	188
Zambia	1859	1669
Zimbabwe	1192	705
South Africa*	18806	777

* Includes Lesotho, Namibia, Swaziland.

Source: United Nations *Statistical Yearbook,* 1979–80, pp. 810–824.

Several large dams — Kariba (Zimbabwe-Zambia), Kafue (Zambia), Cabora Bassa (Mozambique), Kunene (Namibia-Angola) — have not been fully exploited for irrigation and have unused hydro-electric capacity sufficient for the initial stages of industrialisation in the area. As Table XI shows, hydro-electric capacity is already quite adequate in several of the states. In addition to Angola, oil resources are known to be off-shore in Tanzania, while there are known oil re-serves in Botswana, Lesotho, Mozambique and Namibia. Although the largest uranium mine in the area (Rossing in Namibia) is still under South African control, uranium is also found in Angola, Tanzania, and Zambia. Coal deposits are sufficient to serve energy demands of factories where hydro-electric or oil energy is inadequate (with the potential problem of coal pollution). In short, energy for development is not one of the problems for the Southern African region if the potential can be harnessed. Presently, several states are suffering from the high cost of oil which takes as much as 70 percent of the export earnings for some. The vast energy reserves could be unleashed if capital were available.

TABLE XII

IRON AND STEEL PRODUCTION, 1978
(1000 METRIC TONS)

	Iron Ore	Pig Iron	Steel
Angola	1664 (1975)	0	0
Botswana	0	0	0
Lesotho	0	0	0
Malawi	0	0	0
Mozambique	0	0	0
Swaziland	624	0	0
Tanzania	0	0	0
Zambia	0	0	0
Zimbabwe	384	320	350
South Africa	15153	7041	7903

Source: United Nations *Statistical Yearbook,* 1979–80, pp. 208–209, 344–345.

The mineral wealth of Southern Africa has been a mixed blessing for the region. More than in other parts of Africa, intransigent colonial regimes fought to maintain control over the wealth, which was not exploited for the benefit of the majority of the population. The states in the region, after three colonial wars (Angola, Mozambique, Zimbabwe), now hope to be able to turn that wealth to improve the quality of life of the people. Minerals necessary for industrial growth are available in great quantity: iron ore, cobalt, chrome, lead, nickel, zinc, and copper. As shown in Table XII, iron ore is found in several of the states, but only Zimbabwe and South Africa produce steel. Iron ore is also known to be in Tanzania, Mozambique and Zambia but is yet to be fully exploited. The independent states are planning to use the Zimbabwean steel industry as a base for eventual self-sufficient steel production in the region.

The mineral, energy, and land wealth are not even fully documented. As the states mobilise their resources for local needs, more minerals will be discovered. Under colonialism it was not profitable for the colonial power to explore for coal or oil if it were already supplied sufficiently from other sources around the world. For a poor country, long-term benefits overcome short-term costs of exploration and initial investment.

When compared with the potential wealth, Southern Africa's

present underdevelopment does not appear so bleak. It is when its underdevelopment is compared with South African affluence that obstacles loom on the horizon. Presently South African economic dominance is pervasive. The combined GNP's of the nine Southern African states (excluding Namibia) are only one-third of South Africa's alone. Angola, with all the present oil production in the region only refines 4.4 percent, while South Africa with no oil reserves refines 82.3 percent of available refined oil in the region.[9] South Africa's present control of transport and communication infra-structure in the Southern African region is almost complete: as one Rhodesian Front member said in the Zimbabwean parliament, South Africa could crush Zimbabwe with a rail embargo without firing a shot.[10] Several of the states in the region regularly import steel from the South African state corporation, ISCOR. And many are dependent on South Africa for food supplies not only in times of crisis, but on an annual basis. In almost every vital economic sector — agri-culture, manufacturing, transport and communication, energy — South Africa has goods ready to export to its neighbours and capital ready to invest in their economies.[11]

The South African Constellation Of States (CONSAS)

South African reaction to the election of Robert Mugabe was publicly restrained. They were surprised by his tone of reconciliation and confident that their economic strength could foster friendly relations. As the Deputy Minister of Defence, H.J. Coetzee, stated soon after the election, 'Mugabe accepts economic realities. He may decide on a policy of accommodation and that we would welcome. South Africa is in the best position to extend existing economic ties. I maintain that we really hold the key to stability within the region.'[12] This official optimism remained until Zimbabwe announced that it was breaking off diplomatic relations with South Africa and buying out South African interests from the Zimbabwean press and from the third largest bank in Zimbabwe.

These steps angered the South African government even though the Zimbabwean government paid mutually agreed upon prices for the firms and left foreign interests in many productive sectors alone. The South African regime had hoped a politically independent Zimbabwe would be a key factor in the formation of its newly proposed 'Con-stellation of States'. On 11 November 1979 in the Carlton Hotel, Prime Minister Botha had called together prominent businessmen to discuss economic development plans for the Southern African region. The Constellation of States was to be South Africa's solution to poverty and underdevelopment in the region.

The strategy offered by the government to the corporations was to form a constellation, not a solar system of states where one state clearly dominates as the centre. Beyond this analogy, no clear institutional structure was formulated. As depicted by Prime Minister Botha, however, the constellation was to look very much like the present configuration; development plans can work

> provided that we can keep as close as possible to the concept of utilising the capacity of the already existing infrastructure better. Our development strategy must also be aimed as far as possible at letting the advantages of our own well-developed infrastructure extend to the other, less well-equipped states of the subcontinent.[13]

He suggests that the present South African Customs Union could be the prototype for development within the constellation:

> The need here is to create the necessary machinery to handle the many functions of co-operation efficiently, taking into account the specific needs of our developing neighbour states. This latter principle has already been embodied in the Customs Union and other regional agreements.[14]

Finally, the constellation would incorporate the 'independent' bantustans as separate nations:

> No adjustments to the policy framework have in any way altered the high priority that the government has accorded to the economic development of the self-governing and independent national states [bantustans]. On the contrary, for the credibility and effective deployment of a constellation of states in Southern Africa, and later a possible council of states, it is actually more important than ever before that the economic vitality of these Black states be raised.[15]

Choosing to ignore the contradictory political interests in the region, the constellation policy promotes South African technology and know-how as the key to regional co-ordination. It offers South African technology to eradicate underdevelopment in the area.

This call for regional co-ordination is really not new, but it is a more sophisticated tactic of an old strategy. In different ways South Africa has had four previous attempts to normalise relations with the

rest of Africa without changing the domestic policy of apartheid:
1. Outward looking policy – 1963
2. Dialogue — 1968–1971
3. Détente – 1974
4. Muldergate – 1977
5. Constellation – 1979

The 'outward looking' policy began in the early 1960's under Prime Minister Verwoerd, as a diplomatic effort to gain recognition in the international community after the shock of the 1960 Sharpeville massacre. It was an effort to show the newly-independent black African states that South Africa could offer badly needed commodities. This policy became more direct and had somewhat more success in the 'dialogue' of the early 1970's.[16] The African states that responded (mainly Ivory Coast, Senegal, Liberia, and Malawi) stated that more regular political and economic exchanges would show the South African government that Africans are not ignorant and can manage affairs of states. By setting a good example, the black independent states hoped to convince the white minority regime to change its mistaken opinions. The reason behind the rationale was economic. South Africa wanted, as it does now, greater markets on the African continent. Some of the African countries wanted South African expertise and products. Prime Minister Vorster did make a few diplomatic coups by being able to meet with Presidents Senghor, Houphouet-Boigny and Tolbert from May 1974. The economic benefits were modest: landing rights in the Ivory Coast and some commodities exchanged. After the Soweto uprisings in June 1976, Senghor and Tolbert hardened their attitudes toward South Africa; Houphouet-Boigny wanted to retain relations.

The outward looking policy and dialogue did begin a long history of exchange with Malawi, the only African state to establish diplomatic relations with South Africa. A 1967 trade agreement increased imports from South Africa from 6 percent of total Malawian imports in 1964 to 41 percent in 1979.[17] Development assistance programmes have helped to build the new capital of Lilongwe, the railway to Nacala, Mozambique, a sugar mill, fertiliser plant, and tourist resorts.[18] Malawi did not join the Frontline States, but it is now a member of SADCC.

Détente exchanges began in 1974 with envoy communication between Kaunda and Vorster over the Rhodesian settlement. As discussed in Chapter 2, the Frontline States quickly came together to

present a unified policy to South Africa and Rhodesia about Zimbabwean independence. They made it clear that discussions with
South Africa about Zimbabwean independence did not imply accept-
ance of apartheid.

From 1972 for five years, the South African Ministry of Information secretly allocated millions of dollars to convince other countries
that apartheid was changing and that South Africa offered excellent
investment and trade opportunities. In persuading Prime Minister
Vorster and Minister of Information Connie Mulder of the need for a
'massive and secret psychological war of propaganda in a number of
prominent nations of the world', State Secretary for the Department
of Information, Eschel Rhoodie, emphasised the importance of
Africa:

> Africa must be our prime target. If we succeed in being accepted
> as an interlocuter by some moderate black states in Africa, white
> Western countries, such as Sweden, can no longer refuse a
> dialogue with us.[19]

The lack of landing rights in black Africa was costing the South
African airlines about $9 million a year to fly along the coast. One of
the first ventures, therefore, was to obtain permission to land from
Zaire north to Europe. In exchange for some aid and trade, Zaire, the
Central African Republic, and Gabon all secretly agreed to landing
rights. In other dealings, the South African government loaned
$60,000 to the Nigerian daily *West Africa* which then published
favourable articles about South Africa. This campaign spread much
beyond the continent as South Africa tried to legitimise apartheid
around the world. For example, South African agents tried to buy the
Washington (DC) *Star* and the Sacramento (California) *Bee* to
influence their editorial policies. Contributions were given to election
campaigns of American candidates to Congress who were favourable
to South Africa.[20] In short, 'Muldergate' was such a widespread,
systematic divergence of government funds to secret propaganda
projects that it became a major scandal inside South Africa. Prime
Minister Vorster, Minister of Information Connie Mulder, and State
Secretary for Information Eschel Rhoodie all were forced to resign.

The Constellation of States, therefore, has a history, but the new
offer is a more subtle and pragmatic proposal to the neighbouring
states and, therefore, is more difficult to resist. South Africa is
offering important development schemes to entice its closest
neighbours. Botswana will have a heavy duty rail link to western

Transvaal for the export of coal through Richard's Bay. In an unprecedented move, South Africa has offered Swaziland about 2,000 square miles of land from KaNgwane bantustan and the Ngwavuma region of KwaZulu bantustan. Lesotho has begun the huge Highlands water scheme with major financing from South Africa. Although these projects are problematic,[21] they offer capital financing and resources which are hard for these poor economies to reject. Samora Machel admitted the paradox by stating that sometimes new dependencies are necessary to open up possibilities of ending dependence.[22] South African technology could solve many of the region's problems, yet the wealth and organisation necessary to develop such technology are based in apartheid.

The Constellation of States is part of a total strategy outlined by the South African government which consists of three major areas: full implementation of the bantustan policy, the Constellation of States, and massive build-up of the military. In other words, while offering technology and trade to the black independent states in Southern Africa, South Africa is affirming and rationalising apartheid. The regime is reinforcing its attempt to divide the people by ethnic groups by promoting class distinctions among the Africans. By creating a 'permanent' urban labour force, it is trying to create an élite group to acquiese to apartheid.[23] Meanwhile, others who cannot fulfil the requirements for urban residence will continue to be treated like foreigners in the white sectors. Those who do not have jobs in the cities, such as the wives and children of 'migrant' labourers, will be forcibly removed to the bantustans. Strict apartheid could not work because the wealth of South Africa is dependent on African labour; therefore, this latest policy is to separate out an urban élite while removing the others to the bantustans. As the bantustans have more residents, due to the forced population moves, jobs will be needed. The land, as the government's own Tomlinson Commission assessed as long ago as 1955, cannot sustain the people that are already there. Massive infusions of capital are needed.[24] The private sector, therefore, is called in to provide more jobs to try to make the bantustan policy more workable. (Corporate provision of capital and employment is also central to the Constellation plans.) Production, finance, and employment will remain under control of white South Africa; most of the goods made in the bantustan factories will also be for the white South African consumers or for export, because most Africans can barely afford subsistence goods.

The Frontline States call the Constellation of States the 'bantu-stanisation of Southern Africa'. They understand the South African policy as promoting industries in their countries with South African capital and under South African control. The Constellation would formalise and expand the dependence of the Southern African states on South African technology and capital. Economic growth would occur but more to the profit of South Africa than of any integrated development in the Southern African region. The parallel between the bantustans and the Constellation of States has been made by South Africans themselves. At the Constellation discussion, the President of the Chamber of Mines, Mr D.A. Etheredge stated:

> The mining industry has, in terms of Black labour, been a primitive constellation for years as it draws from seven foreign countries, the three independent states (formerly part of the Republic of South Africa), the self-governing states and from the Republic itself.[25]

Botha suggests that the bantustans and the independent African states come together into a Customs Union, similar to the one that already exists. The South African Customs Union gives preferential pricing for South African goods to Botswana, Lesotho, Swaziland, and Namibia, but South African goods are not cheaper in real terms than those on the international market for those four countries. The 40 per cent preferential pricing is eliminated by 1) a ceiling on the ratio of amount payable to imports and 2) a formula which pays proceeds two years in arrears so inflation and real growth eliminate the apparent gain.[26] The tariff walls around the union tie the economies to South Africa as it is the major market for their exports; in addition, transport and finance are controlled by South Africa. The trade arrangements offer some assistance to the poorer countries, but the customs union is detrimental to their industrialisation. Promoting the free flow of goods and capital, the union gives an advantage to the well-established South African firms and retards the development of infant industries in other countries. The South African government, however, avoids any dependence on its customs union neighbours. Available water is becoming a problem for the growing economy and a hydro-electric scheme was proposed using sources from Lesotho. The major concern was whether such a source would make South Africa dependent on a non-white neighbouring government for the vital water resource.[27] The customs union is not a constellation, but more like a solar system where South Africa is the dominant and essential centre of economic activity. It is the only institutional example given by the prime minister as to the nature of the proposed 'constellation'. It appears, therefore, that the constellation would have a central and brightest sun that would forever outshine the lesser bodies.

These economic and political proposals for the bantustans and the Constellation are to protect South Africa from internal and external challenges, denounced by Botha as the 'marxist onslaught'. In case these more palatable tactics do not work, the third part of the total strategy involves preparation for total war to defend the *laager*. Government plans are to increase expenditure on armaments and nuclear defence. This expenditure is coupled with a policy to carry out pre-emptive strikes against its neighbours to warn them of South Africa's ultimate stand.[28] It is similar to the policy of Ian Smith in Rhodesia: pursuit of negotiations while making direct attacks to demonstrate power and will. South Africa attacked Angola, Botswana, Mozambique and Zambia in the first year after Zimbabwe's independence. The regime carries out assassination raids against ANC members in other countries such as the murder of Joe Gqabi in Zimbabwe and the massacre of ANC refugees in Matola, Mozambique and Maseru, Lesotho. The policy of full implementation of apartheid, therefore, is backed by the full militarisation of the white population. Any challenge to the status quo, either from within or without, is crushed with swift ferocity.

This policy of total strategy does not stop at the boundaries of the Southern African region, just as the policies of Ian Smith had international support and repercussions. Concerned about the strategic importance of South Africa, both for its mineral production and its position at the Cape around which the oil super-tankers travel, NATO is promoting negotiations for a South Atlantic Treaty Organisation (SATO). The plan is for South Africa to join Argentina, Chile and Brazil in protecting the South Atlantic. Third in a series of exchanges was an international symposium held in Buenos Aires on 26–29 May 1981. Although privately sponsored by the Institute of American Relations and the Council for Interamerican Security, both in Washington, D.C., and the Carlos Peregrine Foundation and Atenio Deoccidente in Argentina, the meeting was to discuss 'military strategy including the South Atlantic alliance'.[29]

South Africa is increasing its trade, investment, tourism, military and nuclear exchanges with Argentina, Chile and Paraguay. The ex-Chief of Operations of the South African Defence Force has been appointed ambassador to Chile. However, the Brazilian Foreign Minister denied that Brazil plans to join the alliance because of its close ties to Angola and other independent African states which are prospective markets for Brazilian goods.[30] Brazil, in fact, attended the Blantyre SADCC meeting (November 1981) and was vociferously anti-South Africa.

The co-operation is based on a number of mutual concerns: uninterrupted access to minerals of South Africa; containment of national liberation struggles, such as in Namibia and El Salvador; guarding the vast atomic testing area in the South Atlantic; domination of the large unexploited and strategically important Antartic continent. Historically, Argentina, Chile and South Africa have had similar policies: a virulent anticommunism used to retaliate against any opposition with arrests, torture and death. The Western powers have chosen to ignore these domestic policies to solicit support for the defence of strategic interests in the South Atlantic. The Reagan Administration, for example, lifted restrictions on aid to Argentina and Chile which were imposed by the Carter Administration because of those governments' violations of human rights. The Frontline States assert that the two policies cannot be separated. Plans for a constellation cannot be divorced from apartheid and the military arsenal built to defend it. Similarly, plans for defence of the South Atlantic cannot be separated from the repressive policies of the regimes involved. What constitutes 'defence' is also debatable, as the Foreign Minister of Mozambique, Joaquim Chissano, warned the West when they were talking about an 'African' defence force trained and armed by the West:

> We remind the NATO countries directly involved in these manoeuvres ['Pan-African defence'] that those countries which had to fight hard for their independence do not need their opinion to know who is the enemy of Africa. We know all those who were at our side during the difficult times in national independence struggles.[31]

Frontline States' Rejection Of The Constellation

A column in the Johannesburg *Star* by Deon Du Plessis (21 March 1980) declared the constellation a 'dead duck', and the Frontline States share that opinion. Prime Minister Botha was in fact responding to the Fronline States' initiatives for regional co-operation, which started in 1978 and resulted in the first formal conference in

July 1979 at Arusha even before Lancaster House negotiations or elections in Zimbabwe. The declaration for a Southern African Development Co-ordination Conference (SADCC) in Arusha was exactly to reject any or all plans like the constellation which could emerge from the changing status quo in the Southern African region. A statement from the SADCC-II meeting in November 1980 in Maputo best articulates the Frontline States' position:

> South Africa has worked energetically to sell its stillborn proposals for a Constellation of Southern African States centred on the Republic itself. These are not new proposals but merely variations on a well-known theme. None of the states of the region will have anything to do with them. Their object is clear: to tie the countries of the region into a irreversible dependence on South Africa; to turn the free states of Southern Africa into a little more than Bantustans. *Constellation is simply Apartheid as foreign policy.*[32] [Italics mine]

Earlier in Lusaka (April 1980) four countries (Zimbabwe, Malawi, Lesotho, Swaziland) joined the Frontline States to form SADCC. At the meeting President Kaunda declared that they were forming SADCC in spite of South Africa:

> Some people have tended to think that we are forming this economic grouping purely to face South Africa. In our view, this regional grouping is being established despite, not merely because of, South Africa and her concept of a regional constellation of states.[33]

President Samora Machel of Mozambique was careful to articulate that the SADCC nations are not declaring war on South Africa; instead, they are asserting and implementing their own analysis for economic development in the region:

> It is now time for the struggle for economic liberation of our countries, in particular to reduce our dependence in relation to South Africa. We should not have any compunction to say that we want to reduce our dependency on South Africa. However, we want to clarify that we are not declaring a war against South Africa.[34]

SADCC is a rejection of the South African Constellation of States but also of the old patterns of economic integration. The continent of Africa has many examples of failure of economic integration and the co-ordinating conference intends to avoid old mistakes. Its basic premise, in fact, diverges from the assumption of the old pattern, rejecting the idea that economic considerations can be separated from the political. The co-ordinating conference is turning that assumption on its head and asserts that the experience of political co-operation is the basis for economic co-ordination. The designation of economic priorities and strategies is first, political, and then economic variables can be analysed for more technical decisions about implementation.

Customs unions have long been tried on the African continent: the East African Customs Union was formed in the 1920's. The oldest is the South African Customs Union started in 1910. The customs union approach is now viewed as simply a means for continuing neocolonial linkages on a regional basis.[35] They facilitated the growth of the already dominant sectors and further enriched the dominant classes. Setting up protective tariff walls, the unions protected the transnational corporations already in place in the regional economy. Co-ordination of exchange and infrastructure facilitated expansion of production and of sales. The larger producers could take advantage of the economies of scale and, as important, of the reduced competition from outside the union. Fiscal incentives were also usually offered in addition to market protection. The unions tended to create and sustain monopoly production within their borders, which increased inequities among productive sectors. Distribution of goods, as well as production, remained in private hands.

These critiques are not only relevant to the South African Customs Union, promoted still by the constellation strategy, but also the East African Community. The community did not die simply because of the antics of Idi Amin, but because it continued to promote the industrial growth of Kenya, at the expense of Uganda, and especially, Tanzania. Kenyan industries competed with and overcame the nascent industries in Tanzania.[36] Private investors, making short-term decisions about profits, invested in the strongest sector; their pattern of investment reinforced uneven development.

Precursors Of SADCC

The origins of this new Southern African co-operation are older than the Frontline States, although clearly, details could not be formulated until the pivotal state of Zimbabwe was independent under a government not tied to South Africa. And the origins are clearly political. The 1969 Lusaka Declaration, followed by the Dar es Salaam Declaration of 1975, set the political priority of liberation from white minority rule as the path toward 'total' liberation. In working through the political differences and contradictions in support of the liberation of Zimbabwe, the Frontline States were able to move on to economic considerations. As President Machel summarised at the Lusaka conference:

> The experience of the Frontline States in the struggle for support to the liberation of oppressed and exploited people of Southern Africa taught us that to each one of our initiatives and victories, imperialism responds with new manoeuvres . . .
>
> What exists are interests. Therefore, we cannot talk about help, but rather about co-operation . . . It is economic interests which move different countries. They are going to Angola because they want oil, diamonds, and coffee. In Zimbabwe they want chrome and gold. In Swaziland, they want iron and coal. Our natural resources are targets and therefore, they are also tools for co-operation and not for aid. Therefore, we should not wait for aid, but rather for co-operation.[37]

The practical experience of the Frontline States is the political base for the economic co-operation and that base has now been broadened to include the other economies in the region:

> The Frontline States do not envisage this regional economic co-ordination as exclusive. The initiative toward economic liberation has flowed from our experience of joint action for political liberation. The Frontline States envisage regional co-ordination as open to all genuinely independent Southern African States.[38]

This political base to economic co-operation has precedents in smaller multilateral agreements in the region. Specific countries within the Lusaka Nine have been co-operating for a long time, even prior to their independence. For example, the lusophone states held economic summits in June 1979 and in March 1980 to establish principles of basic agreement in finance, trade and transport. This co-operation is a continuation of their collaboration during the colonial period when the present government leaders were leaders of the liberation forces pledged to mutual aid in the Conference of Organisations of the Portuguese Colonies (CONCP). The important collaboration between Tanzania and Frelimo for the Independence of Mozambique is well known. Immediately upon the independence of Mozambique (25 June 1975), the two countries established trade relations. By September they had agreed to set up a Mozambique-Tanzania Permanent Commission of Co-operation.

Although others in the Frontline established several bilateral agreements, the Mozambique-Tanzania Commission is a direct precursor of SADCC and is referred to as the model for agreement in several of the SADCC papers. Therefore, an analysis of the Commission could give some clues about the future directions of SADCC. The first session of the Commission was held in April 1976 in Dar es Salaam; it formed many subcommittees to implement co-operation in specific areas: education and culture, agriculture and natural resources, trade and finance, communications and transport, health information, industry, works and foreign relations.[39]

The first priority was to learn from and build upon their shared political experiences. Both governments set education for the people as a development priority, not just to learn the skill of literacy but to teach national culture and history. In both Tanzanian schools and the Frelimo schools in the liberated zones, African culture was affirmed, and education was based on practical needs such as improved agricultural production. Colonial history and politics which taught the inferiority of Africans were eradicated. The Commission established regular exchange between the two educational systems: Mozambicans wanted to learn how Tanzania achieved universal primary education. Tanzanians wanted to learn more about the programme in the Frelimo schools during the liberation struggle. The political agreement extended to foreign relations too. Mozambique had over 95 per cent illiteracy at independence and did not have enough personnel for consulates which were important for foreign trade relations. Tanzania agreed to act as the Mozambican liaison. In addition, the two have built a diplomatic school where students from both countries are trained for international service.[40]

A second priority was to overcome the legacy of the colonial infrastructure. Shipping between the two countries was still controlled by foreign shipping firms, which would refuse to ferry goods between the two unless the hulls were full. Three ships which had operated on Lake Nyasa in the west were out of order and needed to be put in service. There was no paved road linking the two countries although they have a common border of about 800 km. The Commission started to put the Lake Nyasa ships back in operation and registered ships for service on the Indian Ocean under Tanzanian and Mozambican ownership. A bridge across the Ruvuma River which forms their mutual border has been planned and preliminary surveying and construction plans begun.

In addition to overcoming colonial patterns of exchange, the Commission wanted to reduce competition between the two economies. They have established common export policies for timber, sisal, tea, and cashews, major foreign exchange earners for both. They have also agreed to expand trade between the two. In contrast to outsiders' ideas that the two underdeveloped economies would not have items to exchange because they produce similar unprocessed goods and both need processed manufactures, the Commission found over fifty items for exchange that were immediately available and needed by the other economy. To itemise only a few, Tanzania could export, to meet Mozambican demand, items such as textiles, blankets, corned beef, aluminium, tin containers, cocoa, fishnets. Mozambique had available for Tanzania import goods such as asbestos, water pipes, electric cables, cement, hospital equipment, refrigerators, condensed milk, railway wagons, copra oil. From 1977-78 the volume of trade more than tripled between the two countries. By the end of 1981, tariffs had been removed for several products traded between the two; others will be gradually reduced over 10 years.[41]

The difficulties were not insufficient goods for exchange, but rather three others: high prices, foreign exchange shortages, and the previously mentioned infrastructure for transport. Prices in both countries were higher than prices from outside sources because of a 'low level of productive forces, a situation imposed on our economies by imperialism; the prices of goods produced in both countries are generally higher than prices of similar goods coming from industrialised countries'.[42] Producing on a smaller scale with greater inefficiency, the prices are not competitive. In addition, some governments subsidise goods from their economies so that they are competitive in the international market. The Commission has agreed to try to lower the prices, but they have also agreed to tolerate the higher prices for certain goods in order to achieve greater co-ordination for development. Such a decision is clearly political and would not be made by economies driven solely by the profit motive. For the foreign exchange problem they have set up reciprocal accounts. Goods are paid for in their own currencies so that Tanzania pays Mozambique in shillings and Mozambique pays Tanzania in meticais. In this way they alleviate somewhat the severe restrictions of foreign exchange requirements.

The goal is development, but industrialisation that is mutually beneficial is most difficult to co-ordinate. To industrialise without competition, the Commission called for rationalisation of production and industrial complementarity. The programme of rationalisation is to 'reallocate production lines among industries and to reorganise the application of labour, material resources and technology' for the most efficient use.[43] Co-ordination would not be simply at the level of exchange but of production. Therefore, medium and long term plans for industrial production need to be co-ordinated between the two countries. With such plans, efficient allocation of the productive forces can be achieved on a regional basis. Industrial complementarity also takes co-ordinated planning. Tanzania turned south after the bitter break-up of the East African Community, and the government wanted to make sure that any regional co-operation would not perpetuate its underdeveloped and poor economy; complementarity was proposed as a way to industrialise both Tanzania and Mozambique without competition:

> The basis for industrial co-operation should be that the major gains to both countries will arise from . . . complementarity. This means that integrated industries will be those which require access to some or all of both markets or which have significant forward or backward linkages to other national or joint industries.[41]

With complementarity one economy is not left to provide raw materials for the other to produce. For example, both countries desired to be self-sufficient in cement so production will continue in both. But they then agreed that they could designate the specialised cements to one or another. Both produce batteries but Tanzania produces radio batteries and Mozambique car batteries. Tanzania will produce printing and writing paper and Mozambique will produce panel board. One makes tyres for trucks, the other for cars and vans. Discussions about similar arrangements are continuing for sectors like farm implements, railway wagons, vegetable oils, fertilisers, and textiles. Finally, because of the industrial co-operation, they will collaborate to make joint offers to foreign firms for better terms for machinery. With the complementarity, the industries can take advantage of economies of scale without promoting inequities in the development of the productive forces and in income.

The priorities and goals worked through by Tanzania and Mozambique are emerging as key points in the SADCC negotiations. Similar terms of co-operation between the Mozambique-Tanzania

Permanent Commission and SADCC are the following:
1. political experience as the basis of economic accord
2. transformation of the colonial infrastructure and colonial patterns of exchange
3. reduction of competition within the area
4. rationalisation and complementarity of industry
5. co-ordination of national development plans.

Of the five terms of agreement only number 3 is similar to the traditional customs unions. The others create a new approach to regional integration. Learning from previous mistakes, SADCC is trying to co-ordinate at the level of production, not simply of exchange, to promote development.

SADCC: A Radical Plan For Integration?

The plans and goals of the SADCC group are broad but inclusive:
1. the reduction of economic dependence, particularly but not only, on the Republic of South Africa;
2. the forging of links to create a genuine and equitable regional integration;
3. the mobilisation of resources to promote the implementation of national, interstate, and regional policies;
4. concerted action to secure international co-operation within the framework of [our] strategy for economic liberation.[45]

To transform the colonial infrastructure, transport and communication have been set as the overwhelming priority. First, the road and rail systems are in disarray because of bombing by the Smith forces during the war, flood damage, and mechanical failure. During the height of Zambia's transport difficulties, the turn-around time for the Tazara railroad had increased from 15 days to 64 days for the wagons. The Chirundu Road from Lusaka to Salisbury had a backlog of 100,000 tons of goods. The Kafue Bridge was built in 1906, and trains must slow to 10-12 miles per hour when they cross.[46] The list of examples of outdated or destroyed bridges, rail lines, and locomotives is very long. In addition to this state of disrepair, many of the roads lead to South Africa. Zambia, Botswana, and Zimbabwe are still largely linked to South Africa's rail and port system. To reduce this dependence and to increase exchange among the nine, SADCC has called for the rehabilitation of the existing facilities and the construction of new road, rail, air and lake transport systems. Over 40 percent of the $600 million pledged at the SADCC II conference

(November 1980) was allocated to Mozambique for improvement of the rail and port facilities. Mozambique presently can serve four land-locked countries and with increased capacity could serve six. The pledges also contribute to the Kazangula road and bridge between Botswana and Zambia to overcome reliance on ferry boats for exchange of goods between the two countries.[47] Of the 114 projects planned for SATCC (Southern African Transport and Communication Commission) by the end of 1984, half of the total $3.172 million funds had been raised. Twelve projects had been completed and 31 were underway.

In food and agriculture the immediate problem was eradication of foot and mouth disease. With the curtailment of dipping by the Rhodesian authorities in the rural areas because of the war, the disease spread to Botswana and meat exports dropped by 50 percent. Botswana has set up a regional control programme, including the distribution of vaccines. Research will be co-ordinated for semi-arid tropical agriculture.

The longer term problem was summarised at the Blantyre confer-ence: 'Inadequate food security has led to recurrent foreign exchange and food distribution crises in half of SADCC's members and to dependence on purchases from South Africa for several of them.[48] By 1983, Zimbabwe had co-ordinated proposals for 15 projects with priorities for early warning systems on crop results, food crop storage, and exchange of technical information. The urgency of this co-ordina-tion is second only to the transport sector for several reasons. The use of food as a weapon is well known in the region, for Rhodesia bombed bridges and irrigation systems in Zambia and Mozambique during the Lancaster House talks to convince the Frontline States to stop the guerrilla struggle. Further, drought and floods have alternately devastated food crops in the region. During a severe drought in 1982, only Zimbabwe and Malawi were able to be self-sufficient in food. SADCC co-ordination for food production includes joint actions for procurement, especially for international aid; the states do not want to compete on the international grain market for food if regional production is insufficient.[49]

Technical co-operation is beginning with soil and land utilisation co-ordination. Swaziland also presented plans for the sharing of national training facilities for skilled personnel. Speciality schools will open their doors to all nationals in the region so facilities do not need to be duplicated. Taking the region as a whole, at least one relatively strong secondary and/or tertiary institution already exists in most specialised fields.

Energy represents a major constraint on development for several countries as discussed earlier. Yet in other countries in the region energy resources are exported. Angola is, therefore, leading the co-ordination of energy production and utilisation for the region.

Industrial production is essential to sustain development and SADCC has set a three stage approach to industrialisation. First, national manufacturing with surplus capacity will be brought into production for regional trade and will begin importing materials from the region rather than from outside. Second, a preliminary study identifies sixty clusters of products that could be available for regional trade. Trade planning will be based on the Mozambique-Tanzania annual trade plans as adopted by their permanent commission. As the Maputo report states, no SADCC country can envisage a complete range of industries in the forseeable future because of capital cost, construction capacity, and skilled personnel constraints. Therefore, the third stage in industrial planning will be an effort to co-ordinate projected production plans to avoid duplication and to encourage regional trade. For certain branches of industry more integrated planning will be necessary. Branches of chemicals, pulp and paper, basic metal production, and engineering are areas which could benefit from close examination and discussion about the 'modalities of integrated planning, on durable inter-enterprise relations (joint enterprise or otherwise), and on acceptable balances of product and export gains'.[50]

Discussions have already suggested that Angola could develop a petrochemical industry for the region. Tanzania, with modest deposits of phosphate, but much natural gas, could specialise in fertilisers. Iron ore in Angola, Mozambique, Tanzania and Zambia could be directed to iron and steel development, probably building on the present structure in Zimbabwe, and perhaps, Mozambique. Zambia heads the co-ordination of mining developments and Malawi directs regional planning for forestry, fishing and wildlife.

Regional financial co-ordination is on the agenda but did not receive immediate attention. The project co-ordination must proceed before there is sufficient demand for multistate investment to warrant establishing a financial infrastructure. Zambia is heading a team of financial experts to study the institutional needs in this field. In the interim, each commission is delegated responsibility for mobilisation of finance for its sector. In this way some of the states may be able to use funds as alternatives to South African financing.[51]

The Southern African states point out that their regional plans will efficiently allocate aid for the entire region, but foreign donor response has not been generous. The $600 million offered at Maputo was only a beginning for the $1.5 billion needed simply for the communication and transport infrastructure. *South* magazine summarised that donor response as follows: 'China and the Soviet Union both turned down invitations to attend. Japan, France, and Britain offered nothing. West Germany gave a token $1.5 million. The EEC offered money that must go to the region anyway under Lomé II. The US promised the same as earthquake stricken Italy ($50 million)'.[52] Contributions from donor countries, however, have steadily increased. To illustrate, funds committed to SATCC by the November 1981 Blantyre Conference were only 17 percent of the total pledged at Maputo in 1980. As a result of project development and negotiations, 24 percent ($678 million) of total projects were committed with with $450 million under discussion by January 1984.[53]

As SADCC tries to reduce its dependence on South Africa, it increases its need for foreign capital investment. This dependency is viewed as short-term by SADCC and the nine do not intend to relinquish control, but the problems are real. For example, the major EEC contributions are not new funds, but ones pledged under the Lomé II Convention. However, Angola has not joined the Lomé Convention although Mozambique did at the end of 1984. Under the Reagan Administration, the US clearly prefers bilateral aid to contributions to the region. Zimbabwe is by far the largest aid recipient in the Southern African region; by the end of 1982, Zimbabwe received $162.9 million from the United States and the total for 1980-1983 was to be $225 million.[54] To 1984 the US, in contrast, had only pledged a little over $50 million for SADCC projects, had also cut off aid to Mozambique (except emergency food aid) and would not formally recognise the Angolan government. The Soviet Union attended its first SADCC conference in January 1983 at Maseru. It appears that the Soviet Union also prefers to maintain bilateral aid to its most favoured nations. SADCC was formed in part to ameliorate these political preferences; it remains to be seen if the major donors will co-operate. Certainly several smaller countries (especially Scandinavia) have been willing to give substantial amounts to SADCC. Yet others, such as OPEC, have not been rushing to contribute. Prime Minister Robert Mugabe has already sounded a warning note; he expressed gratitude for the aid but said it was 'disturbing that there is an increasing tendency to give aid with political strings in order to reduce recipients to neo-colonies'.[55]

In spite of the limited donor response and the attendant danger of donor control, progress has been made in SADCC co-ordination. All of the twelve sectors except the development fund are well under way. Each summit and conference produces a new list of projects proposed and initiated. Starting with the urgent but simpler co-ordination of infrastructure, the countries hope to reach the stage where they can actually co-ordinate national development plans. However, the path from a few new roads to co-ordinated national development plans is long and full of obstacles.

Obstacles To Co-ordinated Development

SADCC co-operation is based on two major premises. Colonialism blocked the development of sector linkages among African states. As Samora Machel has emphasised, 'the economies of the Southern African countries were conceived or organised as functions of South Africa'.[56] Therefore, the first premise asserts there is little possibility for 'autonomous' national development. No one economy has both the resource base and the infrastructure linkages to develop without collaboration with its neighbours. Second, given the constraints of this dependent capitalist development, economic co-operation in the region is not a natural consequence of market forces. It must be created.

These conditions enhance the role of the state in economic development. As discussed in Chapter 6, the theories of relative state autonomy suggest that for a weak and dependent economy (with an immature national bourgeoisie), the state can promote economic development to increase its own resource base. This prominent role by the state is tolerated by the dominant class as long as profits are insured.

The SADCC plan for economic integration clearly enhances the role of the individual state, emphasising the sovereignty of each state in several ways. For example, in contrast to the models of integration under colonialism (South African Customs Union and the Central African Federation), membership and participation are voluntary.

Major decisions in SADCC are made only by consensus. The programme also overtly constrains the centralised bureaucratic authority; each state takes control and responsibility for one or two development sectors. Most of the decision-making is, therefore, decentralised and does not threaten national sovereignty.[57] SADCC in no way diminishes the role of individual states for development, but rather, each state will increase its individual and collective resource base from which to promote development. Yet this strength provokes new difficulties for co-ordination.

The prospects for SADCC can be evaluated in three important areas: 1) infrastructure; 2) co-ordination of production; 3) social relations of production. For the first two, there are already broad areas of agreement, with problems arising as the co-ordination is implemented. It is the third area, hardly mentioned in SADCC documents, which will probably be the main obstacle to the success of this economic co-operation.

There is little or no dissent among SADCC members that building of transport and communication links (infrastructure) must be a priority for the region. Greater networks will increase the efficiency of production and exchange. Because of reduced transport blockages, capital investment can be rationalised throughout the region. There is a major obstacle, however, to this plan: sabotage and destabilisation from South Africa.

Within the first year of Zimbabwe's independence, South Africa had openly attacked not only Angola, but also Mozambique, Zambia and Botswana. In 1981 it deliberately delayed oil and/or fertiliser shipments to Lesotho, Malawi, Zimbabwe, Zambia and Botswana to hinder crop production and marketing — in order to increase the region's food dependence on South African production.

By financing commando raids. South Africa finds it easy to attack new SADCC railways and other infrastructures. Much as it has kept the Benguela railroad in Angola out of operation by financing Jonas Savimbi, South Africa is now backing the Mozambique National Resistance to sabotage rail lines to Mozambique. The lines from Beira and Maputo to Zimbabwe and from Nacala to Malawi are regularly attacked, as are major roads.[58] The oil pipeline from Beira to Mutare is regularly blown up. Oil storage tanks in Beira as well as navigation buoys in the port have been sabotaged.

Several thousand Rhodesians are now residents of South Africa, many of whom know the Zimbabwe terrain well because they have served in the Rhodesian army or even the Selous Scouts. It is reported that some are being integrated into the South Africa Army.[59] The Frontline States have pledged joint retaliation in the event of a major South African attack,[60] but clearly the necessity of such military expenditures diverts funds from development. Further, countries like Botswana have very small numbers of defence forces so the mutual defence pact is limited by national capabilities.

As the South African regime is frustrated in its attempt to legitimise apartheid and to succeed in its newest 'outward looking policy', the SADCC countries expect further armed aggression from their neighbour. Through direct sabotage of SADCC programmes, invasion of the independent countries, and raids to intimidate governments (Mozambique, Lesotho, Swaziland, Zimbabwe), the South African regime clearly intends to raise the cost of SADCC.

The goal of co-ordination of production involves co-operation in agricultural planning, marketing of minerals, and complementarity of production in industry and agriculture. In the past, co-operation in Africa meant that those who were already invested in the dominant sectors could expand their operations in a protected market with little or no restrictions. The profits went mainly to international capital, even after colonialism had officially ended. SADCC production complementarity will also reduce competition, but production priorities will be determined by the governments, not the 'market'.

An investor, from within the region or from without, will find it necessary to negotiate the terms of investment with the national government and with the SADCC commission involved. (Pleading economies of scale and efficiency of production, an investor could argue that a single large tyre factory for the region is the most economically viable way to provide this necessity. SADCC complementarity would argue that at least two factories in different countries are more desirable, one to build truck tyres, another for automobile tyres.) The requirements for investors (limitation on the expatriation of capital, training of nationals, etc.) will deter some capital transfers. Other investors may be attracted by the larger market with adequate transport and by participation with local governments who will share the risk. But the outcome is not predetermined. Production complementarity will prompt a struggle between the investors and the governments as they each bargain for the best terms.[61] In some areas, SADCC will favour national capital because of the desire to reduce dependence; in other areas, international capital will be favoured because of the need for advanced technology.

Conflict will also arise among the member states over the terms of local projects which are not SADCC co-ordinated. In Mozambique, Angola and Tanzania, transnational corporations are under strict government regulation of production and of expatriation of profit. The transnational corporations in Malawi or Swaziland would not be under such restrictions so they could well choose to invest there, especially if the land-locked status of the two is ameliorated by the new transport system. Further, labour costs are kept lower in some of the states through strict government control. Finally, many theorists are predicting that Zimbabwe will attract more additional capital because of its relatively developed industrial base, and, therefore, Zimbabwe will dominate all of SADCC. The terms offered to the transnational corporations, in other words, will attract or discourage them from investing in particular states in the region. To avoid this inequality, the regulation of foreign investment should be uniform for similar industries in the area. SADCC could assess how to mobilise its own investible surpluses and introduce a regional tax to stop the outflow of surplus from the region. Is it possible for a uniform policy to be decided upon among states with capitalist relations of production versus those with a mixed economy trying to move to socialism? If not resolved, SADCC plans for industrial complementarity will remain on paper.

The most fundamental obstacles to SADCC are the contradictions which the co-ordinated projects themselves create. In a dialectic sense, the process of resolving underdevelopment and dependence in the Southern African region sets in motion contradictions which could, in turn, destroy the process. SADCC regional co-operation does confront the problems of the underdeveloped forces of production in the region. It does not try to transform the forces of production simply through reforms in exchange, but through regional planning of production. In this way, it is innovative and may avoid mistakes of previous attempts at economic integration. The plans for rationalisation and complementarity of industry and agriculture will greatly help to increase production capabilities. But these plans have not raised questions about the third area of future problems for SADCC: contradictory social relations of production within and among the participating states. As the states come together to resolve the problems of underdevelopment, social problems will intensify. And they will be more difficult to resolve because they do not have ready technical solutions.[62] The contradictions are fundamental, for resolutions in the social conflicts will determine *how* the increased productive capacity will be utilised and *for whom*. The proposed plans to develop the forces of production cannot be isolated from the contradictions in the social relations.

Problems in the social relations of production have already emerged in bilateral agreements, which suggest areas of possible conflict for the wider regional co-ordination. For example, one measurable indicator of basic contradictions is wage differentials. For the Tazara Railroad, Tanzania and Zambia had a major dispute over the wages to be paid to the managers. In Tanzania the wage differential is about 1:10 between the lowest and highest paid employees in the parastatals. In Zambia it is as great as 1:50. The Zambian government wanted to pay the managers of the railroad much more than the Tanzanian government would tolerate. For projects in the Mozambique-Tanzania Permanent Commission, however, Tanzanians are paid pensions which raise their salaries much above the Mozambicans for the same job. These differentiated wages for the same project and same skill levels will create tension not only among the workers, but also among the states. Tanzania, Mozambique, and Angola, with their national policies of keeping managerial and skilled workers' salaries somewhat in line with peasant incomes, will not want to create a large privileged sector among the workers.

Symbolic of this problem was the discussion over the salary of the Executive Secretary of SADCC. The appointment is equivalent in rank to a permanent secretary in the national governments, the annual salaries of which range range from $8,000 in Tanzania to $30,000 in Zimbabwe. A Zimbabwean was appointed as the first SADCC Executive Secretary (Arthur Blumeris), but the salary was set at a compromise $24,000.[63]

More fundamental is the difference in the actual stratification of workers in the various countries. In Mozambique and Angola, the stratification between planners, managers, and producers is under attack. The goal is to include workers in management and planning, to put them in charge of finance and production. Can the goals and methods of producer-planners in Mozambique be co-ordinated with those of specialised technocrat-managers of Zambia or Malawi?

The question is important, for these differences will mean disagreement over development priorities. Priorities could vary over the choice for development for quick economic growth versus development that enhances local control. For example, choice of the level of technology — which determines whether the production is capital or labour intensive — could affect the degree of local control. The choice for high levels of technology would require high levels of skills and most likely more capital. This could require more foreign technicians to run and repair machinery, for even countries like Tanzania, who have insisted that local workers be trained in all aspects of machinery operation and repair, have found that the foreign technicians need to return for repairs and major adjustment. This necessity creates long delays in production and disruption in marketing the goods, which then affect other industries using the products. Planning breaks down. Implementation of the goal of SADCC for national/regional control of production will vary considerably, depending whether that 'national' control is dependent on foreign technicians and based in foreign capital or is under command of the local workers.

Another obstacle is the contradiction between local initiative and regional planning. Zimbabwe, Tanzania, Mozambique, and Angola are committed to encourage local initiative for development projects. Clearly, these initiatives need co-ordination for projects like water or energy supply. The question is to what extent will regional planning discourage local initiative. Will the villagers simply wait for projects to come to them as they have learned to do in Zambia and Tanzania? What does that imply for local political control? Successful state central planning that facilitates local initiative is very difficult to accomplish. Regional planning will be even more difficult to reconcile with local initiative.

To indicate these problems is not to be cynical, but to suggest the extent of the struggle yet to come. The Frontline States scored a major victory with the independence of Zimbabwe, at great cost to their economies. As they unite for economic liberation, they will score other victories. The SADCC plans are innovative and daring and could evolve into a programme for alleviating dependent capitalist links. As the leaders who have fought national liberation wars have often stated, the difficult struggle of economic transformation continues long after the guns are laid down. At the SADCC II conference in Maputo, the participants reminded the sceptics of their determination:

> There are those who do not believe that the countries of the region will have the resolve to carry this struggle for economic liberation to a positive conclusion. Similar voices were heard in

Lusaka in 1969 when the states committed themselves to the political liberation of Southern Africa. Since then Angola, Mozambique and Zimbabwe have been freed at considerable cost to all the countries of the region. Namibia, we hope, stands on the threshold of independence. Only in South Africa do those who propagate the pernicious policies of racial superiority still attempt to project a false image of security and stability. The international community should not be fooled. The cynics were wrong when they underestimated the commitment to political liberation. They will be wrong again if they believe that SADCC is not truly embarked on the road to *economic liberation*.[64] [Italics in original.]

Notes

1. *Tanzania Daily News*, 4 July 1979.
2. The regional co-operation promoted by Nkrumah and Nyerere differed considerably, however. Nkrumah promoted political co-ordination first — on a very large regional scale (e.g., all of West Africa). Nyerere promoted economic co-operation first and then political, both on a regional level.
3. Samir Amin, *Unequal Development* (New York: Monthly Review, 1976).
   Andre Gunder Frank, *Capitalism and Underdevelopment in Latin America* (Harmondsworth: Penguin Books, 1971).
   Clive Thomas, *Dependence and Transformation: The Economies of the Transition to Socialism* (New York: Monthly Review, 1974).
4. Ronald Chilcote, 'Issues of Theory in Dependency and Marxism', *Latin American Perspectives* 8, Nos. 3/4 (Summer/Fall 1981), pp. 3–16.
   Norma Chincilla and James Dietz, 'Toward a New Understanding of Development', ibid., pp. 138–147.
   Lorraine Culley, 'Economic Development in Neo-Marxist Theory' in Barry Hindess, ed., *Sociological Theories of the Economy* (London: Macmillan, 1977).
   John Weeks and Elizabeth Dore, 'International Exchange and the Causes of Backwardness', *Latin American Perspectives* 6, No. 2 (Spring 1979), pp. 62–91.
5. Opinions expressed by several government leaders in Zambia, Tanzania, and Mozambique during personal interviews early in 1979. It is further corroborated by the fact that neither the USSR nor East European countries were able to come to the aid of Mozambique after the intensive bombing of bridges and irrigation systems in late 1979.

6. There is a dispute over the origins of SADCC, with some theorists wanting to give full credit (blame) to the EEC. They caution that SADCC may be just another form of neocolonialism. This study will clarify that SADCC has important precursors in bilateral agreements among the Frontline States and that much of its originality derives from the experiences (positive and negative) of the African states in economic co-operation, not from any abstract European model of integration.
   For the former argument, see Doublas Anglin, 'SADCC vs. PTA-Competitive or Complementary Approaches to Economic Liberation and Regional Co-operation in Southern Africa', paper presented at African Studies Association, Washington, D.C. (4 November 1982), pp. 4–5, 25.

7. Southern African Development Co-ordination Conference, 'Southern Africa: Toward Economic Liberation', Declaration by the Frontline States, Arusha (3 July 1979), p. 8.

8. *Africa News* (14 September 1981), p. 4.

9. Ann Seidman and Neva Makgetla, *Outposts of Monopoly Capitalism: Southern Africa in the Changing Global Economy* (Westport, Conn: Lawrence Hill and Co., 1980), p. 245.

10. Mozambique Information Agency, *Information Bulletin 57* (March 1981), p. 13.

11. For further documentation on South African dominance, see Arne Tostensen, *Dependence and Collective Self-Reliance in Southern Africa — The Case of SADCC*, Research Report No. 62 (Uppsala: The Scandinavian Institute of African Studies, 1982), pp. 15–92.

12. *Africa News* (3 October 1980), p. 9.

13. P.W. Botha, *Towards a Constellation of States in Southern Africa* (Pretoria: Information Service of South Africa, 1980), p. 12.

14. Ibid., p. 15.

15. Ibid., p. 17.

16. Sam C. Nolutshungu, *South Africa in Africa* (Manchester: Manchester University Press, 1975), pp. 114–129.

17. Economist Intelligence Unit, *Quarterly Economic Review: Rhodesia/Zimbabwe and Malawi*, Annuals, 1968 and 1981.

18. Arne Tostensen, op. cit., pp. 40 and 55.

19. Ferry A. Hoogendijk, 'Exclusive Interview of Eschel Rhoodie', *Elseviers Magazine* (Amsterdam) (August 1979), reprinted in *Facts and Reports* 9, Q (31 August 1979), p. 21.

20. Ibid., pp. 22–31.

21. Estimates of the Lesotho Highlands Water Scheme's potential earning power is equal to the present revenue of the entire Lesotho government. However, the scheme will not provide energy self-sufficiency for Lesotho, nor many permanent jobs, nor irrigation for the driest parts in the southwest. *Africa Economic Digest*, 8 January 1982, pp. 2–3.
   New African, May 1982, p. 42.
   The transfer of land to Swaziland will more than double the present population and adds little viable land to the nation. The South African courts have delayed the transfer by ruling against it.
   'The Swazi Case for Border Adjustment', *The Swazi Observer*, 18 September 1982.
   'Mabuza Threatens K-Ngwane People', *The Swazi Observer*, 9 October 1982.
   'KwaZulu Verdict Upheld', *The Times of Swaziland*, 1 October 1982.

'South Africa Tells Tribe of Transfer', *New York Times*, 18 June 1982.

'Clouds Gather Over Swazi-SA Land Deal', *African Business* (August 1982), p. 5.

22. *The Herald* (Zimbabwe), 3 August 1981.

23. Barbara Rogers, *Divide and Rule* (London: International Defence and Aid Fund, 1980), pp. 57–67.

Judy Seidman, *Facelift Apartheid* (London: International Defence and Aid Fund, 1980), pp. 35–62.

24. Report of the Commission for the Socio-Economic Development of the Bantu Areas within the Union of South Africa, Tomlinson Commission Report (Pretoria: Government Printer, U.G. 61/1955).

25. P.W. Botha, op. cit., p. 28.

26. Personal communication from Reginald H. Green, member of SADCC Liaison Committee and an assistant to the Secretary General of SADCC, 9 February 1982.

27. Johannesburg *Star*, 25 August 1980, p. 11.

28. J.E. Spence, 'South Africa: The Nuclear Option', *African Affairs* 80, No. 321 (October 1981), pp. 441–452.

Jennifer Davis, 'The Roots of Total Strategy', *Southern Africa* 14, No. 1 (January/February 1981), pp. 10–13.

Richard Leonard, *South Africa at War* (Westport, Conn: Lawrence Hill and Co., 1982).

See 'Secret US–SA Deal' *The Windhoek Advertiser*, 1 October 1981 for an exposé of how the Reagan Administration has promoted 'far-reaching military and security co-operation' with South Africa.

29. Episcopal Churchmen of Southern Africa (New York), newsletter, May 1981.

30. Brazil's trade with Africa south of the Sahara increased 155% in January-February 1981 over the previous year. Banco Central de Brasil as reported in *Africa News* (7 September 1981), p. 12. Brazil announced in June 1982 the construction of a naval base on Trindade Island, 700 miles from Brazil and on the same latitude as Walvis Bay. The US will help fund it as part of the South Atlantic defence scheme. *New African* (October 1982), p. 54.

31. Joaquim Chissano, speech delivered at United Nations General Assembly, 10 June 1978.

32. SADCC II, 'A Perspective', prepared by Conference Office, Maputo, November 1980 p. 2.

33. Kenneth D. Kaunda, Opening Address, SADCC Summit Conference, Lusaka, 1 April 1980, p. 3.

34. Samora Machel, Address to SADCC Summit Conference, 1 April 1980, p. 2.

35. Ann Seidman and Neva Makgetla, op. cit., pp. 334–338.

36. D. Wadada Nabudere, 'The Politics of East African Federation 1958–65', Political Science Seminar, University of Dar es Salaam, 1 December 1978.

— 'Political Economy of East African Integration', Economic Research Bulletin seminar, University of Dar es Salaam, 6 March 1979.

37. Samora Machel, op. cit., pp. 3–4.

38. SADCC, 'Southern Africa: Toward Economic Liberation', op. cit., p. 6.

39. Mozambique — Tanzania Permanent Commission of Co-operation, 'Reports of Co-operation Agreements', 4–9 April 1976; 6–7 December 1976; November 1977. Further details about the commission are also taken from these three reports as well as from personal interviews with officials in the Ministry of Finance, Tanzania, 1978–79.

40. SWAPO also sends students to prepare for diplomatic work for an independent Namibia.
41. Mozambique Information Agency, *Information Bulletin 64* (November 1981), p. 17.
42. Mozambique — Tanzania Permanent Commission of Co-operation, 'Programme of Action' (4–9 April 1976), p. 1.
43. Mozambique — Tanzania Industrial Co-operation, 'Joint Report' (6–7 December 1976), p. 2.
44. Mozambique — Tanzania Industrial Co-operation, 'Joint Report' (4–9 April 1976), p. 2.
45. Declaration by the Governments of Independent States of Southern Africa, 'Southern Africa: Toward Economic Liberation', Lusaka (1 April 1980), p. 2.
46. Michael Holman, *Financial Times*, 7 June 1979; see also USAID, *Development Needs and Opportunities for Co-operation in Southern Africa: Transport/ Communication* (March 1979).
47. SADCC, 'Record of the Council of Ministers', Luanda (25–26 June 1982), p. 19.
48. SADCC, *SADCC, Blantyre 1981*, Proceedings, Blantyre (March 1982), p. 12.
49. SADCC, Ministerial Meeting Communique, Salisbury (11 September 1980). Further details about SADCC projects are also taken from this document.
50. SADCC II, 'Southern Africa: Toward Economic Liberation, The Strategy', Maputo (November 1980), p. 7.
51. A summary of the allocation of responsibilities for co-ordination of sectoral activities is the following:

Angola	— Energy conservation and security
Botswana	— Animal disease control
	Crop research in semi-arid tropics
Lesotho	— Soil conservation and land utilisation
Malawi	— Fisheries, forestry, wildlife
Mozambique	— Transport and communication
Swaziland	— Manpower development
Tanzania	— Industrial development
Zambia	— Mining
	Southern Africa development fund
Zimbabwe	— Food security
	Security printing

52. 'Surviving a Cold Shoulder from the North', *South* (London), January 1981, p. 53.
53. Pedro Figueiredo, SATCC Technical Unit, Interview 28 March 1984.
54. *Washington Post*, 11 January 1983.
    The Reagan Administration cut the amount by $35 million because Zimbabwe voted 'against' the US on UN Security Council votes.
55. *Los Angeles Times*, 11 January 1983.
56. SADCC, *SADCC, Blantyre 1981*, op. cit., p. 13.
57. Emphasis on *national* efforts for development is found throughout the SADCC documents. At the Salisbury summit, President Masire of Botswana was very explicit: [Specialised co-ordinating bodies] should be created only when there is a proven need for them. This deliberately business-like approach, in which institutions follow achievement, surely promises greater dynamism than a system in

which Member Governments merely react to proposals put forward by technocrats lodged in a centralised bureaucracy.' SADCC, *SADCC, Blantyre, 1981*, op. cit., p. 18.

58. The Mozambique National Resistance operates from Malawi, although Malawi is a member of SADCC and in spite of the fact that its own transport links to the sea through Mozambique are disrupted by the sabotage. Malawi is very dependent on South African investment.

59. Manchester, *The Guardian Weekly*, international weekly, 8 February 1981, p.9.

60. Communique of Emergency Frontline Summit Meeting, 17 February 1981 as reported in the Washington *Star*, 18 February 1981.

61. The accusations have already begun: 'Businessmen are not invited to SADCC meetings or consulted about projects until they are *faits accomplis*. What is seen as an *anti-business ethic* has created distrust of SADCC by local and foreign industries . . .' *Africa Confidential* 24, No. 2 (19 January 1983), p. 1.
    American government officials, however, repeatedly say that they find the governments in the region are open and ready for transnational corporations to enter their economies under acceptable terms. *Transafrica Forum*, op. cit., p. 44.

62. One of the few references found that even mentions the necessity for internal restructuring of economies to make SADCC work is the following, but even here there is only an oblique reference to this need: Yusuf Adam, Robert Davies, Sipho Dlamini, 'A luta pelo futuro da Africa austral: as estratégais de CONSAS e SADCC', *Estudos Moçambicanos*, No. 3, Centros de Estudos Africanos, Universidade Eduardo Mondlane, Maputo (1981), pp. 65–80.

63. *Africa Economic Digest* (21 November 1983), p. 4.

64. SADCC II, op. cit., p. 5.

CHAPTER 9

Conclusion

Internationalisation Of Capital, The State, And Regional Economic Co-operation

Analysing the role of the Frontline States in the liberation of Zimbabwe emphasised the international context of Zimbabwean independence. Because the Zimbabwean economy is dominated by foreign capital, the struggle for majority rule was not simply national. The Zimbabwean people fought a protracted war to eradicate racism and gain control of the state, and their victory is shared by their neighbours who offered vital material and diplomatic support. With the internationalisation of capital, all five of the Frontline States are dependent peripheral capitalist economies, yet they were able to support the Zimbabwean nationalists in their efforts to gain political independence.

Frontline subvention was first a basic moral question; legalised racism not only oppressed Zimbabweans but humiliated its neighbours. But promoting human rights does not distinguish the Frontline. The ruling classes in Malawi and Zaire even criticise white minority rule — while reaping benefits from their favours. What distinguished the Frontline was not the call for one person-one vote, but for an independent state that had juridical power to intervene in the economy. The Muzorewa-Smith alliance was rejected not simply because the elections excluded the Patriotic Front, but because the Zimbabwe-Rhodesia state had no authority over an economy totally dominated by foreign interests; two-thirds of the productive capacity was foreign owned. The Frontline States were not demanding socialism for the Zimbabweans, but were simply trying to guarantee that choices would be open for Zimbabweans to decide their own form of economic relations during the continuing debates after the war — after the elections.

As shown in many ways in this study, control of the peripheral states does not guarantee control over the forces of production. Those who govern are not automatically those who own and control the means of production. However, those in control of the state are also not automatically puppets of the ruling class. In certain instances, under certain conditions, the state can assert relative autonomy from the dominant class. Relative state autonomy does not mean that capitalist relations of production will be overturned. It may mean, however, that the state has a central role in the relations between national and international capital. For example, the state may try to delimit the hegemony of international capital in order to ameliorate crises in the national economy. For situations of revolutionary transformation, control of the state can be even more crucial in delimiting international capital; as the class struggle transforms authority and production relations, new juridical and political conditions can, in turn, promote further transformation of the economy. Further, during revolutionary transformation, the state would be the locus of the class struggle against capitalist relations of production. (See Chapter 6 and 7.)

These conditions, however, may not be fulfilled. The state may be totally captured by the dominant class, for the limits on relative state autonomy are real. When challenged, capital will reorganise and consolidate to reassert its political economic control. The approach of this study has been to separate analytically the state from the social classes in order to investigate (not assume) its role in the class struggle. Analysis of the role of the state is necessary to understand the nationalist struggle in the periphery. The leaders of the Frontline States and the Zimbabwean nationalists were never misled into believing that raising the flag of independence meant the end of foreign economic domination or the defeat of the dominant class.

To overcome the dominance of South Africa and of foreign capital, the states are proposing economic co-operation. Their experience is that no one peripheral economy can industrialise alone; no one state can reduce the negative impacts of the international division of labour and the world capitalist market. They, therefore, are forming regional co-ordination not only at the level of exchange but also of production. This new economic co-operation is an example of *practice which is ahead of theory*. Theorists are offering little hope for weak and subordinate economies to reduce their dependence. Some even declare that political independence is useless.[1] And individual state programmes, financed with massive aid, have not improved the quality of life of the majority. Within SADCC, the states may have begun a process for resolving the dilemma while the theorists are still shaking their heads at the difficulty of finding alternatives to dependence.

Success Of The Frontline States

One reason for the success of the Frontline States in promoting Zimbabwean nationalism is that the goals which defined their success were modest. They demanded internationally supervised elections, with those who won the elections to have full juridical control of the state and of the economy. White privilege was not to block the authority of the state to legislate, execute, and adjudicate. The political leaders, elected by majority vote, were to have the legal right to take full authority over the state apparatuses. Smith and his Western allies were gambling on the outcome that political impotence would reduce this state authority. They analysed that the ZAPU forces, and perhaps even ZANU, would have to form a coalition with Bishop Muzorewa of the UANC. Such a coalition would have inherent political antagonisms and the resulting political instability would reduce state authority. Political impotence would limit the new government's ability to transform the state apparatuses and to intervene in the economy. Their plan did not work. ZANU itself achieved an absolute majority of the vote and needed no coalition to rule. Its political hegemony increased state authority as the party moved to transform the state apparatuses. This transformation is still in process. Although major changes have been made in the military and police, transformation of the judiciary and the civil bureaucracy is slower (for reasons discussed below).

Transformation does not mean simply changing white faces for black ones. The new government is trying to transform the state to serve the people and turn greater control over to them. The health sector can be used as an example, for it is a priority area where changes were noticeable within months after independence. First, the state intervened in the health sector and made health services available for all. Only those earning more than Z$150 per month have to pay modest fees. Health care has become a right, no longer a privilege. The government has also turned the health system 'on its head'. The emphasis on curative health care centralised in the big cities was transformed into a priority for preventive health care in the rural areas. The people are to take charge of their own health. Village health workers, aided by district technicians with expertise in environmental measures, will provide the technical advice to enable the organised villagers to implement health programmes; the goal is to prevent disease, not simply to cure it. Acquisition of state authority by ZANU has allowed this transformation to happen. Private doctors are now legally constrained from discrimination against patients because they are black or poor. Doctors are encouraged to go out of the cities into the rural areas where they are most needed.

Juridical control of the state and the economy does not mean the defeat of the dominant class. From the point of view of all the participants, however, the state was worth fighting for. US Secretary of State Henry Kissinger and British Foreign Minister Anthony Crosland knew, from the historical experiences of their countries' involvements in other nationalist struggles, that the fighting would eventually change the goal to transform the relations of production and would also increase the ability of the nationalists to implement that revolutionary transformation. (See Chapters 2 and 5.) The struggle for Zimbabwe was not a revolution in that the class relations have *not* been transformed. The armed struggle delimited the hegemony of the dominant class of white settlers and international capital; it did not defeat them.

The limited goals were one source of Frontline success. Of course, the leaders of the individual states disagreed with each other and with the Zimbabwean nationalists over the ideal type of state they preferred for Zimbabwe. As discussed in the previous chapters, there were real tensions, and several times the Frontline almost broke apart over serious disagreements. However, the leaders were able to work through agreement for the basic demands of majority rule of a state legally empowered to take control of the economy. The political unity had a material base.

All five states agreed that Zimbabwe was a pivotal economy in the region and the key to reducing the dominance of South African and foreign capital interests over their own economies. These agreements were maintained with concrete support for each other. No one country would have been able to sustain the burden of support for the nationalists alone. Botswana could be a sanctuary for some refugees, but had to transport many to Zambia because the political and economic cost of hosting all of them was too high. Yet Zambia could not have survived without the help of transport links to the sea through Tanzania and Mozambique. Tanzania made it possible for Zambia to enforce sanctions as much as it did. Support for the MPLA government from Kaunda and Nyerere was hesitant at first, but as the South Africans sustained their attacks on Angola and SWAPO, the other four Frontline States rallied political and economic support behind the MPLA government. As a newly independent state,

Mozambique would have had more difficulty in sustaining the struggle without even the minimal outside aid it received. The diplomatic unity of the five states gave credence and legitimacy to the support of the Zimbabwean refugees and guerrillas that might not have been possible if one state had acted alone. The legitimacy of the struggle, from the point of view of the international community, encouraged more aid from the outside for the Frontline.

A goal of all five states is to reduce their dependence on foreign capital, but the decision to aid in the Zimbabwean struggle increased their dependence for the short-term. The states ran the risk that short-term expediency might become long-term necessity. Aiding in the war meant that the states would have to accept more aid from the outside and also go deeper in debt. They took this risk with the idea that such costs were necessary steps toward economic independence in the future. In particular, Zambia and Mozambique in a very real sense mortgaged their future development plans for the liberation of Zimbabwe. Yet a Zimbabwean government not beholden to South Africa for its victory was necessary for their own economic struggles. They achieved the political goal desired and evaluation of the continuing economic struggle is for the future.

The risk of increasing dependency taken by the Frontline was politically feasible because although the policies were developed by leaders in each of the five states, the Frontline policy was not taken in isolation from the people. In all five states the Frontline goals were consistent with the national ideology. Chapter 7 discusses the various expressions of nationalism in support of the Frontline, and it is not necessary to repeat that analysis here. It is sufficient simply to summarise the contrasting degrees of support within Mozambique versus Zambia to illustrate that the Frontline policy retained legitimacy among the peoples of Southern Africa.

The Mozambican government could take the risk of increasing dependency because the people were mobilised to understand and support the nature of the struggle. Frelimo explained that Mozambique could not ameliorate its own economic crises without joining the Frontline. The Mozambican struggle over the economic crises and the dynamic of change of the state structures were part of the struggle for Zimbabwe.[2] Rhodesia held joint operations with the Portuguese against Frelimo and bombed Mozambican villages during the Frontline struggle for Zimbabwe. From the early 1970's Frelimo and ZANU held joint operations. The people of Zimbabwe and Mozambique had a long history of interaction and co-operation to fight colonialism, and a colonial border drawn on a piece of paper could not separate the two struggles.

In Zambia the degree of support varied considerably, but the state did not operate in isolation. Pure rhetoric and propaganda would not have won the tolerance that the people exhibited. The state did have support for its anti-racist and anti-colonial policy. Part of the support was simply nationalist: the Zimbabweans and the Zambians should be able to run their own affairs. Part was economic: greater Zambian economic growth depended on regular outlets to the sea. The Zambian people were not mobilised as were the Mozambicans to struggle in the war, but the nationalist appeal was initially strong. As the costs of the war escalated and individuals had to suffer a decline in their standard of living, the nationalist support wore thin, but did not remove Zambia from the Frontline.

The costs of participating as a Frontline State were high — in terms of lives and foreign exchange; the degree of support by the citizens of each state varied and was a factor in policy differences among the Frontline. (See Chapters 2, 6 and 7.) Yet understanding and support for the nationalist goals by the citizens of the states were basic to sustaining the struggle.

A final reason for the success of the Frontline in supporting the Zimbabwean nationalists concerns the international economic context of the stuggle; vital economic support was available from the socialist countries at a time when the crisis in advanced capitalism constrained the ability of the Anglo-Americans to intervene militarily on behalf of Smith. As the five confronted the dominant powers in the region, they turned more to Scandinavia and to the socialist countries for material aid. The aid and trade came at crucial junctures, such as the building of the Tazara Railroad. Mozambique and Angola, while still integrated into the advanced capitalist market, began diversifying their international economic linkages; the socialist countries provided important support. This alternative support was effective because the Frontline struggle occurred during serious political and economic crises of advanced capitalism. Britain would not have been able politically or economically to support any major armed intervention on the side of Rhodesia. The United States, fresh from its defeat in Vietnam, was also constrained politically and economically. (See Chapter 5.) The economies of the Frontline States were weak, but the crises in advanced capitalism weakened their adversaries.

Negotiated Settlement — A Truncated Victory?

Critics of the Frontline States accuse them of cutting short the military victory of the Zimbabwean guerrillas and strapping them not only with a neocolonial economy, but also with a neocolonial state. They claim that political independence is no victory when the white minority still retains 20 percent of the seats in parliament, when full pension compensation must be paid to civil servants who may choose to abandon Zimbabwe, and when full compensation must be paid for nationalised land that had been stolen by the whites in the first place. Further, the new government is constrained in legally changing these provisions in the constitution. (See Chapter 3 for a discussion of the constitution.)

To assess this accusation we must refer back to the goals of the Zimbabwean nationalists and the Frontline States. As discussed in previous chapters, the nationalists and the Frontline did not always agree, but, as in any war, the parties compromised to sustain the alliance. The nationalists supported fully the idea of negotiations with armed struggle; negotiations were the 'second front' of the war. Committing one's brothers and sisters to war is not taken lightly, and negotiations on the part of the nationalists were serious attempts to end that war. The goals of the conflict were basic: majority rule with the state having full legal right over the economy. Those limited goals were not truncated by the Lancaster House settlement.

As discussed earlier, Smith and his allies hoped to truncate the goals politically — after the elections. A coalition government would reduce state authority and consequently its ability to intervene in the economy. They lost that goal with the majority victory of ZANU. However, economic constraint on the legal rights of the state are still in order: the necessity to pay full compensation for nationalised property and to honour pensions. The land question is not resolved and remains a struggle inside Zimbabwe. The demands are real; the Africans fought for land and many still do not have access to sufficient land for production. The constitution leaves such terms as 'full compensation' undefined so one alternative would be for the state to give a modest definition to full compensation. Yet there are economic constraints to that political choice; the state needs the food production that the large commercial farmers provide. Further, the Frontline allies also need Zimbabwe's food exports. The dilemma is to redistribute land without seriously curtailing marketed food production. A longer war would have probably solved the land redistribution problem; it would also have precipitated a food crisis — increasing Zimbabwe's dependence on South African or other foreign food imports (as happened to Mozambique and Angola). Power does come from the barrel of a gun as Mao stated, but in a very real sense food is also power. Even for the very crucial land question, it is not clear that the Lancaster negotiations truncated the goals; a military victory could have created a food crisis just as serious as the present land problem. With the political authority that ZANU enjoys, the new government may be able to solve the land redistribution versus food supply contradiction with minimal economic dislocation. The contradiction is real and will require political struggle in Zimbabwe, yet the government does have the authority and legitimacy to deal with it.

The Southern African Development Co-ordination Conference (SADCC) was formed because the states knew that the political independence of Zimbabwe was not sufficient to challenge South African and foreign economic dominance over the Southern African region. There are many obstacles to the success of SADCC (see Chapter 8.), but its institutional form is innovative. Aggregation of their strengths helped reduce Frontline weaknesses in the fight for Zimbabwean independence. Now economic co-ordination at the level of production will be tried to achieve a greater degree of local economic control. Political agreement to reduce the dominance of foreign capital in the region and to ameliorate the negative impact of the vagaries of the world capitalist system is the basis of the economic agreement. These political goals will direct economic decisions and will be added as criteria of evaluation along with cost-benefit analysis. The single criterion of profit will not define the projects. SADCC is a format for amelioration of economic dependence which merits close observation as it proceeds.

Lessons From The Frontline Struggle For Zimbabwe

As the Frontline turns toward Namibia and South Africa, the lessons from Zimbabwe are many. Both sides in the struggle for Namibia are clear that control of the Namibian state means eventual control of the economy. State intervention in the economy is such that almost any form of majority state control could use the state to modify the productive relations of apartheid. The South African government has not, therefore, been countenancing majority rule. Ian Smith changed the definition of majority rule. He brought Africans into the government, while taking executive power away from their offices and never discussing African control of the economy. When forced by the armed struggle to negotiate at Lancaster House, Smith and his allies hoped to force the coalition government. Learning from the failure of Bishop Muzorewa to win enough seats to demand a coalition, the South African regime has been trying to guarantee a coalition government before elections.

One plan promoted by South Africa is that majority rule should not be based on one person-one vote. The South African regime's definition of majority rule has been representation by ethnic group; one is to relate to the state, not as an individual (which is the basis of Anglo-American law defining the liberal state), but as a member of an ethnic group. This definition accomplishes two important goals for the Afrikaners. First, the *volk* are not a minority but one of many 'nationality' groups; their cultural identity retains its separate legal and political status. Second, group representation will require a coalition form of government which weakens any one group beyond the ability to maintain authority, to regulate the economy and eventually, to sustain legitimacy. At best, the state is constrained in its ability to take control of the economy; at worst political instability because of competing factions results in chaos. Whether this plan is formally implemented or not, South Africa hopes to restrict a majority government through support of ethnic divisions which could result in instability and a possible take-over by a segment of the military . . . or by the South African army 'invited' to step in by one of the factions.

Since the independence of Zimbabwe, South Africa has followed the same tactics for which it had criticised Ian Smith. It has negotiated the Namibian crisis, making few concessions while escalating aggression both externally against neighbours that support SWAPO and internally against the African majority. The game of negotiations allows the regime to claim that it is the other side which is stalling. As with Smith, talks of progress and of concessions are simply paper covers to sustain minority rule.

The Frontline States, now joined by Zimbabwe, are promoting negotiations with armed struggle. SWAPO fully agrees and made negotiated concessions as long ago as 1978 to show its willingness to compromise. But again, free and fair elections for a state with legal power to take control of the economy remains the demand. Majority rule is to be based on one person-one vote, not on a vote tied to ethnic allegiances. Perhaps, once again, the continuing armed struggle will be necessary to convince the white minority and its Western allies to negotiate seriously a settlement for majority rule.

The Frontline States provided crucial material and political support for the Zimbabwean nationalists. Still the struggle for Zimbabwe is not yet resolved, as the Zimbabwean people try to consolidate their political victory of independence for national control of the economy. Because of the continuing economic struggle in the whole Southern African region and because of the quest for majority rule in Namibia, and then South Africa, the Frontline States have not dissolved their alliance. They have strengthened the alliance with the addition of Zimbabwe and extended it into the regional economic co-operation of SADCC. With these new alignments, which effect new strategies, the challenge to imperialism continues in Southern Africa.

Notes

1. Barry Munslow, 'Is Socialism Possible on the Periphery?' *Monthly Review* 35, no. 1 (May 1983), pp. 25-39. Munslow argues that world systems analysts and Trotskyite theorists think that achievement of state power is only a tactical option.
2. This analysis was given to me not only by leaders of Frelimo, but also by villagers in Cabo Delgado who would discuss the war in detail and the goals of the Zimbabwean nationalists as one with their own.

Selected Bibliography

(For a more complete listing, see notes at the end of each chapter.)

Official Documents and Papers

The Bingham Report. *Report on the Supply of Petroleum and Petroleum Products to Rhodesia* (London: HMSO. 1978).

Botswana, Government of. 'Transition Plan for Social and Economic Development' (Gaborone, 1968).

Commonwealth Heads of Government. Final Communique, London, 8–15 June 1977, *Africa Contemporary Record 1977–1978* (New York: Africana Publishing Co., 1979).

———. Final Communique, Lusaka, 1–7 August 1979, *Africa Contemporary Record 1979–1980* (New York: Africana Publishing Co., 1981).

Dar es Salaam Agreement. 'Unity of the Patriotic Front', mimeo (9 April 1979).

East African Community, East African Customs and Excise Department. Annual Trade Reports (1964 and 1977).

East and Central Africa, Heads of States and Governments. 'Lusaka Declaration', Fifth Conference (April 1969).

———. 'Mogadishu Declaration', Seventh Conference (October 1971).

Food And Agriculture Organisation, United Nations. 'A Study of Constraints on Agricultural Development in the Republic of Botswana' (Rome 1974).

Free and Fair? The 1979 Rhodesian Election: A Report by Observers on Behalf of the British Parliamentary Human Rights Group (London: Parliamentary Human Rights Group, May 1979).

Frelimo. 'The Third Party Congress of Frelimo', mimeo, Maputo, 1977.

International Bank for Reconstruction and Development. *Tanzania: Basic Economic Report*, no. 1616—TA Main Report (December 1977).

———. *Basic Economic Report: Zambia* (3 October 1977).

Moodley, Judge M.M. 'Trial within a Trial Ruling, The People versus Joseph Siwela, Josiah Tongogara, Sadat Kufamazuba, HP/67/1976, High Court for Zambia (Lusaka, 20 October 1976).

Mozambique, People's Republic of *Economic Report* (Maputo, January 1984).

Mozambique–Tanzania Industrial Cooperation. 'Joint Report', (4–9 April and 6–7 December 1976).

Mozambique–Permanent Commission of Cooperation. 'Programme of Action' (4–9 April 1976).

———. 'Reports of Cooperation Agreements' (4–9 April 1976; 6–7 December 1976; November 1977).

Organisation of African Unity, Council of Ministers. 'Declaration of Dar es Salaam on Southern Africa', Ninth Extraordinary Session (7–10 April 1975).

Organisation of Economic Cooperation and Development (OECD). *Economic Survey: United Kingdom* (February 1980).

'Report of the Special Commission on the Assassination of Herbert Wiltshire Chitepo' (Lusaka, March 1976).

'Rhodesia: Draft Constitution of Zimbabwe Rhodesia' (1979).

'Rhodesia: Proposal for Settlement' (Anglo-American Proposals) Presented to Parliament by the Secretary of State for Foreign and Commonwealth Affairs (September 1977).

South Africa, Union of. 'Report of the Commission for the Socio-Economic Development of the Bantu Areas within the Union of South Africa — Tomlinson Commission Report' (Pretoria: Government Printer, U.G. 61/1955).

Southern Africa, Government of Independent States of. 'Southern Africa: Toward Economic Liberation' (Lusaka, 1 April 1980).

Southern African Development Coordination Conference. 'SADCC II, A Perspective', prepared by Conference Office (Maputo, November 1980).

_____ . *SADCC, Blantyre 1981* (Blantyre: March 1982).

_____ . 'Southern Africa: Toward Economic Liberation', Declaration by the Frontline States, Arusha (3 July 1979).

_____ . 'Southern Africa: Toward Economic Liberation, The Strategy' (Maputo: November 1980).

Tanzania, United Republic of. *Economic Survey* (Dar es Salaam: Government Printer, annuals).

_____ . *Third Five Year Plan for Economic and Social Development, General Perspectives*, Part I (1 July 1975–30 June 1981).

United Nations Centre Against Apartheid: Report of the International Mission of Enquiry. 'Acts of Aggression Perpetrated by South Africa against the People's Republic of Angola (June 1979–July 1980)' (New York; January 1981).

United Nations Economic and Social Council. *Assistance to Botswana: Report of the Secretary General* (A/32/287, S/12421) 26 October 1977.

_____ . *Assistance to Mozambique: Report of the Secretary General* (E5812) 30 April 1976.

_____ . *Assistance to Mozambique: Report of the Secretary General* (A/32/96), 9 June 1977.

_____ . *Assistance to Mozambique: Report of the Secretary General* (A/33/173) 12 July 1978.

_____ . *Assistance to Mozambique: Report of the Secretary General* (E/1978/114, 5), Annex, 5 July 1978.

_____ . *Multinational Corporations in World Development* (New York: United Nations, 1975).

United Nations High Commissioner for Refugees. 'Report on Assistance Activities in 1979–1980 and Proposed Voluntary Funds Programmes and Budget for 1981' (A/AC.96/577) 14 August 1980.

U.S. Agency for International Development. *Development Needs and Opportunities for Co-operation in Southern Africa*, 7 vols (March 1979).

U.S. Department of Agriculture, Economic Research Service. 'Angola's Agricultural Situation', mimeo (Washington, D.C.: 23 March 1982).

U.S. House of Representatives (H.R.), Committee on Foreign Affairs, Sub-Committee on Africa. 'Political Developments in Southern Rhodesia' (4 October 1977).

_____ . 'The Rhodesian Sanctions Bill, H.R. 1746' (24 February 1977).

_____ . 'US.Business involvement in Southern Africa', Parts 1–3 (May–June 1971; September–December 1971; March–July 1973).

_____ . 'US Policy Toward Rhodesia' (8 June 1977).

U.S. Library of Congress, Congressional Research Service. *Imports of Minerals from South Africa by the US and OECD Countries*. Prepared for the U.S. Senate, Foreign Relations Committee, Subcommittee on Africa (1980).

U.S. Senate, Committee on Foreign Relations (The Clark Report). 'US Corporate Interests in South Africa' (January 1978).

U.S. Senate, Committee on Foreign Relations, Subcomittee on African Affairs. 'Rhodesian Sanctions' (9–10 February 1977).

_____ . 'A Rhodesian Settlement? Analysis of Agreement signed by P.M. Ian Smith, Rev. N. Sithole, Bishop A. Muzorewa, and Senator J. Chirau, on 3 March 1978' (Washington, D.C.: U.S. Government Printing Office, June 1978).

Zambia, Republic of. 'Dear Mr. Vorster . . . Details of Exchanges between President Kenneth Kaunda of Zambia and Prime Minister Vorster of South Africa' (Lusaka: Zambia Information Services, 23 April 1971).

Zambia, Republic of. State House. 'Sequence of Events Leading to Decisions to Open Southern Railroad Route for Transportation of Fertiliser and Cotton' (6 October 1978).

Zimbabwe Patriotic Front. 'Statement on British "Proposals for a Settlement" in Rhodesia' (12 September 1977).

'ZIPA Denounces the Geneva Perfidy', mimeo (20 November 1976).

Books

Amin, Samir. *Unequal Development* (New York: Monthly Review Press, 1976).

Andrade, Mario de and Marc Ollivier. *The War in Angola: A Socio-Economic Study* (Dar es Salaam: Tanzania Publishing House, 1976).

Anglin, Douglas G. and Timothy Shaw. *Zambia's Foreign Policy: Studies in Diplomacy and Dependance* (Boulder: Westview Press, 1979).

Anti-Apartheid Movement. *Fire Force Exposed* (London, 1979).

Arrighi, Giovanni. *The Political Economy of Rhodesia* (The Hague: Mouton, 1967).

Avirgan, Tony and Martha Honey. *The War in Uganda: Legacy of Idi Amin* (Dar es Salaam: Tanzania Publishing House, 1983 and Westport, CT: Lawrence Hill 1982).

Bailey, Martin. *Oilgate: The Sanctions Scandal* (London: Coronet Books, 1979).

Barkin, J. and J. Okumu, eds. *Politics and Public Policy in Kenya and Tanzania* (New York: Praeger, 1979).

Bender, Gerald. *Angola Under the Portuguese: The Myth and the Reality* (Berkeley: University of California Press, 1978).

Bernstein, Henry et al, eds. *Development Theory: Three Critical Essays* (London: Routledge and Kegan Paul, 1980).

Bloomfield, Jon, ed. *Class, Hegemony and Party* (London: Lawrence and Wishart, 1977).

Blue, Richard and James Weaver. *A Critical Assessment of the Tanzanian Model of Development* (Washington, D.C.: USAID Development Studies Programme, 1977).

Boavida, Americo. *Angola: Five Centuries of Portuguese Exploitation* (Richmond, B.C.: LSM Press, 1972).

Boesen, J.; B.S. Madsen and T. Moody. *Ujamaa: Socialism from Above* (Uppsala: Scandinavian Institute of African Studies, 1977).

Botha, P.W. *Towards a Constellation of States in Southern Africa* (Pretoria: Information Service of South Africa, 1980).

Brett, E.A. *Colonialism and Underdevelopment in East Africa* (London: Heinemann, 1973).

de Brunhoff, Suzanne. *The State, Capital and Economic Policy* (London: Pluto, 1978).

Burawoy, Michael. *The Colour of Class on the Copper Mines: From African Advancement to Zambianisation*, Zambian Papers no. 7 (Lusaka: Institute of African Studies, University of Zambia, 1972).

Cabral, Amilcar. *Revolution in Guinea* (New York: Monthly Review Press, 1969).

Cardoso, F. and E. Faletto. *Dependence and Development in Latin America* (Berkeley: University of California Press, 1979).

Chilcote, Ronald, ed. *Protest and Resistance in Angola and Brazil* (Berkeley: University of California Press, 1972).

Clarence-Smith, W.G. *Slaves, Peasants and Capitalists In Southern Angola 1840–1926* (Cambridge: Cambridge University Press, 1979).

Clarke, Duncan. *Foreign Companies and International Investment in Zimbabwe* (London: Catholic Institute for International Relations, March 1980).

Clarke, Simon. *Changing Patterns of International Investment in South Africa and the Divestment Campaign* (London: Anti-Apartheid Movement, 1978).

Colclough, Christopher and Stephen, McCarthy. *The Political Economy of Botswana: A Study of Growth and Distribution* (Oxford: Oxford University Press, 1980).

Commonwealth Secretariat. *The Front-Line States: The Burden of the Liberation Struggle* (London: Commonwealth Secretariat, 1979).

Coulson, Andrew, ed. *African Socialism in Practice: The Tanzanian Experience* (Nottingham: Spokesman, 1979).

Cronjé, Suzanne; Margaret Ling and Gillian Cronjé. *The Lonrho Connection* (Encino, CA: Bellwether Books, 1976).

Davidson, Basil. *In the Eye of the Storm: Angola's People* (Garden City, NY: Doubleday, 1973).

Davies, Robert. *Capital, State and White Labour in South Africa 1900–1960* (Atlantic Highlands, NY: Humanities Press, 1979).

Day, John. *Internationalism: The Extra-Territorial Relations of Southern Rhodesian African Nationalists* (New York: Humanities Press, 1967).

Draper, Hal. *Karl Marx's Theory of Revolution* 1 and 2 (New York: Monthly Review Press, 1977).

Duffy, James. *Portuguese Africa* (Cambridge: Harvard University Press, 1959).

El-Khawas, Mohamad A. and Barry Cohen, eds. *NSSM 39 — The Kissinger Study of Southern Africa* (Westport, CT: Lawrence Hill, 1976).

Evans, Peter. *Dependent Development: The Alliance of Multinational, State and Local Capital in Brazil* (Princeton: Princeton University Press, 1979).

Frank, Andre Gundar. *Capitalism and Underdevelopment in Latin America* (Cambridge: Cambridge University Press, 1971).

Frederikse, Julie. *None But Ourselves: Masses vs. Media in the Making of Zimbabwe* (Johannesburg: Raven Press and Harare: Zimbabwe Publishing House, 1982).

Gabriel, Claude. *Angola: le Tournant Africain?* (Paris: Editions la Breche, 1978).

Gilmurray, John and Roger Riddell, David Saunders. *From Rhodesia to Zimbabwe: The Struggle for Health* (London: Catholic Institute for International Relations, 1979).

Girvan, Norman. *Corporate Imperialism: Conflict and Expropriation* (White Plains, N.Y.: Sharpe, 1976).

Green, Reginald H.; D.R. Rwegasire and B. Van Arkadie. *Economic Shocks and National Policy Making: Tanzania in the 1970's* (Hague: Institute of Social Studies, 1980).

Green, Reginald H. *Toward Socialism and Self-Reliance: Tanzania's Striving for Sustained Transition Projected* (Uppsala: Scandinavian Institute of African Studies, 1977).

Greenberg, Stanley B. *Race and State in Capitalist Development* (New Haven: Yale University Press, 1980).

Hamilton, Nora. *Mexico: The Limits of State Autonomy* (Princeton: Princeton University Press, 1982).

Hartland-Thunberg, Penelope. *Botswana: An African Growth Economy* (Boulder: Westview Press, 1978).

Heimer, Franz William. *The Decolonisation of Conflict in Angola, 1974–76, an Essay in Political Sociology* (Geneva: Institut Universitaire de Hautes Etudes Internationales, International Studies in Contemporary Africa Series, 2, 1979).

Henderson, Lawrence. *Angola: Five Centuries of Conflict* (Ithaca: Cornell University Press, 1979).

Hindess, Barry, ed. *Sociological Theories of the Economy* (London: Macmillan, 1977).

Holloway, John and Sol Picciotto, eds. *State and Capital* (London: Edward Arnold, 1978).

Houser, George and Herb Shore. *Mozambique: Dream the Size of Freedom* (New York: Africa Fund, 1975).

Isaacman, Allen. *Mozambique: The Africanization of a European Institution: The Zambezi Prazos 1750–1902* (Madison: University of Wisconsin Press, 1972).

Isaacman, Allen and Barbara Isaacman. *Mozambique and the Twentieth Century* (Boulder: Westview Press, 1984).

Isaacman, Barbara and June Stephan. *Mozambique: Women, the Law and Agrarian Reform* (Addis Ababa: Economic Commission for Africa, 1980).

Ishemo, S. *Some Aspects of the Economy and Society of the Zambezi Basin in the Nineteenth Century and Early Twentieth Centuries* (London: Institute of Commonwealth Studies, 1978).

Janke, P. *Marxist Statecraft in Africa — What Future?* (London: Institute for Conflict Studies, 1978).

Jessop, Bob. *The Capitalist State* (New York: New York University Press, 1982).

Kaplan, Barbara Hockey, ed. *Social Change in the Capitalist World Economy* (Beverly Hills: Sage, 1978).

Kilson, Martin L. and Robert I. Rotberg, eds. *The African Diaspora: Interpretative Essays* (Cambridge: Harvard University Press, 1976).

Kim, K.S.; R.B. Mabele and M.J. Schultheis, eds. *Papers on the Political Economy of Tanzania* (London: Heinemann, 1979).

Kimambo, I. and A. Temu, eds. *History of Tanzania* (Nairobi: East African Publishing House, 1969).

Klinghoffer, Arthur J. *The Angolan War: A Study in Soviet Policy in the Third World* (Boulder: Westview Press, 1980).

Legum, Colin. *Southern Africa* (London: Rex Collins, 1975).

Lemarchand, René, ed. *American Policy in Southern Africa: The Stakes and the Stance* (Washington, D.C.: University Press of America, 1978).

Leonard, Richard. *South Africa at War* (Westport, CT: Lawrence Hill, 1983).

Leys, Colin. *Underdevelopment In Kenya — The Political Economy of Neo-Colonialism* (London: Heinemann, 1975).

Loney, Martin. *Rhodesia: White Racism and Imperial Response* (Middlesex: Penguin, 1975).

Machel, Samora. *Mozambique: Revolution or Reaction?* (Richmond, British Columbia: Liberation Support Movement, 1975).

_____ . *Sowing the Seeds of Revolution* (London: Committee for Freedom in Mozambique, Angola, and Guinea, 1975).

Mapolu, Henry, ed. *Workers and Management* (Dar es Salaam: Tanzania Publishing House, 1976).

Marcum, John. *The Angolan Revolution, Vol. I: The Anatomy of an Explosion (1950–62)* (Cambridge: MIT Press, 1969).

_____ . *The Angolan Revolution, Vol. II: Exile Politics and Guerrilla Warfare* (Cambridge: MIT Press, 1978).

Martin, Anthony. *Minding Their Own Business: Zambia's Struggle Against Western Control* (Harmondsworth: Penguin, 1975).

Martin, David and Phyllis Johnson. *The Struggle for Zimbabwe* (London: Faber and Faber and Harare: Zimbabwe Publishing House, 1981).

Miliband, Ralph. *Marxism and Politics* (Oxford: Oxford University Press, 1977).

Minter, William. *Imperial Network and External Dependency: The Case of Angola* (Beverly Hills: Sage, 1972).

_____ . *Portuguese Africa and the West* (New York: Monthly Review Press, 1972).

Mittelman, James. *Underdevelopment and the Transition to Socialism: Mozambique and Tanzania* (New York: Academic Press, 1981).

Mondlane, Eduardo. *The Struggle for Mozambique* (Harmondsworth: Penguin, 1969).

Moran, Theodore. *Multinational Corporations and the Politics of Dependence* (Princeton: Princeton University Press, 1974).

Mushi, S.S. and K. Mathews, eds. *Foreign Policy of Tanzania 1961–1981: A Reader* (Dar es Salaam: Tanzania Publishing House, 1981).

Muzorewa, Abel. *Rise Up and Walk* (Nashville, Tennessee: Nabingdon, 1978).

Newitt, M.D.D. *Portuguese Settlement on the Zambezi: Exploration, Land Tenure and Colonial Rule in East Africa* (Harlowe: Longman, 1973).

Nolutshungu, Sam C. *South Africa in Africa* (Manchester: University Press, 1975).

Nyagumbo, Maurice. *With the People* (London: Allison and Busby, 1980).

Nyangoni, Christopher and Gideon Nyandoro, eds. *Zimbabwe Independence Movements, Select Documents* (New York: Barnes and Noble, 1979).

Nyerere, Julius. *The Arusha Declaration — Ten Years After* (Dar es Salaam: Government Printer, 1977).

Obichere, Boniface. *Crisis In Zimbabwe* (Boulder: Westview Press, 1979).

O'Connor, James. *Fiscal Crisis of the State* (New York: St. Martin's Press, 1973).

Ollawa P. *Rural Development Policies and Performance in Zambia* (The Hague: ISS Occasional Paper, 59, 1977).

Ottaway, David and Marina. *Afrocommunism* (New York: Holmes and Meier, 1981).

Palmer, Robin. *Land and Racial Domination in Rhodesia* (Berkeley: University of California Press and London: Heinemann, 1971).

Petras, James. *Critical Perspectives of Imperialism and Social Class in the Third World* (New York: Monthly Review Press, 1978).

Potholm, C. and Richard Dale. *Southern Africa in Perspective* (New York: Free Press, 1974).

Poulantzas, Nicos. *Classes in Contemporary Capitalism* (London: New Left Books — NLB, 1975).

_____. *Political Power and Social Classes* (London: NLB, 1973).

Proctor, J.H., ed. *Building Ujamaa Villages in Tanzania* (Dar es Salaam: Tanzania Publishing House, 1975).

Raeburn, Michael. *Black Fire: Accounts of the Guerrilla War in Rhodesia*(London: Julian Friedman, 1978).

Report of the Study Commission on US Policy Toward Southern Africa (Rockefeller Report). *South Africa: Time Running Out* (Berkeley: University of California Press, 1981).

Resnick, Idrian. *The Long Transition: Building Socialism in Tanzania* (New York: Monthly Review Press, 1981).

Riddell, Roger, *From Rhodesia to Zimbabwe — The Land Question* (London: The Catholic Institute for International Relations, 1978).

Rweyemamu, Justinian. *Underdevelopment and Industrialization in Tanzania* (Nairobi: Oxford University Press, 1973).

Saul, John S. *The State and Revolution in Eastern Africa* (New York: Monthly Review Press, 1979).

Seidman, Ann. *Comparative Development Strategies in East Africa* (Nairobi: East African Publishing House, 1972).

Seidman, Ann and Neva S. Makgetla. *Outposts of Monopoly Capitalism* (Westport, CT: Lawrence Hill, 1980).

Shamuyarira, Nathan. *Crisis in Rhodesia* (Nairobi: East African Publishing House, 1967).

Shivji, Issa. *Class Stuggles in Tanzania* (Dar es Salaam: Tanzania Publishing House, 1975).

Sklar, Richard. *Corporate Power in an African State: The Political Impact of Multinational Mining Companies in Zambia* (Berkeley: University of California Press, 1979).

Skocpol, Theda. *State and Social Revolutions* (Cambridge: Cambridge University Press, 1979).

Sousa Ferreira, Eduardo de. *Portuguese Colonialism from South Africa to Europe* (Freiburg: Aktion Drittee Weit, 1972).

Stockwell, John *In Search of Enemies: A CIA Story* (New York: W.W. Norton, 1978).

Stoneman, Colin, ed. *Zimbabwe's Inheritance* (London: Macmillan, 1981).

Struck, Harry R. *Sanctions: The Case of Rhodesia* (Syracuse, NY: Syracuse University Press, 1978).

Swainson, Nicola. *The Development of Corporate Capitalism in Kenya 1918-1977* (Berkeley: University of California Press, 1980).

Tanzer, Michael. *The Race for Resources: Continuing Struggles over Minerals and Fuels* (New York: Monthly Review Press, 1980).

Tordoff, William, ed. *Administration in Zambia* (Manchester, Manchester University Press, 1980).

Tostensen, Arne. *Dependence and Collective Self-Reliance in Southern Africa — The Case of SADCC,* Research Report no. 62 (Uppsala: The Scandinavian Institute of African Studies, 1982).

Turok, Ben, ed. *Development in Zambia* (London: Zed Press, 1979).

University of Eduardo Mondlane, Centre of African Studies. *The Mozambique Miner* (Maputo: 1977).

Van Onselin, Charles. *Chibaro* (London: Pluto Press, 1976).

Vengroff, Richard. *Botswana: Rural Development in the Shadow of Apartheid* (London: Associated University Press, 1977).

Von Freyhold, Michaela. *Ujamaa Villages in Tanzania — Analysis of a Social Experiment* (New York: Monthly Review Press, 1979).

Warren, Bill.*Imperialism — Pioneer of Capitalism* (London: NLB, 1980).

Western Massachusetts Association of Concerned African Scholars, eds. *US Military Involvement in Southern Africa* (Boston: South End Press, 1978).

Wheeler, Douglas L. *Republican Portugal* (Madison: University of Wisconsin Press, 1978).

Wheeler, Douglas and René Pélissier. *Angola* (New York: Praeger, 1971).

Wilmer, S.E. *Zimbabwe Now* (London: Rex Collings, Ltd., 1972).

Wolfe, Alan. *The Limits of Legitimacy* (New York: Free Press, 1977).

Wright, Erik Olin. *Class, Crisis and the State* (London: NLB, 1978).

Articles

Adam, *Yusuf; Robert Davies and Sipho Dlamini.* 'A luta pelo futuro da Africa austral: as estrategais de CONSAS e SADCC', *Estudos Mozambicanos* (Maputo), no. 3 (1981), pp. 65–80.

Angola debate. *Review of African Political Economy* 14 (January–April, 1979), pp. 105–110; nos. 15–16 (May–December 1979), pp. 148–153; no. 19 (September–December 1980), pp. 6–7, pp. 69–76.

Angotti, Thomas. 'The Political Implications of Dependency Theory', *Latin American Perspectives* 8, nos. 3–4 (Summer–Fall 1981), pp. 124–137.

Baylies, Carolyn. 'Emergence of Indigenous Capitalist Agriculture: The Case of Southern Province, Zambia', *Rural Africana*, nos 4–5 (Spring–Fall, 1979).

Bender, Gerald. 'Comment: Past, Present and Future Perspectives of Cuba in Action', *Cuban Studies* 10, no. 2 (July 1980), pp. 44–54.

Block, Fred. 'Beyond Relative Autonomy: State Managers as Historical Subjects',
    Socialist Register, 1980, reprinted in *New Political Science*, no. 7 (Fall 1981).
Bond, Carol. A. 'Women's Involvement in Agriculture in Botswana,' (Gaborone:
    Ministry of Agriculture, 1976).
Bratton, Michael. 'Zimbabwe in the Making', *Southern Africa* (October 1977),
    pp. 6–8.
Brenner, Robert. 'The Origins of Capitalist Development: A Critique of neo-Smithian
    Marxism', *New Left Review* 104 (July–August 1977), pp.25–92.
Burawoy, Michael. 'State and Social Revolution in Southern Africa', *Kapitalistate*, no.
    9 (Fall 1981).
Caporaso, James A. 'Dependence, Dependency and Power in the Global System: A
    Structural and Behavioural Analysis', *International Organization* 32, no. 1
    (Winter 1978), pp. 13–43.
Chinchilla, Norma and James Dietz. 'Toward a New Understanding of Development',
    Latin American Perspectives 9, nos. 3–4 (Summer/Fall 1981),
    pp. 138–147.
Clarence Smith, W.G. and Richard Moorsom. 'Underdevelopment and Class
    Formation in Ovamboland, 1845–1915', *Journal of African History* 16, no. 3
    (1975), pp. 365–382.
Cliffe, Lionel and Richard Moorsom. 'Rural Class Formation and Ecological Collapse
    in Botswana', *Review of African Political Economy*, nos. 15–16
    (May–December 1979).
Coulson, Andrew. 'Decentralization and the Government Budget' (Dar es Salaam:
    Economic Research Bulletin, October 1975).
Davis, Jennifer. 'The Roots of Total Strategy', *Southern Africa* 14, no. 1
    (January/February 1981), pp. 10–13.
Dias, Jill. 'Black Chiefs, White Traders, and Colonial Policy near the Kwanza: Kabuku
    Kambilo and the Portuguese, 1873–96', *Journal of African History* 42,
    no. 2 (1976), pp. 276–290.
Duvall, Robert D. 'Dependence and Dependencia Theory: Notes toward Precision of
    Concept and Argument', *International Organization* 32, no. 1
    (Winter 1978), pp. 51–78.
Egero, Bertil. 'Mozambique before the Second Phase of Socialist Development',
    Review of African Political Economy, no. 25 (September–December 1982),
    pp. 83-91.
'Elections in Mozambique — The Reality of Liberty', *African Communist* 74, no. 3
    (1978), pp. 60–74.
Fauvet, Paul. 'The Rise and Fall of Nito Alves', *Review of African Political Economy*, no.
    9 (May–August 1978), pp. 88–104.
Friedland, E.A. 'Mozambican National Resistance 1920–49', *Civilisations* 27,
    nos. 3–4 (1977), pp. 332–344.
Georgetown University Center for Strategic and International Studies, 'Background
    Information on Angola', paper presented for Conference on Angola's
    Economic Prospects (Washington, D.C.: 24 March 1982).
Gervasi, Sean; Ann Seidman, Immanuel Wallerstein and David Wiley. 'Why We Said
    No to AID', *Issue* 7, no. 4 (Winter 1977), pp. 35–37.
Goulbourne, Harry. 'The Problem of the State in Backward Capitalist Societies', *Africa
    Development*, 6, no. 1 (1981).
Hammond, F.J. 'Race Attitudes and Policies in Portuguese Africa in the 19th and 20th
    Centuries', *Race* 9, no. 2 (1977), pp. 205–216.
Harvey, Charles. 'Botswana's Monetary Independence — Real or Imagined?', *IDS
    Bulletin* (Sussex) 11, no. 4 (September 1980), pp. 40–44.

Holm, John D.'Liberal Democracy and Rural Development in Botswana', *African Studies Review* 25, no. 1 (March 1982), pp. 83–102.

Hymer, Stephen. 'Is The Multinational Corporation Doomed?', *Innovation* 23, (1972), pp. 16–18.

Isaacman, Allen and Barbara Isaacman. 'A Socialist Legal System in the Making: Mozambique before and after Independence', *Politics of Informal Justice*, 2 (New York: Academic Press, 1982), pp. 281–323.

Laclau, Ernesto. 'Feudalism and Capitalism in Latin America', *New Left Review* 67 (May–June 1971), pp. 19–38.

Lobban, Richard. 'American Mercenaries In Rhodesia', *Journal of Southern African Affairs* 3, no. 3 (July 1978), pp. 319–326.

Lonsdale, John. 'Some Origins of Nationalism in East Africa', *Journal of African History* 9, no. 1 (1968), pp. 131–136.

Machel, Samora. 'Education in Revolution', *Mozambican Revolution*, no. 57 (1973), pp. 20–24.

_____ . 'Women's Liberation is essential for the revolution', *African Communist*, no. 61 (1975), pp. 37–51.

Mandaza, Ibbo. 'Imperialism,the Frontline States and the Zimbabwe Problem', paper presented at seminar University of Dar es Salaam (16 November 1979).

Meillassoux, Claude. 'From Reproduction to Production', *Economy and Society* 1, no. 1 (February 1972), pp. 93–105.

Minter, William. 'Major Themes in Mozambican Foreign Relations, 1975–1977', *Issue* 8, no. 1 (Spring 1978), pp. 44–49.

Mittelman, James. 'State Power in Mozambique', *Issue* 8, no. 1 (1978), pp. 4–11.

Mondlane, Eduardo. 'Race Relations and Portuguese Colonial Policy, with special reference to Mozambique', *Objective–Justice* 1, no. 1 (1969), pp. 14–19.

Mubako, Simbi. 'The Quest for Unity in the Zimbabwe Liberation Movement', *Issue* 5, no. 21 (1975), pp. 7–17.

Munslow, Barry. 'Is Socialism Possible on the Periphery?' *Monthly Review* 15, no. 1 (May 1983), pp. 25–39.

Nabudere, D. Wadada. 'The Politics of East African Federation 1958–65', Political Science Seminar, University of Dar es Salaam, 1 December 1978.

Nursey-Bray, P.F. 'Tanzania: The Development Debate', *African Affairs* 79, no. 314 (January 1980), pp. 55–78.

O'Brien , Conor Cruise. 'The End of White Rule?' *New York Review of Books* (7 March 1978).

Ollman, Bertell. 'Thesis on the Capitalist State', *Monthly Review* 34, no. 7 (December 1982), pp. 41–46.

Palley, Claire. 'The Rhodesian Election Campaign', (London: Catholic Institute for International Relations, April 1979).

Palma, Gabriel. 'Dependency: A Formal Theory of Underdevelopment or Methodology for the Analysis of Concrete Situations of Underdevelopment? *World Development* 6 (July–August 1978), pp. 881–924.

Patankar, Bharat and Gail Omvedt. 'The Bourgeois State in Post-Colonial Formations', *Insurgent Sociologist* 2, no. 4 (Spring 1980), pp. 25-30.

Petras, James. 'State Capitalism and the Third World', *Development and Change* 8 (1977).

Phillips, Anne. 'The Concept of Development', *Review of African Political Economy* 8 (January–April 1977), pp. 7–21.

Pratt, Cranford. 'Tanzania: The Development Debate — A Comment', *African Affairs* 79 (July 1980), pp. 343–347.

Samoff, Joel. 'Crisis and Socialism in Tanzania', *Journal of Modern African Studies* 19, no. 2 (1981), pp. 279–306.

_____ . 'On Class Paradigms and African Politics', *Africa Today* 29, no. 2 (1982), pp. 41–50.

Saul, John S. 'African Peasants and Revolutionary Change', *Review of African Political Economy* 1, no. 1 (1974), pp. 41–68.

_____ . 'Zimbabwe: The Next Round', *Monthy Review* 32 (September 1980), pp. 1–43.

Smiley, Xan. 'Zimbabwe, Southern Africa and the Rise of Robert Mugabe', *Foreign Affairs* 50 (Summer 1980), pp. 1060–1083.

Smith, A. 'Antonio Salazar and the Reversal of Portuguese Colonial Policy', *Journal of African History* 15, no. 4 (1974), pp. 653–667.

Spiliotes, Nicholas J. 'Nigerian Foreign Policy and Southern Africa: A Choice for the West', *Issue* 11, nos. 1–2 (Spring/Summer 1981).

Stevens, Christopher and John Speed. 'Multipartyism in Africa: The Case of Botswana Revisited', *African Affairs* 76, no. 304 (July 1977), pp. 381–387.

Turner, James and Sean Gervasi. 'The American Economic Future in Southern Africa', *Journal of Southern African Affairs* 3, no. 1 (1978), pp. 85–98.

University of Eduardo Mondlane, Centre for African Studies. 'Frelimo from Front to Party: Revolutionary Transformations', paper presented at University of Minnesota African Studies Council (25 May 1983).

_____ . Zimbabwe: Notes and Reflections on the Zimbabwe Situation', mimeo (Maputo, 1977).

Vail, Leroy. 'Mozambique's Chartered Companies: The Rule of the Feeble', *Journal of African History* 13, no. 3 (1976), pp. 389–416.

Van der Pijl, Kees. 'Class Formation at the International Level', *Capital and Class*, no. 9 (Autumn 1979).

Weeks, John and Elizabeth Dore. 'International Exchange and the Causes of Backwardness', *Latin American Perspectives* 6, no. 2 (Spring 1979), pp. 62–91.

Williams, Mike. 'The Theory of the Capitalist States(s)', *Capital and Class*, no. 9 (Autumn 1979).

Wolpe, Harold. 'Towards an Analysis of the South African State', *International Journal of Sociology and Law*, no. 8 (1980), pp. 399–421.

Wuyts, Marc. 'Peasants and Rural Economy in Mozambique', paper presented at University of Eduardo Mondlane seminar (August 1978).

Yaffe, David. 'The Marxist Theory of Crisis, Capital and the State', *Economy and Society* 2, no. 2 (May 1973), pp. 186–232.

Zimbabwe Information Group. *Bulletin*, nos 5–6 (December 1977–January 1978).

INDEX